THE FYLDE GUARDIANS

OF THE POOR

AND THE

UNION WORKHOUSE

Front cover photograph: Workhouse Entrance, Moor Street, Kirkham

With Love and Thanks to my wife Samantha.

Published by Michael Townsend

British Library Cataloguing-in-Publication data
A catalogue record for this book is available from the British Library

ISBN 978-1-9164748-1-9
Proof Reading by Danny Hurstfield: Danielle0801@googlemail.com

Typeset by Carnegie Scotforth Books
Printed and bound by Halstan

Contents

Introduction

The Fylde Union Workhouse was situated at three different sites in Kirkham and Wesham over the years. The reasons will become apparent as you progress through the book.

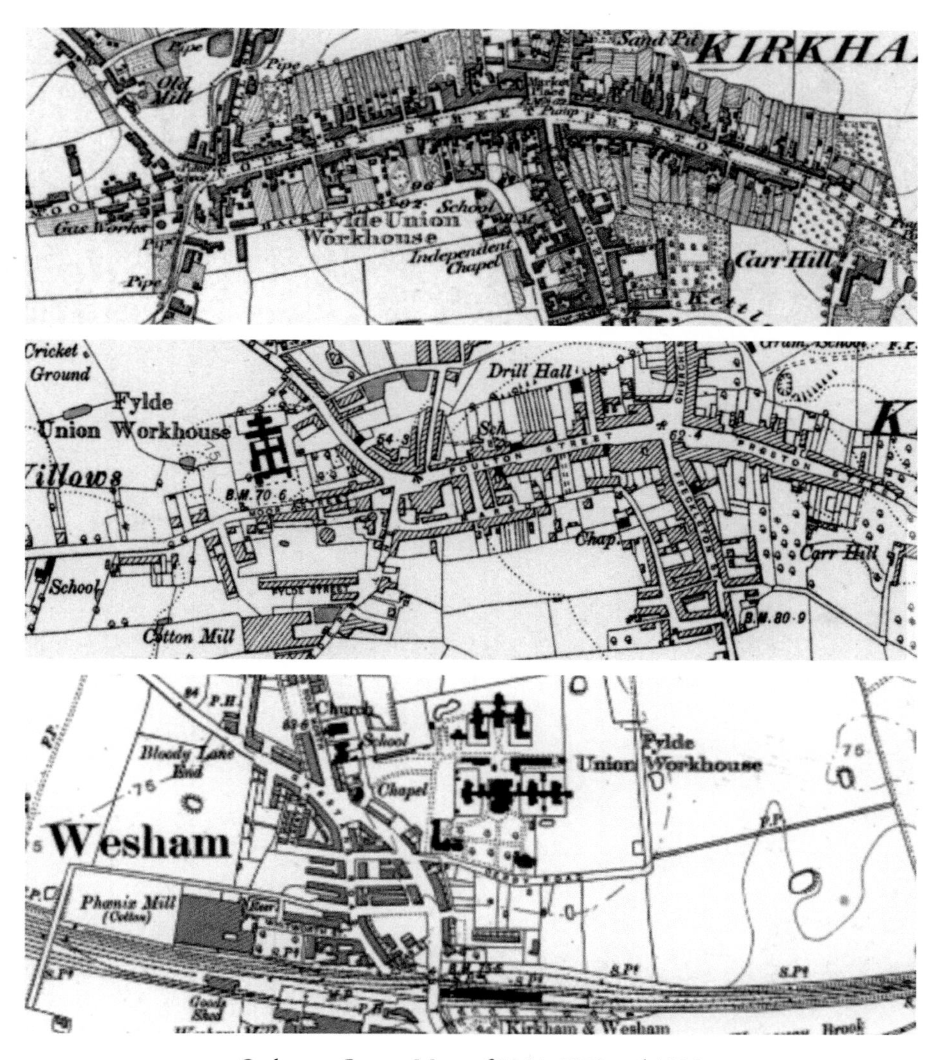

Ordnance Survey Maps of 1844, 1892 and 1909

Under the Poor Law Amendment Act 1834, the Government decided to join parishes together to create unions, who would look after the poor, as one consolidated unit. The Fylde was probably one of the easiest to create. Bordered by the Irish Sea on the west, the River Wyre in the north, and the River Ribble in the south. The Fylde's eastern border was sealed by the creation of the Lancaster, Garstang, and Preston Unions. The union was formed in the days before Blackpool and Fleetwood had existed; the main towns were Poulton-le-Fylde and Kirkham. After the railways arrived, the Fylde changed, and the guardians had to deal with the growth of Blackpool; a large seaside resort, which attracted thousands of travellers looking for work, and Fleetwood; a port town, and the numerous problems all port towns created in the Victorian Era. This is the story of the Fylde Poor Law Union.

In the Beginning

The opening of the new Fylde Union Workhouse in 1845, had its roots firmly set in the Tudor Era. After the 'Dissolution of the Monasteries', the duty of looking after the poor and needy passed to the parish churches. Then, when Queen Elizabeth introduced a law stating that all able-bodied should work, it created the problem of who was deserving of poor relief and who wasn't. These two events created two groups of people.

The first group included people like the elderly, orphans, the infirm, unemployed, or poorly paid workers, unmarried mothers, widows and travellers looking for work. The second group were called 'vagrants' who from the Tudor to the Victorian Era, were the lazy, the work-shy, the criminals, and beggars, the list goes on. Being a vagrant was a criminal offence.

Deciding who deserved poor relief and stopping vagrancy was near impossible and, with the church being by its very nature 'liberal', the cost of poor relief began to climb.

The first attempt at reducing poor relief was the 'Settlement Act'; after which you could only claim relief in the parish where you had lived or work for a set period. If you tried to claim relief in a town where you had no settlement rights, the town's bailiffs would send you back to your place of settlement.

In 1722, the 'Knatchbull's Act' gave birth to the concept of a workhouse. A parish could now build a house, where the sick and infirm could be looked after, travellers could obtain overnight accommodation, orphans could be brought up, and a place where destitute people could go for help. In return, people were set to work to pay for the relief. The work was made hard not out of malice, but it was a test. If you were desperate you would go into the workhouse, if not you wouldn't.

In Kirkham, a workhouse was built on Back Lane (Marsden Street), but before it was built, Bailiff John Langton went around Kirkham, asking the people who were paying the poor rates if they wanted one built. A workhouse would remove the poor from the streets, but the costs of building and running such a place, would be passed onto the rate payers.

22 May 1726.

"Mem. That the town of Kirkham was summonsed from house to house & the inhabitants unanimously agreed to the setting up of a workhouse."

The event was recorded by the Thirty-Men

The three-storey building stood next door to the alleyway 'Union Passage' leading from Poulton Street to Marsden Street. The building was twenty metres long by ten metres wide and came with its own garden, stable, yard, shippon and outbuildings.

Kirkham Parish Workhouse during V.E. Day celebrations 1945 (Photo Courtesy of Christina Salisbury)

The Gilbert Act of 1782 standardised the rules under which workhouses could operate. Boards of guardians were elected to oversee the running of individual workhouses, and small parishes could form unions to share the cost of a workhouse.

The cost of poor relief continued to climb, and vagrancy was still a problem. In the 1830s, government inspectors were sent around the country looking at different workhouses who, despite the Gilbert Act, still administered relief in their own different ways. The inspectors reported back to the Government, and the Poor Relief Amendment Act of 1834 created the workhouse system we now remember.

The main points were as follows

1. No work to be given outside of the workhouse.

There were two types of relief, indoor and outdoor: indoor; when you went into the workhouse, and outdoor; when you received relief but stayed outside the workhouse. Outdoor relief was meant to come to an end after two years, but this never happened. In rural areas like the Fylde, fields could be rented, and the outdoor paupers put to work sowing and harvesting crops. The crops were sold, and the money could be reinvested back into the relief system. Paupers could also be employed on farms at harvest time and the wages taken by the unions.

2. The regulation of workhouses would come under one uniform and responsible authority, with a central board.

The workhouse system was centralised in London, under the Poor Law Commission. To prevent politics influencing the commission's decisions, none of the board could sit in Parliament. This decision backfired. As the cost of poor relief increased by thirty percent over the first thirteen years, Members of Parliament were unable to hold them to account. The commission was extremely unpopular in Parliament and hated in the parishes. To remedy this, the Poor Law Board was created, replacing the Poor Law Commission in 1847. Charles Buller M.P. for Hull was the first president. The other members of the board who represented the Government, were, the Lord President of the Council, the Lord Privy Seal, the Home Secretary and the Chancellor of the Exchequer.

Everything had to be sanctioned by the board: buildings, renovations, loans, staff appointments etc. Workhouse inspectors were sent to the different workhouses, who reported back to the Poor Law Board.

> 3. The board to have the power of incorporating parishes as they think in their discretion as desirable.

This meant joining different parishes together to form a union. The union would then be known by the area it was situated: Preston Union, Bolton Union, Fylde Union.

> 4. The board to have the power of incorporating parishes for the purposes of appointing permanent officers, and of regulating rates.

The first person to be elected to office was the clerk. The clerk established the new union, organised the annual elections of the guardians, and was the constant in the individual workhouses, whereas the guardians, masters, matrons, schoolmistresses, nurses and servants were more fluid.

> 5. The board to have the power at recommending fit persons for parochial officers to the different parishes and also the power to dismiss unfit persons upon complaints being made to them.

Each union was split into different districts, and a relieving officer appointed to look after a specific area. He was the first point of contact for the poor. It was the relieving officer's duty to make sure the people receiving poor relief were the 'deserving poor'.

> 6. Children to take their fathers settlement, or on the death of the father, their mothers until the age of sixteen. After that age, the settlement to be birth only.

People gained settlement through birth, marriage, apprenticeships, regular employment for a full year, renting a house worth ten pounds per annum, paying parochial taxes, or serving as a parish officer. All this was to stop people turning up in a town and burdening themselves onto the local ratepayers. The one year of employment was later extended to three years.

> 7. Illegitimate children until sixteen to follow their mother's settlement and the mother to be required to support her illegitimate children herself or enter the workhouse.

There was no limit on the number of children an unmarried mother could claim relief for. The mother would be given support until the parish could find the father and force him to pay the maintenance. Finding the fathers was difficult and either way the woman received support. Most ratepayers thought the system encouraged illegitimacy. The responsibility for getting pregnant was passed onto the mother.

> 8. The entire abolition of the Bastardy Laws.

Single mothers were seen by some as a particular burden on the ratepayers. Before the new act, the mother of a bastard child could make a claim for maintenance from the father through the Petty Sessions. As from 1834, the mother now had to have evidence and apply at the Quarter Sessions. The cost and complexity involved made it impossible for some mothers to make a claim. Cases of illegitimacy increased, as the law now made it easier for fathers to escape paying for their offspring. It was changed back to the Petty Sessions in 1839.

> 9. The same liability to be upon her getting married, extended to her husband.

When a woman married, she gained her husband's settlement. He now became responsible for her and if the family needed relief, it was the husband who applied to the relieving officer. It was not uncommon for unmarried couples to pretend to be married to gain relief.

> 10. Repeal of so much of the 35th George 111 c.101 section 6 as makes a pregnant, unmarried woman removable and do so much of the 59th George 111 c.51 section 2, as renders a woman liable to be committed to the house of correction.

This put an English woman on the same footing as a Scottish or Irish woman. A pregnant woman could now be sent back to where she had come from and being pregnant didn't stop you from being sent to the 'House of Correction' after being found guilty of a crime.

All these changes started at the end of 1834, but the Poor Law Commission wanted the process to be implemented slowly. The following instructions were sent to the overseers of the poor:

> 1. With regard to able-bodied paupers who are unable to procure employment, you should, if possible, set them to work,

and, in all cases where circumstances permit it, adoption task-work should be preferred.

2. The allowance paid to the pauper in return for parish work, should be considerably less than the ordinary wages paid for similar work to an independent labourer.

3. If it is found impracticable to set the able-bodied paupers to work, one-half at least of the relief given to them should be in food, or in other necessaries of life, and if this rule be applicable to your parish, the commissioners recommend you consider whether arrangements cannot be made for carrying it into effect without delay.

4. If it is practise in your parish to make allowances to labourers in respect of the number of their children, you should not suddenly or altogether discontinue these allowances, but should make them in kind rather than in money.

5. With respect to paupers (if any) belonging to your parish but resident elsewhere, who have been accustomed to receiving from your parish weekly or other payments, such payments, especially as regards aged and infirm persons, should not be hastily withdrawn, but the list of cases of this nature should be carefully revised, with the view to detect frauds and impositions.

6. If your parish possesses a workhouse, which is already in such a state as to admit of able-bodied paupers being lodged, maintained, and set to work therein, you may make the offer of relief within the house to any such pauper who shall apply for parochial aid, and such offer will exonerate you from the necessity of offering other relief.

The commissioners added that; the forgoing suggestions were information only, and not to be mistaken for rules or orders issued by them, under the authority of the Poor Law Amendment Act.

The Fylde Union began taking shape in January 1837, when Robert Bonny Fisher put himself up for the position of clerk.

To the Gentlemen who shall be elected Guardians of the
Poor of the Fylde Union
And to his Majesty's Justice of the Peace, residing within the
Union.

Gentlemen,

In the event of Kirkham, being fixed upon as the place where the meetings of the Guardians of the Poor of the Fylde Union, as at present constituted, shall be held, or should the Poor Law Commissioners think fit to divide the union, I beg leave respectfully to offer myself as a candidate for the Office of Clerk to the Board of Guardians of Kirkham. I am fully sensible of the important duties attached to the office of clerk to your board, and that great personnal attention and active exertion will be required on the part of the officer, appointed to the discharge of those duties. Having, however by an attentive consideration of the provisions of the Poor Law Amendment Act, and of the various rules and orders which have been issued by the commissioners to unions already in existance, (and particularly in the agricultural districts,) made myself practically acquainted with the alterations which will occur in the management of the affairs of the poor, by the introduction of the act into this neighbourhood, and being intimately acquainted with the localities of the different townships comprised within the union, and generally known to the inhabitants, I hope I may with confidence rely on your support.

Should I meet with your approbation, I assure you no exertion shall be wanting to merit your confidence, and as the interest of the union would be best consulted by the residence of the clerk at the place where the meetings are held, I take this opportunity of announcing my intention to reside in Kirkham.

I have the honour to be Gentlemen,

Your very obedient, Servant,

Robert B. Fisher.

Kirkham, 19th January 1837.

Robert Fisher would only take on the role if the union were based in Kirkham. At that time, there were two workhouses in the area: Poulton-le-Fylde and Kirkham. It was decided that Kirkham was to be the base for the guardians and Robert Fisher was elected clerk on the 1st of February 1837. The union was split into two districts at the end of that month.

District number one was comprised of Kirkham, Lytham, Westby-with-Westby-with-Plumton, Freckleton, Clifton,-with-Salwick, Treales, Roseacre and Wharles, Weeton-with-Preese, Warton, Greenhalgh-with-Thistleton, Medlar-with-Wesham, Bryning-with-Kellamergh, Ribby-with-Wray and Newton-with-Scales.

District number two was comprised of Poulton-in-the-Fylde, Marton, Thornton, Layton-with-Warbrick, Singleton, Hardhorn-with-Newton, Bispham-with-Norbreck, Carleton, Elswick and Little Eccleston-with-Larbrick.

Each district had a relieving officer. He would issue instant relief, or an order for admittance to the workhouse. If you were given outdoor relief your name was added to the 'relief lists' which a committee examined before each guardian's meeting for final approval. The relieving officer also took on the role of a registrar of births and deaths and issued medical orders for paupers needing medical care.

Although formed into a union, each parish still had two overseers of the poor, who were appointed annually by the magistrates. The role of administering poor relief was a former role of the overseers, who still assessed property for calculating rate payments, organised guardian's elections and were a voice representing the local ratepayers. Parish overseers looked after the rent from property or land left in trust for the benefit of the poor in their parish; this rent money could be used to off-set the parishes' poor rates.

In some unions, the overseers still collected the poor rates, but the Fylde appointed two paid overseers called 'collectors'. This cost the union more in the form of salaries, but the officer appointed was qualified for the position, worked full time collecting the rates, gave the money to the treasurer on time, and acted as assistant relieving officers. The union treasurer at this time was Mr Henry Jennings manager at the Preston Branch of the Lancaster Banking Company. The rates or 'call' was set by the guardians and included the Lancashire County Rate, Lancashire County Lunatic Rate, Preston House of Correction Rate, Kirkdale House of Correction Rate and Lancashire Rural Police Rate.

The Fylde Union was also split into three medical districts: Poulton, Kirkham, and Lytham. A medical officer was appointed for each district. The medical officer's duties included 'the supply of medicines and appliances, in all medical and surgical cases, midwifery, and the vaccination of children, which may be necessary for all paupers falling ill within the several districts, whether belonging to the union or not, and for which a written order shall be given by the relieving officer, overseer, or other competent authority.'

Attending to the poor during childbirth and paupers injured in accidents was classed as extra work, and the doctors had to claim the costs back from the union. The Kirkham doctor also had to look after the inmates in the workhouse. All doctors had to live in the district they served.

Guardians' elections were held every March, the role was voluntary, and the guardians stood for a year before further elections. If nobody stood against a guardian, an election wouldn't be held in that township. Anybody whose property had the annual value or rental of twenty pounds or more could stand as a guardian. Only owners of rateable property or ratepayers were entitled to vote in the elections. One guardian was elected for each of the small townships, and two for the larger towns of Poulton and Kirkham. The guardians elected a chairman and vice-chairman during the first meeting of the financial year, held in April.

When government inspectors travelled around England looking at the different workhouses, there were two types that they came across. The first was a poor house were a building was rented by a small parish to house the poor, described by the inspectors as, 'a miserable abode, occupied rent-free by three or four dissolute families, mutually corrupting each other'.

The larger workhouses, like Kirkham's, they described as 'usually occupied by 60 or 80 paupers, made up of a dozen or more neglected children, 20 or 30 able-bodied adult paupers of both sexes, and probably an equal number of aged and impotent persons, who are proper objects of relief. Amidst these, the mothers of bastard children and prostitutes live without shame and associate freely with the youth, who have also the example and conversation of the frequent inmates of the county goal, the poacher, the vagrant, the decayed beggar, and other characters of the worst description. To these may often be added a solitary blind person, one or two idiots, and not infrequently are heard from amongst the rest, the incessant ravings of some neglected lunatic. In such receptacles, the sick poor are often immured.'

At the time, it was thought that the paupers bred pauperism and it would be better to split them into different classes. The authorities would then be able to treat the classes differently, the old, infirm, and children with sympathy, and the rest a little harsher.

The Poulton Workhouse was closed, and the Kirkham Parish Workhouse became the Fylde Union Workhouse. Under the new poor laws, the paupers were separated into seven different classes.

The seven classes were:

1. Men infirm through age or any other cause.
2. Able-bodied men and youths above the age of fifteen years.
3. Boys above the age of seven years and that of fifteen.
4. Woman infirm through age or any other cause.
5. Able-bodied women, and girls above the age of fifteen years.
6. Girls above the age of seven years and that of fifteen.
7. Children under seven years of age.

The different classes lived in separate wards and had separate exercise yards; with a number of undesirable paupers entering the workhouse, it provided some protection for the vulnerable inmates, especially the women and children.

Old married couples who were infirm could live together and were provided with separate sleeping accommodation. In 1866 there were three couples living together in rooms in the infirmary: Old Man Cassidy and his wife, the Butlers and the Fishers, but if the infirmary became overfull, which it often was; they were sent into the main part of the building.

The class system also allowed the master to treat the classes differently in terms of work and their daily routine.

Able-bodied female paupers could be employed as assistants to the matron, looking after the children and helping with the household chores, as long as they didn't come into contact with able-bodied men and boys. If they were employed as a nurse on the sick wards, they could nurse all classes of females and boys under seven years. An infirm male pauper could be assigned by the master as a supervisor in the ward of boys above seven years. All children under seven years were placed in a female ward, and the mothers of this class were allowed to visit their children regularly throughout the day. The parents of children above seven years were allowed to visit their children once a day, and a room was provided for this daily meeting.

The vagrants, casuals or wayfarers were treated separately from the seven classes. They stayed for short periods and were given the hardest work to pay for their bath, shave, food and overnight accommodation. They had their own sleeping cells and baths and didn't enter the main parts of the workhouse. They were a difficult class to provide for as their numbers fluctuated, sometimes they were just put up in the local lodging houses at a cost to the union.

The last group, 'paupers of unsound mind' entered the workhouse and after being assessed were sent to a lunatic asylum, either Lancaster or Haydock Lodge at this time. Some stayed in the workhouse for long periods, because the asylums were constantly full. Dangerous lunatics, however, had to leave for the asylums within fourteen days.

FORMS REFERRED TO IN THIS ORDER.

(Form A.)

	Time of Rising.	Interval for Breakfast.	Time for work.	Interval for Dinner.	Time for work.	Interval for Supper.	Time for going to Bed.
From 25th March to 29th Sept.	½ before 6.	From ½ past 6 to 7.	From 7 to 12.	From 12 to 1.	From 1 to 6.	From 6 to 7 o'clock.	8 o'clock.
From 29th Sept. to 25th March.	½ before 7.	From ½ past 7 to 8.	From 8 to 12.	From 12 to 1.	From 1 to 6.	From 6 to 7 o'clock.	8 o'clock.

The daily routine was fixed and set by the Poor Law Commission.

All classes had to rise at the time stated on Form A, except the sick, insane and infirm men and women and children under seven. The times on the form 'winter and summer' reflected the working day of a weaver in towns like Kirkham. All able-bodied adults and children over seven, were woken by a bell, and half an hour later they all had to be by their beds for a roll call.

All paupers except the sick, young children, persons of unsound mind, vagrants, and infirm paupers had their meals in the dining or day rooms, none of this group were allowed to go into their sleeping rooms during the working day or at mealtimes without the master's permission.

To put this practise of splitting the paupers into different classes into action, it would require the building of a new workhouse. It would be built at the edge of the town on an elevated position with space for gardens. One side would be for the male inmates, the other for the females.

In 1843, the guardians purchased three acres of land off Moor Street, Kirkham for £800 from Hugh Hornby of Liverpool, who had two tenants on the plot. William Aspinall was renting the land on Moor Street, where he had a cottage, gardens, stable and a weaving shop. Behind him was Margery Whalley who rented Plumpton House; Margery's land bordered Wrangway, which was to become Station Road

Margery's cottage and barn were demolished, along with William's buildings, and the guardians spent another one-thousand pounds levelling the site. They then erected the building for two hundred paupers and brought new furniture and fittings. The only furniture taken from the old workhouse to 'avoid any filth' was twelve iron bedsteads.

The house part of the Fylde Union Workhouse.

The building consisted of two parts: the 'house' the administration block; a two-storey building facing Moor Street , and the 'home' the body of the building where the paupers lived. Downstairs in the house, on the left of the main entrance, was the guardians meeting room, and on the right were the reception rooms 'union offices' for male and female paupers with baths and equipment for fumigating the clothing and a laundry. The paupers were bathed and given workhouse clothing before entering the main building, to try and prevent the spread of lice and vermin. Upstairs were the offices for the clerk and officials, and the living quarters for the master and matron.

A central corridor left the house, connecting it to the H-block shaped 'home'. This corridor and the stem of the H contained the kitchen, dining room, storerooms, vagrant cells, and workrooms. The bakery was in the cellar beneath the dining room. On the right side of the H, there were two wards for males, separated by a central staircase leading up to two further male wards, one of which was the sick ward. On the left, it was the same, but for females. The wards were a mixture of small rooms and communal bedrooms with dayrooms.

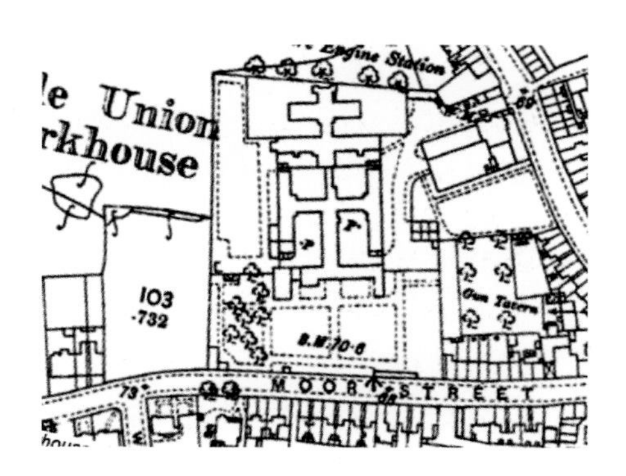

Ordnance Survey

The heating and cooking were all done with coal fires; the water was supplied from two wells: one in the males' yard and one in the females' yard. The building was brick-built with flagged stone floors. It was a cold, damp, place to live, with the small windows low in the wall, making it poorly ventilated.

The inmates slept on large iron beds with straw mattresses, which they had to share when the workhouse was full. The vagrants slept on boards.

The building cost £5,400, nearly £700,000 in today's money. The loan to pay for the building was paid back over a twenty-two years period.

The inmates were set work each day; the type of work depended on the class of paupers. The able-bodied males were set to work breaking stones or oakum picking.

A typical pebbled pavement in Victorian Kirkham. All the roads as well as the pavements in Kirkham were cobbled with workhouse stones. Dr Shaw thought the town was obsessed with them. (Photo Courtesy of Frank Smith)

When stone breaking, the weaker able-bodied inmates' wheelbarrowed stones into the breaking room, where inmates broke them with a sledge-hammer. The broken stones were then hand-chiselled mainly by the vagrants into smaller stones to pave the roads and streets of the Fylde. These were wheelbarrowed away to the stores.

Oakum picking is when old rope was cut into two feet lengths and beaten with a wooden mallet to remove the tar. It was then cut into short lengths, and the inmates unravelled the lengths into single strands. The strands were then mixed with grease or tar to create oakum. The oakum was then used as caulking to fill the gaps between the wooden planks on ships to make them watertight.

The older and weaker inmates worked in the gardens, where vegetables were grown. When the Bolton Union was planning on building a new workhouse, their clerk visited Kirkham. It was cited as an example by their guardians.

The Bolton Clerk stated that, 'The old people, who were as large a proportion of the inmates as was the case here, were all engaged, some carrying manure for cabbages, others in hoeing potatoes, or in doing something else, on the land in question and they were much fresher in appearance than were the old people of Bolton.'

The vegetables grown in the gardens could keep them supplied for up to six months. The guardians also bought in supplies, and contracts lasting three months were issued for shambles meat, potatoes, wheat bread, meal, flour, milk, butter, groceries, coals, and clogs. The diet for the paupers had to be no better than the average for a labourer in the area.

The females were employed to scrub and clean the building, wash clothes, sew, bake, look after the children and nurse the sick.

Children were also set to work, but for three hours each day, they were instructed in reading, writing, arithmetic and the principles of Christian Religion. They also undertook 'industrial training', which for the girls meant training for a future life in service, and for the boys shoe repairing or tailoring, ready for being apprenticed. A cobbler and tailor were employed two half days a week to instruct the boys. On Sundays nobody worked except for the ones involved with the daily chores; paupers could go out for the day, but had to be back before five o'clock.

The cost of the wages in 1841 when the present master and matron, Thomas and Esther Barton, were first employed, totalled £554; the cost of outdoor relief for the union was £350, and indoor relief cost the union £1,550. That year the union spent £3,375 on poor relief (£440,000).

On the 8th of April, the guardians stopped meeting in a building on Freckleton Street, and they held their first meeting in the new workhouse boardroom. The minutes of the meeting went as follows.

Board Room 8th April 1845

The newly elected Board of Guardians met this day at 2 o'clock in the afternoon at the boardroom Kirkham New Workhouse, for the first time to the order made at the last guardians meeting.

Present, The Rev. Richard Moore and William Birley ex officers and John Butcher, Thomas Smith, Joseph Hodkinson, John Miller, Robert Mayer, Robert Walker, James Fairclough, James Rogerson, Richard Ward, Thomas Salthouse, John Poole, Richard Cookson, Richard Bilsborrow, Jas. Loxham, William Catterall, William

Cookson, Thos. Jackson, James Smith, James Kirby, and John Ward, elected Guardians.

William Birley esquire was called to the chair, and on the motion of the Rev. R. Moore, seconded by Mr James Rogerson and unanimously carried, William Birley Esquire was again elected chairman of the board for the coming year.

Moved by Mr James Rogerson, seconded by the Rev. R. Moore and unanimously carried that Mr Richard Walker be the vice-chairman of the board for the coming year.

The clerk stated that he had duly complied with the terms of the Poor Law Commissioners General Election Order and that as there was no opposition to any candidates nominated in any of the townships within the union, he made out the lists of guardians elected in the 27th instant including therein the last years elected guardians for the townships of Clifton with Salwick, Layton with Warbrick, Marton and Singleton having received no nominations from any of the said townships which list together with the nominations papers he laid before the board having previously signed and certified the same and forwarded a copy thereof to the Poor Law Commission.

Order that the lists of guardians and nomination papers be preserved within the public papers of the union.

The following is a list of the townships and guardians forming the board.

Bispham with Norbreck	John Butcher
Bryning with Kellamergh	Thomas Smith
Clifton with Salwick	(no nom.) Archibald Scott (cont.)
Carleton	Henry Fisher
Elswick	Joseph Hodkinson
Little Eccleston-with-Larbreck	John Miller
Freckleton	Robert Mayer
Greenhalgh-with-Thistleton	Robert Walker
Hardhorn-with-Newton	James Fairclough
Kirkham	James Rogerson & Richard Ward.
Lytham	Thomas Salthouse
Layton-with-Warbreck	(no nom.) John Poole (cont.)

Marton	Richard Cookson (cont.)
Medlar-with-Wesham	Richard Bilsborrow
Newton-with-Scales	James W. Loxham.
Poulton	William Catterall & Richard Singleton
Ribby-with-Wrea	William Cookson
Singleton,	(no nom.) James Luxton
Treales, Roseacre and Wharles	Thomas Jackson
Weeton-with-Preese	James Kirby
Warton	James Worthington
Westby-with-Plumpton	John Ward

Resolved, that the fortnightly meeting be held as usual at 2 o'clock in the afternoon.

Resolved, that Messers James Rogerson, Richard Ward, William Cookson, James Loxham, and Richard Bilsborrow shall be the Kirkham Workhouse Visiting Committee for the coming year and that they shall have the direction and charge of all matters connected with the removing the pauper inmates and the furniture of the workhouse from the old to the new workhouse.

Order that no ward bedsteads be removed from the old to the new workhouse but that for the present ten single and ten double iron bedsteads be ordered by Mr Finch, and that should anymore be wanted the workhouse visiting committee are to purchase the same.

The clerk stated that the Hon. Clements, Inspector, Poor Law Commission, visited and inspected the new workhouse on Friday the 21st ultimo and that since his visit he had stated in a letter to the clerk the pleasure his visit had afforded him – the letter which is dated the 29th ultimo also stated that several small matters were required to be done before the building could be considered to be finished.

The letter having been read was taken into consideration when it was resolved that all the matters required in the completion of the new workhouse as suggested in the Hon. Mr Clements' letter except the wall as a boundary fence shall be done, and that it is the opinion of this board that a thorn quickset hedge will be more ornamental, less expensive and quite as useful for a boundary fence as a wall if properly protected by wood railings until it became a sufficient fence.

Mr John Loxham appeared before the board and stated that Mr Hornby of Liverpool had no objection to let land for twenty-one years, the remaining part of the field of which part of the workhouse was sited, provided the guardians would also leave therewith the three cottages and gardens adjoining and get possession of the same themselves.

Resolved that the consideration of the above proposition be deferred for the present.

The clerk stated that at the request of the chairman he had visited Lancaster Workhouse for the purpose of enquiring into the methods adopted in the establishment respecting the clothing and the discipline of the inmates, but unfortunately the governor thereof was sick in bed and, therefore, the information received was not so extensive as it might have been -- for the particulars see a short report in the file of letters.

The clerk laid before the board a letter from the Poor Law Commission dated the 5th instant acknowledging the receipt of the return of the guardians of this union for the current year -- see file

The clerk laid before the board resolutions of the Blything Haithies Union and a petition from the Liverpool Select Vestry respecting James Grahams Settlement Bill now before Parliament also resolutions of the Blackburn, Salford, Wigan and Preston Unions respecting the Commission's Order regulating non-resident relief and non-settled poor. order to be filed.

The books of the relieving officer for the Kirkham District was examined.

The amount Expended in the 1st week of the quarter for resident poor, £19 12s. 3d.

The amount Expended in the 1st week of the quarter for non-settled poor, £2 6s. 4d.

The amount Expended in the 2nd week of the quarter for resident poor, £19 6s. 4d.

The amount Expended in the 2nd week of the quarter for non-settled poor, £1 18s. 6d.

Ordered that forty-two pounds, seventeen shillings and five pence be credited in his account, that a cheque for sixty pounds be given him for resident and non-settled poor and debited in his account and that the treasurer's account credited with the same.

The books of the relieving officer for the Poulton District were examined.

The amount Expended in the 1st week of the quarter for resident poor, £17 6s. 3d.

The amount Expended in the 1st week of the quarter for non-settled poor, £2 15s. 0d.

The amount Expended in the 2nd week of the quarter for resident poor, £15 1s. 1d.

The amount Expended in the 2nd week of the quarter for non-settled poor, £3 4s. 0d.

Ordered that thirty-eight pounds, six shillings, and four pence be credited in his account that a cheque for forty-five pounds be given for resident and non-settled poor and debited in his account and that the treasurer's account be credited with the same.

Certificates under the hand of Mr Finch for the following amount were laid before the Board, ordered that cheques be made out and signed for the same, on account of the new Workhouse.

To:

James Armstead for stonework,	£33 0s.0d.
Mr Thos. Catterall for flagging and slating,	£200 0s.0d.
Geo Hodgson & Sons Plumbing,	£112 0s.0d.
Holland and Matthews Brickwork,	£100 0s.0d.
Mr Morgan,	£10 0s. 0d.
Thomas Turner for woodwork,	£150 0s. 0d.
Mr Stevenson Iron safe,	£10 9s.10d.
Mr Finch for Superintendence,	£25 0s. 0d.
John Whitehead,	£80 0s. 0d.

From the minute book, we know William Birley was the chairman, Robert Walker was vice-chairman and the meetings were held at two o'clock in the afternoon every second Tuesday. The workhouse visiting committee formed at this meeting; were to work closely with the master and matron and had to visit the workhouse at least once a week. The committee was tasked with moving the paupers into the new building and then had all the old furniture and articles of worth cleaned and auctioned off raising, twenty-four pounds, eight shillings, and nine pence. John Whiteside was instructed to cart five loads of manure from the old house to the new house gardens, where potatoes and vegetables were planted by the inmates.

The committee gave the damaged bricks, lime, and rubble left after building the workhouse to the highway's surveyor, who in return used it to make a path along Moor Street leading up to the workhouse. One side of the workhouse faced Moor Street and one Station Road; these were walled and topped with iron railings. The other two sides were open and faced into the countryside. As we know from the minutes, Mr Clements, the government inspector, thought these two boundaries should also be walled. The guardians thought it would be too expensive, so decided instead to build a wooden fence, then planted hedges which would be ready to form a boundary in five years' time.

The contractors were asked to leave the site by the end of June, and the finishing touches were made to the workhouse. The guardians purchased ten double and ten single bedsteads, a new pulpit, and a dresser for the kitchen. Brick pigsties with flagged floors were built and pigs were bought. Richard Moore, Kirkham's solicitor, was employed to sell the old workhouse.

Inside the workhouse, Christmas was always celebrated by having a meal of roast beef and plum pudding. The Christmas meal was held on Boxing Day and the leading families of Kirkham, mainly the Birleys, would donate gifts of beer, tobacco, tea and snuff for the adults. The children received fruit and toys. People who had family members in the workhouse could also send gifts to their relatives. In later years, the old people and children would have 'Blackpool Day' to look forward to, when they went on a day trip to Blackpool. On a weekly basis though, it was a dreary existence with only the Friday church service to look forward to.

One person who would not be at the first Christmas meal in the new workhouse was 80-year-old Thomas Fairclough of Medlar-with-Wesham. Thomas had tried to take his own life by cutting his throat. Doctor Gradwell the workhouse doctor treated him straight away, and he survived his injuries.

The guardians asked Thomas why he had tried to take his own life, but he could not give a reason. Dr Gradwell, however, could.

The doctor said, 'The pauper is not insane, but his attempt of suicide arose from his depraved disposition by being known as a despicable bad character for a long time.'

Thomas was sent out of the workhouse to family members, who were given an allowance to look after him.

The workhouse, was a multipurpose building: people entered for many reasons. The institution was an orphanage, a children's home, an old people's home, a hospital for the poor, a lying-in-hospital, an assessment centre for the mentally ill, and a homeless refuge.

When somebody entered the workhouse, their circumstances were looked into by the clerk, who tried to recover the cost of their maintenance from family members; men who deserted their families were summoned to court for neglect. In August this year, John Langured and James Blackburn were summoned for neglecting their families and leaving them chargeable to the union. What happened to the men in court is unknown, but there were three usual outcomes. The worst outcome was a one- to three-month prison sentence. The second was a prison sentence, deferred, if they agreed to pay the maintenance, or if they were lucky, the accused would come up with a good excuse and have the charges dropped.

The asylums charged the Fylde Union for the care of their patients. In 1845, the costs for the Poulton and Kirkham Districts were twenty-two pounds and nine shillings. Family members were expected to pay the maintenance of their relations in the asylums. Thomas Bennet, a Kirkham shoemaker, was summoned for not contributing to his son Richard Bennet, who was in the Lancaster Asylum after shooting the Reverend Moore of Lund Parish Church.

On the Fylde, unmarried mothers, depending on which district they lived in, applied either to Poulton or Kirkham Court for an order of maintenance from the child's father.

Date of Order	Mother of Bastard Child	Father of Bastard Child
3rd Feb	Ellen Simpson	James Smith
3rd Feb	Grace Carter	James Greenwood
3rd Mar	Betsy Butcher	John Hodgson
3rd Mar	Jane Topping	Christopher Charnock
7th April	Isabela Thornton	William Rawcroft
7th April	Grace Bamber	William Gardner
5th May	Elizabeth Thornley	John Leary

The court order lists from Poulton Court, early 1845.

Paupers who didn't have settlement on the Fylde could be removed to their place of settlement. The clerk applied for a court order, and the paupers had twenty-one days to appeal. In November, Widow Harrison and her children were removed to Blackburn. Margaret Jones and her two children were removed to Halkyn Flintshire.

Removing paupers to their place of settlement was a two-way street. Jane Brewer, widowed whilst living in Leeds, was returned with her three children back to Kirkham. Orphan Ellan Keighley was sent to Kirkham from Lancaster.

The paupers entered the workhouse through the male and female receiving wards. Here they had a bath and were given a workhouse uniform; their own clothes were cleaned and stored away until they left. Old people who would be staying a long time or would probably never leave, were now ordered, to wear their own clothes out first before being given a uniform.

To leave the workhouse, you had to have permission from the master and give three hours' notice. If you didn't, it was classed as absconding, which was illegal, and if you left wearing the uniform, it was also theft. The only enclosed spaces were the four yards attached to the building.

In this year, 1846, Agnes Brown, aged sixty-seven, decided to scale the wall and abscond from the workhouse.

The master told the guardians, 'She's gone to continue her lifelong occupation of begging.' The master passed her details to the police.

The guardians understood that the workhouse could be a poverty trap, as people entered without any money and would therefore also leave without any.

To help, people could ask for casual relief to see them through the journey home. Elias Huff asked to leave with a new set of clothes; he also received five shillings to travel to Fleetwood and then by ship back to Ireland. Richard Miller asked for twenty shillings to take his family back to Norfolk. James Ainsworth of Kirkham his wife and three children asked to leave with fifteen shillings casual relief.

Paupers who claimed outdoor relief, 'on the parish or on the rates' had their circumstances checked every two-weeks. The Poulton relieving officer decided that James Ainsworth now earned enough to support himself and his family, and his relief was stopped. William Hodgson had his relief reduced from five shillings to four shillings weekly.

Richard MacKinnon applied for casual relief of five shillings, so he could go and find work. Ellen Rigby, who had been in confinement with her 'bastard child', asked for money to go home to her parents in Lancaster. All requests were granted.

Some paupers took advantage of the guardians' goodwill. William Hodgson, who was back in the workhouse, asked for seven shillings of casual relief plus a pair of shoes to go in search of work. He left his wife and five children in the workhouse, saying he would be back to collect them within two weeks. William never returned and left his family chargeable to the union. After the relieving officer found no trace of him, an advert was placed in the Poor-Law-Gazette, offering a reward of one pound for information on his whereabouts. He would turn up again at some point; men like William Hodgson were constantly in and out of the workhouse with their families.

Another type of outdoor relief was called 'non-residential-relief' which was there to help people leaving their place of settlement (usually the agricultural districts with high unemployment) for the new industrial towns desperate for labour. They could claim relief from the union they had moved to, and that union would then send a bill for the relief to the person's place of settlement.

The Fylde Union's bill for non-residential relief in June 1846 was:

Birmingham Parish, Three pounds and five shillings

Bradford Union, One pound, seven shillings, and six pence

Carlisle Union, Nineteen shillings and sixpence

Preston Union, Eleven pounds and six shillings

The guardians sent cheques every three months via the post office.

After the arrival of the railways, the new towns of Blackpool and Fleetwood were starting to grow. So, three new medical districts were created in 1846. The union doctors were now appointed every March. The districts doctors were William Gradwell, Kirkham Number One Thomas Shaw, Kirkham Number Two; Harrison Bowness, Fleetwood; William Moore, Blackpool; and Charles Kelan, Lytham.

In the workhouse infirmary the guardians had to convert a room, 'To securely confine anyone that may be affected with temporary insanity.'

The problem the workhouse had was that the two Lancashire asylums; Lancaster and Haydock Lodge were always full. The husband of June Elson asked for his wife to be sent to an asylum after she became insane. The clerk wrote to Haydock to see if there was a place for her. They replied that there was no space except in the private wards costing fifteen shillings per week. The husband was asked to pay six shillings towards her care and the union paid the rest until a vacancy arose in the pauper side of the asylum. She was sent to Haydock, which cost the union two pounds and seven shillings in travel costs.

In April, two more people needed sending to the County Asylum, Lancaster: Isabella Salisbury, an inmate, and William Buckwell of Westby-with-Plumpton. Once again, it was full, and they stayed in the workhouse until two places became available. They were both sent to Lancaster on Monday 7 June.

Orphans or children of paupers claiming indoor or long-term outdoor relief were removed from their parents' care at the age of thirteen and apprenticed until they were twenty-one. William Threlfall, an orphan aged fifteen, was apprenticed to Kirkham shoemaker Richard Winder for six years. Christopher Whiteside, aged seventeen and the child of paupers, was apprenticed to James Robinson of Lytham for four years. They both took a bond of ten pounds.

Girls usually went into service, Mary Bond, aged thirteen, was sent for a month's trial as a servant to Henry Nightingale, a shopkeeper of Liverpool.

Some children were claimed by their siblings. One Irish boy, John Gallagher, left to live with his sister.

Chairman William Birley was also a judge at Kirkham Court. He missed a lot of the meetings, which were held at the same time as the court hearings. It was therefore decided to have two vice-chairmen – one from the Kirkham District, who would be the senior vice-chairman, and another from the Poulton District. After the April guardian's elections of 1847, Robert Walker of Greenhalgh was elected vice chairman of the Kirkham District and John Poole of Layton-with-Warbrick for Poulton.

The Kirkham District Relieving Officer, Thomas Breckell, resigned, and five people applied for the position. The guardians then voted on who they wanted in the post.

> James Davies of Kirkham, fifteen votes.
>
> J. Gardner of Fleetwood, five votes.
>
> James Butcher of Lytham, one vote.
>
> Robert Waddington of Kirkham, one vote.
>
> James Thompson of Elswick, one vote.
>
> James Davies was appointed relieving officer for the Kirkham District.

There were some more removals. James Lincoln and his wife were removed to Walton-le-Dale. John Clemmisson his wife and five children were removed to Preston. Salford Union ordered the removal to Kirkham of Margaret Hackett and her two children. She asked the Fylde Guardians for two shillings and sixpence weekly non-residential relief so she could stay in Salford, which the Fylde Guardians agreed to.

The Fylde was an agricultural district, and farm labourers were often without work during periods of bad weather, when farm operations stopped. It was cheaper to pay them two-weeks relief, than put hundreds of labourers temporarily into the workhouse. This was another reason why outdoor relief never ended on the Fylde.

The town of Kirkham had a flax and cotton industry which was hit badly in October 1847 and how the guardians reacted shows why outdoor relief was a better tool for dealing with short term economic distress.

Railway Mania had come to an end, the price of cotton went through the roof, and access to quick money ended. The economy collapsed, and with the Potato Famine in Ireland thousands of desperate people turned up in Lancashire to add to the woes. The 'Commercial Distress' had hit the Fylde.

The guardians acted quickly. The meetings went from fortnightly to weekly. The outdoor relief lists became permanent; prior to this, the lists were examined every second week. The clerk ordered new clogs and clothing for the outdoor paupers.

To create extra work, the guardians rented six acres of land from Hugh Hornby of Liverpool on Orders Lane for sixteen pounds a year plus rates and tax. The contract for the two fields: Wet Acre and Skellants Meadow, was for seven years. At the time, the fields were grass meadows, which had to be sown with clover and grass, in the last year of the contract.

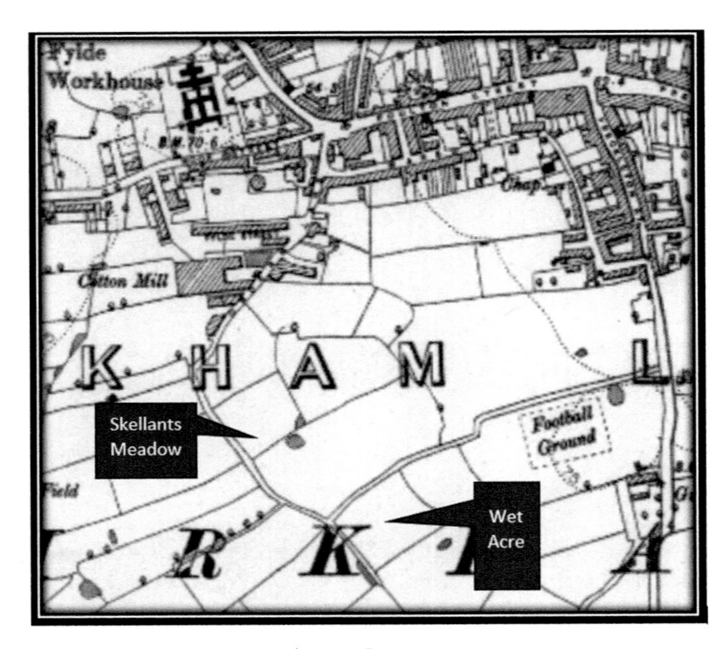

Ordnance Survey 1892

The guardians then advertised for a labour master. James Bickerstaff of Poulton and George Rossall of Greenhalgh applied. James was awarded the position by ten votes to nine, on a salary of fifteen shillings per week, for as long as needed. The paupers in need were now set to work digging drainage ditches and carting the soil away for one shilling a day. This work was called 'spadework' which was created so that the guardians had a pretext to offer outdoor relief.

The second thing the guardians did was reduce the amount paid in outdoor relief but made up the difference with bread. Bakers were asked by the guardians to bring samples of bread to the workhouse. Robert Rawlinson of Lytham, and John Noblett and John Brindle; both of Kirkham, brought some samples. The contract was awarded to John Noblett.

The guardians would decide at Tuesday's meetings how much bread was needed and John would have to deliver it on the following Monday. The average weekly order for December was ten c.w.t (five-hundred kg), delivered in 'shilling and sixpence loaves'.

In the workhouse, to cope with the extra pressure, ten single and twelve double iron bedsteads were purchased along with blankets and quilts. The vagrant wards were also overfull, and the guardians wanted to use the old windmill on the Wrangway (Station Road) near the rear entrance as overnight tramp accommodation. The windmill had been recently used as a warehouse and a cottage, but because of his neighbours' objections, the owner refused the guardians permission. Despite the times, the old workhouse was finally sold to Kirkham pawnbrokers, James Radcliffe and John Whiteside for three-hundred and seventeen pounds, twelve shillings.

At the start of 1848, the bread was still needed, but the amount ordered dropped from nine c.w.t in January to five c.w.t by the end of February. The distress had eased, and the meetings were moved back to fortnightly on 29 February. After being dug, the land was sown with oats, and then the labour master's services were dispensed with. The outdoor relief lists were reverted to fortnightly.

During the winter, the guardian's meetings were held at one-thirty in the afternoon and in the summer at two. At ten-thirty in the morning the finance committee met and went through the relief lists which showed who the relieving officers had granted relief to, during the past two weeks. It was the committee, not the relieving officer who had the final say who would be granted relief, how much, or who would have it taken away or reduced.

The workhouse children were inspected each year by the Poor Law Board's school inspector. The inspector, Mr Brown, recommended that the guardians employ a teacher and open a school in the building. The matter was left on the table, the term the guardians used to say, 'ignore it.'

The workhouse infirmary was limited in terms of the medical help it could offer. When somebody needed to have surgery, the only place to go was the Manchester Infirmary. Mary Brown of Kirkham needed an operation (the reason unknown), and her husband asked the guardians for help. She was sent to Manchester and treated at the cost of twenty-four pounds and fourteen shillings. Her friends raised ten pounds, twelve shillings, and five pence and the guardians paid the Manchester Infirmary the outstanding fourteen pounds, one shilling, and five pence.

The new clerk William Thompson told a Lytham shipwright that he must repay the relief his daughter-in-law had received and to continue to support her and her children in the future; all of whom were resident in the workhouse. He replied to the guardians, saying that he would support his two young grandchildren and pay to bind the third apprentice but would not support the mother who was 'rather untowardly'.

John McGuiness and Gereil Murphy, who had been working weekly at Westby, applied for an order to be sent home. The clerk, in consequence of their destitution, granted an order for payment of their passage back to Belfast from Fleetwood.

In August, the oats grown on the Orders Lane Farm, as it was now known, were auctioned off at the New Black Bull Inn, Kirkham. John Taylor and John Billington purchased the oats at eight pounds, seven shillings and sixpence per acre paying the union fifty pounds, one shilling and ten pence in total for the oats. The cabbages grown in the workhouse gardens were also auctioned off in November to save them being damaged by frost, raising one pound, four shillings, and four pence. More money was raised for the union when Mr Whinneiah of Burn Hall asked for his crop of peas to be assorted by the old inmates of the house.

It was commonplace for persons to donate gifts for the use of the inmates.

Reverend Moore gave a selection of books for the pauper inmates of the workhouse, 'to read at suitable times and that a catalogue was received therewith out of which selections could be made when requisite.'

When the price of potatoes became too expensive, or crops were blighted, the guardians would change the diet. After a large increase in the costs of potatoes in November, the potatoes were substituted with rice, barley and peas.

There were some alterations to the workhouse.

The sleeping rooms in the male and female sick departments were comprised of small rooms. The doctors advised taking down the partition walls to create four large rooms to separate the sick from the fever cases. The walls were taken down, and new water closets were put into each of the four rooms. Richard Tripier was paid ten pounds to make some tables; so all the inmates could dine together. The master ordered some new pigs, a fire gate for the laundry, and all the doors inside the building were numbered.

In 1849, William Birley left his home Hillside House in Kirkham to work in London and his nephew, Charles Birley of Ash Tree House, Kirkham, was appointed chairman. In July the workhouse visiting committee inspected the workhouse, 'finding the house clean and in good order.' The committee ordered all windows, doors and waterspouts to be painted, and made a few more alterations. They moved the water closet attached to the board room into a room in the union office. The former water closet was converted for the use of the relieving officers. The female vagrants' bath in the union office was removed to the washhouse, and the room was now to be used as a waiting room for paupers. Finally, they asked the master to attend to the laundry attached to the new waiting room to stop it from smoking.

The guardians were responsible for dealing with complaints about unsanitary practises in the different townships, whether inside buildings or outside. They decided to appoint an inspectors of nuisances and the two relieving officers were chosen for the role, John Parkinson and James Davies. This role was separate to the role of relieving officers, and they received an additional salary.

The inspectors of nuisances were asked to deal with a problem at the dog kennels belonging to the Kirkham Harriers Hunting Pack on Bloody Lane

End, Wesham. There were complaints regarding the flaying of carcases on the highway side of the kennels, the stench from cooking food for the dogs, as well as the carrion becoming putrid. The inspectors ordered the above stopped or a court order would be obtained. The hunting pack obeyed the inspectors requests regarding the complaints.

The guardians were also responsible for the containment of diseases, especially smallpox. They reported a case of English Cholera to the General Board of Health. Mary Harrison, aged seventy, years came down with the disease on 20 August 1849 and died the same day.

Outdoor paupers were kept busy on the farm. The master ordered twenty-five bushels of oats, and the new labour master John Sawyer set them to work digging the land and sowing the oats. The master also ordered seven new pigs costing £3 19s. 11d. plus carriage. The pigs used up the kitchen slops and kept some of the indoor paupers busy. The pigs, when fattened up, and the oats, when ready, would be auctioned off. Mr Langton Birley purchased the oats for forty-seven pounds, seventeen shillings, and six and a half pence.

Another person was sent to the Manchester Infirmary.

John Anson, an orphan, who was seventeen-years-old, was taken to Manchester by the clerk where he later died. The cost to bring his body home plus the coffin would cost four pounds and eight shillings. John's friends raised one pound, and the union paid the remaining three pounds and eight shillings, so he could be buried in St Michaels graveyard Kirkham.

The year ended with inmate Steven Nixon of Bryning absconded from the workhouse and leaving his wife and two children chargeable to the union. He was apprehended and sentenced to two months hard labour at the Preston House of Correction.

In 1850, a new committee was created, the 'labour committee' consisting of the chairman Charles Birley, the two vice-chairmen Robert Walker and John Pool and guardians John Loxham, Richard Bilsborrow, Henry Fisher, James Ramsey, and Thomas Jackson. Their remit was 'to give direction about all matters connected with the cultivation and produce of the land belonging and occupied by the union.'

The labour committee, which was later renamed the farm committee, organised the sale of the crops grown on the union's farm on Orders Lane. Potatoes were sold for sixteen pounds and nine shillings, mangold wurzel for sixteen pounds and nineteen shillings, and cabbages and turnips for one pound, ten shillings, and eight pence.

This year's 'call' for the rates was nine and a half pence in the pound which raised six-thousand, seven-hundred and seventy-seven pounds. This figure included the county and police rates, lighting, watching and highway rates and repayments of workhouse loans and officers' salaries. When you took these figures out, the cost of poor relief was three and a half pence in the pound. This figure was the mark of how successful the union was in controlling the cost of poor relief.

The number of paupers in the Fylde excluding vagrants in 1846, was eight-hundred and eighty-eight paupers; 1847, one thousand and thirty-six paupers; 1848, one-thousand, four hundred, and thirty-two paupers; 1849, one thousand, three hundred, and forty-eight paupers ;1850, one thousand, one hundred, and ninety-five paupers; and 1851, nine-hundred and seventy two paupers. These figures show how the increase in pauperism climbed due to the commercial distress before reducing back to normal levels in 1851.

Low numbers were not always a good thing in the workhouse. During the summer, the number of able-bodied women in the workhouse was so low that it caused a problem for the matron, who didn't have sufficient help to run the workhouse properly. The guardians decided to hire a temporary female servant to help the matron.

Some more children left the workhouse, to start their apprenticeships, go into service, or left to live with relations.

Orphan Peter Taylor of Freckleton was apprenticed to Thomas Salthouse of Fleetwood; who was a plumber, glazier, and painter. He took a seven-pound bond with a four-pound fee and a suit of clothes. Elizabeth Baines, eleven years old, an inmate from Lytham, was sent to Mr Holmes Green, Preston as a servant.

William Gardner also an orphan was apprenticed to tailor and draper Charles Hankinson of Southport for seven years. He left with an eight-pound fee and a new suit of clothes.

When a child was apprenticed, only half the fee was paid. After twelve months the apprentice and his master came before the board and if both sides were still happy with the arrangement, the second half of the fee was paid. Charles Hankinson 'produced' his apprentice before the board after twelve months. The board was satisfied with the statements from the master and the apprentice, and the remaining fee was paid.

In November, Mary Taylor complained to the guardians that her son Edward, who had been apprenticed to shoemaker George Gregson of Marton, was being ill-treated. They were both asked to explain themselves at the next guardian's meeting. Edward and George both accepted both sides had been a little to blame, and for the future, both parties promised to do their duty to each other.

The workhouse master said, 'I have no fear of a good understanding existing between him and his apprentice, if the boy's mother would not interfere.'

At Christmas time, William Chadwick, a pauper of weak mind, was sent to live with his Uncle William Chadwick of Carnforth.

In the infirmary, there were three Irish vagrants who were sick with the fever. They were to be sent back to Ireland as soon as they were fit to travel. There were a lot of Irish people in the area, as at this time English companies would use people from Ireland as cheap labour to fill unpopular jobs.

A company called Waitman & Holme Mills of Westmorland had brought a number of females over from Ireland and told them if they didn't like the work, they would pay for the journey back home. This, however, never happened, and three women turned up at Fleetwood in a destitute condition. They applied for relief and asked to be returned immediately back to Ireland. Mr Parkinson, the relieving officer thought the company had ill-treated and deceived the women and should pay for the relief and cost of travel. The clerk was ordered to recover the money from the firm.

In 1851, the guardians helped two families leave the workhouse. James Luick and his wife applied to be discharged on 8 April with two shillings and sixpence weekly relief and four shillings casual relief; which the board agreed to. However, before he left, he became ill and wasn't well enough to leave until June. James asked again for the same relief, but then requested to live in the workhouse whilst working as a weaver until he had earned a few shillings to buy some furniture. The guardians agreed. Thomas Wilding his wife and two children were discharged with a one-pound loan from the guardians. The loan was to be repaid in weekly instalments, or otherwise as may best suit Thomas' convenience.

Adam Wright, the workhouse doctor, went to visit the Lancaster Asylum and returned with three released paupers, Nancy Baines and Isabella Salisbury of Kirkham and Alice Bragg of Layton. The quarterly costs for the care of the Fylde's lunatics at Lancaster at the time was fifty pounds and three shillings.

The school inspector visited the workhouse and examined the children; he found them unsatisfactory. The guardians sent copies of the remarks he placed in the visitors' book to the three Kirkham schools, all run by churches. Copies were sent to the Vicar of Kirkham, Father Sherbourne of the Willows and Reverend Best of the Zion Chapel.

A workhouse was not an ideal institution to raise children, and one of the best ways to remove girls was to put them into service. Some girls left at an early age.

Jane Davies asked to take eight years-old Jane Norman from the workhouse to act as nurse and servant to her father John Davies, 81 North Road, Preston. She said she would find meat and clothes, treat her as one of the family, and not allow her to leave their service without first informing the guardians. The decision was left up to Jane Norman, and she agreed to go. It didn't work out, and she returned to the workhouse two weeks later. In July, she left again on her own will to take up a position as nurse and servant for Richard Burton of Blackburn.

Inside the workhouse, new armchairs were purchased for the aged and infirm to sit more comfortably. In the laundry, a new floor was laid, and pipes were fitted for drying clothes during the winter months.

In order to be fair to the ratepayers, the relieving officers would refuse relief to persons he felt were undeserving. Some people could take great offence at being refused relief. When Mr Parkinson refused to grant two Irish vagrants sisters Mary and Ann Smith relief, they smashed his house windows causing three shillings worth of damage. The guardians paid for his windows to be repaired.

The call on rates was set biannually in March and September and was paid in four instalments. This year the rates had to be paid by 28 May, 2 August, 23 October, and 22 January.

Bispham with Norbreck	£50	£25	£25
Bryning with Kellamergh	£33	£17	£16
Carleton	£70	£35	£35
Clifton with Salwick	£148	£74	£74
Little Eccleston with Larbreck	£62	£31	£31
Elswick	£54	£27	£27
Freckleton	£130	£65	£65
Greenhalgh with Thistleton	£68	£34	£34
Hardhorn with Newton	£110	£55	£55
Kirkham	£380	£190	£190
Layton with Warbrick	£112	£61	£61
Lytham	£120	£60	£60
Marton	£198	£100	£98
Medlar with Wesham	£56	£28	£28
Newton with Scales	£56	£28	£28
Poulton	£120	£60	£60
Ribby with Wray	£68	£34	£34
Singleton	£72	£36	£36
Thornton	£310	£155	£155
Treales, Roseacre and Wharles	£147	£79	£68
Warton	£71	£36	£35
Weeton	£126	£63	£63
Westby with Plumpton	£138	£70	£68

These figures show the 'call' for the Fylde's Parishes in 1852.

The school inspector again found the children's education unsatisfactory. Some guardians thought it was time to appoint a schoolmistress, but some thought they should visit the schools to see if the inspector was being fair to the children.

The workhouse visiting committee went first to the national school. They reported, 'There was only one pupil 8 years-old Elizabeth Whiteside who reads pretty well, and, in all aspects behaves. She was treated the same as the other children of the school. We couldn't visit the infant school because the master was away, and it was closed.'

In the Willows Catholic School, there were four pupils. Ellen Keely, fourteen years; June Norman, nine years; Mary Hall, ten years; and Jane Hall, eight years.

The committee reported, 'The girls acquitted themselves in reading in a satisfactory manner. Ellen Keely's right hand is disabled and appears to have made some progress in writing with the left hand. None of the other girls could write. The girls were taught to knit and sew, as well as to read and write. The pauper children were treated the same as the other students.'

The problem the teachers told the committee was that, 'The children are generally on admission into the schools extremely ignorant and their attendance at school is generally of a short duration, and it was impossible to make any progress in learning.'

No decision was made at this time, about opening a school in the workhouse.

The guardians had the power to detain children under the age of sixteen unless they had somewhere to live. One of the reasons they were sent into service or apprenticed is that they were provided with accommodation.

Pauper children or orphans were often used to fill unpopular jobs; one was in the cotton mills. To get around the question of accommodation, mills like John Birley's and Sons, Kirkham, built poor houses where children could live and be cared for by a matron whilst they trained in aspects of weaving. Robert Thornton, fifteen years old, was taken by the master to Birley's Flaxfield Mill to find employment for the boy. The boy said he was willing to do anything and after finding a position, he moved into the poor apprentice house. Robert now had somewhere to live, learnt a trade, earned a wage and eventually, escaped the poor law system.

Some children were just abandoned by the parents. Three sisters Catherine, Ellen, and Jane Judge, all under twelve years of age, entered in May this year. They had been found alone and destitute in Fleetwood. Their mother had put them on the train at Preston and then disappeared. When the mother never returned, the girls were removed to their place of birth, Glasgow.

John Birleys Poor Apprentice House, Barnfield, Kirkham (Photo Courtesy of Neil Heslip)

The asylums continued to be overfull. Agnes Ward arrived at the workhouse in 'a rather unsound mind' without the knowledge of her husband Thomas. The doctor detained her to see if there would be any improvements in her mind. Agnes' husband, a labourer, was told he must endeavour to find work and do what he can to contribute to her maintenance. She was released in June after a four-month stay.

The guardians were struggling to find enough accommodation for the vagrants. Once the vagrant ward was full, they were sent to local lodging houses at the expense of the union. This practice was to end as the board thought it encouraged the tramping. They were to be fed and lodged in the workhouse after being well cleaned by bathing. The food and board given to them while under the care of the workhouse master would be paid for by being set to work breaking stones. The families of tramps were to be given work according to their age, sex and strength.

The only information remaining about the early days of the Fylde Union are the minutes of the guardian's meetings, where this information is gleamed from. Unfortunately, part way through 1852 and until March 1858 the minutes are missing.

The last thing mentioned in the minutes was that two pigs were killed in September 1852, for the use of the workhouse, and two new pigs were purchased to replace them. Until this point the pigs were sold at auction, but now they were butchered and consumed by the inmates and staff.

Thomas Barton, the master and his associate John Chadwick (63) of Kirkham saw this as a chance to make some money and started selling the bacon in the town. By the time, the thieving had been discovered, 200lbs of bacon had been sold. The workhouse master who was the 'principal delinquent' died the week before his trial aged 52, so John Chadwick, faced the music alone. He was sentenced to four months' imprisonment at Preston Sessions. A new master and matron were appointed Mr and Mrs Lord on a joint salary of £40.

March 1858, Charles Birley was still the chairman. Mr and Mrs Lord were the master and matron, William Thompson, clerk, and life continued as usual. The guardians had decided that all able-bodied receiving outdoor relief would now be set to work breaking stones at two-thirds of the normal rate paid to normal stone breakers. They would work with the surveyor of the highways, to deliver the stones to the townships where they would be broken.

Running costs of the union were published every March and September. It showed the broken-down costs of the entire union and the costs for each individual township. One figure is the common fund which was for the running costs of the union; salaries, purchasing, building's general maintenance and loans. The rest of the figures represent the general fund, and when you took out the county rate and the common fund charge, the figures showed what an individual townships paupers had cost the union (Kirkham's being the example). This information was important because a three-year average could be taken for each township, and if this figure was below what the township had paid for its paupers, the overseers could apply for a discount.

	Entire Union	Kirkham
Indoor relief	£271 19s. 8d	£48 13s. 8d
Out-door-relief	£998 13s. 81/2d	£99 3s. 9d
Maintenance of Lunatics	£142 1s. 6d	£27 13s. 8d
Extra medical costs	£12 5s. 4d	£1 10s. 0d
Vaccination fees	£41 17s. 9d	£10 8s. 6d
Registration fees	£36 19s. 0d	£7 3s. 0d
County Rate	£1461 1s. 6d	£74 3s. 10d
Collector Rate	£60	£5 6s. 0d
Common Fund Charge	£547 10s. 4d	£74 10s. 0d

When the cost per head at the workhouse had increased without reason, the guardians suspected that the paupers were stealing things from the workhouse to sell in Kirkham. This was proven when it was discovered that Alice Wilkinson had taken a ball of yarn from the workhouse and sold it in the town. The police were informed, but they found no evidence to take her to court.

The master told the guardians, 'The paupers leave the workhouse premises without my permission, and I do not have the controls necessary to prevent such conduct.'

The guardians reprimanded him 'for such a state of discipline' and insisted upon him carrying out strictly the regulations for the governance of the workhouse. He had from then on to keep a record of all paupers who were temporally absent from the workhouse on leave of absence. They also suspected that some paupers were stealing the property of the dead and from then on, any paupers who had died, had to have an inventory of their clothing and personal articles made.

There was a high death rate in the workhouse. This year new tenders were put out to joiners to build the coffins for the workhouses' dead. John Eccleston, Richard Ward, Thomas Royale, John Catterall, and Richard Whiteside replied. Mr Whiteside was awarded the six months contract at ten shillings and sixpence per coffin for paupers over seven years and six shillings for paupers under seven years.

Some paupers left for the colonies. Margaret Rogers of Lytham applied for assistance in buying a new set of clothes for herself and her children to join her husband in Australia. He had paid her passage money to the

Emigration Committee. The guardians agreed, but the Poor Law Board declined to sanction it, as it wasn't a case of pauperism.

Robert Rainford, whose wife Alice was in prison, was summoned for not contributing to his children in the workhouse. In situations like this, the guardians could make the person share their children's fate and enter the workhouse. It turned out, however, that he'd sent the money by carrier who had failed to deliver it. He intended to pay the five shillings a week and was allowed to remain out of the workhouse.

On the farm, the oats were sold to Mr Loxham for ten pounds and one shilling per acre. The farm committee planned to plant mangold wurzel and turnips for next year, so they had the land ploughed and drained in preparation. The farm was a quarter of a mile away, and when land came up for sale next door to the workhouse, the farm committee went to the auction at the Black Horse Hotel, but it was too expensive.

The following year, 1859, the guardians asked Arthur Leyland Birley if he would sell one acre of land on the east side of the workhouse. He wanted two hundred pounds for the land, but the guardians only offered one hundred and fifty pounds. Mr Birley then proposed one-hundred and eighty pounds. The guardians again offered one-hundred and fifty pounds which Mr Birley finally agreed to. The guardians borrowed the money from the Public Works Commission and wanted to pay it over a twenty years period, but the Poor Law Board told then that such a small loan must be paid over five years; in five equal payments.

The guardians now moved the workhouse eastern boundary in line with Station Road, and new gates were built. The rear gates were kept locked except on board days and for deliveries. The front gates were open between eight in the morning until dark in winter, and eight in the morning until eight at night in the summer. At the same time, the master was told to keep the paths in the gardens cleaner and in better order. Inside the workhouse, handrails were fitted on either side of the stairs leading up to the women's department in the infirmary.

There was a refractory ward, in the workhouse, a number of small rooms, where patients were sent for punishment. The master had the following list of wrongdoings which deemed a pauper 'disorderly', which were published in the book, *General Orders and Instructional Letters of the Poor Law Commission* (1845).

> Punishments for Misbehaviour of the Paupers.
>
> Art 34. Any pauper who shall neglect to observe such of the regulations herein contained as are applicable to and binding on him;-
>
> Or who shall make any noise when silence is ordered to be kept;
>
> Or shall use obscene or profane language;
>
> Or shall by word or deed insult or revile any person;
>
> Or shall threaten to strike or to assault any person;
>
> Or shall not duly clean his person;
>
> Or shall refuse or neglect to work, after having being required to do so;
>
> Or shall pretend sickness;
>
> Or shall play at cards or other game of chance;
>
> Or shall enter or attempt to enter, without permission, the ward or yard appropriated to any class of paupers, other than that to which he belongs;
>
> Or shall misbehave in going to, at, or returning from public worship out of the workhouse, or at prayers in the workhouse;
>
> Or shall return after the appointed time of absence, when allowed to quit the workhouse temporarily;
>
> Or shall wilfully disobey any lawful order of any officer;
>
> Shall be deemed DISORDERLY.

These offences would usually mean six hours with a diet of bread and water, but it could be up to forty-eight hours. If a pauper repeated the offence or any other offence in article thirty-four, within seven days or any of the below; he or she was classed as a 'Refractory Pauper'.

The other offences which deemed you refractory were:

> Or who shall by word or deed insult or revile the master or matron, or any other officer of the workhouse, or any of the guardians;
>
> Or shall wilfully disobey any lawful order of the master and matron after such order shall have been repeated;
>
> Or shall unlawfully strike or otherwise unlawfully assault any person;
>
> Or shall wilfully or mischievously damage or soil any property whatsoever belonging to the guardians;
>
> Or shall wilfully or mischievously waste or soil any provisions, stock, tools, or materials, for work belonging to the guardians;
>
> Or shall be drunk;
>
> Or shall commit any act of indecency;
>
> Or shall wilfully disturb the other inmates during prayers or divine worship;
>
> Shall be deemed REFRACTORY.

A refractory pauper could be held in solitary confinement for up to twenty-four hours maximum. If the offence was such that confinement above twenty-four hours was deemed insufficient punishment, the person was sent before a magistrate.

Mary Rainford was deemed a refractory pauper and was kept separate from the other paupers because of her bad behaviour. One day she smashed thirty-five panes of glass in the workhouse and was summoned to Kirkham Court. In court, the case was dismissed because she said she was unwell and had been kept in the refractory ward for five nights and days by the master, Mr Lord; which was illegal. Mr Lord admitted this in court. The guardians talked about the case at the next meeting and thought the master was wrong and pointed out to him that she was not in the refractory ward, but kept separate from the other paupers in a proper room.

The relieving officers and master's accounts were made up on Mondays, but this didn't give the clerk the chance to read through the reports in time for the guardian's meetings. As from now, the accounts had to be ready by Saturday so they could be examined by the clerk before the fortnightly meetings.

It was common for men to join the army or navy and leave their families chargeable to the union.

William Edward had joined the Army and left his son in the workhouse. Flemming Croft had also left his family and joined the Navy, Boarding *H.M.S. Hastings* in Liverpool. The clerk wrote to the admiralty and the war office for claims against their wages. They both replied to the guardians, saying poor unions had no legal claim on the wages of sailors and soldiers.

The farm committee confirmed what they would plant over the next three years on the farm. Oats in 1860, barley and grass in 1861, and in 1862, and 1863 only grass. The last order of the decade was that 'no weak-minded inmates were allowed to leave the workhouse, without the company of another adult'.

1860–1869

In 1860, Robert Walker replaced Charles Birley as chairman, and Ellen Carter replaced the previous servant Betsey Wray after she gave a month's notice and left for a new position at Great Brighton.

Ellen was offered the position as servant on a salary of eleven pounds plus rations. This offer of employment had to be sanctioned by the Poor Law Board who refused the appointment because Ellen had an illegitimate child. The guardians were of the mind that if she worked, she could support the child herself and not be a burden on the ratepayers. The illegitimacy was a fact that wouldn't change, and they wrote back to the board saying they thought the appointment was a proper one. The board relented, and she was given the role as servant.

The visiting committee reported that the privies needed ventilation. They also had the bakehouse external door bricked up to stop the wind blowing in; a new doorway was made from the room next door to gain access to the bakehouse; and a cupboard was built in the nest cavity in the master's bedroom.

The guardians also looked into ways of stopping the inmates leaving the workhouse without permission. They thought about locking the front gate by fitting a bolt and lock, and building a porter's lodge at the rear gates. However, instead of building a porter's lodge, the guardians went for the cheaper option and fitted a bell to the front gates. The front and rear gates would be locked each night at nine p.m.

Mr Farnell inspected the workhouse in September. He found the house clean and tidy and recommended that old married couples above sixty be allowed to live together in private rooms. The guardians and medical officer who weren't present at the inspection, asked to be informed in future of the time and date of inspections so that they could be present.

Mr Shaw, the workhouse medical officer, thought that the idiot inmates of the house needed to be in separate wards to have the proper care they needed. He also recommended that Robert Woods and Johnathan Titterington be sent to the Lancaster Asylum. Robert was sent, but Johnathan, who was only eight, was too young to enter an asylum and had to stay in the workhouse. He was finally sent to live with James Wignall of Newton, who would look after him for five shillings a week. Being sent out to live with a family was called boarding-out and was one way of taking children out of the workhouse.

District medical officers were asked by the guardians to nominate a substitute in case of absence or inability to perform their duties. They also gave an order to the master that in future children had to be accompanied by an adult when they went out to one of the Kirkham churches.

On 26 August 1861, the house master, Mr James Lord died, aged fifty-seven; his wife Mrs Lord stayed on as matron for fifteen pounds per year. An advert was placed for a new house master on a salary of twenty-five pounds per annum, plus rations. Eight men applied for the master's post, which was reduced down to three applicants; James Salisbury, Whitehaven; Thomas Latham, Liverpool; and W. Liddel, Preston. The guardians went through rounds of votes to decide on the new master.

Round one: the votes went Liddel: eight; Latham: five; Salisbury: five. Therefore, Liddel went through.

Round two: the votes went Latham: nine; Salisbury: eight. Therefore, Salisbury went out.

Round three: the votes went Latham: ten; Liddel: eight. Mr Latham got the job.

It was finally decided by the guardians to open a school in the workhouse and employ a teacher on a salary of thirty pounds. There were two applicants, Miss Cooke and Miss Dennis. The guardians voted eleven for Cooke and three for Dennis. Not all the guardians thought a workhouse school would be for the better. Guardian William Segar Hodgson moved that no appointment be made. The chairman refused to put the motion, and Miss Cooke was appointed. The number of children who went to the new school was forty-one.

In August, there was one-hundred and three inmates, but one was leaving to start his five-years apprenticeship, thirteen-year-old James Hornby. He was bound apprentice to Mr Whiteside of Poulton-le-Fylde, together with a premium of five pounds.

The Reverend W. L. Hussey of St Michael's Church, Kirkham, donated one-hundred and forty volumes of books from the Christian Knowledge Society to the workhouse.

Poor Law Inspector, Mr Mainwaring, enquired about the coming winter regarding the depressed state of trade, due to the approaching Cotton Famine, the clerk replied.

> My Dear Sir,
>
> I have acknowledged the receipt of your letter of the 9th inst, requesting to be informed of the prospects of this union for the ensuing winter, in consequence of the present state of the cotton trade. There are at Kirkham three mills engaged in the cotton trade, all of which, for some weeks, have been running short time. The flax mill here runs full time, and so far, as I am aware, there is no immediate prospect of any alterations in the hours of labour, either in the flax mill or the cotton mills. The partial closing of the cotton mills had not hitherto the effect of materially increasing the application for relief, and unless the mills should entirely closed, it appears to me that the rates in this union will not, to any great extent, be affected by the state of trade. The guardians have not taken any steps to meet an emergency, and so far as the prospects of the union are concerned, I am glad to believe that it will not be necessary for them to do so. I am, my dear sir, yours truly
>
> Wm. Thompson Clerk.

In April 1862, Roger Charnock Richards was elected the new chairman; the former chairman had lost his seat of Thornton. Mr Richards' first task was to oversee the formation of a new committee, the 'assessment committee' which was to investigate and supervise the valuations of the property of the ratepayers.

The committee had to have at least nine members, but no more than twelve. The first meeting of the assessment committee was on Tuesday 23 September 1862, meeting at twelve noon on the day of the guardians' meetings. The overseers would work out the value of each parish. Land was assessed at five per cent, land with buildings at seven and a half per cent, houses at fifteen per cent, cottages valued under six pounds at twenty per cent and mills at twenty-five per cent.

The main mills valued were:

> Richards and Holden, Kirkham, at sixty-four pounds, eight shillings, and zero pence.
>
> John Birley & Sons, Kirkham, at seven-hundred and eighty-four pounds, sixteen shillings, and zero pence.
>
> Richards and Holden, Wesham, at seven-hundred and sixty-two pounds, zero shillings, and zero pence.
>
> Whitworth & Barrett, Wesham, at two-hundred and forty-two pounds, twelve shillings and zero pence.
>
> Henry Hall, Freckleton, at one-hundred and fourteen pounds, six shillings and zero pence.

The rateable value of the railways was set at five pounds per mile from Kirkham to the Preston Union boundary. The Lytham Branch to the main line was set at two pounds per mile and all other parts of the Fylde's Railways four pounds per mile.

The overseers and collectors of the Kirkham District were called to a meeting with the finance committee, and the new assessment lists were set as follows for the district. It shows an increase in the rateable value of the Kirkham District of three-thousand, one-hundred, and ninety-five pounds.

	A	B	County Valuation 1854	Rateable Value 1862	New Gross Estimated Rentals	New Rateable Value	Change
Kirkham		50s. 5d	£5737	£6442	£7721	£7346	£375
Bryning	28s. 5d	29s.	£1617	£1559	£1771	£1721	£50
Clifton	28s. 10d	29s. 1d	£5487	£5703	£5957	£5754	£203
Freckleton	30s.	35s.	£3792	£4001	£4438	£4189	£249
Greenhalgh	26s. 1d	27s. 7d	£2880	£2757	£3113	£2970	£143

	A	B	County Valuation 1854	Rateable Value 1862	New Gross Estimated Rentals	New Rateable Value	Change
Lytham	26s. 8d	33s. 6d	£13359	£14139	£16676	£15595	£1081
Medlar	26s. 10d	28s. 3d	£3245	£4362	£4805	£4641	£164
Newton	37s.	35s. 7d	£2332	£2347	£2634	£2526	£108
Ribby	32s. 2d	36s. 11d	£2549	£2737	£3046	£2897	£149
Treales	23s. 8d	25s. 2d	£5285	£5921	£6512	£6254	£258
Warton	30s. 3	33s. 6d	£2638	£2636	£3209	£3027	£182
Weeton	37s. 2d	28s. 1d	£3803	£4235	£4969	£4797	£172
Westby	31s. 8d	32.s 7d	£5866	£4995	£7080	£6819	£261
Totals			£58590	£61834	£719311	£68536	£3395

A=Estimated value of a statue acre on farms above forty acres.
B=Estimated value of an acre on farms above forty acres as per overseers.
Kirkham District Valuations 1862.

The Poulton District's parishes were re-assessed the following month.

By October, the Cotton Famine had begun to bite in Kirkham; Phoenix Mill, Selby Mill, and Freckleton Street Mill closed, putting five-hundred and sixty people out of work. The outdoor relief reached one-hundred people in Kirkham; in better times it would have been forty. This figure of one-hundred shows that most mill workers turned to their friendly societies for help. Those receiving outdoor relief were paid weekly, which included one shilling and sixpence to pay their rent and one shilling for 'fire'.

In Kirkham, a relief committee was set up to provide additional help for the unemployed. The relief was in the form of the distribution of food, clothing, and necessities including coal and additional relief payments. A soup kitchen was set up in the National School. In October, the Kirkham Relief Committee raised four-hundred and fifty pounds from house to house canvassing. A further three-hundred pounds were raised from donations. One-hundred pounds was donated by Thomas Langton Birley; a guardian and owner of the Flaxfield Mill, Kirkham which was still running full time. A further one-hundred pounds came from Richards Holding and Co., owner of the closed Wesham spinning mill, Selby; and another one-hundred pound came from Whitworth and Barrett, of the Wesham weaving shed, Phoenix Mill, also closed. In the first month, the committee distributed bread, meal and potatoes to thirty families.

Forty unemployed men were found work by breaking stones. Mr Ogden of Station Road was employed as 'labour master' for fifteen shillings a week. A sewing shop was opened in the town for unemployed females.

Due to the type of work, the male inmates wore a uniform made from fustian: a hard-wearing twilled cloth. It was proposed by Mr Barrett that twenty-five new suits be procured for the men and boys immediately.

He said, 'The fustian had been washed and worn till there was neither goodness nor warmth in it.'

The visiting committee was ordered to procure the suits.

In the workhouse, was a pauper called Christopher Hall, who was a member of the Oddfellows Friendly Society. The clerk applied to the society to pay for Mr Hall's maintenance, whilst he was sick in the infirmary. Dr Shaw, the oddfellows, and workhouse doctor, didn't think he was sick and refused to write a sick note. The oddfellows only paid out for sickness, so the clerk couldn't claim from the society for Christopher's maintenance. The guardians, who disagreed with Dr Shaw, called him before them.

Dr Shaw said, 'Christopher was a 'sly bird' and up to 'foxing', that he was not sick, but infirm from old age and general debility, and that it was contrary to the rules for him to give him a certificate, and he could not conscientiously grant him one and therefore would not.'

It wasn't uncommon for paupers to feign sickness, in order to have an easier life in the workhouse.

Despite the Cotton Famine, Christmas was still celebrated in the customary way. The one-hundred and fifty paupers including forty-one children had the usual Christmas meal of roast beef and plum pudding. Mrs Langton Birley also donated a barrel of beer.

In 1863, the guardians thought that all the pauper's clothing was in a very bad state, and used it as a way to create work. They decided to purchase material and use tailors, who were without sufficient work, to make the clothing. More unemployed men were found work picking oakum at Freckleton Street Mill, Kirkham. Some guardians questioned whether this was viable, as it only brought in a penny a day per worker.

Mr Ogden, the labour master resigned.

'A good man, who had resigned through meddlers who did not understand the matter.' thought Mr Barrett, and regarding unemployed men he said, 'They could be employed in the agricultural line in filling up pits, riddling fences, but the agriculturists had no faith in factory hands at their work.'

In July, the economy was beginning to pick up, and the new labour master's services were dispensed with. The unemployed were now to provide for themselves. The upturn was short lived. Messrs Whitworth and Barrett's Phoenix Mill, Wesham, closed again and then Bowlderstone Mill, Freckleton, closed after a fire, this mill reopened four weeks later.

The board received a letter from Dr Whitgreave, of Kirkham Number One District, enquiring why three items on his bill were not paid. The first item was attending an old woman called Rawlinson, who'd fractured a thigh, the second a boy named Cross who'd broken his arm, and the third for attending a woman named McMahon in a midwifery case. The items were disallowed by the guardians because it was rumoured that Mrs Rawlinson's thigh was not broken and second because he had had no medical orders for the cases from the relieving officer, Mr Raby.

The guardians held an inquiry at one of their meetings. Mr Raby was called into the boardroom.

Mr Raby told the guardians, 'The people at the woman's house told him that the old woman's thigh was not broken. The boy's father Cross was in full-time work and therefore did not require relief in my opinion. The third case, this was the woman's first child, the husband was in full work and, therefore, able to pay himself.

Mr Birley proposed that Dr Whitgreave be brought in.

On being questioned, the doctor said, 'The old woman's fracture was in the socket at the top of the thigh bone, and that such a fracture did not need spells of bedding up. In such cases, the patient was able to walk a little, but not with ease, in a fortnight or three weeks. As regards to the boy, the father had been chargeable to the town a short time previous, and I did not consider it necessary to obtain a fresh order, as for McMahon, the man was earning only 7s. 6d. per week and I did not think he was able to pay.'

The guardians refused to pay the doctor, so Dr Whitgreave appealed to the Poor Law Board in London over the disputed claims, but they supported the guardians.

Dr Whitgreave wrote another letter the following year, asking for something extra for attending a boy at Clifton who was scalded on the leg some time ago. The board told him, 'Little ones pay for the big ones, it was all in the bargain,' therefore nothing extra could be allowed. By July he'd had enough and resigned. Dr John Ireland replaced him as medical officer for the Kirkham District.

The present chairman, Roger Charnock Richards, like two of his predecessors, William and Charles Birley, were mill owners and judges in Kirkham. All three men were involved with all the Kirkham institutions; the only difference was that the Birleys were Church of England and Mr Richards an Independent. Inevitably the different roles they had overlapped, none more so than sitting on the bench at Kirkham Court, a role the three men prioritised, which was on the same day as the guardians' meetings. So, it was motioned and carried that the guardians now me every Wednesday at ten o'clock in the morning.

On 10 March, it was party time in the workhouse, celebrating the royal wedding of the Prince of Wales. The workhouse master had only requested the treat for the fifty children because he thought the adults didn't deserve it. However, by the day of Prince Albert Edward's wedding to Princess Alexandra of Denmark, the master had relented, and the adults could also celebrate.

The Preston Chronicle recorded the event.

> The children were 'regaled' by the guardians with a plentiful supply of tea, coffee, currant bread and oranges. Each child received a toy and medal from Mrs Wentworth. In the evening, the adults sat down in the decorated dining room to a meal of roast beef, mutton, veal pies, cheese. There was tea and coffee plus an abundant supply of good ale all provided by Reverend J. W. Birley, Thomas Langton Birley, Arthur Leyland Birley and Mrs Parson, who are always foremost in every good and charitable work connected with the town of Kirkham. A good evening was had by all.

Every August, the children, although still in the workhouse, had a two-week holiday where they didn't have to work or go to school. During these two-weeks, they would have a day out in Blackpool. 'Blackpool Day' was the highlight of the year when they were escorted around the resort by the matron and schoolmistress.

The year had been a busy one and now that the pressure on the workhouse had receded the matron applied for a week or ten day's leave of absence for the purpose of visiting her friends. The guardians readily granted the application, providing she left a proper and suitable substitute. They considered she highly deserved a little recreation for her past valued and untiring service.

Christmas dinner was becoming a grander affair with more of the women of the leading Kirkham families donating gifts. Mrs Langton Birley and Mrs Leyland Birley supplied each adult with a pint of ale. After the meal, the older people were presented with a quantity of tobacco and snuff and the children an orange. The remainder of the evening was spent in dancing, singing and recitations.

1864 started with the school inspection by Edmund Wadshouse, Her Majesty's Inspector of Union Schools.

He said, 'I have examined the school children, and they have passed a fair examination in reading and spelling, but the girls are somewhat backward in arithmetic. I beg to recommend that some Bibles be provided for the use of the school, which is at present entirely without them. Some of the Irish reading books, 2nd series are also required. It is much desired that some systematic and regular industrial training be given to the boys.'

The problem of the Bibles was sorted out when Mrs Langton Birley of Carr Hill House donated two dozen prayer books and two Bibles for the use of the inmates.

D. Corbett, Poor Law Inspector, also visited the workhouse. On 7 April 1864, he wrote the following report in the visiting book.

I inspected the workhouse this day. I much regret to find the classification so indifferently preserved throughout the house, especially as regards the children, it being with the existing internal arrangements, impossible to prevent communication between the girls and able women, and also, between the boys and them. I have requested Mr Thompson to bring this under consideration of the guardians at their next meeting (together with another matter which came under my notice at the time of my visit). And I shall feel obliged if the guardians will appoint a committee to consider what alterations will be requisite and can best be carried out, with a view to prevent the evils above alluded to; I shall be glad if the visiting committee will regularly visit the workhouse for the future and answer the queries in this book after each visit.

The visiting committee had already made plans to create extra space before Mr Corbett's inspection. The guardians had met with Mr Catterall, a local builder, and drawn up plans for greater sleeping accommodation at the least expense. The plans had been passed by the Poor Law Board in June last year. At that time adverts for the work were placed and Mr Sephton of Ormskirk Road, Preston, was awarded the contract for the proposed alterations.

A new infirmary was built. Now at the point where you turned right to the male wards or left to the female wards, you could now go straight along a corridor into the new two-storey infirmary. There were two female wards on the ground floor, one for the fever cases and one for the sickness cases. The wards were divided by a staircase that led up to the male fever and sickness wards.

The extension work left space in the old part of the building for an extra 60 inmates. The visiting committee could now, using the former sick wards, reorganise the accommodation to separate the adults from the children, as demanded by the poor law inspector.

The committee recommended:

> That room number one in the men's ward, now used as a potato and straw store, be cleaned and occupied as a men's work room.
>
> That the building at the bottom of the garden be used for storing the potatoes.

> That a shed be erected near the piggeries for a straw store and also for men to break stones in during wet weather.
>
> That the room in the boy's ward, now used for a men's workroom, be appropriated for the use of the boys as a play and washing room.
>
> That the door between the boy's and men's ward be kept constantly locked except when required for the boys to come to meals and attend school.
>
> That a room be partitioned off at the end of the new female dormitory for a bedroom for the school mistress, and that the girls occupy the sleeping rooms adjoining.
>
> That the women be removed to the dormitory originally intended for them, but now occupied by the children.
>
> That a male receiving ward be provided east front wing and a female receiving ward on the west front wing and necessary alterations to prevent communication with the other parts of the building.
>
> This will prevent the admission of the women into the girl's ward, and by keeping the doors separating the two locked, will keep the classes distinct. The committee are of the opinion that the adoption of the above recommendation will answer all the purposes alluded to by the Poor-law Inspector, and with ordinary care of the master and mistress will, in a great measure remove the existing evil.

The workhouse could now hold two-hundred and sixty paupers, at that time there were one-hundred and thirty-eight inmates. New iron bedsteads were purchased for the extra accommodation. Other work this year included connecting to the local water supply. Until now the workhouse used two wells for water. They received quotes to connect to the Fylde Water Company's supply. The cost for the main pipes and three hydrants was thirty-two pounds, thirteen shillings, and sixpence. The rest of the pipes would be charged by weight, plus labour.

In the April elections, R. C. Richards remained the chairman and Mr T. Parkinson and Mr Hodgson were chosen as vice-chairmen. Mr Hodgson from the Kirkham District took precedence but refused to serve unless Mr Parkinson took precedence, because Mr Hodgson felt he was too young, aged thirty-one, to preside in the case of the chairman being absent.

Mr Bilsborrow didn't agree with him, he said, 'A person could not be put into business too young, if he be active. Mr Hodgson had served with both zeal and energy and was well deserving of the honour conferred on him.'

Mr Hodgson still refused to stand, and the guardians relented allowing Mr Parkinson to take precedence.

The chairman's first concern was which bread to bake, flour or oatmeal. Some samples of each sort and equal value were tried. The bread was dried in the oven, weighed and subjected to other experiments, but still, a decision could not be met. A committee was formed of R. C. Richards, T. L. Birley, W. S. Hodgson, R. Cookson, and J. Barrett to decide the 'knotty point'. They held a private meeting and oatmeal was chosen.

Early in the year, a deputation from the Kirkham Local Board of Health asked permission to build a house for the Kirkham fire engine in the corner of the gardens on Station Road. The permission was granted subject to the plans being laid before them and passed. They received the plans, and the land needed was fifteen by twelve yards. The guardians agreed to the fire engine house and yard for the local board of health. It had a frontage of forty-five feet, extended eighty-eight feet and narrowed to twenty-six feet, and the rent was set at one penny per square yard for ninety-nine years or one pound, seven shillings and seven pence per year.

At harvest time, the paupers were used as labourers on farms; the wages were paid directly to the union.

On Monday 18 July 1864, seventy-four-year-old Joseph Blacoe left the workhouse to make hay for the landlord of the Old Black Bull Inn on Preston Street. Joseph slept inside the inn's barn for the week. The following Saturday he was carried back to the workhouse injured. He died on Sunday afternoon.

His face and body were swollen. Blacoe's friend, John Walsh, said, 'I do not know how he had got hurt or where he had been to.'

The guardians held an inquiry.

Dr Shaw who was called to the granary of the Bull Inn and saw the deceased, told the guardians, 'He was laid in the granary, his ear was split open.'

Richard McCall, an 'ostler' (a man who looked after the horses of people staying at an inn) at the Old Black Bull Inn, found him.

He told the guardians, 'On Saturday morning, about half-past six o'clock, I went into the stable belonging to the Bull Inn and heard someone on the scaffold. I called out, and the deceased said he had had a very bad night of cramp at the stomach and asked me to fetch him a bottle of ginger beer. I did so. I found him laid amongst some straw.'

Mr Shaw had examined him in the workhouse. He said, 'The deceased had got a severe bruise on the right shoulder, and that there was an escape of air from the lungs, and I suppose that a lung was wounded. The escape was all over his body. He was sensible when I first saw him and remained so till he expired. I asked him twice how he had been bruised, but he said he could give me no information about it. The deceased died from the effects of the escape of air from the lungs; how he was injured remains a mystery.'

Thomas Latham, the master resigned and left the workhouse. He was replaced by William Mullins. When another pauper was sent out to work, he spent the wages he was meant to give to the new master.

Joseph Allanson, an old man, had been working for Mr Thomas Billington of Wrea Green as a brick setter. Billington gave him five shillings in wages, which he was to give to the master. Instead, Allanson spent some of the money getting drunk and lost the rest. He then sprained his ankle and had to be taken back to the workhouse in a wheelbarrow by a policeman and another good Samaritan. He was deemed a refractory pauper and reprimanded for 'appropriating money to his own use that he ought to have given to the master'.

In June, a young woman of thirty-five years went to Blackpool in search of work but was taken ill with smallpox. She was sent in a covered carriage to the Kirkham Workhouse. The workhouse matron gave an account of events to the guardians.

She said, 'Susan Sykes, the woman, brought from Blackpool 'in the small pox', had died on Thursday last, the day but one after she had been brought into the house, she was covered with eruptions when she came, and in a state of constant delirium from the time of her arrival until her death. The straitjacket had to be used.'

The board wanted an inquiry into whether she was in a fit state to be moved to the workhouse, and whether it was a case for the overseer of Blackpool Mr Fisher to be involved with, as she was not in distressed circumstances. The guardians were very strict when it came to smallpox cases because they didn't want it spreading inside the workhouse. Alice Catterall and Elizabeth Greenbank, the two women who helped the matron with Susan Sykes, both caught the disease from her; both recovered.

The workhouse, with the extension work, had a modern infirmary building, but no nurses.

Dr Nairn's inspected the workhouse infirmary; his report was not very satisfactory. It went, 'Some rooms were not kept sufficiently clean, the floors not thoroughly washed as they ought to be and, the sick and infirm were not properly tended. I recommend that the board procures and employs a duly qualified paid nurse.'

The only medical staff at the workhouse was the visiting doctor, Thomas Shaw. The sick and infirm were looked after by their fellow inmates good or bad.

Thomas Langton Birley took up the story. He said, 'I have seen the necessity for one for some time. When the inmates were left to nurse each other, the sick and infirm were badly treated, especially when they fell into the hands of such men as Bradshaw, a man who not only robbed them of their money but took two sticks belonging to a sick old man and sold them in the town for 6d. One old man was allowed a little gin each day, and he would leave them to judge how much he would get of it when left to the tender mercies of Bradshaw.'

Bradshaw was later sent to the Preston House of Correction for absconding from the workhouse with union clothing.

The guardians discussed the possibility of recruiting a nurse. Mr Bilsborrow thought the matron should look after the sick.

Mr Benson asked, 'What the nurse was to do.'

Mr Hodgson replied, 'Mrs Lord, said she was to be a lady.'

Mr Benson said, 'Our wives at home are harder worked than the servants at the workhouse and make longer hours. I shall decidedly vote against it.'

The matter was passed to the visiting committee, who recommended employing a nurse for a salary of fifteen pounds. The guardians decided to trial a nurse for three months; her duties were 'to attend the sick and be generally useful.' Two parties applied for the position of nurse, Ellen Cookson of Kirkham and Ann Burgess of Blackpool. Ellen Cookson was appointed.

When Mr Swarbrick of Blackpool applied for an apprentice, he was invited to look at the boys, and he selected Luis Massey 'a fine-looking boy of eleven'.

The guardians were interested in why Luis, a French boy, had ended up in the workhouse.

The master told them, 'Luis had been placed in the French Academy at Blackpool by his mother a French Lady, who had since got married and gone to America. The boy heard from her for some time, and then all correspondence ceased. A remittance for his board, when due was not coming, and the boy was sent to the kitchen at the academy to clean boots, knives amongst other things and eventually was sent to the workhouse. He seemed to be an exceedingly fine boy and was willing to do anything. He stated that he had an aunt in Manchester'.

The guardians decided not to have him bound for the time being and asked the clerk to write to his aunt to see if she would help the boy. Whether she helped him is unclear, but having a member of your family in the workhouse was a stain against your character. Luis' name wasn't mentioned again so its presumed his aunt took him in.

Paupers from Ireland or Scotland could be removed from England and left in specific ports in their country of origin. The master reported that he had removed according to orders Patrick Garrity, his wife, and two children to WestPort, Ireland, the entire cost of which was eleven pounds, one shilling, and two pence.

Finally, this year saw the new practice of inviting workhouse children to events happening in Kirkham. Sanger's Circus visited in April, and the circus tent was erected in the croft behind the New Bull Inn on Poulton Street. All the workhouse children were admitted for free.

The year 1865, started off with the death of the workhouse coffin maker, Richard Whiteside, of Marsden Street, and a charitable donation was made from Arthur Leyland Birley, who donated twenty hares and twelve gallons of ale. The hares were duly cooked and the beer drunk. The inmates, reported the master, were highly delighted with the present and made the walls re-echo with three cheers for so kind and liberal a gentleman.

To appoint better teachers to the workhouses, the Poor Law Board made them sit exams. If they passed, they received a certificate and were then paid a premium on top of their salaries. In February, the schoolmistress, Miss Cooke, sat an exam in front of the schools inspector, Mr Wadsworth. She passed and received her certificate and her salary was increased to twenty-four pounds per annum.

Whilst Mr Wadsworth was at the workhouse, he inspected the school.

His report went, 'The children passed a satisfactory examination, and the progress they have made since my last visit is very creditable to Miss Cooke. The schoolroom is not large enough for the number of children, and I should be much obliged to the Guardians if they would consider whether it would not be desirable to throw down the wall between the schoolroom and the schoolmistress's retiring room, and thus make the two rooms into one. I am informed that Miss Cooke seldom makes any use of this room and would willingly give it up for the purpose of the school. I am very glad to find the boys are now instructed in shoemaking and tailoring, and I hope that, during the spring and summer months, they will be employed as much as possible in the garden.'

In the last few months of the year, Miss Cooke gave a month's notice and left. She was replaced by Miss Mary Ann Hunt of Newton Blue Coats School.

The two rate collectors for the Poulton and Kirkham Districts asked for a pay rise of twenty pounds each. Mr Birley proposed that those townships which had increased in size make up the extra twenty pounds in the following proportion:

Kirkham District: Lytham, ten pounds; Medlar-with-Wesham five pounds; Kirkham, three pounds; Freckleton two pounds, making twenty pounds in total.

Poulton District: Layton-with-Warbreck, thirteen pounds; Thornton, five pounds; Bispham-with-Norbreck, two pounds; making up the other twenty pounds.

After some debate about the legality of the pay rise, Mr Bilsborrow said, 'Some time ago I'd been in the company of the collector for St Michaels in the Garstang Union, and he told me that he had £40 a year and was well satisfied with it. He said it took him eight weeks in the year to make out and collect the rates, thus leaving 42 weeks in the year for himself. We propose to add £5 a year to Wesham, and for that sum, I would be glad to do all the collecting in my township myself, and never mind the salary that's paid at present.'

In March, the Blackpool fire engine the 'Waterwitch' visited Kirkham, for a display alongside the new Kirkham fire engine.

Mr Hodgson said, 'The Poulton collector was at Kirkham on Monday last with the Blackpool Volunteer Fire Brigade, playing with the engine and by such proceedings was not paying due respect to the board.'

Mr Birley countered, 'If he was at Kirkham with the brigade, he still has 364 days left in the year.'

The collectors received a ten-pound pay rise. The best place to collect the rates was Kirkham, as nearly every house in the town was owned by just three people: the mill owners.

The three months trial had expired for the Nurse Ellen Cookson. She was asked if she was willing to stay for the time being which she agreed to. It was a dangerous job being a workhouse nurse, and Ellen had made the wrong decision. She was in charge of a normal sick ward, plus the two infectious diseases wards, where there were three cases of Typhus fever. In April, Ellen caught Typhus fever, succumbing to the disease; she died on 23 April 1865 aged sixty years.

The workhouse was inspected on 10 May. The report went, 'I inspected the Workhouse yesterday. Notwithstanding the minutes being kept in a separate book, it is desirable that the visiting committee should answer the questions in the book, and I should feel much obliged to them if they will do so for the future. The provision for fever and infectious cases as I have before mentioned to the guardians are very defective and insufficient, and I do trust that they will lose no time in considering the best mode of effectively adding to it. At the present time, not only are both the fever wards full, but there is one woman suffering from fever in an ordinary sick ward, with other women.

D. Corbett Poor Law Inspector.'

There weren't any alterations on the workhouse this year, but Mr Barret of the Kirkham Local Board of Health came up to the workhouse on a dark night and found the entrance very dark, and he thought that a lamp was 'requisite'. He reported this to the Kirkham Local Board of Health, who decided to place a lamp at the gates for next winter.

Mr Mullens, who had been the master since June 1864, was found guilty by the workhouse visiting committee of a great irregularity and neglect of duty. He was frequently out all night and often in a state of insobriety. The committee also believed he was guilty of improper conduct with Rebecca Appleby, a female inmate. He was allowed to resign to avoid an investigation.

The guardians decided it would be better to replace him with a married couple, but first, they had to deal with Mrs Lord, who after the death of Mr Lord, they had kept as matron and employed a single man as master. Mrs Lord, who had worked at the workhouse for seven years, was offered a pension of ten pounds a year plus a five-pound reward for her faithful services. Mrs Lord accepted the offer, but the Poor Law Board refused to sanction the pension, so she stayed as matron. Adverts were placed in the papers for a new master. Mr Finley Ringland of Preston was appointed the new master, whilst his wife was to have the role as a nurse.

Mr Mullens left the workhouse owing money. People who were owed money had to apply to the guardians.

A girl named Jane Ward lived in the workhouse but worked in a mill. Mr Mullens regularly received her wages. He had ordered clothing from Miss

Hardman for the girl to the amount of one pound and three shillings. The girl received the clothing, but Miss Hardman did not get paid. The guardians paid the bill from Mr Mullen's one-hundred pounds sureties.

When Mr Ringland took over the workhouse, the first thing he did was upset the woman servant; who handed in a months' notice. Mrs Lord went sick, suffering from an abscess in her side. She was sent away to Bury, by order of the doctor for ten days. She didn't return after ten days, as she was now suffering from chronic bronchitis and sciatica.

Mrs Lord never returned and was offered a superannuation allowance of ten pounds per annum. This time the Poor Law Board agreed to the pension. To receive a pension, you had to have had twenty years' service or retire through grounds of 'infirmity of body or mind.' Mrs Lord could now retire, the decision, however, was ultimately hers.

In December the workhouse staff, who received free rations had their dietary allowance listed. Each, irrespective of sex was to have weekly, six pounds of bread, one pound of flour, five pounds of meat, one pound of butter, one pound of sugar, three ounces of tea, three ounces of coffee, eight ounces of cheese, eight ounces of bacon, three and a half pints of milk, and unlimited vegetables.

In 1866, the Reverend R. Doyle requested that the guardians allow the Roman Catholic children in the school to be absent when the mistress was giving the Protestant children religious instructions and teaching them their catechisms. They left the matter in the hands of the master. The priest also wanted the children to attend nine o'clock mass instead of at ten-thirty.

The master decided that the Catholic children would be excluded from the workhouse school during prayers and religious instruction each morning, which lasted from nine a.m. until nine-forty. The same children would be allowed to go to confession at the Willows Church, the last Friday in each month at eleven a.m. The adults would be allowed to go at the same time, the last Saturday in the month.

The master gave inmate Richard Lakeland the role of teaching the Roman Catholic children their prayers and catechisms. This decision removed at once the protection that the class system provided. Lakeland was later caught taking improper liberties with two young girls and was reported by the nurse. After an inquiry, the visiting committee found this a 'prima facie' case of assault. He was summoned to Kirkham Court.

The only other case of abuse mentioned in the guardian's minutes was in July 1868, when William Fisher, aged thirty-nine, was charged with improper conduct with some female inmates. The workhouse committee could not find sufficient evidence to take him to court, and he was removed to another part of the workhouse.

Mr Ringland's management of the infirmary, fell short of Doctor Shaw's expectations; leading him to write two letters of complaint.

To the Poor Law Board, he wrote:

> My Lords and Gentlemen. As surgeon of the Fylde Union Workhouse, I beg most respectfully to call your attention to the nonfulfillment of my orders as regards the dietary of the sick in the house. Having had from time to time so many complaints about the food supplied contrary to my orders, I consider it my duty to inform you that on Thursday last, bacon and beef was supplied to two patients in place of beef or mutton.
>
> I spoke to the master some months since upon the subject of not carrying out my orders. He then gave me to understand that such irregularities should not occur again. It appears to me that he is determined not to carry it out. I am informed, he told one of the inmates a short time since, that he did not care for my orders, I gave, for he would please himself, or something to the same effect.
>
> There is another subject which I wish to draw your attention to, and which is of a most serious nature in an establishment of this kind, and that is the changing of stockings worn by the inmates. It has come to my knowledge, and so far, as I can ascertain, weekly changing is the exception; one man wore the same dirty stockings eleven weeks, others seven weeks, one ever since Christmas, and some change once in a fortnight.

I am, my Lords and Gentlemen, your most obedient servant Thomas Shaw.

And to the guardians:

Gentlemen, I beg most respectfully to ask you to allow the surgery in the workhouse, to be fitted up with a table, chair, and a supply of ink and pens, for I have of late, found so much difficulty in writing up my sick list in consequence of the ink, etc being removed out of the porter's room, where it had been since the house was erected.

There is another subject gentlemen, which I consider it my duty to draw your attention to, that is the necessity of appointing a nurse, who can devote the whole of her time to the sick. For on Sunday, the 11th I found a man suffering from bronchitis, had left his bed and gone downstairs to the water tap for the purpose of obtaining something to quench his thirst. There is another case of a woman who had been forbidden to take potatoes. I find that some had been given to her by another patient in the same room, which made her much worse for a time.

There is another subject which comes more under the comforts of the house. I saw a man a few days since, taking his dinner, consisting of meat, bread and potatoes, without either knife, fork, or spoon, pulling it to pieces with his hands, and by the same means conveying it to his mouth. Another man I saw with nothing more than a knife and his fingers taking his meat, bread, and potatoes, I am, gentlemen, your obedient servant.

Thomas Shaw.

The letters were forwarded to the workhouse visiting committee, and a meeting was held to discuss the complaints along with Doctor Shaw, Mr Ringland, and some inmates.

Mr Ringland defended himself, "With regard to the stockings, the washerwoman had been in the habit of putting dirty stockings belonging to the other inmates, on the inmates, who were having their stockings washed. There is no proof that any other irregularity exists; clean clothes are provided weekly.'

After interviewing some of the inmates, the committee found that lice were present in both clean and dirty clothing and that there was a problem in the regularity of washing. The men who used to strip to the waists and wash once a week, now just wash their hands and faces. The women who are able went into the washhouse on Saturday and washed themselves. Two imbeciles are washed regularly by one of the inmates. There was, however, no supervision of the inmates washing.

Females on admission were not stripped and washed in the receiving ward, provided for that purpose, but this was done in the dry house. Their dirty clothes were tied up in bundles, stored away dirty, and returned to them in the same state on leaving the house. The males on their admission were stripped and washed in the oakum room, and their clothes tied up in bundles and deposited in the store without being cleaned, and again returned to them in the same state when leaving. Some inmates were allowed to wear a portion of their own clothing during their stay.

Mr Ringland said, 'I admit that bacon had been mixed with the beef, and this was done without my knowledge by a pauper assisting in the kitchen. Soon after my appointment, the cook, the only paid servant in the workhouse left, and I was for some time without any servant in the establishment. Mrs Ringland, who is the nurse, had to also officiate as matron, leaving the attendance to the sick upon two paupers. Any irregularities was down to want of proper and sufficient staff.'

He went on to say, 'The female pauper in charge of the women in the infirmary uses every endeavour to do her duty to the sick; but having no discretionary power as to food, beyond the dietary laid down by the doctor, the sick and dying might be better cared for by a regular paid nurse, to whom the medical officer might confide some discretion as to the character of food applicable to individual cases. The pauper in charge of the sick males stated that if a person is sick and ill and wants a little tea, or anything else it cannot be furnished until the doctor comes and orders it.'

The committee recommended that in future strict attention is paid to the changing of clothes, that all paupers on admission are stripped and washed in the receiving wards and not admitted into the main building until properly cleaned and supplied with union clothing. The clothing of the paupers must be purified before being sent into storage. The master and matron must see that inmates, both male and female, especially the old people bath regularly.

A few months later, after Mrs Lord had still not retired or returned to work. The committee suggested that either Mrs Ringland returned to her duties as nurse and superintendent of the infirmary and lying-in-wards, or a competent person engaged for that situation. The guardians decided to employ a new nurse and give Mrs Lord a pension of six pounds.

Mrs Lord declined this pension, saying she wanted the original offer of ten pounds per annum. The guardians asked the Poor Law Board for advice, who said the most she could receive is two-thirds of her salary of ten pounds. The board had to wait for Mrs Lord to resign from her post, as she was still on sick leave which the guardians had sanctioned. The guardians would only pay her six pounds per-annum, and she finally accepted that figure and resigned in August 1866. Mrs Ringland could now officially become the matron. Mrs Swarbrick was employed as a nurse.

Johnathon Titterington, who was now aged twelve, was back in the workhouse. He absconded on 20 January. He often escaped and came back with something of value. The master searched his locker and found an old verge watch, and a scarf, which he thought he'd probably stolen.

A few days later, Johnathon Titterington returned to the workhouse with 'another cargo of pilferings'. There were items of clothing and a photograph with a likeness to himself. The guardians found it highly amusing as they passed the photograph from one to the other, all agreeing that it was a capital likeness. He'd also stolen two half-crowns from a house. It was decided to send him to an asylum.

Johnathon returned to the workhouse from the asylum in April, after being found not sufficiently insane and returned to his old tricks. He escaped from the workhouse again and stole a dead-beat watch valued at seven pounds and ten shillings from Pointer House, Singleton; where a Mr Harrison lived. The master questioned the boy who admitted stealing the watch.

He said, 'I tried to set the watch and broke the hands. I then took out the insides and threw the pieces in to a ditch and threw the case over the wall on Station Road into Milbanke grounds.'

The master took him to Milbanke and searched the grounds for the case. Whilst searching the grounds the gardener came up to them and asked if they'd lost something. The gardener then explained that he'd found a watch case and some of the works at that spot. The theft was the boy's last chance and he was handed over to the police.

His case was reported in the Preston Chronicle.

> Watch Stealing, Johnathon Titterington, of workhouse notoriety, was charged with stealing a watch on Friday, the 30th inst. from the house of Mr James Harrison Singleton, value £6 6s. The boy admitted having taken it. He broke the pieces and threw them away. Part of the case and part of the works were produced. The boy is considered insane. He was sent to the asylum, Lancaster, but sent back to the workhouse in consequence of not being sufficiently mad. He is beyond control in the workhouse, and is too young to be sent to a reformatory, but was discharged and sent back to the workhouse. He is constantly running away from the workhouse, and he invariably commits some depredations before he returns. A short time ago, he returned with a portrait of himself, taken by Mr. Oglesby, and some other things.

The following year, Johnathon was back in court and sent to the Preston Sessions, again his case was reported in the newspapers.

> A Singular Lad, Johnathon Titterington was found guilty of stealing at Warton, on the 7th February, a silk handkerchief, the property of Matthew Hardman. Mr Knowles, who appeared for the prosecution, said the prisoner had been brought up at the workhouse, but he had acted singularly of late, that they did not know what to do with him. He went about different people's houses and seemed to have a great passion for clocks and watches. He was constantly in the habit of winding up every clock he came across, and was in the habit of taking out the insides of watches when he could lay his hands upon them. He was ordered to be imprisoned for a month and then sent to reformatory school for four years.

Some changes were made to the paupers' diet by the guardians. The paupers' diet was a fixed one and had to be approved by the Poor Law Board. The only exceptions were for the sick, suckling women and infants under two years of age, whose diet was fixed by the doctor. There were different diets for the different classes, and for paupers undertaking strenuous work.

The guardians decided to give the inmates some wheaten bread each day in lieu of oatcake. The men would receive five ounces per day, the women four ounces. However, due to complaints from the women paupers, the wheaten bread ration was raised to five ounces per day for women. Female inmates also now received twenty-two ounces of meal to the gallon of water, instead of eighteen ounces. The women in the washhouse received extra rations because of the harder work; this came in the form of one pint of tea, nine ounces of bread and butter twice a day.

The finance committee would set certain dates in the year for people to object to the valuations of their property. On 18 April, the following dates were given for appeals. They were all on Wednesdays; 30 May, 11 July, 3 October, 14 November, 26 December, 6 February, and 20 March.

At the meeting in August, Thomas Poole objected against his assessment: number four-hundred and fourteen. The gross value was reduced from twenty-five pounds to sixteen pounds.

Messers Catterall and Harrison's spinning mill, Wesham, was assessed at three-hundred and seventy-one pounds. The mill's representative, Mr Whittaker, suggested a reduction of ninety-six pounds ought to be made because one of the spinning rooms was closed. The reduction was agreed to.

Captain Westby of Mowbreck Hall asked for a reduction on his three-hundred and thirty-acres estate. He had his rates reduced by fifty pounds.

A tramp, a former soldier, aged thirty-eight years, got a night's lodging in the workhouse. He fell ill and stayed for ten nights in the workhouse infirmary. The man asked the guardians for a shirt and a pair of stockings to leave with. Mr Crook agreed to the request saying, 'It's very unfeeling to turn a man out without shirt or stockings on a frosty morning.' Some disagreed, saying it only encouraged his tramping. A vote was held, ten for his request and five against. He was given the clothing.

The workhouse was audited in June. Two things were disallowed, one pound, three shillings, and four pence, which the master had paid for the lodging of three boys, and two pounds and eight shillings for the porter. Doctor Shaw took exception to the 'porter' as a ratepayer (a dark brown bitter beer brewed from malt, which people in strenuous jobs drank). Mr Ringland explained to the guardians that the porter was given to the men cleaning out the sewers in the men's yard, and some to the paupers nursing the sick. The boys 'factory boys' worked in a Kirkham mill, but didn't earn enough wages to pay for their board, which Mr Ringland made up with the one pound, three shillings, and four pence. The guardians were satisfied with these explanations.

The workhouse was inspected in November by Inspector Crane, and the report wasn't favourable.

He reported, 'This workhouse has not been constructed in such a manner as to afford full accommodation and proper classification by day as well as by night for all classes of inmates; that many of the wards are low and some of them, neither well lighted nor well ventilated, and that the windows are, for the most part, too small for one purpose, and not sufficiently near the ceiling for the other. Also owing to the unclean habits of some of the boys and to the defective ventilation, their bedrooms was at the time of my visit extremely offensive; that the privies were likewise offensive and require entire reconstruction; and I advise that the floor of the children's day-rooms and school-rooms, which are of stone, also should be boarded.'

'I draw attention to the fact that owing to want of room, the men sometimes slept together two in a bed, which the board consider a most objectable practise. Owing to the same reason, namely want of space, the two fever wards of the infirmary are sometimes used for the reception of other patients, and that so great has been the pressure for accommodation for the sick, that it has even been found necessary to place a patient on the landing from the stairs. The wards in the infirmary are, moreover, stated to be small, ill-ventilated, and at times overcrowded. They appear also to be most deficient in general comfort, and very defected as regards convenience, whilst the inmates are at present in charge of pauper attendants, who are quite incompetent to perform the duties of nurse. I advise that a new and capacious infirmary is urgently required.'

The guardians responded to the report. They ordered the girls' day room and the schoolroom floors to be boarded. Instructed the master to properly ventilate the boys' bedrooms and where possible stop the paupers from sharing beds. They also ordered two reclining chairs for epileptic patients.

In 1867, the guardians introduced the new system, where the children or grandchildren of inmates were asked to contribute to their relations keep in the workhouse. The guardians wanted to charge the three children of Mrs Roberts fifteen shillings weekly for the support of their mother, who required a person to take care of her. The children wrote to the guardians saying they could not afford fifteen shillings per week but would pay two shillings each. The guardians decided that, as a nurse was about to be appointed, they would be able to take care of Mrs Roberts for seven shillings and sixpence per week. The children were ordered to pay two shillings and sixpence each.

The practice of letting factory boys go out of the house daily was against union rules, and the Poor Law Board ordered it to be stopped. The guardians appealed the decision saying the boys worked in the mills but didn't earn enough to live on their own. The guardians thought sending boys out to work would enable them eventually to work their way out of the workhouse and in the meantime, they could contribute to their keep. The board would not relent, and the guardians gave the one months' notice required on behalf of the four boys.

The problem of vagrants was a major problem, especially during the summer when many were attracted to Blackpool. The vagrants were usually given a ticket for a lodging house for overnight accommodation to keep them off the streets. From July, the Police Sergeants at Kirkham, Poulton, Lytham, Blackpool, and Fleetwood would act as assistant relieving officers for the relief of vagrants.

In April complaints started arising about the master and matron again. Mary Livingston had become ill on Friday 26 April. Alice Latin and Fanny Lothium both informed the matron who took no action. They told her again on Saturday, but she still took no action. On Sunday morning, Mary was moved to the infirmary where she immediately died.

The guardians investigated the incident and found the matron responsible for Mary's death: she was reprimanded.

On 7 May, the visiting committee found that Catherine McGwin had been without food from being admitted in the afternoon until eleven o'clock the following day. They also found out the female paupers were weaving their own 'stays' when it was part of the uniform. They ordered the master to buy a dozen stays.

Dr Shaw sent another written complaint to the guardians.

> Kirkham 18th Sept 1867.
>
> Gentlemen, having heard complaints, I beg most respectfully to draw your attention to two matters with reference thereto. In the first place, I am informed that the milk supplied to the officers and inmates of the house is deposited in the same vessel or vessels and that the officers' table is furnished with about half a pint of cream twice every day. I have also to draw your attention to the butter supplied to the inmates. From observation, and having very frequently weighed the quantity, I say without hesitation that the correct quantity is never supplied, although they are debited with it in the accounts; and I can also say that the porter is frequently short measured. I beg to ask you to allow stays, to two inmates of the infirmary; one of them complained to me a few days since of being cold; the covering of the chest they are at present wearing is insufficient.
>
> There is another matter I cannot pass over without naming, for I am satisfied from what Mrs Ringland says, that there must be something radically wrong, either in her ideas, or the management of the house, for she stated to one of the inmates that the workhouse was worse than a nanny shop.
>
> I am gentlemen, your most obedient servant Thomas Shaw.

The guardians forward the letter to the Poor Law Board in Whitehall, London, asking for a commissioner to visit Kirkham and investigate the matter. The board didn't send a commissioner but wrote back saying, 'In consequence of frequent complaints that have arisen through the non-agreement of the Medical Officers and the Master of the Workhouse, the Poor Law Board, finally decided that both parties had better resign.'

Both parties tendered their resignations, and an advert was placed for a new medical officer and for a new master and matron.

FYLDE UNION.—ELECTION OF MEDICAL OFFICER.—The Guardians of the Poor of the Fylde Union are in WANT of a duly-qualified MEDICAL MAN to fill the office of Medical Officer of the No. 2 Kirkham District of the Union, vacant by the resignation of Mr. Thomas Shaw. The district comprises an area of 12,264 acres, and contains a population of about 3,000 inhabitants. The Union Workhouse is also included in the district. The salary will be £53 7s 6d per annum; no extras. Applications must be sent in to the Clerk on or before Tuesday, 12th November next.—By order of the Board.

WILLIAM THOMPSON.

Kirkham, 31st Oct., 1867.

This advert was placed in the *Preston Chronicle* for a district doctor.

FYLDE UNION.—ELECTION OF MASTER AND MATRON.—The Guardians of the Fylde Union intend at their meeting to be held on Wednesday, the 27th November next, to APPOINT a MASTER and MATRON of the Workhouse at Kirkham. Joint salary, £40 per annum, with rations, and furnished apartments in the Workhouse. Candidates must be man and wife, without incumbrance, and between the ages of 25 and 45 years. The Master must be competent to keep the books and accounts required by the Poor-law Board and the Board of Guardians, and will be required to give security in the sum of £100, with two sureties for the due and faithful performance of the duties of the office. Applications in the candidate's own handwriting, stating age and occupation, accompanied by testimonials, will be received by the Clerk until Tuesday, the 12th November next. Selected candidates will receive due notice when their attendance will be required.—By order of the Board.

WILLIAM THOMPSON, Clerk.

Kirkham, 31st October, 1867.

The one placed in the *Preston Chronicle,* for a new master and matron.

The new master and matron, Mr and Mrs Ramsbottom, started on 11 December. Doctor Boyle replaced Dr Shaw. The schoolmistress resigned in November; Esther Charnley became the new schoolmistress. Nurse Dorothy Bleasdale left to take up the post of nurse and assistant matron in Beverly; Mrs Jane Gee replaced her.

The year 1868 started with a complete change of staff, and in response to the November 1866 inspection, plans to build a new infirmary which could hold forty patients, twenty of each sex, were drawn up. In the meantime, the workhouse ordered two water beds for the infirmary. John Cookson, a paralytic, was first on the bed but was scalded when the inmates filled the pillows with boiling water. Reverend Webber Birley also donated an 'invalids perambulator.'

The curate of the parish church, Reverend John Atkinson, decided to brighten the whitewashed walls of the infirmary with scripture texts. The scripture texts, in large print, were donated by the Society of Christian Knowledge: much to the annoyance of the Catholics. As far as they were concerned, the workhouse was a public institution, and the scripts were seen by them as being sectarian.

Some guardians wanted the scripts removed, but Thomas Langton Birley said, 'If the scripts are removed, I will motion to have them put back up.'

Richard Cookson countered, "I now give notice that I will at the next board meeting, move, that the Catholic clergyman who attends the Catholic poor, be allowed to place crucifixes and other religious prints etc. wherever he may deem consolatory to the sick around the beds of the Catholic poor in the infirmary and that this as regards the said Catholics, be his exclusive right."

The priests from the Willows Church got involved and wrote two letters to the guardians.

> Gentlemen,
>
> First, we the undersigned priests of St. John's Church, the Willows, beg to ask if it were by your authorisation that the

> walls of the Kirkham Workhouse have been recently posted with religious doctrines.
>
> Secondly, we are of the opinion that it would have been much wiser if the character of this house, as an institution for the general public, had been maintained and that this show of sectarianism had been left undone.
>
> Thirdly, we are of the opinion that a Protestant clergyman ought not to post, or cause to be posted, religious doctrines which he is pleased to admire, around the beds of Catholics' as they are attended to in religious matters by the priests of their own church.
>
> Fourthly, we regret to have to address to the board this document, but we are anxious that the workhouse should be continued to be directed, as it had been hitherto, in a fair and objectable manner, and that it should not in any way be made odious to the house. Requesting the favour of an answer
>
> We are, gentlemen, your obedient servants, signed Frederick Hines, Jno. O'Meara.

Mr William Segar Hodgson suggested that any Catholics objecting to the texts should be moved to another room.

Chairman R. C. Richards added, 'I understand that with Catholics, everything was sectarian except Cathology; therefore, anything put forth by any other professors of Christianity was sectarian.'

The voice of reason came from Reverend Brown, Vicar of St Michael's who was also a guardian.

He said, 'The Church of England had no more right to interfere with the Catholic's poor than the Catholic priests with the Church of England's poor.'

The scripts were left up, and the Catholic sick were allowed to place Crucifixes at their bedsides.

In April, Dr Doyle was appointed to Kirkham Medical District Number One, and Dr Shaw was reappointed to Kirkham Number Two District;

which included the workhouse. Nurse, Jane Gee, asked for a pay rise from fifteen pounds to twenty pounds, in the end, it was agreed to raise it to seventeen. The nurse then resigned saying she'd gained a place of employment at the Salford Fever Ward but was willing to stay if she received the twenty pounds. The guardians, who were impressed with her services, agreed to the raise; although, they didn't like her forcing system. However, by the end of the year, she was having disputes with the master over the care of the sick. The guardians thought these disputes amongst the officers was bad for the workhouse. Blaming the nurse, she was asked to resign.

Reverend Brown (Lancashire Archives)

In July, the clerk received a letter from the Beverley Union, about the former nurse, Dorothy Bleasdale.

> Dear Sir,
>
> We have, unfortunately, a great quarrel between the master and nurse in our workhouse. When the nurse was appointed here, she produced what the guardians considered high testimonials from yourself and several gentlemen connected with the Fylde Union. The master here produced before our guardians at their meeting today a letter he wished to be read, seriously reflecting on the character of Mrs Bleasdale, a copy of which with her consent I enclose. If the statements therein are true, our guardians feel they have been greatly deceived. They wish me to ask if your testimonial was a genuine one and if you believe there is any truth in what is stated in Mr Ringland's letter.
>
> I am dear sir yours truly F. Hobson.

A copy of Mr Ringland's letter was enclosed. The clerk was ordered to reply to the Beverley Union that the testimonials were quite correct and that Mr Ringland's letter was a complete fabrication from beginning to end. The clerk was also instructed to write to Mr Ringland informing him that the guardians highly censured his conduct in attempting so maliciously to slander and traduce the character of an officer who had satisfactorily performed her duties.

Mr Crane inspected the infirmary. A patient Mary Ireland told him that her petticoat had not been washed for six months. Mr Crane also complained of a deficiency of knives and forks in the infirmary. Many of the inmates were suffering from fistula. The medical officer thought the fistula was caused by the tanks about the premises being full of stagnant soft water. Mr Crane suggested that the master ordered a moveable iron pump, take the water out and use it for watering the plants.

The work of claiming money for the support of inmates from their families was the responsibility of William Thompson the clerk. He was also responsible for the removals: mainly back to Ireland. This was extra work, which he had to submit a claim to be paid for. He asked the board for a yearly fixed sum of twenty pounds per annum to save submitting the claims, the board agreed, and his yearly salary was raised to one hundred and twenty pounds. He had three removal cases in December to deal with.

To prevent Irish Immigrants from becoming chargeable to the union, those unable to support themselves, would be sent back to Ireland.

In the Summer, two Irishmen were walking along the railway line when one was killed and the other severely injured. The injured man was taken back to Fleetwood, where he was nursed back to health. The cost to the union for his care was between nineteen and twenty pounds. When the man recovered, he was sent back to Ireland.

Francis Ratican and his family of Westby were ordered to be removed to Ireland, their native place. They had been in the receipt of seven shillings per week. They could have avoided being sent home if they had stopped claiming relief like Jane Stafford, who received a similar order. She refused to go and declined any further relief.

James Bryon, his wife and child, all tramps, also received a similar order. They'd been in the workhouse for about three weeks when his wife became ill and was sent into the infirmary. After she had recovered the husband refused to leave the house until spring.

The master told him, 'You will find out your mistake. You have got a free trip to Ireland coming up, as a Christmas present.'

The family quickly packed up their things and fled the workhouse.

When a union decided to order a family back to their place of settlement, the twenty-one days' notice given was to give them a chance to appeal the decision. The twenty-one days also gave the union who was going to receive the paupers the chance to investigate the case and decide whether to accept responsibility or appeal: this was again the role of the clerk.

Joseph Houseman from Freckleton was in the Militia when he married in 1856. He later enlisted into the regulars and was sent out to Malta with his family. Whilst abroad his wife died, and he returned to England and left his children, the eldest ten in the Newcastle Workhouse. Newcastle wrote to Kirkham and asked them to look after their own, as the father was away with his regiment, he did not contribute to their keep. The clerk accepted the case and the children were moved to Kirkham.

The year ended with the one-hundred and sixty-one paupers enjoying a Christmas dinner and drinking two nine-gallon casks of ale provided by Mrs Langton Birley.

In 1869, James Hibbert's plans for a new infirmary; drawn up by the same architect who built Preston Harris Museum, were finally passed by the Poor Law Board.

The contracts were awarded as follows:

Mr Thomas Singleton: brickworks, costing six-hundred and fifty pounds and flagging and slating costing two-hundred and seventy-three pounds.

R. Parkinson: joinery, at the cost of seven-hundred and one pound.

Westby and Woods: plumbing and painting costing three-hundred and ten pounds.

Mr Steward: heating, at the cost of one-hundred and fifty pounds.

John Rigby: plastering at the cost of ninety pounds.

Ingram and Co.: masonry, costing four-hundred pounds.

The total cost of the new infirmary was put at two-thousand, five-hundred and seventy-eight pounds, and fifteen shillings. It was built at the north end of the grounds; attached to the sick and fever wards for easy access to the kitchens. It was divided from the rest of the workhouse by a wall. The loan from the Building's Finance Committee was paid back over fifteen years. The building opened in June, and the master was sent to Manchester to buy some sample flock to use as bedding. He returned with two samples, one which cost one and a quarter pence and one which cost two pence. The guardians went with the two pence flock. The contract to supply the bedsteads, at nine shillings and two pence per pair, was given to Mr Woods of Kirkham. Miss Eliza Heath became the new nurse, on a salary of seventeen pound raising in yearly increments of one pound until reaching twenty pounds. Eliza became ill and never took up the post; Mary Sharp was appointed nurse in May.

As well as treating the poor, the union was responsible for vaccinating children and trying to eradicate smallpox. At this time, the vaccination was compulsory, and the inspector of vaccinations charge three people, who all ended up in Kirkham Court charged with not vaccinating their children: George Williams of Blackpool, Thomas Tobay and William Forrest of Fleetwood. They were fined one shilling each, plus costs or could choose seven days imprisonment.

The workhouse's 'odd job man' Thomas Fish wrote to the guardians on 31 March 1869.

> Mr Chairman and Gentlemen,
>
> I hope to be excused writing to you. My motive is this: I consider myself entitled to a little more money, 2 shillings for the work I have to do is very little. I am baking seven packs of flour in a fortnight and twice oat cake. The remainder of my time is occupied in painting, whitewashing and colouring. I was promised 1s. per week more if I would learn to bake oat cake. I have done that six months since, my tuition costing me 2s. 6d. The season has again commenced for renovating, and I presume to ask your honourable board for an advance of 1s. 6d per week. If you will allow it, I humbly thank you, and if not, I hope there is no offences. Thanking you for past favours, I remain your obedient servant, Thomas Fish.

There was no mention of whether he received the rise or not.

The clerk took William Ward of Bispham to court because he would not pay three shillings towards his father's maintenance, as he had nine other brothers and two sisters who could also contribute. The court refused to give a summons until all family members were brought before the judge. The case came to court three times, but the guardians lost each time. In August, James Ward wrote to the guardians saying he and two of his brothers would pay one shilling to their father's keep which they accepted.

Mr Hodgson said, 'I do not think the old man would live above a fortnight, so they would not have to contribute long.'

James Ward senior, lived for another four months, he was buried in St Michaels, aged eighty years, on 15 December.

The master had to give a six-monthly report to the guardians, this is a breakdown of costs for October of 1869.

The average number of inmates was one-hundred and twenty-two, and the average number of vagrants per week was twenty. The expenditure for the half-year, ending on 5 October, was for: provisions, three-hundred and seventy pounds, fourteen shillings, and seven and a half pence; necessaries, sixty pounds, eighteen shillings, and seven pence; clothing, sixty-one pounds, two shillings, and three pence; outfits three pounds and fourteen shillings; funerals, seven pounds and three pence; gas, ten pounds and three shillings. The overall total for the half-year was five-hundred and thirteen pounds, twelve shillings, and eight and a half pence. Making the average cost per head each week at three shillings and one-half penny.

The clerk could use these figures to work out how much to charge a person for the cost of their family members maintenance.

Two 'unnatural sons', as the court called them, went before the Kirkham Bench in December. Daniel and William Dewhurst were summoned for refusing to maintain their mother, seventy-two-year-old Peggy Dewhurst. She lived in Hardhorn-with-Newton and was receiving two shillings and sixpence per week in relief. The bench made an order against both farmers, Daniel was to pay one shilling and one penny and William was to pay one shilling per week.

Two guardians, Robert Parkinson and Mr Bilsborrow, were sent to visit the lunatics belonging to the union at the Lancaster Asylum. They use to send a medical officer with the guardians, but last time that happened the committee lived in 'good style'.

A guardian said, 'At that time the visiting committee charged three pounds and three shillings for the journey and ran up a bill of about ten pounds, returning with pockets full of champagne bottle corks.'

The Poor Law Board sent a circular letter reminding the unions that all able-bodied vagrants be set a task of work and bathed. The master was ordered by the guardians to make sure that all able-bodied men in the house were kept at work breaking stones, and that a certain quantity be allotted to each man; in the case of any refusal or neglect, the guardians were to take the case before the magistrates.

The master was asked by the guardians why there were so many vagrants in the area and what was their diet.

He said, 'The Fylde was a warm place for them, for the stages were easy and the plunder rich in consequence of their being so many visitors at the watering places. The vagrants received, according to the order of the guardians, a quart of porridge at night and 7oz of oatcake, lodgings, and porridge and bread in the morning.'

Mr T. L. Birley thought they should receive a pint of porridge and four ounces of bread.

Reverend Brown said, 'If people were not so ready and willing to relieve vagrants there would not be so many.'

Mr Hodgson agreed, 'Whenever they went to a cottager's door, they seldom went away empty handed.'

Workhouse Inspector, Mr Basel Cane, inspected the workhouse in August, he reported; 'I suggest to the guardians that at this time of the year the meat should be delivered more frequently at the workhouse, so that it may be perfectly fresh when served for meals. At present, I find on examining the meat that there are some grounds for the complaints made to me by two of the inmates in this respect. Means should be taken for carefully keeping the inmates' own clothes, so that on leaving the clothes may be returned to them in a good a state as they were when the inmates entered the house.'

'I strongly advise the guardians to direct the cesspools to be done away with and to avail themselves of means, which I am told exist for placing the drainage of the premises in a thoroughly satisfactory condition. The emptying of one of these cesspools on a recent occasion has been described to me as attended by a stench which was almost insufferable, and which could not but have been most prejudicial to the health and comfort of the inmates and especially to the inmates of the sick wards, closely adjacent to the place where the heap of soil now lies. I am bound to say however that this heap having been covered with soil was free from offence today.'

'I notice that the medical officers' book has not been kept duly made up. I shall feel much obliged to the committee if they will regularly answer the questions in this book at every visit. There are various other things which may be noticed, such as the improvements that have been made and which I refer to with satisfaction. Other improvements are dependent upon the works in progress, which will be a great advantage to the establishment and for which the guardians deserve credit.'

The guardians decided that a room in the vagrant's ward would be made into a receptacle for the clothing of paupers during the time they are in the house. It was heated and would keep the clothes dry.

Donating to the workhouse inmates, especially the children, was becoming a regular thing.

Reverend Brown, asked for permission, which was granted, to take the children to Weeton Parsonage to receive a treat of buns, coffee, and oranges from the Reverend Cookson. Mrs Louisa Brown of Lytham sent a number of children's 'very nice picture books', and Reverend Webber Birley gave thirty shillings towards the children's annual trip to Blackpool. The master reported that gifts of various kinds were becoming very common in the house, such as money, food, wine and spirits, particularly in the infirmary and he did not like to interfere without the sanction of the board. The board decided that no wine or spirits were allowed, but with regards to other things a discretionary power was left with the master.

On Saturday 13 of November, John Lee, a vagrant, entered the workhouse. On Sunday he tore his clothes up saying he was destitute and couldn't get work. The master gave him another set of clothes, and on Monday morning he was handed over to the police. In court, he was sent to the Preston House of Correction for twenty-one days, with hard labour. The court case was one of the last acts of the master. He later resigned.

1870–1879

The first thing the guardians had to do in 1870 was to appoint a new master. There were four applicants for the position. Three were experienced masters: James Walmsley, Stockport Workhouse; Samuel Stancliffe, Preston Workhouse; and Herbert Hawkes, Toxteth Park Workhouse. The fourth was a farmer – Henry Penswick of Newton-with-Scales, who was appointed.

In February, blacksmith, John Singleton entered the workhouse. Some said to get away from his wife and some to get better food. However, according to the guardians, he was typical of the able-bodied man who was too lazy to work. He wanted to come into the workhouse, have his free lodgings, food, a bath, and a shave, and expect the hardworking ratepayers of the Fylde to pay for it. The guardians decided to make these 'idle fellows' break one ton of stones per day. The guardians thought at one ton the vagrants would not be overworked.

In the opinion of the guardians, a man accustomed to the work could break three tons a day. The workhouse paid between one shilling and three pence to one shilling and sixpence per ton for the field stones. They could also get a supply of shore stones from Fleetwood for three shillings per ton. Shore stones cost more, as they were harder to retrieve. The guardians agreed that the able-bodied would break the stones and their weaker brethren take the stones to the breaker and then carry them away. In November, the Lytham Improvement Commission ordered between fifty and one-hundred tons of stone which were to be delivered by rail.

Blackpool was growing rapidly, and the ratepayers association wrote to the guardians asking for an extra rate collector.

> Gentlemen, Your attention is earnestly called to the following resolution, unanimously passed at the annual meeting of the ratepayers of the township of Layton with Warbrick, the 22nd March 1870. Resolved, 'That in the opinion of this meeting a considerable amount of rates are being annually lost, for want of a sufficient number of collecters, and that the present collector has more duties to perform than he can possibly

get through in consequence of the increase of ratepayers in Blackpool.'

Joseph Smith, Chairman.

Miss Charnley, the schoolmistress, passed her exam, and her salary was increased to twenty pounds. Despite this, she later decided to resign to take up a post at the Knutsford Union. She left in April and was replaced by seventeen-year-old Miss McGhee of King's Norton. Miss McGhee settled in nicely with the twenty-one boys and seventeen girls under her charge. In November she asked the guardians for an easy chair or sofa for her sitting room: which was granted. She then asked the guardians to consider the question of allowing beer at dinner. Mr Slater was quite surprised at the request, 'A girl, seventeen years of age, talking about ale.'

The workhouse was also used as a place of refuge for victims of domestic abuse.

Mary Hardman left her husband, and sought refuge in the workhouse with her children. She told the master, 'I do not dare live with him, he ill uses me so much.'

William Hardman of Kirkham refused to support his family in the workhouse, and Mary refused to leave. The clerk had him summoned before the magistrates. The clerk lost this case because Mary had walked out on her husband, not the other way around; therefore, the union had to prove she was destitute before an order could be made.

Another woman who had left her husband was Deborah Eaves of Marton Folds, who received nine shillings per week in relief from the union. William Eaves, who was a joiner and wheelwright, was told by the board that the relief, which his wife had received for the past two weeks, would stop, and he would have to support her. If he neglected to do so proceedings would be taken against him. Whether William started supporting his wife is unknown, but the threat of court action was usually enough to get a man with an income to start supporting his family.

A third case of 'neglect of family' involved Thomas Rawthorne, a widower, who was charged with neglecting his two children, one nine, the other seven years old. The relieving officer found the children living in destitution.

He said, 'They had nothing in the house but an old pan, an old bedstead, and some filthy rags for bedding. Their father earned upto one-pound per week and never less than sixteen shillings but spent it nearly all on drink.'

The children were taken into the workhouse, and their father was ordered to pay five shillings per week for their maintenance. He was warned that if he neglected, to pay he would become a 'sojourn with the King' at the Preston House of Correction.'

Mr Baldwin Fleming, Sub Poor Law Inspector, inspected the workhouse on 15 November.

He reported, 'I beg to express my satisfaction with the new infirmary and the many improvements which have recently been carried out. The inmates made no complaints to me, and the general condition of the establishment is clean and proper.

P.S. It is desirable that a bell should be provided to afford a means of communication between the vagrant's ward and the master.'

In 1871, the Government created the Local Government Board, who took over the roles previously undertaken by the Poor Law Board. In reality it was the Poor Law Board with a different name. Transferred to the new board was the work previously under taken by four different government departments to prevent duplication. Public health, prevention of diseases, vaccination, registration of births, deaths and marriages, baths and washhouses, public improvements, artisans and labourers' dwellings, local-taxation returns and roads were all transferred to the Local Government Board.

After one-year, the master and matron, Mr and Mrs Penswick, resigned. They were replaced by Raby Anderson and his wife, Mary. George Smart, a pauper, didn't like the new master. He complained about the master using very abusive language such as 'devils, sneaks and scamps'. The master was called before the guardians and asked to explain the complaint.

He said, 'I called George Smart a sneak because he had been sneaking out of the gate and getting drunk, and I called a man named Coward a scamp because he came in the house and said he must not be left by himself because he had fits. I told him I would see about that and shortly afterwards I was fetched to him. I found the man was lying down on the floor. I put my thumb nails under Cowards thumb, and he immediately jumped up.'

The guardians excepted Mr Anderson's explanations, and no further action was taken.

The population of the Fylde coastal towns was growing faster than the old country townships. Fleetwood and Blackpool had received an extra guardian in 1867, giving them two gardians each. In June, the Blackpool ratepayers who paid nearly a quarter of all the Fylde's poor rates, asked for another representative on the Board. They argued that Poulton-le-Fylde had just over one-thousand inhabitants and two guardians, but only contributed one-tenth of the rates. The request was refused by the guardians.

POPULATION OF THE FYLDE UNION.

Townships.	Population.				
	1831.	1841.	1851.	1861.	1871.
Bispham-with-Norbreck	313	334	354	437	556
Bryning-with-Kellamergh	164	152	195	116	115
Carleton	319	378	401	363	433
Clifton-with-Salwick	598	585	470	447	447
Eccleston Little, with-Larbreck	230	199	205	209	192
Elswick	327	303	307	290	254
Freckleton	909	992	968	879	930
Greenhalgh-with-Thistleton	408	371	382	383	365
Hardhorn-with-Newton	409	357	358	385	436
Kirkham	2469	2903	2799	3380	3593
Layton-with-Warbreck	943	2165	2503	3908	7092
Lytham	1523	2047	2695	3189	3881
Marton	1487	1400	1650	1691	1982
Medlar-with-Wesham	242	209	170	563	880
Newton-with-Scales	381	324	299	286	292
Poulton	1025	1127	[illegible]	1141	1161
Ribby-with-Wrea	482	442	406	444	466
Singleton	499	391	293	338	317
Thornton	842	3765	4041	6029	5122
Treales, Roseacre, and Wharles	756	709	695	632	625
Warton	531	500	473	446	444
Weeton-with-Preese	477	545	465	465	433
Westby-with-Plumptons	686	643	707	601	535
Totals	15930	20774	21905	25823	30534

This newspaper article shows the growth of the original townships that made up the Fylde Union. Blackpool was part of Layton-with-Warbrick. Fleetwood came under the Thornton township.

One year after the workhouse inspector had said a bell should be placed in the vagrant's ward, nothing had been done about it. The Local Government Board wrote to the guardians.

> I beg again to request that the guardians will provide a means of communication from the vagrant's ward to some responsible officer. It appears that on two former inspections of the workhouse, Mr Baldwyn Fleming brought this defect in the workhouse under the notice of the guardians, and the board, therefore, I trust that the guardians will, at once, remedy it. If a vagrant should be taken ill during the night, there is apparently no means of obtaining assistance. I am your obedient servant, W. G. Lumry assistant secretary.

The last thing the guardians wanted was this bell.

The clerk said, 'The responsible officer whoever he is will have no rest if there is a bell affixed, for it will be pulled, during the whole of the night.' A member suggested they should put a cap on it.

Mr Hodgson said, ' We should put one inside it, then it might be always out of order.' The guardians decided to do nothing about the bell.

The inmates accidentally burnt a hole in the new infirmary floor. Sawdust in a wooden box had caught fire and caused the damage. Smoking was now banned in the workhouse, except in the dayrooms. For some months, the guardians had been trying to get the plans for the infirmary off Mr Hibbert to send to the Local Government Board. He refused to hand over the plans because they were his, but he was willing to make copies. In the end, the guardians had to accept the copies.

Mr Slater said, 'There ought to be a plan of the bad workmanship, repairs have been going on ever since completion.'

Another guardian remarked that if such was the case, it was surprising, as Mr Gibson was there as clerk of the works.

'Mr Gibson would surprise a great many folks if they had aught to do with him,' added Mr Hodgson.

Mary Sharp, the nurse, resigned to take up a post in the Haslington Union. Miss Mary Massey of Preston replaced her on a salary of eighteen pounds increasing by one-pound a year until reaching twenty pounds; she took up the post at the end of July.

On 25 April, a man who lived near Thornton Church died from smallpox. The case was taken up by the guardians because preventing the spread of diseases in the rural townships, came under their list of duties. The man had been working away from home and returned to Thornton 'following a horse from Yorkshire', he travelled in his own compartment of the carriage because nobody would sit with him on account of his looks. On the day of the funeral, the man should have been buried at nine o'clock, but the relieving officer couldn't get anybody to go within two-hundred yards of the house. He was eventually buried at four o'clock in the afternoon, and the grave was covered with lime.

The guardians discussed how best to disinfect the house. One idea was to burn a little brimstone for a while; another was to place iodine in a saucer and burn it to kill the organic poison. Dr Williams, who had attended the man, agreed the house should be disinfected, and advised that the house be white-washed and the clothes of the wife and children burnt. The guardians decided to hire a bathing van from Lytham, for the family to live in until the house was cleaned. The bathing van was used to keep the wife and children in isolation and out of the workhouse.

Guardian, Mr Noblett, was put in charge of cleaning the house. At the next guardian's meeting, the smallpox case was discussed.

Mr Noblett said, 'All the man's clothing was accordingly burnt under my personal supervision, and part of the furniture was also burnt. The house was disinfected with chloride of lime and white-washed, and the children had not ailed anything since.'

The guardians replaced all of the man's furniture they had burnt. There was a second case of smallpox in May involving an Army Officer, called Steeds, who was staying at the Clifton Hotel Blackpool. The officer had recovered from smallpox but had passed it onto his servant. The relieving officer gave the servant a ticket to enter the workhouse infirmary. Mr Birley complained that as the man was employed as a servant, he was not destitute, and his officer was charge one pound a week for the man's care. These were the only cases, and the district was declared free of smallpox by the end of June.

In May, a young lad, named Smethhurst, was sent under the boarding out system to Preston tailor Mr Ryding. Six months later, he was dropped back at Kirkham Station, in a dirty state, with his clothes in tatters.

The guardians inspected the clothes which were full of holes. The boy told the guardians that he had been thrashed for stealing money, but he'd lost it going to the shops. The guardians agreed that money could easily be lost with those tattered clothes. The clerk added that when the boy left the workhouse, he had two suits: one for Sunday and one for weekdays. The clerk was ordered to write to the tailor for an explanation and money to pay for the damaged clothes.

The tailor's wife replied in writing.

> I was not aware that the lad had been returned to the workhouse in his second suit, and I never intended him doing so. My husband is a traveller on that line, and he left the lad at Kirkham Station. It was my intention that the clothes should be put in proper repair, and I would be happy to do anything you might suggest. The lad did not like the trade, and he would rather do anything else. Many times, in going on errands, he had lost both money and articles. He had been well treated as one of the family. He was regularly sent to Christ Church School on Sundays with my boys and had frequently found fault with the master for setting bad examples to others, and he also urged my boys to conduct themselves improperly. I feel obliged to send the lad back on account of his conduct. I am exceedingly sorry that it should have happened, but I would do anything the guardians thought proper.

The master added, 'She does not like the lad, and the lad's master has been two or three times to say that he did not like him so well, but he has kept him until now.'

The chairman was satisfied with the explanation. He ordered the clerk to claim ten shillings from Mr Ryding for the damaged clothing.

It was the relieving officer's duty to periodically check on the condition of boarded out children. Because this boy was sent to Preston, he was outside of the Fylde Union, therefore, it was the duty of the Preston relieving officers to check on his wellbeing. These checks didn't happen. The children would from now on only be boarded out within the Fylde Union, so that they would stay under the guardian's protection.

In September, Blackpool fishmonger, James Duerdon, applied to the board in person for an order to take his wife into the workhouse because of her drinking.

He claimed, 'She started sending the children out during the day with money to buy drink for her. I told the children not to buy the drink but to bring the money to me. The next time, my daughter brought the money to me, but she received a thrashing from her mother when she returned home empty-handed. I have one child already dead because of my wife's neglect. The police threatened to lock me up if I didn't put my wife somewhere, and when I went to the police to ask what I should do with her, they told me I had no right to be there, and if I did not go away, they would lock me up. I would be very much obliged if you would keep her at the workhouse, and I would pay for her maintenance.'

The guardians sent him out of the room to discuss the man's request.

Mr Birley said, 'The case was a very sad one, but they could not make the workhouse a receptacle for drunken woman, If they did, they would soon need to enlarge it.'

The chairman remarked there should be a place between a workhouse and an asylum for such persons. The guardians agreed that the case was one of an extremely sad character, but they could not do anything in the matter. The man was called back in and was told the guardians decision.

He again appealed, 'My wife was willing to come, she told me that she would go anywhere. One night I turned her out, and she smashed the windows.'

The chairman replied, 'That's a case for the police, could you not take her to someplace, a cottage for instance, away from where any drink was sold? Or could you not get some strong woman in the house to see that she did not carry on?'

James said, 'Both my sister and her sister came to the house, and she bundled them out, telling them that she was the Missis!'.

The chairman replied, 'Well I'm sorry, but we cannot do anything for you in this matter.'

The case was reported in the newspapers. Thomas Birley, who was suspicious, decided to go to Blackpool to speak with the policemen involved. James Duerdon was a known drunk by the Blackpool police.

A police constable told Mr Birley, 'About a month ago he came to us drunk, at around 10 o'clock in the evening and made an application to get his wife in the workhouse. He was told that it was not the business of the police, and that the relieving officer was the proper person to apply to. He then became very abusive and said that it was the duty of the police to get her there, that she was drinking all the money she could get and that she was starving the family. He was again told to go home and get some friends to look after her until he saw the relieving officer, Mr Fisher, when he was sober. I saw him again at 11'o clock on Bank Hey Street, and asked him if he had seen Mr Fisher, when he replied, 'Find it out.' I told him at once to go home; he was not setting a good example to his wife, and if he would not go, I would be obliged to lock him up. With that, he went away grumbling.'

Mr Birley later told the guardians, 'I have made inquiries into the case, and I find that he came to Blackpool at Whitsuntide, and from his ill-treatment to her, it has driven her to drink. I thought that the affair should not go by without being contradicted.'

Back in 1870, James Catterall had been deemed a refractory pauper and taken to court. He was jailed for twenty days with hard labour for creating a disturbance in the house and using obscene language. James, who thought he was a highly educated man, wrote a letter to the Local Government Board complaining about the work and day rooms. The board forwarded the letter to the Fylde Guardians, which the clerk read out much to the 'mirth' of the guardians.

> Honoured Sir,
>
> I beg to ask you if I should be compelled to work any. I am above 70 years of age, and I suffer much through infirmity, which the doctor says I must bear to my grave. He cannot remedy it, and my son proposed 1s. 5d, towards my maintenance to have a little clemency shown to me, and it is more than he is able to spare. I do not blame the Master at present, but I did Penswick on that account. I work as much as I am able on my own account, and through infirmity,

> I beg to ask if you could permit me to sleep with my wife, as others do. I am going in 72, and she is above 40 and has never had any off springs. I cannot pull one stocking off these two years. I have to sleep in it, and she is willing to assist me with anything that I was not able, and we conduct ourselves with reference enquire. Her work is more available than the others by extra work, so if you take this into consideration. I remain your humble servant, James Catterall.

> I wish you to arrange the men dayrooms, they are jumbled together anyhow. There is a few old men in our room while we cannot sit down comfortably, and the discourse is very disagreeable to me and the others of the same class. I remain your most respectfully, James Catterall.

The guardians dismissed the letter, as they thought that he was a born complainer.

James Catterall wrote another letter to the guardians asking to be allowed out of the workhouse to stay with his son for Christmas.

> Gentlemen of the Board. Honoured sirs: I beg leave to inform you that I applied for a small favour of the committee, to go either to my dinner or tea, could not be granted, and others some 3 or 4 days, which is wholly supported from the union, which I am not. I am surprising astonished, which I am obliged to trouble you on the subject for I work hard and exercises good conduct enquire, and my wife to with no incumbrance, it is considered, I am not legally dealt with. My son troubled himself last Christmas to come and ask the master, and I thought I could save him that time, as it is precious wasting it must be prodigality, so I beg you judge of the matter and leave me an answer in the affirmative, and I remain your most humble servant,
>
> James Catterall.

When the guardians had finished laughing, the clerk told them he had already spoken to his son, who didn't want James to leave the workhouse. He said that last time he was out, he turned up drunk at the house and created a disturbance. The son said he would send him his sherry and Christmas pie to the workhouse.

In 1872, with a growing population, Blackpool asked again for more representation by increasing its number of guardians from two to five. The clerk wrote to some unions similar to the Fylde, to make some comparisons.

	Population	Rateable Value	Guardians
Preston	83,000	£212,900	16
Ormskirk	59,000	£330,000	29
Fylde	30,000	£180,000	27
Oldham	127,000	£329,000	12

Blackpool, with a population of seven-thousand, had a rateable value of forty-nine-thousand pounds.

When the guardians discussed the subject, Mr Thomas Langton Birley said, 'There is no doubt Blackpool is entitled to some increases. Still, I think the number of guardians which they ask for is sadly too many. In my opinion you should not decide the question of representation, either by the rateable value or population; but if you take the number of paupers relieved you will have a better chance of seeing which township requires additional representation. In the year 1871, in Kirkham, the total number were 311, whereas in Layton-with-Warbreck they only numbered 147, consequently they ought to ask for additional guardians for Kirkham, before they ask at Blackpool, because they have a greater number to attend to. If we look at the gross value of Thornton, which combined Fleetwood, we shall see that Thornton ought to have precedence of Blackpool in the election of additional guardians. They only return two guardians, and it will be exceedingly unequal if Blackpool has to return five and Thornton only two. At Lytham, the number of paupers is not great; but still the value is one half of what Layton-with-Warbrick is. Blackpool is in my opinion entitled to some increase; but three are too many.'

Mr Wade, gave some other reasons for Blackpool's request.

He said, 'You must remember that Blackpool is something like three miles in length, that the two present guardians reside in the centre of the town, and its not convenient always for the relieving officer to come from the south shore to consult these guardians, as they frequently do in difficult cases of relief. Then, there is the north end of Layton-with-Warbrick, which extends a good way from Blackpool. I think if we had more guardians the business of the township would be more efficiently and satisfactorily transacted. Two guardians are insufficient for the extent of the duties in the township, and I have great pleasure in moving that we have three extra guardians according to the voice of the ratepayers.'

The guardians decided to leave the decision to the Local Government Board, who gave permission for an extra three guardians, two guardians for Blackpool and one guardian for Lytham.

Mr Cane, poor law inspector, received a letter from an inmate called Robert Leech. Robert alleged that the master had ordered two men to pull him out of bed when he was in the infirmary and put him in a room without a fire, and had otherwise badly treated him. The complaint was passed to the workhouse committee.

The master was called before the guardians at the March meeting.

He said, 'The only bad language I used was calling him soft. The man had been in bed from eight in the morning until two o'clock in the afternoon, and he was ailing very little. Another inmate was brought in, and there not being any room at liberty, I asked the man to go into the room below and make a place for the other inmate. The man said he would not go unless he was made. I then went to speak with the doctor about the matter and asked him if it was not right that the man should be removed. The doctor then told the man this. He still refused to go out. I took him by the shoulders for the purpose of putting him out, and when the man saw I was determined to remove him, he went quietly and was put in the other room.'

The guardians accepted this, but there was a more serious complaint, this time about the matron, from an imbecile girl. The sixteen-year-old had burnt her petticoat, and as a punishment for this the matron took her downstairs, put her in a cold bath, washed her head in cold water, and afterwards, left her alone in the receiving ward for three hours. The matron was reprimanded by the guardians. She expressed her sorrow and promised not to renew that sort of punishment again.

In the workhouse, there was a growing ill-feeling between the master and matron, and the workhouse staff. The nurse was reprimanded in March for leaving the workhouse without permission. In July she was reported by the master for neglecting her duties. The staff were brought before the guardians for an explanation.

The master complained that he'd found William Brown, cleaning the steps on the female side of the infirmary which was against the rules.

The nurse said, 'I put him to that work because I was short of assistance in the female side. I stayed with him all the time and never asked him to go to the female side unless I was with him. He has never assisted since the master complained.'

The next complaint was that the nurse had sent dirty clothes to be washed on the wrong day.

The nurse said, 'On Friday last I sent some dirty clothes to the washhouse. After I had sent them, an inmate, called Cassidy, came back and asked me from the matron what they were. I did not send an insulting message to the matron, nor did I wish to expose the patients. Thursday is the day I usually send the dirty clothes down, except the bad clothes, which went down on the Monday. In dirty cases, they were sent more frequently.'

The next complaint involved a man called Henry Simpson, who went to the infirmary kitchen to get his neck poulticed. He waited half an hour but went away without getting it done.

The nurse said, 'About six weeks ago Simpson came to the infirmary and told me he had a carbuncle. I poultice it, twice a day and it was improving. The day Simpson complained of having to wait, I was busy, and when I came down, I found he was gone. I sent for him, but he never came.'

The third case involved an old lady called Ellen Bibby, who had died in the infirmary, the matron claimed she had been neglected by the nurse.

The matron said, 'I saw Ellen outside her bed at 10 o'clock, trying to dress herself. The nurse was by the bedside of a patient named Paddock, playing tunes with her fingers on a table. I helped the old woman to get up. She had been in the infirmary for six weeks.'

The nurse replied, 'When the matron assisted Ellen Bibby to dress, I was busy with another patient, and I thought the matron was seeing to the old woman, seeing that I was busy.

The matron and master then involved Doctor Bowness.

The matron said, 'One night, after ten o'clock, after Ellen Bibby had been taken to the infirmary, I asked the doctor to see her. He never answered. I told the doctor the woman was helpless. She was on a special diet, and not on the sick list.'

The master said, 'I have asked him several times to enquire whether or not Ellen Bibby could go out of the house. The doctor never gave me a satisfactory reply, whether she might or not. She complained once or twice of being ill to the doctor, and he gave her nothing. She was on No. 4 diet.'

The doctor was called before the Guardians.

He said, 'I think I have only seen her once or twice before she went into the infirmary. The second time I was called to see her, she was in her own bed, and I did not consider it necessary to have her removed to the infirmary. She was able to walk before being brought into the infirmary.'

The nurse agreed, 'She could walk before being brought into the infirmary. When she came in the infirmary, she was very feeble. I had to lift her out of bed when they changed her.'

Ellen Bibby died of old age in the doctor's opinion, eight weeks after being put into the infirmary.

The guardians were split on who was at fault. Some thought the master and matron were and should resign, whereas some thought the nurse was to blame. William Hodgson thought they all should resign. In the end, they decided the nurse should go; she was replaced by Jane Lockley, who had worked in the Chorlton Union and the Lancaster Workhouse. Miss Lockley only stayed for a few months and was subsequently replaced by Miss Garson.

Mrs McGee, the school governess, also resigned and left for the Salford Workhouse. On 22 March, the school was inspected by Mr Mosley, who wrote in the visitor's book.

I have inspected the school today. The children passed, on the whole, a very fair examination. There ought to be more attention paid to their arithmetic, and I recommend the use of arithmetic cards with the numbers written in words in rotation.

Miss Rachel Bennet became the new school governess, in August she resigned and asked to leave straight away. Miss Bennet left due to the matron and wrote a letter of complaint to the Local Government Board.

In the letter, Miss Bennet stated that she had at one time been called a liar by the matron, had been subjected to several petty annoyances and that an imbecile had been put under her charge. She believed she had enough to do looking after her school, without being troubled to look after an imbecile. Miss Bennet added that 'three weeks together' sheets on some beds had not been changed and that her own bed had to be made by one of the larger boys. She also stated that the boys did not get the soap they needed to wash the floors.

She was replaced by Miss Blythe of Hungerford, Berkshire. The new governess complained almost immediately to the guardians about the matron.

She said, 'My orders to the boys were countermanded by the matron; the consequence was I cannot receive due respect from the lads. The rooms of the lads were not kept clean and, therefore, I would like sole superintendence of them, as was formerly the case. One of the lads is improperly dressed; in fact, I'm ashamed to take him out, his coat being composed of five different coloured materials.'

The guardians gave the governess sole responsibility of the children, but her request to dine alone and not with the master and matron was declined by the guardians.

Things didn't improve for the governess, and she wrote a letter to the guardians.

> Fylde Union Workhouse, 9 October 1872.
>
> To the Guardians of the Fylde Union, Gentlemen, I regret being compelled to bring under your notice the conduct of Mrs Anderson, the matron. Since the last meeting of the board, it has been a question with me whether I should take this course, or at once tender to you the resignation of my

office. I have adopted the former, believing that you would, by your kind interference, be able to put a stop to the abuse to which I am daily subjected. Whenever I see the matron, she invariably begins to quarrel and use bad language. As a sample of it, I may tell you that when I saw her yesterday, she began (without the slightest provocation) by saying, 'I'll prove you to be a liar. You are a brute and a mischief-making thing.' This is not a casual occurrence, but one of the kind that happens daily. Trusting to receive at your hands such redress as my case requires.

I am your obedient servant, H.N. Blythe.

The guardians discussed the matter.

Mr Noblett said, 'I have nothing against the master, but the matron is a very mischievous woman.'

The chairman said, 'I suppose the master took the matron for better or for worse.'

The guardians passed a motion that if any more complaints arose, all three would be asked to resign. On 29 November, Mary and Raby Anderson resigned. Forty couples applied for the post, which was given to John and Alice Billington of Blackburn.

The yearly cost to the union of patients in the Lancaster Asylum reached six-hundred and eighty pounds. The guardians started making sure people who had relatives in the asylum contributed to their keep and sent a visiting committee to bring back to the workhouse the patients who could be released. Sarah Harrison, Margaret Ward, Ann Cookson, Margaret Dobson, John Bond, and Alonzo Ford were fit to leave the Lancaster Asylum and were removed to the workhouse. In October, the guardians received a report from the asylum regarding the union's remaining charges.

1. Sarah Slater is paralysed in her lower limbs, and usually, she is quiet and tractable. She has been an inmate so long that no change for the better can be expected.

2. Mary Titterington is an irritable person and is apt to be violent to those around her. She requires the controlling influence of an asylum.

3. Robert Webster is a criminal patient, not yet tried at the sessions. He was returned 'to the castle' (Lancaster Prision) in July last but was sent back as his insanity had returned. I hope by a longer trial, he may be quite recovered.

4. W. H. Moon is making considerable amendments in his mental symptoms, and his discharge may be looked forward to very shortly.

In November, the Government passed an act making the unions responsible for sanitation. The union appointed a doctor, Dr Shaw, as the sanitary officer for the Fylde. Kirkham, Blackpool, Lytham, and Fleetwood were exempt because they had their own Local Boards of Health. There was a report of a typhoid outbreak in Wesham. Doctor Shaw was asked for a report by the guardians. He reported that it was gastric fever caused by the unclean piggeries in the back yards of the houses.

Lavinia Hyde, a mother of five children, lived in London but had settlement in the Fylde from when she was the landlady of the Halfway House, Blackpool. She wrote to the board asking for relief, so she could maintain herself and her children where she was living after she was refused relief from the London authorities. The woman had been offered a place of employment by her son, but she had refused to take it. The guardians thought the test should be applied and offered her a place in the Kirkham Workhouse; if she were desperate, she would accept the offer. Like many so called 'desperate' people, when the test was applied nothing more was heard of from Lavinia.

The master asked about bathing the vagrants.

One guardian remarked, 'If we wanted to keep them, away we must bathe them.'

The master didn't want to bathe the vagrants in the normal baths because they bought vermin into the house. The matter was referred to the visiting committee, who decided to build a new bathhouse for the vagrants. They also extended the boardroom to accommodate more guardians. The room was widened by eight feet; it was now twenty-five feet by twenty feet. Two new windows were put in. Seventy-six pounds and forty shillings was spent on hot water pipes for heating the boardroom, and the boiler was repaired for twenty-one pounds and six shillings.

James Catterall wrote another letter.

> Gentlemen of the Board, I beg to lay case before you, which is considered of a shameful nature for last Sabbath morning week. A tumult arose in the bedroom by two inmate persons, which is in charge of all the bedrooms, which is ill neglected for want of knowledge of their offices, and the most blaspheming profane language I never heard in my life, I rose from my prayer and directed my steps as far from the hearing as I could, but it would reach to the outer doors.
>
> It is commonly so, without check or reprimand and when prayer time came on, an inmate came into the room where I sat and said, I have no one to go with me to church to day, so I sayed, I'll go with you, for I have heard Mr Brown preach several times, and he took my attention very much, I sayed. So I went in the afternoon, and it so happened that Mr Atkinson officiated at the sermon and I enquired if Mr Brown would preach in the afternoon, and I was told in the affirmative, so I was going with a few other inmates, but the master came in such a fury that he made me tremble and bid me come back and would not show any reason, and when I reached the front, the dame began with most insulting language and falsehoods, but I passed by on the other side.
>
> I often want to know the reason of the spite and malice, but they won't answer, or else I would abolish the error for I work hard and conducts myself with good behaviour and I am not kept wholly from the union, methinks I should have a little favour shown me, instead of ill treatment for I am prepared at any period to show more infirmity to Mr Bowness on my body than any inmate that pretends to work, any so, I beg for you to try remedy my case and I remain your obedient and most humble servant.
>
> James Catterall.

The letter was ignored. The guardians received a letter from John Livesey, who had lost the contract to supply coal to the Workhouse.

> To the Guardians of the Fylde Union, Gentlemen,

> I hope you will excuse the liberty I am now taking in bringing before your notice the following remarks. I, having supplied you with coals for the last six months without complaints, whatever, being made, and at a considerable loss which you must be all aware. I am quite at a loss to know the reason why I have not been asked to tender for the next three months, as there have not been the least complaints made about the coals I supplied. I never should have brought the case before your notice, nor yet did I know that I would receive tenders for that term, nor yet ever asked to tender for three months. I could tender now, but I consider that it would be both irregular and dishonourable to do so long as I had not been invited to do so. I may also add that I think other parties have been solicited to send tenders by someone or other, as no respectable tradesman would tender without being asked to do so. Gentlemen, hoping you will excuse the liberty I have taken, and that you will give the case the consideration it merits. I beg to remain, gentleman, yours truly John Livesey.

They gave it some consideration. John Livesey was supplying the workhouse with coal at twenty-five shillings a ton but supplying private individuals with coal at twenty-one shillings and sixpence, which is why he lost the contract.

Mr Walker, 4 Lowther Street, Lytham, donated some books to the workhouse and Mrs Willacy of Kirkham, whose brother had formerly been in the workhouse, but who had since died sent ten pounds as an acknowledgement for their kindness to her brother, while he was in the workhouse.

In April 1873, R. C. Richards, who had been the chairman since 1862, was again nominated to the position. He declined the nomination and William Segar Hodgson, who had been a dedicated guardian of 12 years, was elected chairman. The guardians at the meetings asked and moved all sorts of things. Here are three examples from this year.

> 1. Mr Noblett wanted to know the nationalities of the paupers in receipt of relief. The clerk stated that two-hundred and fifty-one able-bodied paupers were receiving outdoor

relief, two-hundred and fifteen of which were English, fifteen were Irish, and twenty-one were Scottish. In the workhouse there were one-hundred and nine paupers, ninety-six of which were English and thirteen were Irish. The indoor and outdoor paupers, of all classes, were counted at four-hundred and twenty-three Englishmen, one-hundred and two Irishmen, and twenty-one Scotsmen: a total of six-hundred and fifty-four.

2. Mr Bilsborrow moved that in future the boy's clothing be made not as at present by piecework but by contract. He was of the opinion that it would be better and cheaper to have it done in that way than to have a tailor in the house, to whom they had to pay three to four shillings a day. Mr Slater seconded the motion to take effect in a fortnight, and it was passed by the guardians.

3. Mr Slater told the guardians that two women from the workhouse had been allowed to go out for the day. One was married and had a child. In due time after this permission, she had been 'delivered of a bastard child.' He wanted to know whether or not women should be trusted in that manner in future. The question was referred to the consideration of the visiting committee.

The present nurse, Miss Garston, resigned in January to avoid an inquiry after the Toxteth Board of Health claimed she had been discharged from the Toxteth Workhouse, in consequence of her intemperance in 1867. Mr Birley thought it would only be fair to write to the people who wrote her testimonials, which he said were very good. One was from a clergyman and the other from a doctor. The doctor of the Toxteth Park Union wrote back saying, in all the time she had been at the union, she had never been charged with that offence.

Miss Lockley, the former nurse who had left Kirkham, applied for the job, as she felt she was being mistreated at her new position in Leeds. The other applicant was Matilda Orme of the Bradford Nurse Training Institute. Miss Lockley was given the position.

The following patients were removed from the Lancaster Asylum, for Miss Lockley to look after.

1. Sarah Slater, aged fifty, who had been in the asylum for ten years.

2. Ellen Broughton, aged forty-two, an epileptic case who had been in the asylum for five years.

3. Peter Brady, aged forty-six, had been in the asylum for seven years and was harmless.

4. Noblett Gregson, aged fifty-two, a patient in the asylum for one and a half years and was fit for release.

5. Mary Wilson, aged thirty-one, had been in the asylum eighteen months, but still required care.

The nurse had one less patient when Peter Brady's wife asked the guardians for her husband to be released into her care, which they agreed to. She would bring him back if she couldn't manage him.

The Lunacy Commissioners visited the workhouse on 14 April.

I have today seen 15 inmates of this workhouse who are classed of unsound mind, 13 males and 2 females. William Webster is an idiot, Elizabeth Whiteside, a congenital imbecile, both cases for the Albert Asylum Lancaster if their admission could be procured. Many of these patients are employed in various ways, and with two or three exceptions amongst the men, they were personally in a satisfactory state, and I was assured that all were regularly bathed. James Garlick, in consequence of his destructive propensities, wears a strong dress, but the master promised to try the effect of giving him a good suit of ordinary clothing and sending him out for walks. All the men now sleep singly, and the present large bedsteads should be replaced by smaller ones, such as are generally used in workhouses. The beds were clean, and the rooms well ventilated and in proper order. I recommend the substitution of horsehair or woollen flock for straw in the pillows generally, and that an under blanket be placed on all straw beds. The visiting committee book is signed at irregular intervals by the guardians, and no certificates have been given by the medical officer under the provisions of the 20th section of the Lunacy Act Amendment Act, 1862 in reference to these patients.

The workhouse had a horse and cab in which people travelled in during their daily business. They also used it as an ambulance to convey sick people to the workhouse. This year an inmate caught a contagious disease in the cab, as it had been previously used to carry an infectious case. The board decided to buy a separate cab, lined with a removable cloth to transport sickness cases.

Mr Fair joked, 'We should paint 'The Workhouse Sick Removal Cab' on the side.'

The chairman thought they'd better not, as it might frighten the people. A cab was purchased for ten guineas, and a horse was rented when needed. They also built a small building to house the cart.

It was now twelve years since the school had been open. Education was accessible for most children in the country, and it was getting difficult to recruit decent schoolteachers. The Preston Union had advertised for a teacher for a salary of twenty-five pounds, but nobody applied. When it was increased to thirty pounds, they still only had one applicant.

In April when the schoolmistress resigned, Mr Bilsborrow thought it might be time to close the school and send the children out to the Kirkham schools.

He said, 'They have good schools in Kirkham, within two or three minutes' walk of the workhouse of different denominations, where the children could be sent with advantage. It would be more conducted to their health, and they would thus get more exercise. There would be the advantage of the children mixing with others at the school, and this would tend to elevate their ideas and thus cause them to become useful members of society like other boys. Looking at it from a financial point of view, it would be also very advantageous; they had 24 children in the house at present seven of whom were under three years of age, and who could not be expected to attend school. This reduced the number to ten boys and seven girls. There would also be an application that day for one boy to go to service, and if he went it would reduce the number to 16.'

He continued, 'To the present schoolmistress they paid a salary of £25 per year, but she was certificated, and the Government paid about £16 of this. Her rations cost them £16 4s. 7½d. per year and other necessaries £13 3s. 5d, so that she really cost the Board £38 17s. 0d. If the children were sent to the schools in town, the school wage (fee) would not cost above 2d. each per week, and thus the fee for each would be 8s. per annum. The 16 children would only cost £6 8s. 0d. They would be as well and better educated then they were at present. So, there would be a clear saving of £32 9s. 0d.'

He added, 'I think it would be the means, to a certain extent, of stopping the quarrelling amongst the officers, who seemed to have got in their head that it was their sole work to disagree. Some they had discharged, others they had asked to resign, and they had constantly been changing officers.'

Mr Birley could not agree with Mr Bilsborrow.

Mr Birley said, 'With regards to sending the children to school, being only three or four minutes' walk, the distance at least to any school was half a mile and to send such children as those in the house, both winter and summer, I do not suppose would be right. I also think it would hardly be right to permit little children to go by themselves. It is true that at present there were only 16 children, and this they should be very thankful; but two years ago, we had double that number. I know no reason why they might not have the same number again. With regards to the conduct of the present mistress, I had nothing to say, but I would say that Miss Hunt and Miss Ghee were both as good mistresses as possibly could be had and did credit to the children. A great portion of the quarrelling referred to was owing to the incapacity of the late master and matron. He thought that the children would be better cared for at home, and it was an unusual practice for children in the workhouse to be sent out to school.'

The guardians decided to write to the Local Government Board to see if they could send the children out to school. Reverend Brown told the meeting that the schools would charge three pence a week per child for six months, but if they went all year, they would receive a government grant, and it would cost one and a half pennies per week. The Local Government Board agreed for the children to be sent out to school for a six-month trial.

The Fylde had changed since the union had been formed. The area had new large towns, which hadn't existed in 1844. The Thornton township, which included Fleetwood, now a large port town. Layton with Warbreck, which included Blackpool, was now a major seaside resort. Lytham was also in the same position, incorporating the new towns of St Annes and Ansdell and Fairhaven.

In 1874, to give better representation to the ratepayers, Thornton and Lytham were both split into two wards, one ward comprising the urban part and one ward the rural part of the townships. Each town was to get two guardians for the urban area, and one for the rural part. Layton-with-Warbreck was given an extra guardian. To offset this, two guardians were removed by uniting Elswick to Little Eccleston-with-Larbreck, and Bryning-with-Kellamergh to Warton.

In 1839, the new Fylde Union had set the poor rate collectors pay at sixty pounds per annum. The current collector for the Kirkham District was Robert Thompson. He had been doing the job since 1846 and was still being paid the original sum of sixty-pounds. In March, he asked for his salary to be increased to one-hundred pounds. He informed the guardians that in 1846, there was one-thousand, nine-hundred and ninety-five ratepayers in the Kirkham District and the rateable value was fifty-six-thousand, nine-hundred and fifteen pounds. Now there were three-thousand, two-hundred and nineteen ratepayers and the rateable value was seventy-six-thousand, nine-hundred and four pounds. Some guardians pointed out that he collected the rates only twice a year, whereas, earlier it had been four times, so his workload had decreased. After some debate, the guardians decided to raise his salary to eighty pounds: which the Local Government Board sanctioned.

Ann Bamber became the new nurse in January after Mrs Lockley had again resigned. The new nurse had a case of smallpox to deal with when Jane Wilcock was admitted to the workhouse. She arrived in Wesham after leaving the Preston Workhouse in an infectious state, with scales on her face and arms. Dr Shaw, who thought she was in a state to give the disease, ordered her into the infections ward. The question for the guardians was whether she was discharged from the Preston Workhouse before she was fit, or whether she came out herself, and in that case, proceedings would be taken against her for exposing others to the disease.

That June, two guardians, Mr Slater and John Wade, along with Dr Bowness, visited the Lancaster Asylum.

They reported, 'We found the patients, 21 in number, looking very well upon the whole, clean in person and neat in attire. In their mental conditions, little had occurred. There was only one Mary Titterington, who could be fairly be said to be likely for withdrawal from the asylum and even this is doubtful. The opinion at which the board arrived, in the case of Susannah Porter, seems to be amply justified, by her personal appearance and also by the decided opinion of the medical officers. It is much feared that in nearly all the cases now in the asylum, there is not likely to be much further mental improvements.'

The daily running cost of the Kirkham Workhouse was four shillings and nine and a half pence per head, compared with four shillings and one and a quarter pence average for Lancashire. After William Hodgson had become chairman, great effort was made in reducing the running costs. One way of reducing costs was to take as many cases as possible out of the asylums and making sure the relatives paid for the remaining ones.

The cost per week to the union for each patient in the asylums was ten shillings and sixpence, and the guardians wanted the relatives to pay at least seven shillings towards this. The Local Government Board wrote to the guardians and pointed out that if the relatives paid seven shillings or more, that board forfeited the Government grant, but if the relatives paid six shillings, then the Government allowed four shillings in each case.

To meet the Local Government Board requirements, the guardians had a room inside the workhouse converted into a padded cell for violent lunatics,

The Local Government Board wrote to the guardians, asking how it was going sending the children out to school.

Mr Slater said, 'That with regards to children going out to school, everything was going on in a satisfactory manner. The children were much healthier, and better attended to; besides, it was to them a saving of £50 per year.'

Although the school was closed the workhouse school inspector, stilled examined the children. His report didn't back up Mr Slater's report.

> 20 March 1874.
>
> I examined the children on the 18th inst., in reading and arithmetic. The supply of slates in the house was so limited

> that I was unable to examine their writing (except in a slight degree). The arithmetic was, in general, a failure; the reading pretty fair. The children with two exceptions seemed dull and shy; these two I should add were those who had been in the union the longest time (both indeed were born there). These children went to various schools according to creed and sex.
>
> J.R. Mosley.

John Westhead, aged twelve, absconded from the workhouse, whilst on his way to school. The workhouse master, Robert Billington, wasn't concerned about him absconding, but the fact that he took the workhouse clothing he was wearing with him. He was wearing a jacket, a waistcoat, a pair of trousers, a pair of stockings, a shirt, a pair of clogs, a cap, and a scarf, worth twelve shillings. Sergeant Jackson found the lad at his father's house at Blowing Sands, Marton. When John was charged with absconding, he replied, 'I came to see my father.'

At Kirkham Court, he was sentenced to fourteen days imprisonment in the Preston House of Correction.

Another boy, an apprentice named Sharples, appeared before the board to complain at not being taught his trade properly. He complained that he was kept solely to mending and not making shoes. In the five years he'd been an apprentice, he had only made three pairs of shoes. He asked if he could leave Thomas Walmsley's Bootmakers, Lytham, and serve as a miller under Mr Cookson. Mr Raby, the relieving officer, had visited Mr Walmsley and another of his apprentices. He found him a respectable man and a proper person to engage lads from the workhouse.

The chairman said, 'We have no power to deal with the case. He was apprenticed and had better serve his time out honourably, and afterwards, if he did not like his trade, he could become a miller.' The workhouse master was ordered to escort him back to Lytham, for fear of him running away.

Irishman Bernard McGowan was asked to pay ten shillings towards his son's maintenance: he refused.

He said, 'I do not object paying 6s. or if the board put the lad in my care, I would ship him off to the 'ould country'. As for myself, I have given up my business in Fleetwood and intend going over the waters to America.'

The boardroom's stone floor was replaced with wood, and the guardians had to decide on the floor coverings. Mr Moore and others thought oilcloth or linoleum, in point of cheapness, durability, usefulness and neatness.

Mr Rushton, to much laughter, said, 'Carpets in point of softness, neatness, cheapness and warmth.' The guardians chose linoleum.

By January of 1875, Robert and Alice Billington had been master and matron for two years. After gaining the position, they said that they wouldn't ask for a pay raise for two years. Now that the two years were up, they asked for a raise of ten pounds, taking their pay to sixty pounds per annum: which was granted. Despite this, they both resigned three months later, after receiving a better-paid position. John O'Neil and his wife, managers of Leeds Workhouse Infirmary, replaced the Billingtons.

The Lancashire Asylums were constantly full, until 1873 when Whittingham Asylum, near Preston, opened. The opening of Whittingham Asylum led to some competition between the old asylums, which led to a reduction in the cost of maintaining patients. The largest reduction was at Lancaster Asylum, which by August had dropped from above ten shillings to seven shillings and seven pence per person per week. Prestwich's cost per person also dropped slightly to nine shillings and four pence. According to the clerk, Whittingham's and Prestwich's costs stayed high because they treated more complex cases.

In spite of this reduction, the guardians still pushed for as many patients as possible to be released from the asylums. However, this was being detrimental to the sick in the infirmary. John Cleaton, the Lunacy Commissioner, visited the workhouse.

> 13 March 1875.
>
> I have, this day, personally examined the inmates as of unsound mind at this workhouse. They are at present 15 in number, 12 of the male and 3 of the female sex. I have besides had my attention drawn to a woman named

> Margaret Dobson, who has been insane and an inmate of the Lancaster Asylum on three previous occasions, having been discharged therefrom the last time in 1872. She is at present, much agitated, and depressed without any adequate cause and disturbs the inmates of the infirmary by her continuous irrational conduct and conversation. I recommend her to the special observation of the medical officer that he may determine whether she should not be sent again to the asylum. I shall report further to the Local Government Board.

Margaret Dobson was sent back to Lancaster Asylum, where the Fylde Union had twenty-one patients. There were a further two patients at Prestwich and five at Whittingham.

The visiting committee visited Lancaster on 2 June.

There are 21 patients belonging to the Fylde Union now in the asylum, decidedly a smaller number than usual. Of these 13 are male and 8 female. The ages vary from 13 to 76. There are three under 30, 16 between 30 and 60 years, one of 68, and one of 76 years. We found the patients generally in tolerable health and evidently well cared for, but some more debilitated than at our last visit. One Mary Ann Jamison is in the infirmary, suffering from a severe dropsical affection. Her age, 58 years, makes her recovery very improbable. We regret that we cannot recommend anyone for present discharge; Ann Seed and Margaret Dobson are improving and will probably soon be better but cannot as yet be removed from the asylum.

In the six months ending September, the orders for admittance into the workhouse totalled three-hundred and sixty-five. Of these orders, one-hundred and fifty-three people were refused entry. Of the two-hundred and twelve admitted, ninety-seven paupers stayed less than one month, sixty-two paupers stayed between one to two months, and the remaining fifty-three stayed for over three months. When men entered the workhouse, they were shaved. Mr Nickson, the barber, charged the union ten pence per dozen paupers

Basil Cane Inspected the workhouse.

> Sir, I made an entry in the visitor's book calling the attention of the visiting committee to the trapping and the ventilation

of the workhouse drains and asking them to make certain entries in the visitor's book. I think the guardians should re-arrange the sewering of the house. The water closets are drained into the town's sewer, but some of them were foul, and the smell from the discharge pipe of the bath in the female receiving ward was unendurable. The cesspools ought certainly to be done away with.

In 1876, the Manchester Union had adopted the following set of regulations to help with the administration of outdoor poor relief:

1. Outdoor relief shall not be granted or allowed, except in cases of sickness to any of the following classes:

a) Single able-bodied men.

b) Single able-bodied woman.

c) Able-bodied widows, without children or having only one child to support.

d) Married women (with or without families) whose husbands having been convicted of a crime and are undergoing a term of imprisonment.

e) Married women (with or without families) deserted by their husbands.

f) Married women (with or without families) left destitute through their husbands having joined the militia and being called up for training.

g) Persons residing with relatives, where the united income of the family is sufficient for the support of all its members, whether such relatives are liable by law to support the applicant or not.

2. Outdoor relief shall not be granted, in any case, for a longer period than thirteen weeks at a time.

3. Outdoor relief shall not be granted to any able-bodied person for a longer period than six weeks at a time.

4. Outdoor relief shall not be granted on account of sickness of the applicant or any of his family, for longer periods than two weeks at a time, unless such sickness shall be certified in writing, by the district medical officer as being likely to be of a long duration or to be of a permanent character.

The guardians discussed adopting the regulations in January; Mr Cane, the workhouse Inspector, was at the meeting to give advice. The main sticking point was regulation (e) the guardians thought it was unfair to punish a woman who'd been deserted by her husband.

Mr Cane said, 'This was the most important in the whole number. Without this rule, there was the greatest inducement to husbands to desert their wives and go roaming about the country as long as they knew they had a home to come back to. The wife consented to the departure, and the husband sent her a little money now and then, and with the relief she obtained as 'a deserted wife', was able to keep the house open. They could not punish such a husband by law without the consent of the wife, but if rule (e) were enforced they would have a ready witness in the wife, and the law could take effect.'

The chairman thought these regulations would remove twenty-five per cent of their pauperism and were unanimously adopted; a copy was printed and hung in the boardroom.

The cost of pauperism on the Fylde continued to fall. The 'call' for the rates in the first half of last year was five pence, and in the second half, it was three and three-quarter pence. By 1876, rates were reduced to three pence.

The workhouse master and matron received a pay rise of twenty pounds early in the year after promising to stay for at least two years. In December, they both resigned along with the nurse. Mr Slater was named as a reason for the resignations, due to his interference in the running of the workhouse.

Mr Slater spoke about the accusations.

He said, 'I was ordered, by the workhouse committee, to look at the premises and inspect some work about the workhouse, some time ago. I did so, and when performing my duty, the master had been very insulting and said that he would have this thing and the other done and also ordered me off the premises. Also, there has not been a single month without some visitors of the master at the workhouse being there. The master had disobeyed the orders of the workhouse committee, and his conduct has been anything but respectful.'

The chairman said, 'I am sorry that such a disagreement should have arisen between the master and Mr Slater. If Mr Slater had interfered with the master, then he was to blame, unless it had been by the authority of the board. If we kept having such disturbances, they would never have a master worth anything there.'

An animated Mr Slater said, 'When he came here last Saturday, the master called me a liar.'

The chairman said, 'I'm of the opinion the master and matron were the best officers that they had had for twenty years, and furthermore, that the published reports laid on the table some short time ago were the best they had had. More orders and fewer inmates had been called to the house, and the inmates had been better tested. I consider the master to be a very intelligent man.'

Mr Slater countered, 'He is the worst that has been here for 12 years.'

The chairman, 'Well, Mr Slater, we had perhaps better not dispute the point, or we might be no nearer next week at this time.'

Mr Tyler and some of the guardians agreed with Mr Slater. Mr Tyler asked if the inmates got the food they formally did. They received the ordinary diet according to the chairman. Another guardian remarked that the inmates complained of not being allowed sufficient food. The chairman cut the discussion short by saying the resignations had been accepted.

Mr Slater again complained about visitors coming to the workhouse and stopping all night. He moved that no visitors be allowed to stay all night, without the consent of the Board, which was carried.

On 26 May, Margaret Brown of Lytham died in the workhouse from Typhus Fever. When she arrived at the workhouse, the workhouse doctor, Thomas Shaw, was called but refused to come out. The matron wanted to admit Mrs Brown, but the husband being indignant at Dr Shaw, took her back to Lytham. The Lytham medical officer went to see her and sent her back to the workhouse, where she later died. The guardians thought Dr Shaw had neglected his duty and wanted an explanation.

Doctor Shaw refused to help because Lytham was not part of his medical district. He wrote to the guardians.

> Kirkham 27th June 1876.
>
> Gentlemen, I duly received a communication from your clerk informing me of the result of your deliberations on the case of Margaret Brown. I infer that you consider that I am the only person in fault, but I contend that I am the only person faultless, for the following reasons.
>
> 1. Margaret Brown was not an inmate of the workhouse; consequently, she did not come within the sphere of my duties.
>
> 2. The matron, acting under advice, refused to admit Margaret Brown into the workhouse; consequently, she went back to Lytham.
>
> 3. The master and matron had no authority to call me to the workhouse to any sick person who is not an inmate of the workhouse.
>
> 4. Sick persons seeking admission into the workhouse, and requiring medical assistance, belong to No.2 Kirkham District.
>
> 5. Had Margaret Brown been admitted into the workhouse I contend that I would of went to the workhouse within a reasonable time, taking into consideration the nature of her case.
>
> 6. I have been the Medical Officer of the Fylde Union Workhouse for upwards of 30 years, and I believe this to be the first case in which my attendance has been requested in No.1 Kirkham District.
>
> I am gentleman, your obedient servant Thomas Shaw.

The visiting committee recommended that the medical officer should attend the workhouse once daily, as far as practicable, and that the nurse should keep a book for entering the time of such attendances. The committee also advised that a medical certificate should, in all cases, accompany a sick pauper on admission to the workhouse, and that such certificate should state whether the sickness is of an infectious nature, so as to enable the workhouse master to deal properly with the case.

Dr Shaw's reply to the recommendations was, 'I have received notice to attend daily at the workhouse. I hope you will give me adequate recompense for the extra duties by adding £30 a year to my present salary.'

Dr Shaw was the medical officer for Kirkham Number Two District, and the workhouse doctor: two separate roles. The position as number two district doctor was awarded annually, but the role as workhouse doctor was permanent. The first role wasn't in question, it was the latter, but as a permanent role, the guardians could not dismiss him, it had to come from the Local Government Board in London. The complaint was accordingly passed to the Local Government Board, who took no action.

Despite Margaret Brown dying of typhus, the union was doing well in terms of smallpox vaccinations. There were six-hundred and forty-four births, of which five-hundred and twenty-six were successfully vaccinated. Of the ones not vaccinated sixty-three had died, twelve vaccinations had been postponed for medical reasons, twelve had moved to other districts, and nineteen were unaccounted for.

Throughout the workhouse, there were fifty coal fires, which between them burnt one ton of coal per day. The board started looking into heating the house and cooking using steam. They asked Mr Stevenson of the Canal Foundry, Preston, for advice. He thought one boiler would be sufficient for the whole building.

The chairman said, 'We have three fires in the boiler house, besides two other fires for cooking, and with an outlay of about £300 they would make a considerable saving.'

In July, the guardians advertised for tenders to fit a steam boiler, cooking apparatus, and heating pipes.

On 4 October, James Walton was found dead in bed by the workhouse master. He was seventy-seven years of age and had been afflicted with softening of the brain. There had been a recent increase in the number of vagrants entering the workhouse. Mr Slater thought it was because they were being too well fed. He moved that male vagrants above fifteen years of age be allowed only eight ounces of bread and water, and no porridge, or six ounces of bread and a pint of gruel. The motion was carried.

In 1877, the decrease in the number of paupers receiving outdoor poor relief continued. In the first week of 1877 three-hundred and fifty-six paupers were receiving outdoor relief, as opposed to four-hundred and ten in 1876; four-hundred and ninety-seven in 1875; five-hundred and eleven in 1874; five-hundred and ninety-nine in 1873 and 1872. These, compared with the one-thousand, one-hundred, and eighty-two paupers receiving outdoor relief in 1863, when the population of the union was much smaller, which was a significant decrease.

The master and matron were still at the workhouse. A letter from the master was read out at the guardians meeting on 10 January.

> The master and matron will feel obliged if the guardians will kindly liberate us from our duties as master and matron of this workhouse, as we have no control of the house through the interference of Mr Slater, a member of the board. On Thursday last, the nurse took herself away from her duties the whole day, saying that Mr Slater had given her leave and that she did not care for me.

To that Mr Slater said, 'I never said she must go at all.'

The chairman, 'The woman [nurse] we know is a liar, we have evidence sufficient already that she is a great liar.'

The master said, 'She snapped her fingers at me and said she did not care for me as she had had Mr Slater's leave. The workhouse visiting committee have no power to give anyone leave of absence.'

Mr Slater, 'You know very well that the workhouse committee never would of done it. They have never given it without the knowledge of the master.'

The matter ended there, two weeks later the master and matron, left the workhouse and were replaced by Mr and Mrs Farr. The first thing Mr Farr did was to employ a cook on a salary of fifteen pounds per annum. He was ordered by the guardians to buy stones at four shillings per ton and sell them for six shillings when broken. Mrs Disley, the widow of the late Preston relieving officer, was appointed the new nurse.

The new matron complained straight away that Doctor Shaw only visited the workhouse once a day; generally, about nine o'clock at night. She also stated that several children were 'in the whooping cough' and he had not properly looked after them. The guardians ordered the medical officer to look into the cases immediately.

When William Wright was released from Whittingham Asylum, he had several injuries on him. William's family reported it to the guardians. The contingent that visited Whittingham, in October, asked Dr Holland about William Wright's injuries. The doctor told them that there was hereditary scrofula in the family, and when in the asylum he had an outbreak, he would keep injuring his head with his fingers.

In towns without school boards, the Fylde guardians were now responsible for helping the children of the poor to attend school. Poor families could now apply to the guardians for the 'school penny', which you had to pay for your child to attend school.

Elizabeth Fenton, South Shore, Blackpool, who had six illegitimate children, was ordered by the school inspector to send her children to school. The father of the children, John Fisher, earned eighteen shillings per week, but Miss Fenton had no earnings herself and was entirely destitute. However, she had to act on the inspector's orders. She didn't have the sufficient means to pay the school penny, and unless the children 'took the pence', the school master or mistress would not have them. Mr Broadbent moved that Fenton be allowed the school pence for three children, which was carried.

Reverend Johnstone, of Poulton-le-Fylde, complained that Bridget Manning had been taken out of school and had been sent out to service underage. Mr Gaultier looked into the matter and reported back that the girl was fourteen years of age on the 17th of last May. She was born in Yorkshire and christened there. Bridget liked her placement very well, and Mr Parkinson, the relieving officer, said he saw the girl's mother, a widow, who received three shillings a week in relief, and she was contented with her daughter's situation._

In August, the inmates were treated to the annual trip to Blackpool. They visited both piers, the Aquarium, and Raikes Hall. They were admitted for free into the four attractions, by the owners.

In the workhouse, the new boiler got so hot that it heated the bricks in the wall until they were red hot, which the master thought was very dangerous to the surrounding buildings. The visiting committee was asked to look into it. They also ordered the pumps in the kitchen to be removed, as the water in them was unfit for general use. A new men's day room was built for thirty-five pounds and five shillings by Robert Cross of Kirkham. The Reverend Mason, who conducted the services on Friday evenings, asked the board for a harmonium, which the workhouse committee purchased for ten pounds. Robert Nixon, the baker, asked for a two shillings pay rise, the board agreed, and his wages were raised to ten shillings per week.

In 1878, Mr Raby, who'd been employed by the poor law for eighteen years, died. He had had four different roles and earned over one-hundred and twenty-five pounds a year. He was the relieving officer, which earned him eighty-pounds; registrar of births and deaths, earning an additional thirty-five pounds; union collector, which earned him a further ten pounds; and inquiry officer, which was paid as assigned by the guardians for the Kirkham District. Mr William Shorrock replaced him.

The present nurse, Mrs Disley, resigned and was replaced by Miss Strickland of Ribby Row, Kirkham. Before she took up the post, Basil Cane inspected the workhouse.

> I inspected this workhouse and found it admirably clean and in excellent order throughout all its wards and offices. This is more creditable to the master and matron, for, during the nurse's absence, everything devolves upon them, and they have no assistant officer of any kind. Even when the nurse is present the duties of the master and matron must be exceedingly heavy, and although they seem to perform them most willingly as well as efficiently, I do not think they can find time for the rest and repose which I am sure they require. The guardians could not afford better encouragement to meritorious servants then by affording them some permanent aid in the discharge of their duties.
>
> R. Basil Cane, 10th May 1878.

In reaction to the inspector's report, a servant was recruited.

FYLDE UNION WORKHOUSE.—WANTED, a general SERVANT, wages £15; one who understands plain cooking preferred.—Apply to the Master of the Workhouse, Kirkham.

The infirmary was meant to be for the use of the inmates and the poor who couldn't afford to pay medical fees, but it was slowly becoming a general hospital. Dr Shaw wrote a letter of complaint to the guardians, regarding the extra work this created.

> Gentlemen,
>
> I beg, most respectfully, to draw your attention to the fact of sickness cases, having from time to time been admitted into the union workhouse, and having required my attendance, for which I have never received any pay, although they are not paupers, but have the means of paying for their maintenance, whilst in the house. I feel I am duty-bound to ask whether or not I can be paid for sick cases, for the salary I receive for my attendance at the workhouse is something less than 1s. 9d, a day for more than a daily attendance and supplying all medicines (except cod liver oil) to a list of patients far exceeding an average of 20 per week. I hope you will look favourably upon my case and give me a salary such as my case requires, and allow me to be paid for those non-pauper cases, which are charged for their maintenance in the house.

The guardians resolved that any person in possession of money when received into the workhouse, who was then taken ill, should pay the doctor's expenses out of that money. On 8 February, a man was admitted into the infirmary with burns. He died a month later. Dr Shaw had attended him twenty-nine times and wanted two guineas for the work. The guardians paid Dr Shaw one pound from the five pounds found in the man's possessions after his death.

How to treat paupers with fever was a growing concern at the workhouse. Dr Shaw complained that there was no way of separating the fever patients from the other patients in the infirmary. The distance paupers with fever had to travel also raised concerns. Ellen Meredith was moved from Blackpool to Kirkham with fever but later died. The guardians thought moving seriously ill patients nine miles to Kirkham was detrimental to the patients' health and began looking into using the Blackpool Sanitarian for paupers from that area. They also decided to look into building two fever rooms, attached to the infirmary, for three patients of each sex to address Dr Shaw's concerns.

After writing to the Blackpool Sanatorium, the guardians were told that the hospital would apply the following charges to admit fever patients of the union. Ordinary fever cases at fifteen shillings each per week and smallpox cases twenty-one shillings per week, both exclusive of wine, medicine, and medical attention. The guardians agreed to the terms._

The union paid an annual subscription to the Manchester Royal Infirmary; 1878's was three pounds and three shillings. The subscription gave the union the right to have, at any one time, one in-patient and two out-patients. The Manchester Hospital could carry out operations or give treatment far beyond that of the workhouse infirmary.

At the Manchester Hospital, Thomas McEwen had to have his hand amputated after an accident. He told the hospital that the Kirkham Board of Guardians would pay the two guineas for an artificial arm. The hospital asked the guardians if this was the case. One guardian thought two guineas should not be laid out for such a useless man.

The chairman said, 'The man would not do work, and he was determined to let everybody know that he would not.'

Another member of the board said, 'If we bought McEwen an artificial arm, he would probably sell it.'

It was resolved that the board give no countenance to such a matter.

The master asked for leave of absence, in order to go to an interview for a position at the Aylesbury Union, Buckinghamshire. He telegraphed the guardians, from Aylesbury, to inform the guardians that he had received the position and would have to commence his duties on 29 September. He was replaced by Mr Griffiths, aged forty-two, clerk to the Fairfield Local Board, Whalley Bridge.

In December, there were one-hundred and forty paupers in the workhouse, compared with one-hundred and six in the corresponding week of last year.

Mr Broadbent, the chairman of the workhouse visiting committee, told the board they were short of beds and that one man had to sleep in the infirmary. He recommended that they purchased twelve new bedsteads: which was agreed to. He also reported that some of the paupers had been going into Kirkham, getting drunk, and generally misbehaving. Mr Broadbent thought a man should be placed in a cabin at the rear gates to stop the paupers from leaving. It was decided to build a cabin at the gate and place a trusted pauper in it as a guard.

In January 1879, the matron and two paupers came down with the smallpox. Dr Shaw ordered the entire workhouse to be cleaned with disinfectants. The matron recovered, but one of the paupers died.

In March, the yearly appointment for the role of doctor for Kirkham Number Two District came up before the guardians. Thomas Shaw had held this position for a number of years, as well as the position as the workhouse doctor. The main reason he held both posts was that there was no other doctor in the Kirkham Number Two District, and a doctor had to live in the district to hold the post. This year, however, Sidney Wigglesworth of Wesham qualified as a doctor and he was given the position as district doctor. Dr Shaw remained the workhouse doctor and received a pay rise from thirty pounds to forty pounds.

The different unions were active in politics and would send each other circulars to ask for support in certain causes. Outside organisations would also lobby the unions. One circular this year was from the Protestant Alliance London, asking the board not to appoint Roman Catholic clergyman as workhouse chaplains. This circular was irrelevant for the Fylde Guardians.

Chairman, William Hodgson, explained, 'Our clergyman visited the workhouse for nothing. Ministers of all denominations rendered their services gratuitously, and therefore we were never put to the necessity of appointing a regular chaplain.'

In 1879, the Lytham District was split into three wards. Two guardians were appointed in the urban wards, one for Lytham and one for St-Annes-on-Sea. A third guardian was appointed for the rural ward.

In May, new plans were passed for the two fever rooms by the guardians. Basil Cane told the guardians that the rooms could only be used for scarlet fever and typhoid cases, smallpox cases had to be treated separately. He advised the guardians to buy a wooden shed that they could erect during a smallpox outbreak. After the outbreak had cleared, they could dismantle the shed, and store it away. Basil Cane then changed his advice and informed the guardians that the rooms could now only be used to isolate patients with itch, syphilis, and offensive cases, and not fevers cases.

The guardians disregarded Inspector Cane's advice. They sent the plans to the Local Government Board, who asked for the plans to be changed because the new toilets would not be separate from the interior of the building by a cross-ventilated lobby. The plans were changed, and the rooms built.

There are no plans of the Kirkham Workhouse. Most of the plans of the workhouses were destroyed in a fire. If the London Board had taken James Lewis' advice, the plans might have survived.

> James Lewis Inspector for the General Register Office.
>
> I can well understand that it is much trouble for you to go downstairs to the strongroom whenever occasion arises, for referring to the register books, but it is my duty to point out to you that your practice at keeping certain amount of such register books in a wooden press, or cupboard in the register office upstairs is open to strong objection on the score of danger to the books from fire, and moreover it is contrary to the regulations. That the strongroom, is not fireproof and the mildew on the covers of many of the volumes conclusively proves that it is not damp-proof either. I should be justified on both of these grounds in asking the Registrar General to call upon the guardians to make better provisions for the safe custody of the register books, and it is obvious for the convenience of the guardians, that something should be done.

Reports like this give clues to the layout of the building. We now know the clerk's office was upstairs and that it was a cold and damp building. Responding to the report, the guardians purchased a fireproof safe to keep the books in.

The district doctors had to send in their vaccination reports before the guardian's meetings. Dr Orr had not sent his reports for the meeting on 25 June.

Reverend Moore said, 'We have had more trouble with him than anyone else, it was quite time something was done.'

The guardians held an inquiry. They found the doctor had sent the parcel on Tuesday by the six p.m. train from Fleetwood. The railway company said the only explanation for the parcel not arriving for the Wednesday meeting was the heavy rain, as the porter was afraid that it might get wet.

The clerk thought it might be better to send the vaccination books by post, which cost two-pence compared to four-pence by the railway. Mr Tyler added that he'd known documents delayed by post. The chairman suggested that the doctors be requested to send in their returns by the proper time, and if they did not, the clerk should write to them. Mr Noblett moved that the medical officers send in their returns before nine o'clock on the morning of the board meetings. The chairman couldn't accept the motion, because a rule to that effect was already in place.

To which Mr Noblett replied, 'Very well, I hope you will carry it out.'

Blackpool, which attracted hundreds of tramps, had a by-law which stopped lodging houses being used as common lodging houses for tramps. So, tramps had to go to the tramp ward at Poulton or Kirkham Workhouse. During the winter months of 1879, three-hundred and thirty-two tramps passed through Kirkham, five-hundred and twelve through Poulton, and four-hundred and ninety through Fleetwood. In Lytham, they only numbered forty-seven. The cost to Kirkham and Lytham was nine pounds, and the cost to Poulton and Fleetwood was sixteen pounds.

The tradition in Kirkham had been for the police to give tramps a ticket to enter the workhouse up until nine o'clock. After that time the workhouse gates were locked, and the police gave the tramps a ticket for the lodging houses, which cost the ratepayers four pence per tramp.

The tramps began waiting until after nine before reporting to the police to avoid being sent into the workhouse. The police discovered this by placing a plain-clothed policeman in the vicinity of the lodging houses, where he remained until a little after nine when a number of tramps turned out of the pubs and went to the police station for tickets. The constable followed the tramps and detained them, and on one being searched, fivepence was found in his possession. That man was taken before the magistrates and the others sent to the workhouse.

To stop this, the guardians gave the police inspector a key for the workhouse gates to let the tramps inside after nine. They also decided to ask the Blackpool Corporation to allow some lodging houses to be used by the tramps to relieve pressure on Poulton.

The master reported that Bryan Cassidy, aged eighty-four, an inmate of the workhouse, was dead. If he had lived, he would have been in the house twenty years in March next. He was a very useful man, and a tried and trusted servant. Bryan knew he would never leave the workhouse and used the system to his advantage. He had an easy job in the infirmary and slept in a private room with his wife.

Thomas Coward, aged fifty-six, was the opposite of Bryan: an unpopular character in the workhouse and a born troublemaker. He was constantly in and out of the workhouse. He would get drunk, fall ill, and end up in the infirmary. In 1879 he turned up and never left. After Coward was given some bread for dinner, he demanded that it was weighed, thinking he'd been short rationed. After the bread was weighed and found to be right, he said that the scales and weights were wrong. He became abusive to the matron; he used offensive language, and after being deemed a refractory pauper, was summoned to Kirkham Court. The case was dismissed because the master was in court, not the matron, and therefore there was a deficiency in the evidence.

Every Christmas the outdoor paupers received the Christmas sixpence, which cost the union ten pounds in 1879, but the new auditor Mr Edmund Bird now disallowed it. The guardians resolved that, in future, the money should be paid out of the interest fund. The new auditor tried to ruin Christmas again, this time by refusing money for a Christmas tree and the annual Christmas dinner. The guardians again resolved to use some money from the interest fund.

1880–1889

Workhouse Master, Thomas Griffiths, died on 10 September 1880, aged forty-five, from chronic enlargement of the prostate gland. He was buried at Fairfield Church, Buxton, where he was formerly the schoolmaster, organist, and clerk to the local board. Leonard and Mary Tomlinson, porter and the sick nurse of Burnley, became the new master and matron. Mrs Griffiths left when they took up their new post, in October; she received a ten-pounds gift from the guardians.

Mrs Griffiths could have stayed on as matron, and the guardians just find a new master; the salary of fifty pounds was divided into thirty pounds for the master and twenty pounds for the matron. The preference, however, was a married couple, without children, who were Church of England.

Basil Cane wrote to the guardians after the workhouse had been inspected by his assistant.

> On referring to a report, which I have received from Mr Stevens after his inspection of the Fylde Union Workhouse, I found that a fever case, there in the hospital was attended by a pauper inmate. I would remark on this that fever cases especially should be attended by a responsible officer, named and skilled in the management of such cases. The disinfecting apparatus is placed in the men's receiving ward. This is a very dangerous arrangement and is calculated to destroy the use of the receiving ward as protection against the introduction of disease into the ordinary wards of the workhouse. The disinfecting store will, I trust, be removed to someplace where it can be wholly detached and set apart at some distance from the workhouse.
>
> The boys get no exercise out of the workhouse during the holidays, and they do not seem to be under control when in the workhouse. Some of them, it is said, climb over the wall at times into the yard attached to the fever ward. The guardians will no doubt give such directions as these circumstances require.

> There are no 'bed cards' in use at the hospital, as required by the regulations. These cards should be supplied and used. The vagrants are not bathed. The regulations in this respect should be carried out. I doubt whether vagrant women and girls are attended by a female officer and whether the night bell connected with their ward communicates with some female officer. I shall be obliged if the guardians will give their attention to this subject, as well as to the other questions mentioned in this letter.

Mr Philips, Commissioner of Lunacy, also visited the workhouse.

> There were nine men and three women in this workhouse on the imbecile list, none of whom required asylum treatment. They were, with one exception, on the 'aged and infirm' diet of the house, which gave scouse on three days, soup on the fourth day, and only two dinners of solid meat. It would be an improvement if solid meat were substituted for one of the scouse dinners. The general appearance of the patients was satisfactory; the rooms occupied by them being clean. The inspector regretted to find that straw pillows were still used at the workhouse and suggested that flock be substituted

Blackpool was still attracting large numbers of tramps, and the amount of them visiting the Fylde was getting out of hand. In 1879, the year ending midsummer, there were one-thousand, seven-hundred and eighty-two vagrants in the Fylde Union. By 1880, at the same time of year, it was three-thousand, eight-hundred and eighty-nine: an increase of two-thousand, one-hundred and seven. To make matters worse, in August, the Chief of Lancashire Police, Captain Moorsom stopped his officers from handing out vagrant tickets during the summer months. He also stopped the single policeman based at Poulton from giving out tickets for good.

Captain Moorsom wrote to the guardians,

> I regret, I cannot see my way to help the relieving officers by the issue of tickets to vagrants by the police in Blackpool, during the summer season, when their time is more than occupied by the performance of their legitimate duties. If the guardians will tell me what hours, say in the evening, they would be glad of help during the winter in Blackpool. I shall be

> happy to consider if some temporary arrangement can be tried with the view of affording any help in the power of the police.
>
> I am sorry to say, enquiry into this matter fully shows the impropriety of tickets being issued by the police at Poulton le Fylde, there being only one constable there, whose proper rest is disturbed, and consequently his efficiency interfered with by attending to the applications for tickets. I am therefore obliged to give notice that, after the end of September, the issue of these tickets must be discontinued by the police at Poulton, and I understand the relieving officer lives there, I trust it will not cause inconvenience to the guardians to do this with their own means at hand.

A labourer, by the name of Donnelly, came to the workhouse to collect his wife and three children, but she refused to leave with him. He went before the board to say he wanted to take her, but if they thought it right to keep her, they were quite welcome to her.

The chairman asked him if he ever abused her. He said he had not. The fact of it, he said, was that she was rather fond of the bottle, but that was her only fault, and, if she would come, he would make her a comfortable home. The clerk told the guardians that the woman could tell a very different tale to that told by her husband. Donnelly was told to collect his wife and children on Saturday.

In August, the water bill for that quarter was twenty pounds, eight shillings, and nine pence. The bill being larger than usual, the master was asked to keep a daily register of the water used. The first week the workhouse used eight-thousand seven-hundred gallons and in the second week used ten-thousand gallons. The bill for the last quarter had been for three-hundred-and-nineteen-thousand gallons. The visiting committee pointed out that the water passed through the meter into the cisterns, which leaked allowing the water to run away. They suggested placing an engine in one of the old wells on the site and filling the cisterns themselves. The engine would cost about twenty pounds; the workhouse paid, on average, forty pounds a year for water. The guardians decided to ask the Local Government Board for advice.

At the next meeting, the chairman said, 'The consumption last Sunday was 1,000 gallons, whilst on Monday, which was washing day, it was 2,700 gallons. This was higher than usual because the water tank, which collected the rainwater, was empty because of the dry year. The dry weather meant they could only use the Fylde Waterworks water, which caused consumption to rise from 8,000 to 12,000 gallons.'

An engine was purchased for filling the cisterns.

The guardians had two main bank accounts, the general fund and the common fund. The interest paid from these two accounts went into a third account, the interest fund. The guardians used the interest fund, to pay for the annual day trip to Blackpool, the guardian's end of year dinner, the Christmas dinner, and decorations. Auditor, Edmund Bird, however, thought the money from the interest fund belonged to the Local Government Board, and he tried to stop August's trip to Blackpool. To get around it, the guardians asked Dr Shaw to say it would be good for the children's health to have a day at the seaside. Dr Shaw's recommendation was then motioned at a guardians meeting, passed, and now they could use money from the common fund to pay for the trip.

Reverend J. Wayman of Blackpool sent a parcel of books for the workhouse children. He stated that his children had read them, and they afforded them great amusement; he hoped they would give similar pleasure to the poor children in the workhouse.

It is worth noting at this point that in April 1881, Poulton-le-Fylde returned a new guardian called William Hodgson, who is not to be confused with his cousin William Segar Hodgson.

In 1881, the guardians asked William Thompson for a return on the stones broken for the last five years. The clerk stated that there had been one-thousand, two-hundred, and fifty-three tons of stones delivered to the workhouse over the last five years, and there had been one-thousand, one-hundred, and fifty-six broken stones sold. The amount paid for the stones was two-hundred and seventy-five pounds, and the money raised by the broken stones was three-hundred and thirty-seven pounds. On average two-hundred and fifty tons a year were broken, or about five tons per week.

Every year, the North-Western Poor Law Conference was held in a different town in Lancashire. The auditor disallowed the four pounds, one shilling, and eight pence the delegation had spent at the 1881 conference. In his view, it was on a voluntary basis that guardians attended the conferences. The costs consisted of one pound, sixteen shillings, and eight pence of railway fares, one pound and ten shillings general expenses and fifteen shillings for dinner tickets. The conference for 1881 was in Rochdale, but none of the guardians attended.

The vaccination returns from January to June 1880 showed that, in the Kirkham District, there were one-hundred and seventy-one births. Of these infants one-hundred and forty-eight were successfully vaccinated, ten died unvaccinated, five were removed to places unknown, and eight were unaccounted for. In the Lytham District, there were eighty-two births, of which seventy-four were successfully vaccinated, six died unvaccinated, one was removed to a place unknown, and one was unaccounted for. In the Poulton District there were four-hundred and thirty-five births, of which three-hundred and sixty-seven were successfully vaccinated, forty-nine died unvaccinated, four were removed to places unknown, and eight were unaccounted for. An additional nine were postponed by a medical certificate.

In April, just before the start of the season in Blackpool, a vagrancy committee was formed to look into solving the vagrant problem, especially now that they would have no help from the police. They decided that the only solution was to build a vagrant's ward. In November, Mr Wilding, the chairman, went through the plans for the new ward, which was to be built on the workhouse land in Kirkham. The ward would contain fourteen sleeping rooms for males, fifteen working cells for males, ten sleeping rooms for females, and a room for picking oakum. Additionally, there would be a waiting rooms for males and females, a disinfecting room, a porter's lodge and a room for the relieving officer. The cost for the ward was estimated to be one-thousand-three-hundred pounds. The plans were sent to the Local Government Board.

Able-bodied paupers in Blackpool, who were out of work, were found work breaking stones in a yard belonging to the Blackpool Highways Committee. If a man needed relief, he could go to the yard, take a barrow, wheel some stones to one side of the yard, and break as many as he liked. He would then receive two shillings and sixpence for each cubic yard he broke.

Some paupers attended the services in the Kirkham Churches.

After the workhouse paupers had left the Parish Church, James Collins saw his chance and escaped from the workhouse group. He went to Preston where he sold his workhouse jacket for six shillings to Lucy Dewhurst, a clothes dealer on Lancaster Road, Preston. He then sold his workhouse trousers to Richard Bamber, a beer seller, on the High Street, Preston for one shilling in money and two shillings worth of beer. The trousers didn't have a workhouse stamp but being suspicious Richard took the trousers to P.C. Joseph Maitland. P.C Maitland arrested Collins on 21 April. He was charged with theft and imprisoned for three months with hard labour. Thieving also happened inside the workhouse. Thomas McEwen stole two pounds of sugar and a quarter pound of tea from fellow inmate George Longworth. George left his allowance of tea and sugar in another inmate's cupboard for safe keeping. After the cupboard was found broken open, a search was carried out, and the goods where found in Thomas McEwen's quarters. He was summoned to court, where he was committed to the Preston House of Correction for six weeks with hard labour.

In 1882, Edmund P. Bird, the auditor, wrote to the guardians with some good news.

> 27th March 1882, The Local Government Board, having entirely rearranged the audit districts in Lancashire, your board will no longer form a part of my district. In taking leave of you after our short connection, I have to express my thanks for the uniform courtesy and kindness that have been shown me by all with whom I have been brought in contact.

Chairman, William Segar Hodgson, being diplomatic, said, 'I believe Mr Bird was a man who considered it his duty to try to set them right. If the law is wrong, it should be altered. I think we should acknowledge the receipt of the letter, and say they were sorry they had lost him, even though some of our members did not feel so. He was a very nice gentleman, who did nothing underhand and did not wish to do anyone any injury. I myself am sorry we are losing him because he had simply wanted to show them where they were wrong.'

The master and matron resigned.

> To the Guardians of the Fylde Union, June 21st, 1882.
>
> Gentlemen, having been appointed to the office of master and

> matron at another union, we beg most respectfully to tender our resignation. The guardians wish us to ask if you will kindly allow us to enter upon our duties this day fortnight, as the master is dead, and the matron is seriously indisposed and wishes to be relieved of her duties as soon as possible. Hoping that you will grant our request, we beg to thank you for the many kindnesses that we have received at your hands and for the great assistance you have given us. We beg to remain your obedient servants, Leonard, and Mary Tomlinson.

The couple was well thought of by the guardians, and they were released early to take up their new position at Chepstow. Mr and Mrs Chambers of Prestwich replaced them. The new master could start on Wednesday 23 July, but his wife wouldn't be able to come until the end of the month. He asked if his wife's sister could stand in for her. The guardians were not happy but agreed to his sister-in-law being the temporary matron.

Nurse Isabella Strickland also resigned, after securing a place at Leeds Infirmary. Instead of advertising for a new nurse, Mr Broadbent said that the cook, Mary Hindle, was willing to accept the office as nurse. She had the same experience as the last one when she started and was willing to learn. Mary Hindle was given the position on a salary of twenty pounds. At the next meeting, two weeks later, Mr Broadbent admitted making a mistake. The old nurse had a bit of experience when she started as the nurse, but the cook had none. Mary Hindle was asked to resign as nurse.

The Local Government Board wrote back to the guardians, regarding the plans for the vagrant ward.

> The women's sleeping cells make no provision for women with children. The women's bathroom is small and imperfectly lighted and ventilated. As regards the accommodation for males, the bathroom is very small, and the one proposed bath is scantily accommodation of the kind for the number intended to occupy the cells. The work cells are rather narrower than usual, and it would have been more convenient, for an administrative point of view, if these cells had been arranged in direct communication with the sleeping cells, so as to avoid the necessity for the attendant conducting each vagrant from one to the other.

It is not explained where the commodes in the cells will be emptied and cleaned, nor whether proper means of communication will be provided for the sleeping cells to the attendants' apartment. Neither is it stated what disinfecting apparatus will be adopted. It might be worth considering whether it would not be advantage to provide a certain amount of accommodation on the associated system, in order more rapidly to deal with the extra vagrants when the cells are full. The proposed position for the relieving officers, affording as they will, an entrance to enter and exit from the workhouse independent of the entrance under the control of the porter seems questionable.

Contracts.

FYLDE UNION.

THE Guardians invite TENDERS for the Erection of NEW VAGRANT WARDS, &c., at the Workhouse, Kirkham. Whole or departmental tenders will be received. Plans and specifications may be inspected at the Offices of the Architect, Thos. P. Worthington, Clifton Chambers, Blackpool, or at the Board-room, Union Workhouse, Kirkham, on and after the 27th June inst. Bills of quantities may be obtained from the Architect on deposit of two guineas, which will be returned on receipt of *bona fide* tender. Tenders, endorsed "Workhouse Additions," may be sent in to me until 12 o'clock on Tuesday, the 4th July. The Guardians do not bind themselves to accept the lowest or any tender.—By Order,

Kirkham. WILLIAM THOMPSON, Clerk.

The guardians placed adverts in local newspapers, inviting builders to send in tenders.

The contracts were awarded.

John Haslam, Kirkham: brickwork, masonry, flagging, and slating – eight-hundred and seventy-five pounds and sixpence.

James Bennett, Kirkham: plumbing, glazing, gas fittings, and bell hanging - two-hundred pounds.

Thomas Royle, Kirkham: woodwork – three-hundred and twenty-three pounds.

William Forshaw, Lytham: plastering – thirty-six pounds

The total cost for the new building was expected to be one-thousand, seven-hundred, and three pounds, nineteen shillings, and three pence. The guardians borrowed one-thousand-five-hundred pounds which was to be paid back over fifteen years.

The engine used to pump the water from the wells did not work as expected and was turned off. The guardians asked the water company for a reduction in the tariff they paid. Going through Queen's Court was a case, asking for workhouses to be classed as a dwelling and not businesses when it came to the tariffs for water supplies. With this in mind, the Fylde Water Board said it would provide water at nine pence per one-thousand gallons from 1 March, previous it was one shilling and three pence per one-thousand gallons. To help save more water, a manual water pump was placed in the well in the men's yard.

Mr Broadbent said, 'We have a man who never tires of pumping.'

The Local Government Board sent a circular.

> I am directed, by the Local Government Board, to inform you that it has been brought to my notice that, in some workhouses, where cases of smallpox had been under treatment, persons not properly protected by the vaccination have been placed in attendance upon patients, and that the neglect of this precaution has in some instances resulted in the spread of the disease, not only among the attendants, but also among ordinary inmates of the workhouse. The board, therefore, thinks it necessary to point out that, whenever cases of smallpox occurs or are introduced into the workhouse, it is of great importance that the nurses and other persons employed to attend upon patients or brought into personal contact with them should at once be re-vaccinated as a protection against the disease, unless they have themselves had the smallpox or have been successfully re-vaccinated within a sufficiently recent period.
>
> The board desires also to impress upon the guardians the

> necessity of strict measures being taken to prevent communication between the inmates of the fever wards and those of the workhouse, as the spread of the disease, even when the wards referred to were themselves properly isolated, as been traced to the absence of this precaution. The board are also desirous that whenever there is an outbreak of smallpox or any other dangerous infectious disease, in a workhouse the fact should immediately be reported by the medical officer, with a statement showing what provision has been made for the isolation and treatment of the patients, and for preventing the spread of the disease among inmates.
>
> John Lambert, Secretary.

The year ended with the master and matron Mr and Mrs Chambers, giving three months' notice of their intention to resign.

In 1883, the guardians decided to change the guardian elections from yearly to triennially. They thought triennially would be better because in their first year a guardian would just sit quietly learning the role. It would also save money; the election of 1882 cost Blackpool alone thirty-three pounds. The decision was ultimately that of the ratepayers and a poll was held in February that year. Of the nine-thousand, seven-hundred, and sixty-one people eligible to vote five-thousand-six-hundred voted. The result was three-thousand, six-hundred, and fifty-five for triennially and one-thousand and forty-five against.

The chairman and vice chair's elections stayed yearly. In April, Mr Hodgson was re-elected chairman, Mr Tyler was elected senior vice-chairman, and Mr Wilding was elected junior vice-chairman. The following committees were also formed yearly: workhouse committee, finance committee, assessment committee, school attendance committee, building committee, and the visiting committee.

Blackpool, which now paid one-third of all poor rates, asked for two extra guardians. The guardians were reluctant to grant the request because the power of the board could lie in the hands of one ward. After some discussion, it was decided to allow Blackpool one extra guardian.

The Chief Secretary of Ireland wrote to the different unions enquiring into the recent decrease in the number of Irish migratory agricultural workers.

> I would be much obliged for any information which you may be pleased to give me, on the following points.
>
> 1. Have you observed any decrease in the number of Irish migratory agricultural workers during recent years?
>
> 2. If there has been any decrease, do you attribute such decrease to a lessened demand for their services, or a falling off in supply?
>
> 3. If the decrease has arisen from a lessened demand for their services, do you consider that such decrease is likely to be temporary or permanent?

After discussing it, the guardians came to the conclusion that there had been a decrease this year. They put it down to the present unsettled state of Ireland and partly to emigration to America.

Mr and Mrs Girvin, from the Blackburn Union Workhouse, were appointed the new master and matron. They started in February, and the old master and matron were free to leave when they wished. The first master's report, from the week ending 22 May, stated that there were twenty-three elderly and infirm men and twelve women in the workhouse. There were thirteen able-bodied men and twenty-seven able-bodied women, plus forty-nine children, and twenty-three vagrants.

The new master and matron's first inspection went well.

> I find the workhouse today in an extremely neat and tidy state, and the inmates apparently well looked after. I have asked Mr Thompson, to mention the matter of the workhouse drains to the guardians. When it can be avoided, it is better not to have any inlet to a drain inside a bakehouse.
>
> Henry Stevens, Assistant Inspector, June 18th, 1883.

In May, the guardians advertised for a porter for the new tramp ward. Three people were chosen for interviews, from the sixteen applicants. Jonathan Titterington of Newton, Stephen Wignall of Preston and John Clay of Clayton-le-Moors, who was offered the position.

To complete the new vagrant's ward a new entrance to the workhouse was built on Station Road where the porter's cabin had been erected; the Moor Street gates were now locked permanently. The hedge along the west boundary was taken down and a wall built. The workhouse was now sealed off with only one way in or out. The new ward opened on Monday 25 August, from now on any vagrant in the Fylde wanting somewhere to stay was sent to Kirkham.

The building on the left with the tower was the vagrant's ward.

The vagrants arriving at Kirkham would receive a meal, a bath, and be shaved. In the morning, they would have to break a set amount of stones before being released. The 'test' being that if they were desperate, they would go into the vagrant's ward, most however didn't, and the numbers of vagrants began to decline.

The guardians also appointed a temporary police officer as assistant relieving officer for Poulton, whose salary, of eighty-one pounds and ten shillings, was paid by the union. The clerk reported that he had looked at the officer's book for the first four weeks of the current quarter, and there was an average of ten vagrants per night, an average of over seventy a week. For the last, six weeks there had been none. This was saving the union three shillings and four pence per night in tramp tickets.

In August, the inmates had their annual trip to Blackpool. They visited the main attractions in a vehicle placed at their disposal and had a short sea trip on the steamer 'Wellington'.

The guardians decided to allow the inmates fish once a week. They would receive half-a-pound of fish in lieu of potatoes. Fishmonger, Mr Leadbetter, would deliver the fish at three and a quarter pence per pound, including carriage. The variety of fish was; cod, fresh haddock, hake, ling ray, skate and fluke, depending on the season.

The paupers would have their fish dinner on Friday, much to the annoyance of Mr Bradley who thought the Protestant inmates would rather have beef or mutton on a Friday.

He said, 'We are a professedly Protestant Board of Guardians, they had a Protestant Queen at the helm of affairs, and while they seemed as a board, to be adopting the Roman Catholics usages, they seemed to think, or were showing the world that they thought them better than Protestants.'

A bemused chairman said, "I think Mr Bradley suspects that we shall make all the Protestants into Roman Catholics by having fish dinner on a Friday."

Mr Broadbent assured Mr Bradley that, at the visiting committee's meeting, there was not the slightest thought of religion, or about Roman Catholics either. They respected Catholics as well as Protestants, but they did not take that into consideration; they were merely doing the best for the inmates. Mr Finch added that the reason Friday was chosen was because the fish would be fresh on that day.

The old weighing machine at the workhouse was replaced with a larger one. The new one could weigh the horse and cart at the same time. It was supplied by Pooleys and Sons for sixty pounds; they paid the guardians fifteen pounds for the old one. The guardians also bought a large water filter, after Mr Broadbent reported that the water supplied by Fylde waterworks was impure and required filtration. Porter, John Clay, left the workhouse and, in December, the cook resigned. The guardians ended the year advertising for a man and wife as cook and porter.

FYLDE UNION.

PORTER AND COOK WANTED.—The Guardians are in Want of a MARRIED COUPLE, to undertake the offices of PORTER and COOK at the Workhouse. Joint salary £86 per annum, with rations and furnished apartments.—Applications, stating age, with present and previous occupations, accompanied by copies of Testimonials of recent date (not exceeding three in number, which will not be returned), to be sent to me not later than Tuesday, 1st January next.—Selected candidates will be informed when their attendance is required.—By order of the Board, WILLIAM THOMPSON, Clerk.

Kirkham, Dec. 20, 1883.

Guardian's advert for a new porter and cook.

To start the year 1884, the workhouse held a New Year's Day party. They decorated the dining hall, with evergreen bushes hanging from the ceiling and hung lengths of tissue paper chains from the walls. Evergreens were dotted here and there, and on the walls were seasonable mottos. Mrs Birley of Milbanke House lent the workhouse a magic lantern (an early Victorian picture projector). She also gave each man two ounces of tobacco and gave the women some tea and sugar. All the children received a toy each, which had been placed underneath the Christmas tree.

The Visiting Commissioner in Lunacy, Mr Frere, visited the house on 26 April.

> There are, on the list of the imbecile poor in this workhouse, the names of seven men and five women. All the men and three of the women were here at the last visit paid by one of my colleagues; indeed, all the men have been here for many years on the list. I could not see the certificates of the two last cases placed on the list, and as far as I could gather the medical officer had not complied with the 20th sec. of the Lunacy Acts Amendment (1852), and I desire to draw his attention to the matter. Some of the patients complained of

> the want of sufficient food, and I hope an extra meat dinner may be ordered for the class in one day of the week.
>
> The patients were all properly dressed, and the accommodation provided for them is not uncomfortable. I found an epileptic woman, Ann Kirby, who is also paralysed, sitting in a room with a stone floor, and she sleeps in a room, the stone stairs leading to which are steep and decidedly dangerous for a woman subject to fits and cripple as she is. She ought to be moved out of her present room, as she and another woman (who though not classed as an imbecile is certainly weak-minded) are constantly quarrelling.
>
> Throughout the workhouse, the pillows, as well as the beds, are of chaff. I think in the hospital, at any rate, the pillows should be of flock. I saw no patients whose removal to an asylum appeared necessary. All who can be are usefully employed, and they appear to be kindly treated.

There would be no more visits from Mr Richard Basil Cane, who died in October at his home Stanton Woodhouse, Bakewell, at the age of seventy-six. Mr Cane was the local government inspector not just for Lancashire but also Chester, Cumberland, Derby, Westmoreland, and the West Riding of York. Mr J. J. Henley was appointed his successor.

The board began subscribing to the Manchester Eye Hospital which gave them access for two inpatients, who could stay six weeks in the hospital, and twenty outpatients. The first person sent there was John Price of Queenstown, a hawker.

The Fylde Coast had changed dramatically. When Dr Sharp started working as the medical officer for Blackpool in 1868, the population was five-thousand, six-hundred, and ninety-six. Now it was fifteen-thousand, two-hundred, and ninety-one and he asked for a pay rise from forty-three pounds to fifty pounds, which the guardians agreed to. Dr Orr then asked for a rise as his area, Fleetwood, had increased from one-thousand-eight-hundred to seven-thousand in the twenty-five years he had worked there, his salary went from twenty-six pounds and ten shillings to forty pounds.

Since 1876, women left destitute whilst their husbands were in jail were refused outdoor relief. After Ann Singleton's husband was jailed for poaching, she applied for outdoor relief for herself and six children. She was refused relief and ordered into the workhouse. The relieving officer then received a letter stating that,

If no relief be granted, and anything befall the applicant or her family, such as death from destitution or want, a coroner's inquest may presume you responsible after receiving this notice.

She was threatening to commit suicide by drowning herself. One of the guardians, Mr Tyler, added that the husband did nothing but drink and poach when he was out of prison.

The unconcerned chairman said, 'That having given the woman an order to the workhouse they were not responsible for anything that happened, no matter whether she drowned herself or not.'

To further deter tramps, vagrants arriving at the workhouse would now have to stay for two nights. However, the person in charge of the ward could, if he felt that the tramp was a genuine case, release them after one night.

Anthony Bradley became the new porter on a salary of twenty pounds.

The hospital accommodation again came under scrutiny. Dr Shaw thought it was too small. He recommended that the guardians build a new infections ward, totally separate from the workhouse building. He also asked the guardians to place a lamp in the westerly corner of the vagrant's ward, create additional accommodation in the lying-in ward and a covered walkway from the nurse's day room to the lying-in wards.

The guardians agreed and tried to buy an acre of land from Mr John Leyland Birley to build a new infections ward. Mr Birley would not sell the land to the guardians. In his opinion the hospital could be placed somewhere better. Undeterred the guardians decided to build the new ward facing Station Road. The new infirmary would have four rooms, two for each sex, for cases of smallpox and typhoid. The building would therefore hold eight men and eight women, with accommodation for the nurse.

It was common for ladies in various towns to create visiting committees. A ladies visiting society was formed that year in Kirkham by Mrs Birley, Mrs Richards, and Miss Shaw, who applied for permission to visit the workhouse and read to the girls one night per week. They also promised that when they found the girls were able for service, they would find them suitable situations. The permission was granted.

The numbers in the workhouse in January 1885 were high at one-hundred and seventy, but the year would turn out to be a quiet one, which was good for Clerk William Thompson, who was confined to his room suffering from rheumatic gout. The guardians ordered the master to make sure the tramps in the workhouse broke ten c.w.t of stones a day. The old workhouse entrance on Moor Street could now be used on Wednesdays for the board meetings. At all other times, it was padlocked. Father Hines of the Willows asked for a key to the padlock to save him walking around to the Station Road entrance, which the guardians agreed to.

After an inspection, the inspector asked the guardians not to build the new infections ward. He told them that it was the duty of the sanitary authorities and not that of the guardians to provide for non-pauper infections. If the ward were built, it would be a burden on the union. The present accommodation was adequate for the union's pauper fever cases.

The main problem with the infirmary was that the women's wards were overcrowded. The plans for the new fever ward was abandoned. Instead, the guardians built two rooms at either end of the women's ward, connected with glass corridors, with the windows facing towards the gardens to stop infections blowing into the workhouse. The fever cases went into the two new rooms – this left room inside the ward to create more space for lying-in-cases and general medical cases.

The Local Government Board sent a circular in reference to married couples. After some complaints about married couples being forced to live separate, the board reminded the workhouses that married couples above sixty could not be compelled to live separately in the workhouse.

Chairman William Segar Hodgson said, "The last couple they had in the house would not live together; in fact, they would not speak to one another."

At Christmas, Mrs Langton Birley gave two casks of beer to the inmates for Christmas. The porter and cook left, and twenty-five couples applied for the post, which was narrowed down to three: Mr and Mrs James Adams, Mr and Mrs W.C Crompton, and Mr and Mrs McKinnell. Mr and Mrs McKinnell were appointed.

At the start of 1886, the Marton ratepayers asked for an extra guardian, which would give them two. The guardians agreed to the request, but the Local Government Board disallowed it because they could not see how Marton could be split into two wards. The guardians appealed this decision and won. Mr James Cardwell became the new guardian for Marton.

Blackpool was growing rapidly, and the collector was struggling to collect the rates, so he employed an assistant collector. The guardians asked for a report from the clerk, which showed Blackpool had lost five per cent of the rates. This, however, was better than the eight per cent average for the rest of the Fylde.

Prescot Union wrote to the Fylde Union asking for support in their protest against foreign watch movements being placed in English and Irish marked watchcases. The inhabitants of the Prescot Union were mainly engaged in the watch trade and were suffering due to this practice. The Kirkham board decided to support the protest, which was sent to the Board of Trade.

The guardians received a circular from the National Provident Society. The society wanted the board to support their petition for a compulsory insurance scheme. The scheme, if adopted, would mean every person between the ages of eighteen and twenty-one paying ten pounds, in return, they would receive eight shillings a week in case of sickness and a pension of four-shillings when they reached seventy. This they thought would do away with all paupers except orphans and imbeciles who could not look after themselves.

Kirkham Vicar W. H. Mason donated the fruit from his orchard to the inmates, and in November, the children were invited to a concert held in the Co-operative Hall Kirkham.

In 1887, significant differences in the relief paid out in the Poulton and the Kirkham Districts were becoming evident. The Poulton District had a population of thirty-thousand, eight-hundred, and ninety-seven whilst Kirkham had fifteen-thousand, seven-hundred and seventy-three. In the Poulton District, one-hundred and twenty-one people received indoor relief compared to one-hundred and forty-seven in Kirkham, of these, one-hundred and sixty-two came from the town of Kirkham. There were six-hundred and eighty-nine people receiving outdoor relief in the Poulton District, one-hundred and two in the Kirkham District, of which eighty-eight were from the town of Kirkham.

All these relief cases were examined by the relief committee who met at nine-thirty in the morning before the ten-thirty guardian's meeting. They often struggled to go through the relief lists by ten-thirty and asked if the guardians meeting could be moved to the afternoon, at three-thirty but the request was refused.

Some outdoor relief could be paid out to families on low incomes, but there was no form of 'test' with this system of payment, and it encouraged employers to pay low wages. Mr Henley, the government inspector, was against this system and told the guardians to put part of the family in the workhouse and leave the rest to live on the weekly earnings.

Mr Bagot, Visiting Commissioner in Lunacy, visited the workhouse on 17 February.

> I have examined the eight males and seven female inmates of this workhouse who are, at present, classed as of unsound mind. They are all persons who may be properly retained in the house. Two of the men and one woman were in the hospital, in which the accommodation was very good, the rest are lodged with the ordinary inmates in the body of the house, which was not very cheerful. However, there was a certain amount of rough comfort, and imbeciles are sufficiently clad and fed and had clean beds. Flock pillows had been introduced into the hospital and given to some of the old and infirm, but not yet to the imbeciles, I hope their turn would soon come. Some of them were usually employed, all of which were capable of being so. I think all are kindly treated.

Dr Walker, the medical officer for Kirkham Number One District died this year, he had held the position for over eighteen years. When Dr Walker was appointed in 1869, he treated two-hundred and eighteen pauper patients. Ten years later, in 1879, he had one-hundred and twenty-five cases, whereas, in 1886, he treated only twenty-eight patients of the union. At the time of his death, Dr Walker had a salary of seventy-nine pounds, but, because of the reduction in the workload, the new medical officer would only be paid forty-five pounds. Dr Shaw took on the role. This year, the board stopped subscribing to the Manchester Eye Hospital and paid the three pounds and three shillings to the Preston and County of Lancaster Royal Infirmary which was more convenient. In the summer, the guardians restarted the Manchester Hospital payments, alongside the payments to Preston Royal Infirmary.

Under union laws, the inmates were meant to be given butter as part of their diet, but for the last two years, they were given butterine (an imitation butter or margarine) which the inmates preferred. The butter cost one shilling and one penny per pound whereas the butterine cost seven and a half pennies per pound. Not only was butterine cheaper, Dr Shaw thought it was healthier. After some discussion about whether to change to butter the guardians voted, eleven for butter and nine for butterine, putting quality before cost. The inmates refused to eat the butter, but the decision stuck. Mr John Hardman of Kirkham was given the contract at one shilling and two pence per pound of butter.

In September, the contract for the supply of butter was coming up. Mr Whiteside proposed that the workhouse officers, as well as the inmates, be supplied with margarine instead of butter. Mr Gardner indignantly opposed the motion saying that some guardians seemed inclined to make the officers paupers and the paupers prisoners. The motion was negative by a large majority, and they stuck with butter.

The inmates' annual trips to Blackpool were getting better. In 1886, they were given a free meal by 'Mr Memory', Followed by visits to the North and South Piers, the Aquarium, and the Winter Gardens; travel was free on the trams courtesy of the Tramway Company.

It was becoming common for people to donate books and magazines to the inmates. Messrs Sharple, Catterall, and Ward donated a number of periodicals to the workhouse, and Miss Matthews of the Carrs, Kirkham, and Mr Wardle of St Annes-on-Sea donated some magazines.

The guardians didn't have the power to remove their officers or set their salaries; they could only advise the Local Government Board. In January 1888, the Amersham Union sent a circular to ask for the guardian's support in passing a motion, to have the full power and authority, like all other local authorities, to determine the remuneration of all officers appointed, employed, and paid by them, and also that such officers should be removable by the guardians at their pleasure. They also asked that the master should still have the power to let the casuals out as soon as he thought fit.

Over the last decade, there appeared to have been an increase in pauperism, but, when the increase in the population was taken into account, the numbers and costs had actually dropped.

	Indoor Relief	Out Relief	Total	Proportion of Population	Numbers in the asylum	Cost of all types of relief	Rate in the pound
1878	105	364	469	1 in 65	29 paupers	£2,405	2 1/4 d
1888	155	500	655	1 in 62	32 paupers	£3,038	2d

The Chief Constable of Blackpool complained that a lot of tramps arrived in the town when it was too late to send them to Kirkham. He thought an allowance of four pence ought to be made by the board to allow the tramps to find lodgings.

The chairman said, 'If tramps found that they could get 4d. by going to Blackpool, they would have them all walking past Kirkham.'

The board decided the best plan would be to send vagrants from Blackpool by train when it was found too late for them to travel by road.

The year ended with the present nurse, Eliza Ingol, asking for an increase in her salary from twenty pounds to twenty-five; Her pay was raised to twenty-two pounds and ten shillings. The porter and the cook resigned. There were three applicants for the position; Mr and Mrs Weall of Kirkham, Mr and Mrs Clarkson, and Mr and Mrs Hodgkinson both from Preston. The latter were offered the position.

Mr Monk asked the chairman, at the start of 1889, if it was right to make a man break stones when his maintenance was paid by his family. He also wanted to know if a man's family did not pay for his maintenance, at what age was he considered too old to break stones. William Hodgson replied that no distinction is made as to whether a pauper is paid for or not. He is only declared not to be able-bodied when the medical officer certifies to that effect. Mr Monk had asked on behalf of a man verging upon seventy years of age who was of the opinion that if his maintenance was paid, he didn't need to work. The man took it personally that he had to break stones. He thought he had been made to work to drive him out of the workhouse.

In 1899, the Poulton District was divided into two separate districts: Fleetwood and Blackpool. The Blackpool District consisted of Bispham-with-Norbreck, Layton-with-Warbrick, Marton, and Hardhorn-with-Newton. The Fleetwood District consisted of Carleton, Little Eccleston-with-Larbreck, Elswick, Poulton, Singleton, and Thornton. Thomas Dixon, the former relieving officer of the Poulton District, became the officer for the Blackpool District, and a new officer was appointed for the Fleetwood District.

There were twenty-nine applicants for the post which was whittled down to five. The five were H. Parkinson, from Poulton; J. Jolly, from Weeton; A. Clarkson, from Fleetwood; W. H. Fox, from Coniston; and R. H. Charlton, from Kirkham. Hugh Parkinson, an auctioneer, was offered the post. Both Mr Parkinson and Mr Dixon were also appointed births, deaths, and marriages registrars; school inquiry officers; and collectors of their respective districts.

In September, the master, matron, cook, and porter all resigned, leaving just the nurse. There were five applicants for the position of master and matron. John Trickey, a prison officer, became the new master. The master, matron, cook, porter, and nurse all lived in the workhouse. They received free accommodation and rations, which cost the union one-hundred and forty pounds a year. This included eight shillings each a week in food, coal, gas, and firing, they also received five pounds of meat a week which cost about nine shillings each.

The guardians would 'board out' children, mainly the orphans, with local families, who received four-shillings per week for each child. A committee, not connected to the guardians, took charge of the children, found them a home, and reported back to the guardians periodically. Mary Dune, aged five, was sent to live with Christopher Wilcock, 35 London Road Fleetwood and Violet Roberts, aged two months, went to live with Wilcock's neighbour, Richard Bennett.

The guardians took an interest in child protection.

William Bowdler mentioned the new act on prevention of cruelty to children.

He said, 'Although the provisions of the act would not apply so much to our district, still in the strict exercise of their duty, we should watch any case of cruelty to children, and, therefore, make the clauses of the act our study and endeavour, so far as possible, to bring offenders to justice. The amount of cruelty to children in this country was something dreadful and horrible for a Christian country. I again urge the members to consider the act, specially the latter clauses, so that we could apply the powers when necessary.'

In June, several inmates of the workhouse started suffering from diarrhoea. The flour was suspected, and was sent away for analysing. Mr Riding sent the flour to the County Analyst, Dr Brown of Liverpool.

He reported that the flour contained twenty-five per cent of matter other than wheat flour. It contained a large proportion of pea flour, some bran, and a quantity of starch which it was impossible to identify in the present state of admixture. It was not genuine wheat flour and would not make genuine wheaten bread. The board reported the supplier, William Seed, to the superintendent of police under the food and drugs act.

In July, the clerk received a letter from Mr W. Banks, a Solicitor.

> 42 Lune Street Preston 6th July 1889,
>
> We have received counsel's opinion herein and shall see our client during the course of next week. We think we informed you that we obtained analyses from two eminent analysts and found that the samples of flour supplied by your servant, for the purpose of analysis, to be a perfectly pure and sound flour. We cannot understand how this sample, submitted to Dr Campbell Brown, and which your servant said was taken out of the same sack as the sample supplied to our client, could be adulterated as stated by him. Have you made any inquiries as to whether the sample sent to Dr Brown was interfered or tampered with? Our client is determined to have the stigma upon his character removed. The action of the guardians by the payment of his account, after the charge had been made of fraud and dishonesty is certainly mysterious. If your guardians were acting in the interests of the public and of their charges, the paupers of your district or union, why if they believed the flour to be adulterated, pay for it? They

> could not have been compelled by law to pay for an article which was not of the kind they had agreed to purchase. A charge publicly made (and utterly untrue) against our client has been fraught with serious and painful circumstances, and we are requested to ask if your guardians mean to make any and what reparations.

The guardians ignored the letter. If the guardians were right, they expected an apology; if they were wrong, they kept quiet. No action was taken against the flour dealer.

There were forty people in the Lancashire Asylums belonging to the union. None of these patients had been visited for years by the guardians. The chairman thought that sending a visitation each year was a waste of money because magistrates, commissioners of lunacy, and relatives already visited them. Mr Bridge begged to differ. He passed a motion that the guardians should visit the asylums once a year: which was carried.

In August, Mr Gorat and six other committee members visited Whittingham Asylum.

They reported back to the Board saying, 'We have 18 inmates in the asylum, all were well cared for. They had a good report from the doctor in several cases. I think if the visits became annual, as in many other unions, it would be better for the board. The steward at the asylum expressed his surprise that the deputation from the Fylde Board of Guardians did not attend oftener.'

It had been nine years since the last visit to the asylum. Mr Sharples visited the Lancaster Asylum. He found the inmates very clean and, in some cases, a change for the better had taken place.

1889's conference for the North-Western District was held in the Guild Hall Preston on Friday and Saturday, 4 and 5 September. The guardians didn't send a deputation, but Chairman William Segar Hodgson went on his own accord.

1890–1899

The decade started with one-hundred and fifty-four paupers in the workhouse. One of them was seventy-three-year-old Thomas Gregson, whose three sons Edward, John, and George were summoned to court to show why they should not contribute to his maintenance. Although all three worked, they didn't pay anything for their father's maintenance. None of the brothers appeared in court to hear the judge order each to pay one shilling and three pence per week.

Also in court, was Thomas Kilcoyne who worked for the London and North-Western Railway Company. His wife was in the Lancaster Asylum. He had previously been ordered to pay two shillings and sixpence towards her maintenance, but, because his daughter was out of work, the guardians didn't charge him between 7 August and 7 November 1889. He was then requested to recommence payments, but he had not done so and was in arrears to the extent of one pound, twelve shillings, and sixpence. After being summoned to court, he stated that he only received eighteen shillings and sixpence per week and had his mother-in-law and five children to keep. His eldest daughter was earning eleven shillings per week. The magistrates W. H. Bowdler and Henry Birley gave him two weeks to pay.

The Vicar of South Shore wrote to the clerk asking the board to assist in the maintenance of the wife of a fisherman who had recently lost his life in Blackpool. The vicar stated that a sum of one-hundred and fifty pounds had already been collected on behalf of the family and had been placed in the bank. The vicar suggested the board should contribute the sum of five shillings per week to the family, and that six shillings a week be given out of the funds collected. The matter was passed to the relief committee.

Most guardians from Blackpool and Fleetwood travelled by train to Kirkham for the meetings. They complained that they had to catch an earlier train and wait for half-an-hour for the board meetings to begin. If the time of the meetings were moved to ten o'clock in the morning from ten-thirty, no time would be wasted. The board agreed, and the meetings were moved to ten a.m.

The vagrants or casuals slept on plank beds to make their stays as uncomfortable as possible. Mr Henley, Local Government Board Inspector, spoke to the guardians about the use of plank beds.

He said, 'It has been the practice of workhouse authorities, throughout Lancashire, to compel vagrants to sleep upon plank beds. First, I will deal with the women, and I don't think there will be any difference of opinion with respect to the question of the sleeping accommodation afforded them. Women who came in should not be required to sleep upon plank beds, with no pillow and nothing but two rugs. It is true that in the workhouse, there was one place fitted with a straw mattress where women and children could sleep. With regards to the others, they were compelled to sleep upon plank beds.'

He continued, 'All the men slept upon plank beds. When I first came to Lancashire, I was astonished at this state of things, but I did not wish to deal with the subject precipitately, so allowed it to remain quiet for some time. I have consulted the Local Government Board, and they agree that it should not be allowed to go on. The order in force by the act of parliament, with respect to this matter, required that there should be separate cells, beds, or compartments, or other arrangements approved of by the Local Government Board, and suitable bed clothing shall be provided in every casual ward, and, except in the case of a mother and infant child or children, not more than one casual pauper shall be allowed to sleep in one cell, bed or, compartment. They were not criminals. They simply came to the workhouse to be relieved and, at present, they were put upon the same footings as criminals who were convicted, and who were compelled as part of their punishment to sleep for a limited time on plank beds.'

He added, 'It is, in my opinion, necessary that better sleeping accommodation should be provided for these people. I do not advocate luxury in workhouses but was decidedly in favour of the provision of decent sleeping accommodation for casuals. You could cover their boards with felt, or provide straw bags, or hammocks, or provide beds similar to those used by soldiers.'

The chairman responded by saying, 'We could supply superior casual sleeping accommodation. The only difficulty would be preventing any spread of infectious diseases, and it would throw more responsibility upon the officers.'

Mr Henley replied, 'It wouldn't be a problem if you used straw mattresses and emptied them out from time to time, and the usual regulations as to cleaning of tramps was adhered to.'

As to the plank beds, Mr Hodgson said, 'We have in this union suffered, perhaps more than any other union, by the influx of casual paupers, and at one time they had as many as four or five thousand, but these had reduced to as many hundreds. Unless all the unions in Lancashire adopted what Mr Henley had recommended, we would again have a large influx of casuals. Casual paupers are divided into two classes, the destitute working man and the professional tramp, the latter of whom made a business of journeying to and from unions. Through having watering places upon our coast, it caused a large influx of visitors, and with them followed casuals, and, provided these casuals were leniently treated, it would cause a large increase.'

The matter was passed to the workhouse committee, who reported back a month later. They proposed that instead of the vagrants being provided with three rugs as at that time, they were to have two rugs and a pillow. The bare planks should also be covered with felt.

Mr Hodgson, the chairman, was against any change.

He said, 'It has been argued that it was inhuman to treat vagrants as criminals, but from my own observation, I can say with certainty, that two-thirds of them were little better, ever praying upon the well-disposed and benevolent persons. Since the easy conditions which had prevailed at the workhouse, about eight years ago had been restricted, he had noticed that outdoor relief had cost considerably less; and it would be a dangerous policy to change it now. What had been the result? Instead of relieving between 4,000 and 5,000 vagrants per year from outside at 4d. per head, they had relieved 1,500 as inmates at 6d. per head. In 1886, the number of vagrants relieved had fallen to 422, and since that time, there had been a gradual rise. The guardians ought not to encourage vagrancy, or they would pretty soon be in as bad a position as ever.'

The guardians voted to make no changes to the vagrant accommodation and disregarded Mr Henley's instructions.

Paupers were in general, buried in the graveyards of the churches where the workhouses were situated. The Fylde's Church of England paupers were buried in the parish church of St Michaels, in Kirkham. On average, fifteen paupers a year were buried in this graveyard. In 1890, the church wardens wrote to the clerk saying the cost of grave digging for the paupers would increase from three shillings and nine pence to six shillings and sixpence. This was because the graveyard was nearly full, and they proposed to dig the graves deeper.

Reverend Mason sent a quantity of apples to the inmates, which had been donated at the recent Harvest Thanksgiving Festival at Kirkham Parish Church. To make it easier for people to donate newspapers and periodicals, the guardians decided to fix a box at Kirkham Railway Station where they would be collected.

When the nurse resigned, four applicants appeared before the board: Mrs Mercer, from Blackburn; Miss Mountford, from Birmingham; Miss Barroll, from Hereford; and Miss E. Barratt, from Kirkham. Mrs Mercer was offered the position but never appeared at the workhouse to take it up, and the master and matron had to perform her duties.

It was becoming increasingly difficult to recruit nurses. A guardian requested that the board subscribe the sum of thirteen pounds and one shilling per annum to the Nurses Homes Association in London. He thought they would then be able to get a nurse immediately, who they could depend on. The board re-advertised for a nurse. Nobody applied for the post, so they offered it to Miss Barrett, who had been turned down at last month's interviews. She accepted the offer but resigned a month later.

Christmas was celebrated in the usual way with roast beef and plum pudding for dinner. Toys, newspapers, evergreens, books, and gifts were donated by Miss Fisher of Blackpool; Miss Parsons of Bartle Hall; Mr Charles Birley; The Feilden Free Library, Fleetwood; and Guardians Mr Greenwood and Mr Sharples. Mrs Ann Birley of Carr Hill House, Kirkham, donated a barrel of beer.

By 1891, the population of the Fylde had changed significantly since the formation of the union. The fifteen guardians of the rural districts each represented an average population of only three-hundred and sixty-eight. Blackpool had only one representative for three-thousand, three-hundred, and sixty-seven, Fleetwood had one for five-thousand-and fifteen, and Lytham had one for three-thousand, six-hundred, and nine. Blackpool had a rateable value of twenty-seven-thousand, seven-hundred and ninety-nine or forty-two per cent of the rateable value of the union. The guardians reorganised the representation of ratepayers to better reflect the changes that had occurred to the Fylde's demographics.

Marton was split into two wards: one rural and one urban with one guardian each. Layton-with-Warbrick, which Blackpool was part of, was split into six wards: Waterloo, Foxhall, Brunswick, Bank Hey, Talbot, and Claremont. Two guardians were assigned to the Talbot Ward and two to the Brunswick Ward, the rest had one guardian. Fleetwood, which was in the urban ward of Thornton, gained an extra guardian giving the Thornton Ward three guardians. Blackpool now had eight guardians, and Fleetwood had two.

On Friday nights, the Reverend Mason of Kirkham's St Michaels Church held a service at the workhouse. He wrote to the guardians.

> January 15th, 1891.
>
> My Dear Sir,
>
> I beg to say that for the last fifteen years it has been a great satisfaction to myself and the curate of Kirkham to perform a service there, evenings of Friday, for the inmates at the workhouse. Mr Kerby will be good as to perform a service there tomorrow the 16th inst, but, after that date, the service will be discontinued, for I cannot but come to the conclusion that it must be on account of this Friday evening service having been performed at the workhouse, that the inmates are now deprived of the privilege of attending the service at the parish church on Sundays, so that our intention of doing the inmates a benefit by the Friday service is simply doing them harm, by depraving them of the opportunity of worshipping at the parish church.
>
> Believe me, very truly yours,
>
> H. William Mason.

The numbers attending church over the last four years ranged from five to eight paupers at any one time. Mr Finch thought it was a disgraceful state of affairs. Mr Sharples thought that the services on Friday nights were more for the sick inmates, for whose benefit it should be continued.

The chairman said, 'The guardians have no power to force the inmates to attend church. A minister of any denomination would be allowed unto the inmates if they chose, and the guardians would allow them the use of the room if they came forward. If such a plan was adopted, he thought more sympathy and interest would be taken in the paupers. It was the duty of parsons, no matter what denomination they belonged, to see that people went to church. It was not the master's business to see that the inmates went to church.'

After some discussion, it was decided that if Mr Mason wouldn't reconsider his decision, they would ask Mr Theobald the Independent Minister from Zion Chapel, Kirkham, who also visited the workhouse, to conduct the services. The clerk wrote to the vicar asking if his decision was final or would he reconsider. The vicar, who was in London, replied.

> York Hotel, Albemarle Street, London Feb 2nd, 1891.
>
> I beg to acknowledge the vote of thanks passed by the Board of Guardians for the gratuitous services rendered to the inmates of the workhouse during the last 15 years. I may observe that Mr Thompson's letter does not attempt to explain why an arrangement, which has worked satisfactory for the last 15 years, and under which the inmates, who were members of this established church, on Sunday has quite recently practically ceased to exist. When the inmates again appear in their places in church, as before, I will readily take into consideration whether it is desirable to resume the service, which has hitherto been performed in the workhouse on Friday evenings.
>
> I remain, very truly yours,
>
> H. William Mason.

The clerk wrote back to Reverend Mason.

> You observe rightly that my former letter 'does not attempt to explain why an arrangement, which has worked satisfactory

for the last 15 years, and under which the inmates, who were members of this established church, on Sunday has quite recently practically ceased to exist.'

The guardians are not aware of the existence of any arrangement in the matter to which your letter appears to refer, but they have instructed me to make inquiries respecting the church attendances and the reason why it has quite recently been discontinued. I have examined the workhouse porter's book from January to December 31st, 1890 and find that the children are taken by an adult inmate to the Sunday school, and regularly throughout the year, and are attending at present. As regards the other inmates, the average attendance for the first three months of the year was one man and three women, for the next three months one man and four women, and for the other three months one man and three women. In October, the attendance was irregular, and in November and December, there was practically no attendance, possibly owing to the severe weather.

The man and three of the women who attended church regularly are all idiots and are not allowed to attend church unless in the charge of an officer. The guardians much regret that the old and infirm inmates of the workhouse are now deprived of these religious services, which, through the kindness of the clergy of Kirkham, have so long been conducted at the workhouse for the especial benefit of this class of inmate.

On Thursday 16 April, Mr Horace H. Theobald, Minister of the Independent Church, Kirkham, held his first service in the workhouse.

Reverend Mason didn't walk away from the paupers. At a meeting of the Fylde Clergy, he set up a committee to raise funds to pay for church services in the workhouse. He wrote back to the clerk.

The Vicarage, May 9th.

Dear Sir, I believe that the committee appointed to consider the spiritual provision for the inmates of the workhouse will shortly be in a position to make suitable provisions. I will thank you to ask the guardians, at their next meeting, if it

> would be in accordance with their wishes that a clergyman should be deputed to perform on weekdays. Care would be taken that their services and ministrations should take place at such hours in the day as not to interfere with the accepted arrangements of the workhouse.
>
> I remain yours very faithfully,
>
> H. William Mason.

Reverend W. R. M. Holme of Weeton Church, began holding Sunday services for the inmates in the boardroom the following month.

Reverend Mason's Church School, Kirkham, which some of the workhouse children attended, raised their fees. The Wesham Church of England School and the National School Kirkham fees were increased to four pence per week for boys and girls, and three pence per week for infants.

There was a significant turnover of nurses in 1891. Miss Green of Liverpool was appointed the new nurse at the start of the year. She resigned after a month, saying her workload was too much. Miss Southall of Lancaster replaced her in February. By June, the nurse had only three people in the infirmary, all of whom were women. The men's wards in the infirmary had been empty for some time. The workhouse was the quietest it had been for years with only seventy-nine inmates. Despite this, the nurse left the workhouse in December and was replaced by Miss Banks of Preston. The porter and the cook also left at the same time for Lytham Hospital.

In the first two weeks of December, six abandoned children were left at the workhouse, four from Kirkham and two from Blackpool. When a seventh was left, the Blackpool relieving officer was called in front of the guardians.

When asked about the seventh child, the officer said, 'The child's name was William Ramson aged, 20 months. He was left in the charge of Mrs Stuart, who lived in Bonny Street, by a young woman who had worked for her in the summer. The baby was now with Mrs Dobson, in Oddfellows Street, and it was she who had made the application for the admission of the child into the house. I have not had time to find out much about the mother but was told that she was known as Miss Ramson.'

The chairman ordered him to find out more about the woman.

The children and adults received an abundance of gifts and treats that autumn. Mr J. Catterall sent some toys and sweets, and Mr R. Catterall sent some illustrated papers. The editors of the Preston Chronicle, Preston Guardian, Blackpool Herald, and the Blackpool Times said they would supply free papers weekly for the ensuing year. The Lytham churches, St John's and St Cuthbert's celebrated harvest festival, and the offerings of grapes, eggs, and apples were donated to the workhouse.

Kirkham Parish Church donated a quantity of tea, and Professor Herr Pareezer entertained fifty adults and children of the workhouse for free at the Co-operative Hall with his diorama. After the show, he supplied them with coffee and buns.

Miss Threlfall of Lytham wanted to donate some books, worth five pounds, to the workhouse. She sent a letter to the guardians.

> Edinfield, Lytham, November 10th, 1891.
>
> Dear Mr Sharples, I enclose a list of books which we have chosen from the catalogue of the Pure Literature Society. There are about 80 books, and many of them are quite small, and so will not take up much room. A large number of them have pictures, and several are printed in a large type. If the guardians have no objections to our giving the books to the workhouse, we will apply to the Pure Literature Society for the grant, and I think we shall have no difficulty in obtaining it.
>
> Believe me, yours truly E.M. Threlfall.

Chairman, William Segar Hodgson, replied, 'Some years ago there was a library, but now most of the books were lost. I think the books should be submitted to the visiting ministers before being brought into the house. It's a necessity to keep sectarian literature out of the house.'

The matter was passed to the visiting committee.

Thomas Coward, one of the oldest inmates and a notorious character, according to Mr Shuttleworth, made a complaint against the master.

The master said, 'Coward was allowed his day out on Saturday, and he had been from door to door begging. He returned to the workhouse, with a quantity of suet, cheese, bacon, ham, bread, and biscuits. The porter stopped this being brought in at the gate, and it had since been destroyed. It was not fit to eat. The consolidated orders said inmates could not bring food into the house of any kind. Through the inmates taking food from the dining-room, the bedrooms were swarming with mice.'

Thomas Coward died the following year and was buried in the parish church on 20 February 1892, aged sixty-nine.

By 1892, the annual cost of pauperism on the Fylde over the last twenty years had fallen from four-thousand, four-hundred and sixty-two pounds, and nineteen shillings to two-thousand, four-hundred and forty-six pounds, and two shillings, despite the population increasing from thirty-thousand to fifty-six-thousand. Pauperism in the Fylde was also one of the lowest in the country at one pauper to every one-hundred and thirteen of the population of the Fylde. The Lancashire average was one in fifty-nine, and in England and Wales, it was one in forty-one.

The guardians held elections that year and two lady guardians were elected for the first time. The two ladies, Mary Ann Ashworth and Mrs Baxter, were both elected to represent Layton-with-Warbrick.

In July, the new workhouse inspector, Mr Jenner Fust, and his colleague, Mr Moorsom, inspected the workhouse.

Mr Fust reported, 'The wards of the infirmary strike me as extremely nice, but the lavatory and bath arrangements were singularly inconvenient. I am pleased, however, that you are going to improve them. I have no doubt the opportunity would be taken advantage of by changing the position of the baths in order to enable the attendants to do their work better and with more convenience. One point I noticed, with the women's side of the infirmary was the absence of a day room. I was told it had been suggested to make a room, now used by the nurse for a storeroom, to answer the purpose of a small day room. The room was undoubtedly small, but a little enlargement of the windows would make it more cheerful. The nurse's stores could easily be accommodated in one of the three rooms now termed lying-in wards, all of which were hardly ever used for that purpose.'

Mr Moorsom's report went , 'Since my last visit there was now two fire hydrants capable of dealing with a fire. As regards to escape, I suggest that, on each side of the house, a door should be open between the rooms occupied by the boys and men on one hand and the girls and the women on the other. If that were done two staircases would be available for each of those classes on either side of the house, and it would only be necessary to open that door, which would be kept locked, and the key of which would be hung close by under a glass.'

He continued, 'I am sorry to find that the children of the house, during the greater part of the time that they were not at school, were under the supervision of paupers. We all know that that was not a desirable thing, and it was even less desirable now than it used to be, because the number of able-bodied paupers in the house were so very much more diminished. The character of paupers rendered it desirable that they should not have control over children. If you could see your way to appoint an additional officer, whose chief duty would be to look after the children out of school hours, look after their clothing, and see that the wards were properly regulated, and the beds were made, and who at the disposal of the matron for general work, it would be a very great improvement.'

Finally, 'There are two lunatics in the house for whom no proper certificates or justices' orders seemed to have been obtained. I understand attention had been called to it, and proper steps will be taken.'

To respond to Mr Moorsom's comments about the children's care, the guardians changed the role of the cook, and she was now the assistant matron. Mr and Mrs Thurnbeck became the new porter and the new cook.

Miss Shaw of the Girl's Friendly Society presented a report on the girls, from the workhouse, who were in service within the district. In all cases, she said they were in good homes and doing well. She asked for twenty shillings for one of the girls for purchasing clothing, which the guardians agreed to. She also said that there were nine girls under the care of the society as compared to seven last year.

A woman turned up at the workhouse, with her fourteen-year-old son after leaving her job, claiming to be destitute. She was granted admission with her son and complained that her husband did not work and contributed nothing to her maintenance. Her plan was that the guardians would take legal action and punish her lazy husband.

The chairman said, 'I do not think we ought to proceed against the man, as it was a question whether his wife and family entered the house because of his not providing them with means of support. If the board took proceedings in such cases, they would have more than one husband to punish a week, and in most instances when the women found their husbands were not summoned, they left the union in a few days and resumed work.'

A communication from the Local Government Board reminded the guardians about the allowance of tobacco and snuff for the inmates. The guardians could allow tobacco only to people who were not able-bodied, or people employed in work of a 'disagreeable character'. The guardians also had the power to decide in what rooms and what time the paupers could smoke.

The Fylde Guardians decided to give the old men one ounce of tobacco per week and one ounce of snuff per week for the old women. They thought this act of kindness would do the inmates a power of good 'when thinking about what they had once been'.

Unions provided casual wards because it was illegal to sleep rough. An example, in the summer of 1892, was William Halon, who was charged with sleeping in an outbuilding, at Bispham. At Kirkham Court, he was jailed for seven days. Begging was also illegal. James Jackson, a tramp, was jailed on 24 December for begging.

Clerk Robert Thompson, received another communication from the Local Government Board stating that casual paupers, who have been detained for more than one night and who desired to seek work, could take their discharge at five-thirty in the morning between Lady Day and Michaelmas, and at six-thirty in the morning from Michaelmas to Lady Day on condition that they had performed their tasks.

There was always a fine line between people travelling in search of work or people being idle. Chairman, William Segar Hodgson, talked about the system of relieving tramps because he thought their system was not in accordance with the law.

He said, 'We treat all tramps as if they were idle fellows, whereas there was no doubt that some of them were really working men in search of work. Our system was this: we only relieved them at Blackpool and Fleetwood by giving them an order for the tramp ward at Kirkham. Men leaving the tramp ward in the morning and walking to Blackpool or Fleetwood arrived there too late to procure work. They had nothing for their lodgings; they had no credit, and, therefore, were obliged either to beg or creep into an outbuilding, where they ran the risk of being caught by the police and being sent to gaol.'

He suggested, 'We should have forms printed, and supply them to the relieving officers, who should give one to any person employing a man that was destitute to fill in, saying that he would be responsible for the relief granted to the man by stopping it out of the first money he earned and paying it to the guardians. It would only cost the guardians 2d. or 4d. for his lodgings. If my suggestion was adopted, it would relieve the guardians of a great responsibility that attached them at present.'

Guardian William Hodgson, from Poulton, thought the difficulty would be to get the employers to see the proposal in the same light as the board. It would entail a great deal of trouble.

He said, 'If we adopt the chairman's suggestion, the result would be a large influx of tramps down at Fleetwood. The more provision they made for the folks of that sort, the more they would have to provide. They must deal with them with a strong hand. I am perfectly certain that if they adopted any course like that suggested, they would simply have a large number, more than they had now, and there would be increased difficulty in dealing with them.'

The chairman's suggestion was put to the vote and adopted. At the next meeting, it was decided that the police would determine whether a person was deserving or not and give out the forms accordingly. Each deserving tramp would receive four pence for lodgings and three pence for a meal.

William Hodgson was still not happy. He thought the only way to keep them away was to strike terror into them. Coming from Poulton, where a former tramp's ward was situated, he remembered that, at one time, hundreds of tramps turned up at Poulton causing major trouble for the town.

Doctor Thomas Shaw

1893 started with the death of Dr Thomas Shaw on 28 January, aged seventy-seven years. When he began working for the union, they were still in the old workhouse on Marsden Street. For many years Thomas Shaw was the only doctor living in the Kirkham District, but now things had changed, and there were four applicants for his position: Thomas Shaw's son, Dr William Wright Shaw; Dr Wigglesworth; Dr Jones; and Dr Corte. Dr William Wright Shaw became the new workhouse medical officer.

The chairman announced, much to his cousin's amusement that the system of outdoor relief for tramps at Blackpool and Fleetwood had failed. Unlike at Blackpool, the police at Fleetwood gave tickets to anybody that applied, instead of who they thought were genuine cases. During the first few weeks, only a few applied. Then, between September and March, eight-hundred and one tramps applied for relief in Fleetwood compared to sixty-one at Blackpool. In the last three days, seventy tramps had applied for relief at Fleetwood. This caused too much excess work for the police, and they refused to issue any more tickets.

Mr William Hodgson said to the chairman, 'I am glad to see that you are converted, and I must congratulate you.'

Chairman, William Segar Hodgson, replied, 'I am not converted that it is not right to provide for these men who have a legal claim upon us. When they are destitute, we cannot refuse them relief.'

Mr W. Hodgson said, 'We had gone through a similar experience at Poulton as they had at Fleetwood, but a special police officer was appointed to deal with the tramps, and soon cleared them out. If they adopted the same course at Fleetwood, they would find that before the officer had been on duty a month, he would have paid his expense.'

Mr Sharples asked, 'If the tramps were not relieved, what had they to do? When they had no money in their pockets, there was no alternative for them but to go on the road and sleep in some barn or haystack, and then they were brought up.'

The chairman said, 'As the case stood at present, tramps were undoubtedly attracted to Fleetwood. The only way out of the difficulty was to build tramp wards, but he could not advise the board to that because the expense would be enormous.'

Mr Tyler added, 'Tramps would not go in such wards if they were built.'

The chairman replied, "Oh, yes, they would."

Mr W. Hodgson declared that, '90 per cent of the tramps they had to deal with were vagrants, and on the lookout for anything they could take up. There was nothing too hot and nothing too heavy for them if they were out of sight.'

The guardians decided to appoint a special police officer at Fleetwood. He was to act as assistant relieving officer and deal with the tramps for a three month period. P.C. Waddington was appointed assistant relieving officer; he was on duty from twelve noon to nine at night. The number of tramps dropped from thirty or forty a week to about twelve.

It had cost the union thirteen shillings and four pence to relieve forty tramps before the three month trial. Now with the policeman's pay included with the relief, a dozen tramps cost the union fifty-two shillings and two pence. The guardians decided to end the trial, and the policeman was given a month's notice from June.

Miss M. B. Trelfall of Lytham wrote to the guardians, asking for help in getting a boy called Rimmer into the Waifs and Strays Home, Kendal. His mother was a widow and was out all day 'charing' and was not able to look after the boy. The home had offered a place if she could raise forty pounds this year and ten pounds next year. Miss Trelfall had raised ten pounds herself and asked the guardians to contribute ten pounds. The board didn't have the power to give the ten pounds, so they wrote to the Local Government Board for permission: who said no.

The boy could have been sent, like many orphans, to the colonies. The Canadian Emigration Bureau had written to the union saying that they were sending another party in a weeks' time and asked if the board had any children they wished to send to Canada. The guardians told the bureau they had nobody to send.

If a women's husband died, she could often find herself turning to the poor law for help. Elizabeth Stones had left her five children in the workhouse after being widowed, but at this time had met another man and had a child by him. The child lived at home with their mother. She was called before the guardians and questioned as to whether she was able to pay something towards the cost of her five children in the workhouse.

She replied that she was a widow with one child living with her. She went out charing one or two days a week, and it took her all her time to pay the four shillings rent of the house she lived in and provide for herself and child. The child at home was from the man who she now lived with.

The guardians accused her of not conducting herself as she ought to do, and that she took intoxicating drink. She denied these allegations. They discussed the case.

Mr Heap said, 'We have evidence before us that she is a careless woman, indifferent to the duties devolving upon her, and this was more than borne out when she appeared before the board when every gentleman in that room must have noticed the very indifferent way in which she behaved. She had thrown all the responsibility of keeping her children upon the guardians, and it would be a very wrong thing indeed if it were to get abroad in the union, that any woman could abandon her children and herself go and live an indifferent life. The woman did not care at all about her children, and if careless women could desert their offspring and let them come to the workhouse, whilst no call at all was made upon the mothers, there was a very great danger of the resources of the union being taxed to their uttermost.'

This was answered with cheers and calls of 'hear, hear'.

He continued, 'If an idea of that sort had to get abroad in Blackpool, the workhouse would be thronged with children deserted under similar circumstances to those which I refer. The woman in question was leading a disreputable life, whilst her children were being maintained by the union, without any call whatever upon the mother. If there was no law to punish her, then they should compel her to come into the workhouse and share the same fate as her children. It had been said that it would be dangerous to bring such a character into the workhouse, but it was their duty to bring her in, and they would be then in a position to deal with her. Here were children who had had the stigma cast upon their life, that they had been thrown upon the union, whilst they were allowing the person who was to blame to go without punishment. I have a very great pleasure indeed in moving that resolution, for I think that it was encouraging crime to allow that woman to abandon her children, throw them upon the resources of the union, whilst she herself was living a life not creditable to herself.'

This case caused a problem for the guardians. She refused to enter the workhouse, and although they could compel her to enter the workhouse or take the children out, they didn't take this option. They thought she was an 'undesirable' person to have in the workhouse and was an unfit mother to take her children. The guardians then motioned to have her charged under the Vagrancy Act, which could be used in cases of child neglect, it carried a three-month sentence. They voted on this course, but it was lost eleven votes to ten. They then reported her to the R.S.P.C.C. Officer who investigated the child living at home, but he reported that it was not a case for him to take on. The guardians, then asked her Father-in-law, James Stones, to take the children. He told them he was unable to look after them, so the children stayed in the workhouse, and became chargeable to the union.

Mrs Ann Langton Birley, of Carr Hill House Kirkham, donated forty quarts of gooseberries and sugar for the inmates to make jam. At harvest time, she sent some apples to the workhouse and just before her death, on 26 November, she left some tobacco, tea, snuff, and beer for the inmates. The Birley family had a long tradition of donating to the workhouse, and her son Henry Langton Birley promised to keep on the family tradition of donating to the inmates.

At Christmas time the master and matron, Mr and Mrs Tricky, decorated the dining hall and some other rooms. The inmates had a dinner of roast beef and plum pudding and, after the meal, Dr W. W. Shaw spoke a few words. Christmas gifts were sent by Miss Threlfall, Mrs Lowe, Mrs Walmsley, and Mrs Barker. During the Christmas week, Samuel Bancroft and his concert party provided a night's entertainment along with Mr Batty with his comic songs.

The year ended with the Nurse Miss Banks resigning and the porter and assistant matron receiving a six pounds pay rise, four pounds for the porter and two pounds for the assistant matron. The porter now earned one and a half pence an hour.

The Fylde Workhouse was changing. At the start of 1894, there were eighty-six paupers, all of whom were either old, infirm, or children. There were no able-bodied people, except in the tramp wards. The workhouse was starting its long and slow transformation into a public assistance institution.

Before that was to happen, the site needed to be expanded. The numbers in the workhouse were historically low, but this was irrelevant, it had to be able to hold one per cent of the population of about sixty-thousand or six-hundred paupers. The plan was to ask the Kirkham Local Board to move their yard, office, and fire station out of the corner of the workhouse gardens. The union would buy some more land adjacent, from Mr Birley, where Kirkham Baths currently stand, and build a new building there. The building would include overnight accommodation for visitors, four rooms for the officers, a board room of eighty metres square, three committee rooms of twenty-four metres square, two rooms for registration purposes, clerk's room, safe room, fumigating room, and receiving wards for male and female paupers.

The present administration block, facing Moor Street, would be demolished and the extra pauper accommodation built on the site.

The guardians still subscribed to the Manchester Eye Hospital; 1894's subscription was three pounds and three shillings. During the previous twelve months, thirty-nine patients from the union had been treated there for free. In the infirmary, Dr William Shaw was told he was not keeping the medical relief book in a satisfactory manner by not entering the days of attendances.

He wrote to the guardians,

> 'In reply to yours of the 21st inst, I consider my books have been particularly well attended to, and they, no doubt, will be maintained in the same state of efficiency.'

On a different matter, he told the guardians, that he considered the diet of the children, between the ages of two to seven, as not very satisfactory. He recommended that they have a half-pint of new milk daily, except on Saturdays, when they should be given some tea, boiled milk, and bread; this was all in lieu of bread, cheese and coffee. He thought these alterations would bring about a healthier condition among the children, who were now constantly coming over to the infirmary, and who under proper treatment and with a generous diet, rapidly got better.

The children had nowhere to play in the workhouse apart from the common yard and, in cases of sickness, they had nowhere at all to go and had to stay inside. To remedy this, the workhouse committee decided to create a green for the children on the west side of the house.

Miss Ellison of Blackpool was appointed the new nurse to replace Nurse Banks, but she couldn't start because she had influenza and pneumonia. The guardians decided to give the position to Nurse Cavanaugh, who had also applied for the job. She didn't stay long and was replaced by Miss Carr of Mirfield in September.

A case came to the guardian's attention of a girl who had been out of the workhouse for thirteen months, assisting on a farm, but had not been paid any wages.

The chairman said, 'In my opinion, it's not advisable that pauper children should be allowed to be put to work for nothing. They ought to have something for pocket money, and something ought to be put by for them.'

The relieving officer was told to look into the case. He reported back saying the girl was happy in the position, but the farmer couldn't afford to pay the girl any money. The chairman declared that the farmer must pay the girl the customary sixpence weekly pocket money and sixpence should be put aside each week for her. In future, the relieving officers was instructed to report quarterly upon the children taken out of the workhouse, and to give the information to the board as to the condition of the children, the amount of money they were being paid, and the amount which was being placed to their credit in the saving bank.

In October, four lads escaped from the workhouse early in the morning. One of them had been sent to the house by the police, and one was a boy who had employed himself in 'turning cartwheels'.

The master was glad to see the back of three of the lads. He said, 'Three of the boys were of a bad character, and I don't want them back, but one called Heywood was a good lad, and I would be glad to have him back.' The matter was passed to the police.

In 1895, the deputy clerk was asked by the guardians to look into whether the regulations concerning vagrants were being adhered to.

He said, 'According to the rules, the vagrants sleep in separate cells. They have to break 10 c.w.t of stones in the first week, 15 c.w.t of stones in the second week and, if they stayed longer, further increases. When they enter the vagrant's ward, they are detained for at least two days. If they returned in the same week, they are detained for four days. The only rule the master does not apply is the changing and disinfecting of their clothes. This is only done on request.'

Mrs Allen wanted to know, at one of the February meetings, whether it was right or the law that when relieving officers went to houses, and especially to those of the aged poor, that they should pry into every corner and pantry. What was particularly disgusting to her was the checking of bedrooms and even the inspecting of the beds on which the aged lay. She thought that when a couple had lived to the age of seventy years, and for the first time then applied for relief, they should have it without insulting inquiries.

Mr Tyler said, 'The relieving officers for the Fylde District were very civil and humane men, (hear, hear) desired to do what was right, and looked up to the aged and poor and infirm. Of course, in all cases, they were bound to make enquiries, and if in this case, the officer went to look at the bed, he did so with a good feeling (hear, hear).'

Mrs Allen said, 'In this case, the officers were a little gruff. They might say 'May I go upstairs?' instead of 'I am going upstairs,' as happened in this case of the Cartmell family of St Annes.'

Relieving Officer, Mr Blacoe, was called into the boardroom.

He told the guardians, 'The old people applied for 5s. a week. I visited them and looked around the house. In the pantry, there was a barrel of beer. I thought it was a deserving case and reported it to the relief committee, but they did not grant relief. There was not a wrong word passed between me and the Cartmells, and I have heard of no complaint.'

Mr Westby asked him if he went upstairs.

He replied, 'Yes. I said, 'Can I go upstairs?' and the people were quite agreeable. Everything in the house was nice and clean. The woman said she had brewed the beer he had seen, and that she was the only one who could do it.'

His explanation was accepted by the guardians, and no further action was taken.

The Catholic Church had built two new orphanages, Leyfields School for Girls, Liverpool, and St Vincent's School Preston for Boys. Father Hines, of The Willows, asked the guardians if the Catholic children could be moved into the orphanages. He thought the children were well looked after in the workhouse, but there was a stigma attached to being a workhouse child.

Father Hines

The matter was passed to the workhouse committee who unanimously recommended that the children stay in the workhouse. Mr Finch, a Roman Catholic, agreed with the priest and motioned that the matter be referred back to the workhouse committee.

Mr Westby, of the workhouse committee, explained the decision, he said, 'The children were well looked after in the house as they would be in a school. They cost 3s. a head now, and there were 10 of them. If they were sent to an institution, it would cost £50 a year more, as the charge would be 5s. a head. If they were not cared for in the workhouse, I would have reported the matter to the board. I can see no benefit to come from referring the matter back.'

The chairman added, 'If we send these particular children away, we would be spending 2s. more a head on one class than another, and if it was advisable to send them, it was the duty of the board to the other children to also send them some other place, so that all might have the same advantage. Whether it was desirable to go to that expense, it was for the board to say.'

He continued, 'I know children in a workhouse were not brought up in the best way that they might be, and I know it was the common opinion of the world that children should be brought up away from the workhouse to relieve them of any taint. We are guardians of the children, and not simply of the purse strings of the public, and why should we not spend a few shillings more if it was to their benefit. Other unions were doing it. These schools had been inspected, and I know that nothing was left undone to make the children happy and content.'

The committee had only considered the matter concerning the Catholic children. Mr W. Hodgson thought the board must consider all children, and if boarding out was to be adopted, it must be for all the children, religion should play no part.

Mrs Allen and Mrs Ashworth spoke in favour of the children staying in the house. When Mr Finch's motion was voted upon, it was lost by nineteen votes to eight.

For the last few years, the workhouse had been quiet, and the guardians had closed surplus wards to save money. In May, there were one-hundred and fourteen paupers in the house, an increase of thirty-six since the same time last year, and some of the closed wards were reopened.

The proposed expansion of the workhouse came up again. When the workhouse was built the population of the Fylde was twenty-one-thousand, but now it was sixty-thousand and growing at a rate of one-thousand-five-hundred per year. As well as providing space for future expansion, they now had to provide space, so that old couples could live together in private rooms; this would reduce the workhouse capacity from two-hundred and sixty to two-hundred paupers.

The board needed to buy land off Mr Birley of Milbanke House to expand the site, but he disapproved of the new plans and was reluctant to sell any land. The board now began to think about building a completely new workhouse on a different site and selling the present one to use as an infection's hospital for the Fylde.

Taking all the problems into account, they sent the proposed plans to redevelop the present site to the Local Government Board, who rejected them for the following reasons.

1. That the present workhouse is not adequate for the wants of the union.

2. That, with the exception of the infirmary and the vagrant's wards, none of the buildings at the present workhouse are worth spending money upon or preserving.

3. That it is important to separate the children from the adults.

4. That there is no space on the existing site, even if the children were removed, to build a workhouse for present wants, and future enlargements to meet potential requirements, could not be made.

5. That no adjoining land can be procured except under restrictive covenants which would render it useless for poor law purposes.

The Fylde Guardians were also advised to ignore the present small numbers in the house and look at providing a workhouse capable of holding five-hundred paupers, excluding vagrants, and to buy sufficient land, to allow further expansion of upwards of eight-hundred paupers allowing for future expansion of the Fylde. The new workhouse should be built a good distance away from the current one, which should be used solely for the children.

The guardians approached Mr Hale, Lord Derby's land agent, asking if they could buy fifteen to twenty acres of land in Wesham, which was within easy reach of the train station. Lord Derby agreed to sell the land for one-hundred and fifty pounds per acre. Some guardians wanted to move the workhouse to Poulton-le-Fylde, but this would be difficult for people travelling from St Annes or Lytham by train, who would have to change trains at Kirkham Station.

The guardians had three options now, expand the present site, build a new workhouse in Wesham, or move to a new site at Poulton le Fylde. A committee was set up, including William Segar Hodgson, William Hodgson, R. Gorst, F. Finch, R. Westby, P. Blundell, I. Wilde, G. Blundell, J. Needham, R. Cross, J. O. Hesketh, and Mrs Ashworth, to look into the expansion.

Mr Wilde complained about margarine being given to the inmates instead of butter.

He said, 'The stuff was made from dead dogs, cats and sewage, and I would not feed a cat on it. There are farmers in this room who were butter makers, and yet they voted such rubbish for consumption at the workhouse.'

The workhouse committee recommended that butter should replace margarine, and English cheese should replace American cheese. They also thought that in future, all inmates, under sixty years of age, be allowed tea or coffee once a day instead of porridge.

During 1896, the numbers in the workhouse continued to climb. In February, there were one-hundred and forty-four paupers in the house.

The guardians finally decided to build a new workhouse in Wesham and wanted to buy twelve acres, one rod, fourteen perches of land from Lord Derby which was freehold and free from covenants. In April, the Local Government Board declined to give permission for the guardians to buy the land because they wanted to know what would happen with the children who had to be housed, in future, completely separate from the adults.

The new workhouse also had to be at such a distance that the adults and the children would never cross each other's paths. The plan was to house the present fifty-one children; forty-six between two and sixteen years of age, and five under the age of two, at the present workhouse and the adults in the new one in Wesham. The chairman suggested that they write back to London, saying that no adult pauper would be employed where the children were housed and leave it to them to decide if the buildings were too close.

It would be the following year before they would get permission to buy the land.

In the meantime, Mr John Clegg, the collector of poor rates in the ten townships that made up the Fleetwood District, asked for more help. The collector stated that the district had grown in the twenty-two years since he was appointed, and he was now sixty-three years old and could not walk the thirteen miles from his residence to the outer edges of the district. He had been paying an assistant out of his miserable salary of seventy pounds. The matter was referred to the finance committee, who allowed him an extra one pound a year to pay his assistant.

Agnes Morrow was admitted into the workhouse, without an order from the relieving officer, suffering from a broken rib. She'd fallen at the house of Mrs Bulcock, St Annes, where she had been employed for ten days. During that time, Miss Morrow had earned five shillings in wages. After she had broken her ribs, Mrs Bulcock was alleged to of taken the five shillings from the injured girl. She took four shillings to pay the doctor's fees, and the remaining one shilling was spent on Agnes' train fare to Kirkham.

Mr Wilde said that it seemed to him to be a case of inhumanity, and another guardian characterised it as a case of cruelty. It was very selfish to take five shillings from the girl. The chairman thought they should wait to hear the other side of the story before taking any action. They asked for a report from Mrs Bulcock.

This story was reported in the papers.

Mr Bulcock of St Andrew's Road, St Annes replied in writing.

Dear Sirs,

The report appearing in the newspapers, with regard to this woman is so misleading and devoid of truth that I must demand an apology, and I ask you, after reading my letter of explanation, to be good enough to see the same is attended to. Agnes Marrow came to us from Lytham on Thursday, February 20th, for only a week as temporary help, my wife, being very ill in bed, and I had no one in the house save my sister-in-law. As soon as we saw her, we told her that she would not do, but she implored us to let her stay a few days so that she might get a place. Six days afterwards, she had a fit and fell downstairs.

This was at 6.15 a.m., and I hurried off for the doctor. He arrived at 6.40 a.m. and stayed an hour with her. We carried her to bed and gave her gruel, brandy, and other nourishments, and placed a hot bottle to her feet. The following day she got up against our wish, and when the doctor saw her a second time, he told her she must go to the hospital. I twice telegraphed to her mother, and she wired back the message 'Take her nearest hospital.' The woman has the telegram in her pocket. My wife had been confined a few days prior to this woman's accident. I paid for the telegrams and the doctor's bill, besides giving the woman a shilling for the fare to Kirkham. As my wife was in great danger on the Friday, the doctor absolutely insisted on the woman going to Kirkham.

I saw Robert Knowles J.P., who told me to send the woman to the relieving officer, as a note from him was necessary in addition to the order from the doctor. The expression of opinions, from a few members of the board, though natural enough from a lack of the correct account, have caused much pain to my wife. Hoping the matter will be contradicted at the next meeting.

J.W. Bulcock.

P.S. I have omitted to say that Agnes Morrow agreed to stay the week for the sum of 4s. and told us if we would keep her, she would stay for 2s. a week. She only worked five days for us, so how can 5s. be owing her?

The chairman was happy with the explanation, but he thought the doctor had been hard on the girl for taking his fee.

He said, 'I think the explanation is very satisfactory. I think Mr and Mrs Bulcock, are more to be sympathised with than anything else, but the doctor or any medical man had no right to give an order for the workhouse.'

Mr Wilde thought the doctor should apologise. The matter was then dropped until Dr Connor wrote to the guardians in April, to clear his name.

Dear Sirs

As my name had been mentioned in reference to the case of Mr Bulcock's servant, of St Annes, I wish to make a few remarks. Mr Bulcock came to my house soon after six o'clock on the morning, February 26th. I went immediately to his house and found the servant suffering from injury to the ribs, the result of a fall from the top of the stairs. I treated her for the injury and recommended her removal to hospital. I wrote the certificate (not an order, as stated in the newspaper) which I gave to Mr Bulcock. Mr Bulcock, who showed every kindness and attention to the girl, called at my surgery four days afterwards and requested to know my fee for attendance on his servant, which was then paid. I was not aware the girl was destitute till I saw the report in the newspapers. In the report of the second meeting of the Fylde Guardians, I noticed that a man named Wilde suggested that I should apologise. I shall feel much obliged if he will inform me to whom I am to apologise, and for what. Considering there was ample time between the two meetings of the board, I think it would have been well if Mr Wilde communicated with me before making such an absurd remark.

Mr Wilde replied, 'We had nothing but the reports to go by. Now he was trying to clear it up. It appears to me that Mr Bulcock cleared him up, and they scratched each other's backs.'

The chairman thought they'd better move on.

Mr Urmson, Visiting Commissioner in Lunacy, visited the workhouse on 28 July.

> By the death of one of each sex, and the discharge home, to her friends, of a woman, the imbeciles, who are classed as such, in the workhouse, have been reduced to six, being one male and five females. They remain suitable for care and treatment in the house. I saw, in addition to the above, several inmates who appear to be of unsound mind, and I commend the cases to the consideration of the medical officer as to whether they should not be classed. The imbeciles live in the body of the house, and their general condition gave evidence of the sufficiency of their diet and of them being properly looked after. Their clothing was, on the whole, neat and tidy.
>
> Due attention is paid to employment, but the imbeciles get no exercise beyond the workhouse premises. The day rooms were clean, but some stone flags in the day room in which the males sit are loose and worn and require early attention. The dormitories were in good order and the bedding very clean. To meet the contingency of the only access, at present, to the male dormitory being cut off by smoke in the event of fire, a canvas shoot had been provided. The inmates, I was told, practise the use of this shoot.
>
> The bathing arrangements are satisfactory, but the baths require to be re-enamelled, and it is a question whether the opportunity should be taken to replace them with baths of the Stourbridge ware. I had no complaints, while more than one imbecile spoke well of their care and treatment. They were looking forward to an excursion this week to Blackpool. I understand that the site for a new workhouse had been acquired. It is situated nearer the station. The accommodation which the present house affords is of a rough and ready kind; no doubt the new workhouse will provide good imbecile wards, such as are found in many of the suburban workhouses in London.

The report was referred to the workhouse committee with particular reference to the flags and baths. It was also decided to bring to the doctor's attention the inmates alluded to.

In June, it came to the guardians notice that vagrants in Fleetwood and Blackpool were applying for tickets but not turning up at the workhouse. During 1894, one-hundred and twenty tickets were given, but only sixty-three persons were admitted into the vagrant's ward. In the first seven months of 1895, ninety-five tickets were distributed, of which forty-four were presented. The vagrants were applying for tickets to get free travel to Kirkham, but not reporting to the workhouse.

Master John Trickey requested that the inmates should have currant cake and biscuits on Kirkham Club Day. The children walked in the parade, but the adults were not allowed out. They were only allowed to watch the parade as it passed the workhouse.

Mrs Allen made a complaint about the women inmates after an inspection found that their clothes were 'not exactly satisfactory.'

She complained, 'A fortnight ago the women were very dirty and untidy. The matter had been long under consideration and was a sore point with some of the committee.'

Mr Woods remarked that the dirtiness was only observed in one or two cases.

Mrs Allen replied, 'Of course that's your idea.'

Mr Woods explained that the women had been cleaning.

Mrs Allen replied, 'It's wrong that the women have to work in the same aprons that they sew in.'

In answer to this complaint, the visiting committee recommended that the women received one clean cap and a clean apron once a week, instead of once a fortnight. In July, Mrs Allen complained again. The master had given one guardian, Mrs Baxter, permission to celebrate her birthday by giving the inmates seed loaves and cakes. Mrs Allen was also planning to celebrate her birthday in the same way, but she was told she needed permission from the master.

Mrs Allen said, 'I was not aware before this morning that it was necessary to obtain permission to bring sweets etc. for the inmates. It's my birthday next week, and I must bring something; therefore, I asked for the requisite permission.'

The chairman explained to her that nothing could be brought to the house without the sanction of the master or matron. It would not do, for instance, to bring spirits into the house.

Guardian William Hodgson hoped it was not going to become a regular thing.

He said, 'We all know the difficulty they had when the master first came with regards to the inmates passing articles of food. As long as it will be only for about three times a year, I have no objection. I do not believe in the inmates being treated better than people outside. No inducements should be offered to people to come here.'

Mrs Allen furiously replied, 'I have never given anything to able-bodied paupers. I give it to the people in the infirmary and would continue to do so. I will not stop and would do it somehow.'

The chairman told her, 'The guardians are very powerful, but as individuals they were powerless. When they propose to act in this manner, they were apt to be stopped.'

Mr Dickinson rebuked the actions of Mrs Allen and said that if such proceedings were allowed, they would have no regulation in the house at all. He then proposed that all gifts sent to the house should be given to the master, which was seconded by Mr Finch.

All the guardians voted for the motion, save for Mrs Allen, who said, 'I will continue to put toffees in the old people's mouths.'

As she was leaving, she said to Mr Westby, 'I would not put toffee in your mouth.'

After she had left the room, a member said, 'If she is going to act like that, she would soon have the board room all to herself. I would not sit on a board when there was a woman like her.'

By the end of the year, the female guardians had formed into a Ladies Visiting Committee in order to have a stronger voice, especially when it concerned the old aged paupers and the children. Mrs Ashworth explained to the board that there were ten or twelve old women anxious to attend the Catholic Church, and she thought they should dress accordingly. She wanted the ladies to be supplied with serge skirts and bonnets. Mr Finch, who always supported motions supporting Catholics, seconded the motion and it was passed.

In January 1897, the guardians finally received permission to purchase the land in Wesham for the new workhouse. Government Inspector, Jenner Fust, suggested building a workhouse to accommodate two-hundred and fifty paupers; with space to expand it to between five-hundred and six-hundred paupers. The children would stay at the Moor Street site.

The guardians instructed Kirkham solicitor, Mr Dickinson, to purchase the land. In May, the twelve acres were staked out, and boundary stones were erected. The guardians started growing wheat on ten acres of the land to keep some of the able-bodied employed. A brickmaking committee was formed, who appointed Wesham Brickmaker, Joseph Hudson. He started excavating clay and asked for an area on the new plot of land to be fenced off for the purpose: he then began brickmaking. The sand and water needed for brick making was found on the site.

The plans for the new workhouse were drawn up and put on display in one of the rooms in the infirmary for the guardians to view. The architects Haywood and Harrison would work with the committee building the new workhouse for fifty-five guineas per year.

The workhouse officers were entitled to free rations, accommodation, and a uniform. Formally, they were issued with a new uniform every six months. From 1897, they would only receive a new uniform once a year; however, they all received a pay raise. The master's salary was raised from forty-five pounds to fifty-five pounds, the matron's from thirty-five pounds to forty pounds. Miss Carr, the nurse, who had received a certificate and a silver medal for three years' service, was also given a raise from twenty-five pounds to thirty pounds.

The infirmary was sometimes used as an emergency hospital.

John Gregson, who was blind, was run over by a horse and trap crossing Poulton Street in Kirkham. The seventy-four-year-old of 18 Marsden Street was brought into the workhouse infirmary with a fractured thigh. He later died in the infirmary; in those days a broken leg often meant death, mainly through infections.

The Flaxfield Mill in Kirkham closed, and many of the Irish employees returned to Ireland. Some left their children in the workhouse until they could find work in Ireland and then sent for them. One was Mary Jane Atkinson, who had found work at a spinning mill in Belfast, she asked the guardians if they would clothe the children and she would send for them soon. Mrs McLean, also from Belfast, asked for her children to be released to her, but for unknown reasons the guardians refused.

Lines of communication were slower in the Victorian Era, but they still worked. If an inmate absconded from the workhouse, a description and reward would be placed in the Poor Law Gazette. Timothy Murphy absconded from the Kirkham Workhouse, leaving an irate wife and three children chargeable to the Union.

FYLDE UNION.
Clerk—Mr. Wm. Thompson, Union Offices, Kirkham.
TIMOTHY MURPHY, a dock labourer, 30 years of age, about 5 feet 8 inches, scar on right of forehead, blue scar on left eye brow, large nose, blue eyes, brown hair, probably at Salford or Preston. Wife and family. W.
Information to be given to the Superintendent of Police, Kirkham, who holds the Warrant.
One Guinea Rewrad.

Notice for Timothy Murphy, placed in the Poor Law Gazette.

Mrs Murphy had the last laugh when she informed the police of her husband's whereabouts. She wrote to the guardians, asking for the one guinea reward: which was sent to her. Timothy was sentenced to three months hard labour.

The year ended with Emily Alderson being removed to the Burnley Workhouse with her children. Emily, who had settlement in Burnley, had entered the Kirkham Workhouse in July after she had been summoned for neglecting to maintain her children in the workhouse; she was ordered to either join them or pay for their maintenance. The family left for the Burnley Workhouse on 22 December 1897.

1898 saw the departure of Clerk William Thompson, after fifty-five years' service, when he resigned. He was replaced by his assistant, Mr Frederick Henry Brown.

Mrs Ashworth, of the Women's Visiting Committee, suggested that an assistant matron be appointed to look after the children. She thought some of the young women in the house were not fit to be around children.

She added, 'They thought it was clever to teach them bad things, and on one occasion they had put a little child on a table and asked it to repeat sentences that were not fit for old people to hear.'

Mr William Hodgson seconded the move, but the chairman disagreed saying, 'There is a great deal of nonsense talked about pauper's influence in my opinion.'

Mr Bradley agreed. He thought that they ought to spend the ratepayer's money as if it were their own, 'We should wait until they got the new workhouse.' The matter was referred back to committee.

The committee also wanted a new organ for the workhouse. They were advised by the chairman not to buy an American organ; the one at Preston Workhouse was often out of order. An organ where the wind was drawn through and not blown through should be procured. Mrs Ashworth, with some committee members and the matron, went visiting warehouses in search of a new organ for the workhouse. They purchased an English pipe organ for one-hundred and thirty pounds from Rushworth and Sons, Mill Lane, Liverpool.

The finance committee recommended that the board contribute ten pounds and tens shillings to Blackpool Victoria Hospital to treat the paupers of Blackpool. Mr Westby then asked about contributing to Fleetwood Cottage Hospital and Mr J. Needham to Lytham Cottage Hospital. Guardian, William Hodgson, thought they should get returns from the various hospitals and maybe consider closing their contributions to the Manchester Eye Hospital and the Preston Infirmary. After seeing the returns, the guardians decided to subscribe ten pounds and nineteen shillings to Victoria Hospital, Blackpool, and two pounds and two shillings each to Fleetwood and Lytham Cottage Hospitals.

Miss Shaw reported that the girls who had been inmates and were now in service, or otherwise maintaining themselves, but who were still under the notice of the girl's friendly society were all doing well.

The guardians purchased more land for the new workhouse; some came from Mr Birley and another five acres came from Lord Derby. This meant they would have to re-route Back Lane, Wesham, which would eventually become known as Derby Road. They also bought a plot of land from a Mr Riley, where the stone braking yard would be situated.

William Segar Hodgson, William Butcher, William Gradwell, Clerk Fred Brown and Architects were elected as a deputation to meet the Local Government Board in London. However, this and the entire project was put on hold because the overseers, guardians, mayor, aldermen and burgesses of Blackpool wanted to split from the union and create their own.

To do this, they needed the support of all the guardians, which they would never obtain as Blackpool paid sixty per cent of the poor rates but only had forty per cent of the paupers. If they left the union, it would mean a large increase in rates for the remaining parishes. The proposal was refused by the guardians, and the matter was sent on to the Local Board, London.

Relieving officers were now appointed vaccination officers and would oversee the immunisations against smallpox and receive payments for each vaccination. The vaccination fees were set by the guardians.

Vaccination Officer Payments.

a. For each child entered in the birth's lists sent to him by the registrar of births and deaths: three pence.

b. For each case of successful vaccination registered by him: nine pence.

c. For each certificate of successful vaccination sent by him to the vaccination officer of other districts: nine pence.

Public Vaccinators Doctors Payments.

a. For each child, whose birth is registered in the district of the public vaccinator, who attains the age of four months: one shilling.

b. For each case of a successful primary vaccination: five-shillings.

c. For each successful primary vaccination of any person, other than a child, successfully re-vaccinated: two shillings and sixpence.

d. In the workhouse and successful: two shillings and sixpence

Medical Officer of the Workhouse.

a. For each successful vaccination or re-vaccination of any person in the workhouse: two shillings and sixpence

John Stauper left three children in the workhouse when he went in search of a job. After he had found work in St Annes, he paid ten shillings weekly for his children's maintenance. Two months later, his children were still in the workhouse, and Mr Blacoe, the relieving officer, was ordered to enquire into the matter. Mr Blacoe reported back saying it was because he had not found a house. To help encourage Mr Stauper, the guardians ordered him to pay an extra five shillings a week and gave him another fortnight. After two weeks, the children were still in the house, and it took him being summoned to court before he finally removed his children.

Ernest Ellis had absconded from Manchester and had left his wife and children chargeable to the union there. He entered the Kirkham Workhouse after he had been living in Blackpool. Instead of keeping his head down after absconding from Manchester, he complained of his treatment at Kirkham, saying he was refused medical treatment and was forced to break stones. The visiting committee asked the master about the complaints.

The master said, 'He had been admitted on the 15th of September from Blackpool and was examined by the doctor, but not sent to the infirmary. On the 12th of October, I found him in the oakum room inciting inmates to insubordination. I then sent him to the stone yard where Ellis asked to see the doctor. I told him he must wait until 6 pm that night, but he declined to go.'

The guardians thought the master had no case to answer. Three days later, the Manchester relieving officer visited the workhouse and apprehended Ellis.

In 1899, the Government Board rejected Blackpool's request to leave the union. The Fylde had less pauperism in proportion to the population than any other union in Lancashire. The average amount paid per pound for poor rates, for the last five years was one and a quarter pence; in January that year, it was one penny. The average in the North-Western District was five and a quarter pence. The board saw no reason to change the union.

Over the last five years, the average number of paupers, excluding lunatics and vagrants, was one-hundred and forty-one. The average number of lunatics was eight, and the average number of vagrants was four. January's number that year, was one-hundred and sixty-eight in the house, which included thirteen lunatics and no vagrants.

The average number in receipt of outdoor relief, for the last five years, was three-hundred and fourteen. In January that year, it was three-hundred and fifteen paupers.

The union was overseen by forty guardians of which ten came from Blackpool. The rateable value of the Fylde was five-hundred-and-ninety-seven-thousand, four-hundred and forty-six pounds, and of that Blackpool paid three-hundred-and-fifteen-thousand, three-hundred and forty pounds. The population of the union was fifty-six-thousand, three-hundred and seventeen, and of that number twenty-three-thousand, eight-hundred and forty-six came from Blackpool. To placate Blackpool, they were given an extra six guardians.

Out of every thirty-nine pounds collected by Lancashire County Council through the rates, the Fylde Union contributed one pound.

After the decision not to split the union, the guardians purchased the extra land for a total cost of one-thousand-four-hundred pounds.

1. Five acres of land, belonging to Lord Derby, along Back Lane, Wesham.

2. A plot of three rods and twenty-four perches, belonging to Mr Leyland Birley.

3. A plot of land along Station Road, from Thomas Riley, of one acre, three rods, and fourteen perches.

Joseph Hudson had been making bricks for nearly two years now. The guardians contracted builder, Mr Haslam, to build a boundary wall along the west side of the land for twenty-eight pounds. The building of the workhouse was not going to start anytime soon, and with the guardians always keen to make money, they began selling bricks to other builders who were working in the area.

In March, the twenty-nine children and forty-three aged inmates of the workhouse were treated to a night at the pantomime, at the Grand Theatre, Blackpool, by Mr Charles Noden. They caught the train at one o'clock to Talbot-Road Station, where they met Mr Noden. The 'feeble' travelled in coaches, and the rest walked all escorted by the Lifeboat Band to the theatre. During the interval, oranges were distributed. After the show, they all travelled the same way with the band to the Coffee Palace where they had tea with the Mayor and Mayoress. The Mayoress gave presents of tea to the ladies, tobacco to the men, and sweets for the children. The railway only charged the party a single fare, which the guardians paid out of their own funds.

The chairman remarked at the next meeting, 'It seems a good thing to be an inmate of the Fylde Workhouse.'

Mr Gill added, 'Yes, if you give them treats like that, it will become a popular place.'

Mr Finch counted, 'Oh, but you must not begrudge them a treat.'

To which the chairman replied, 'No, I don't begrudge them; I only meant I was glad they had so many kind friends to treat them. (To the master). You did not take them all, I suppose, but only the young and old and infirm?'

'Yes', replied the master.

On 19 April, a rare thing happened when William Segar Hodgson missed a meeting after his beloved sister died; this was the only meeting he ever missed.

Mr R. Westby of Fleetwood donated two barrels of fish to the workhouse and a number of books from Fleetwood Workman's Club.

At one meeting, Mr Butcher said, 'I am struck at the small number of vagrants who came to the workhouse. When we remember that there is a shipping port in the union, and a pleasure resort, and the dietary of the union had been improved. It seems remarkable that vagrancy should be decreasing.'

The chairman said, 'Plenty of work was found for the tramps, and if the weather was fine, they kept out of the house.'

The board wanted to start sending rheumatic patients to the Devonshire Hospital, Buxton. The clerk reported the hospital charges, two pounds, twelve shillings, and sixpence a patient for a three-week period. If they paid a yearly subscription of one pound and one shilling, they could have one in-patient and four outpatients per year. William Glover, who received outdoor relief in Blackpool, was the first to be admitted into the hospital, suffering from acute rheumatism.

The final Christmas party of the decade saw gifts given by Miss Bradly, Mr Thompson, Henry Langton Birley, Mrs Fitton, Mr Needham, Mr Le Maire, and Mrs Catterall.

The chairman thought they had been more generous this year.

The master said, 'No sir, there were not so many gifts as in the past.'

The chairman, 'There are more names, I think.'

Mr Westby asked if the night went off all right, very well indeed was the reply from the master.

The chairman asked, 'Did they cheer? I see that in one workhouse the old folks refused to cheer because they had no beer.'

Mr Westby replied, 'How could you expect them.'

The master said that it made no difference at this workhouse.

The year ended with Nurse Carr resigning, so she could go and look after her seriously ill mother. The porter asked for a pay rise, and in return, he would instruct the inmates in repairing boots and shoes. He received a raise of three pounds.

1900–1907

At the start of the new century, fifty per cent of the males and twenty-two per cent of the females in the workhouse were over sixty-five years of age. There were thirty-nine children in the workhouse who made up twenty-five per cent of the inmates. When the Unity Government of 1895, was elected, it promised an old aged pension and to remove the children out of workhouses and into children's homes. This promise was never acted upon, if it had, it would of rapidly reduce the number of inmates from one-hundred and fifty-four paupers, down to seventy-five paupers.

The Government remedied this by dividing the aged paupers into two groups, deserving and undeserving. From August that year, outdoor relief was to be granted to all deserving cases of old people to save them having to enter the workhouse. For the ones who entered the workhouse, a new special class was created the 'deserving aged'. They were to have extra dayrooms, where both sexes could live and have their meals, separate sleeping rooms, retiring hours at night, rising hours in the morning, increased personal liberty, greater facilities for being visited by their friends and families, and private lockers with keys kept in their custody. All disreputable aged inmates were to be kept separate. Guardians were also encouraged to provide cottage homes for children, board them out, or have them emigrated.

Outside of the workhouse, three-hundred and ninety-five paupers were receiving outdoor relief. Of these two-hundred and eighty-one, which made up seventy-one per cent, were over the age of sixty-five. In the asylums, there were thirty-three paupers in Lancaster, forty-six in Whittingham, seven in Prestwich, twelve in Rainhill, and five in the workhouse; this was comprised of forty-six males and fifty-seven females, making a total of one-hundred and three people.

The half year call for rates were two and a half pence in the pound, and when the county rate was taken out the rate for poor-relief, it was only one penny in the pound, the lowest rate in the country.

The Fylde's Poor Law Institution had become a haven for children, the old, and the infirm. There were virtually no indoor able-bodied paupers, with this in mind the guardians were reluctant to build the new workhouse, and it was put on hold for another year. Mr W. S. Hodgson again pointed out that it didn't matter how many were in the workhouse, they had to have enough accommodation for six-hundred paupers, one per cent of the Fylde.

In 1899, the laws on vaccinations had changed. Previously people took their children to a vaccination station, but now the doctor went to the person's home. The vaccination fees were set by the guardians, and the Fylde's were set at the lowest scale.

Before the change, the five public vaccinators were paid forty-eight pounds and five shillings for the whole of 1898. During 1899 they received one-hundred and eighty-five pounds, twelve shillings and sixpence, almost four times as much, and the fee for vaccinating went from one shilling and sixpence to six shillings. Despite this increase in costs, the numbers vaccinated increased. In 1898, the percentage of children vaccinated was fifty-four per cent, and in 1899, it was sixty-two per cent.

In February, Miss Howard was appointed the new nurse, but she had to give a month's notice to her present employer so she couldn't start for five weeks. The matron, who had been without help for seven weeks, asked the house committee to appoint the other candidate Miss Newton: which they did. She didn't stay long and was replaced by Miss H. Redfern of Blackpool.

In May, two patients suffering from pneumonia were sent by Dr Buxton from Blackpool to Kirkham. Instead of travelling in an ambulance, they were both sent in a regular cab. They both died in the infirmary. The guardians wrote to Dr Buxton for an explanation.

> Dear Sir,
>
> In answer to your letter of May 17th reference Joseph Conroy and John Bentley deceased, I wish to make the following special report. On Monday, May 7th, last at 3.30 p.m. Mr Dixon the relieving officer, left an order at my house for me to see Joseph Conroy. I was out. At five p.m., I came in and at once went to him. I found him at Peeney's Lodging House, No. 1. Back Chapel Street, sitting up and evidently ill with commencing pneumonia. In my opinion, he was fit to be removed to Kirkham when I saw him. I considered from the condition under which I found him that his only chance

> of recovery consisted in his removal to a suitable institution, where nursing and attention would be provided. The fact that finding him in a chair, instead of being in bed, helped me to come to that decision, in his case.
>
> With reference to John Bentley, the facts are these. On Monday, about eight o'clock, a woman brought me an order marked "ordinary" to visit John Bentley, at No.3 Whiteside Street. She said she wished him removed to Kirkham at once. I pointed out that it was too late to have him removed that evening, but that I would visit him in the morning and decide what was to be done. I accordingly saw him at noon next day May 8th and found him lying in a very poor and dirty bed, with scanty clothing, and in a very neglected condition. He was also suffering from commencing pneumonia, and in my opinion, was fit to be removed; in fact, I may say that I considered in his removal to be healthier and cleaner surrounding.

Dr Buxton explained in his letter the difficulties he faced.

> Both these cases exhibited in a marked degree the difficulties and dangers a district medical officer has to contend with, in removing serious cases from common-lodging-houses, where adequate attention was simply impossible, to a workhouse infirmary that is twelve miles off, and who is handicapped in addition by the fact that the only means of conveyance is a cab. In moving poor law patients to the workhouse infirmary, I may mention two methods are sanctioned by the guardians. In one, patients go by train with or without a cab as the case may require, and in the other, they go in a cab all the way.
>
> Both these men were removed with the greatest care the existing methods afford, and neither of them were in a dying condition when I saw them. Had either of the cases been an 'infectious case' I should have had them removed to the Victoria Hospital, Blackpool, but neither of these institutions were eligible for them. Again, and again I have been asked by friends and relatives and others to remove patients to Kirkham, and have refused owing to their condition. A case

> in point, John Edwards of 40 Rothesay Road, whom I saw on May 5th. His daughter wished him sent to Kirkham, but as he was being well cared for, I refused.

After discussing the case, the guardians asked Blackpool Corporation if they could use their ambulance in such cases. The corporation refused, pointing out that the ambulance was often used five times in one day. This left the guardians with no choice, and a new ambulance was purchased for ninety-five pounds. The green ambulance was ready to be collected from Liverpool by December. The following year, the guardians bought a horse, and a man was employed as a carter.

Some minor alterations were made at the workhouse. The old meat store was converted into the bakery, as the old bakery was too small. A new oven and chimney were built by James Newall of Kirkham for eighty-one pounds. The wall dividing the master's office from the room next door was demolished to make the office bigger. The room could now be used for committee meetings. The new committee room was papered, and a piled carpet was laid. This encouraged one guardian to point out that the old people still slept in wards with bare brick walls and stone flagged floors.

The telephone rates had been reduced, and the workhouse committee thought it would be a good idea to connect the workhouse to the Kirkham Telephone Company system. The master wasn't keen; he thought it would only be used once or twice a year.

In April 1901, after twenty-eight years as chairman and forty years as a guardian, William Segar Hodgson resigned.

Mrs Ashworth led the tribute, 'As one of the first lady members of the board to come to Kirkham, I would like to thank Mr Hodgson on behalf of the ladies for the courtesy and kindness he had always extended to them. When the ladies first decided to come to Kirkham, they were naturally apprehensive of how they would be treated when they arrived here, but Mr Hodgson was quite agreeable to them coming and at all times had treated them with great consideration and courtesy. Without showing them any favour, he had undoubtedly always given them a fair field, and, at the hands of Mr Hodgson, they had received full justice and consideration. He had made their work quite easy, and she was sure all the lady members would regret that they were losing such a valuable colleague.'

Mr Gill was appointed as the new chairman. Mr William Hodgson was elected senior vice-chairman and Mr Finch, the junior vice-chairman. Under section 20 of the local Government act of 1894, non-guardians could be co-opted onto the board. William Segar Hodgson who had vast experience of poor law was co-opted, and then elected chairman of the new workhouse buildings committee.

A year after the new recommendations were implemented for the deserving aged and children, Mr Jenner Fust wanted to know what steps the Fylde Union had taken. The clerk replied:

1. The guardians contemplate building a new workhouse and maintaining the children in cottage homes.

2. The children attend elementary day schools in Kirkham and mix freely with all the other children.

3. Every child sent into service during the past 10 years can be traced, and all are doing well.

4. It is the opinion of the Fylde Guardians that the children are better in the workhouse than in cottage homes.

5. Outdoor relief is granted on its merit to old persons, in some cases as much as 10s. to 12s. outdoor relief is 25% higher than last year.

6. Inside the house, the deserving poor are employed in minor roles and allowed extra rations, tobacco, and leave of absence in their own clothes. We feel if we kept them idle when detained, it would be more of a hardship than a favour to them. Separate old age cubicles will be provided in the new workhouse.

The half-yearly returns on 1 January 1900 showed one-hundred and fifty-four persons in the workhouse and three-hundred and ninety-five receiving outdoor relief. That year on 1 January there were one-hundred and forty-four paupers in the workhouse and four-hundred and seventy-four receiving outdoor relief. This reduction in numbers of indoor-relief and an increase in outdoor relief cases showed that the guardians were implementing the new regime.

The county rate, which was outside the guardian's control, had risen by one-thousand-two-hundred pounds in a year. The finance committee recommended setting this year's rate at one and a half pence in the pound. This amounted to four-thousand, two hundred and seventy-two pounds for poor law purposes and six-thousand-seven-hundred pounds for the county rate, totalling ten-thousand, nine-hundred and seventy-two pounds.

Ellen Krauss fractured her leg and ended up in Blackpool Victoria Hospital for several weeks. Her bones would not join and, as she would be bedridden for the rest of her life, she was removed to the workhouse.

When Ellen entered the workhouse, she had eighty pounds in the London and City Bank. Before the changes made for elderly people last year, this would have been taken away from her and placed in the general fund, but now, as a deserving case, she kept the money and just had to pay seven shillings weekly for her care. The money was taken from her bank periodically by the clerk, who had hold of her bank book.

When Ellen Kraus entered the workhouse, her daughters told the guardians that they could not look after her or contribute to her keep, but they still wanted to know if they could have one pound each that their mother gave them every Christmas. The guardians told the daughters the decision was their mother's.

Paupers in St Annes had to travel between three to five miles to visit the Lytham District Medical Officer. The guardians decided to appoint a new doctor for St Annes on a salary of fifteen pounds, but nobody applied for the post. Some guardians wanted to increase the salary offered, but William Hodgson thought the London board would not sanction it. St Annes was such a wealthy town that the doctor would have hardly any cases.

Clerk Fred Brown listed the district doctors salaries and how many cases they had dealt within the last two weeks.

District	Doctor's Salary	Medical cases for the last two weeks
Fleetwood	£40	9
Kirkham No. 1	£45	4
Kirkham No. 2	£25	2
Lytham	£30	1
Blackpool	£80	36

St Annes came under the Lytham District, which had had only one medical case. The guardians couldn't act, no doctor would work for such a low salary, and there weren't enough cases to warrant an increase in the amount paid. The London Board refused to let them pay more, so a doctor was not appointed.

The workhouse infirmary consisted of general wards, sickness wards, fever wards, and lying-in wards. Medical officer, William Shaw, stated that they had a large number of pulmonary cases in the hospital and that a new ward was needed for 'phthisis', the old term for pulmonary tuberculosis.

Building a new ward was a problem the guardians could do without. The female side of the hospital had been empty for ten out of the last twelve months. Plans were in place for a new infection's hospital for the Fylde at Moss Side, near Wrea Green, and with the new workhouse under consideration, they didn't want to build new wards.

Mrs Ashworth, of the visiting committee, said, 'There was not room in the workhouse fit for consumption cases and, as in the new treatment of these cases sunlight and fresh air were deemed of primary importance, if a new ward was erected, it would have to be built on a certain side of the house.'

The committee reported back in June that they could only find one room suitable, but it was on the upper floor of the male infections ward, so the problem remained concerning the female inmates. The visiting committee recommended building a single-storey wing attached to each end of the large sick wards.

This work was not carried out as, later in the year, the Fylde Isolation Hospital Committee erected a temporary hospital at Elswick. The hospital committee erected a building with twenty-four beds to deal with the infectious diseases from the Fylde, Preston, and Garstang Unions.

The Lancashire Asylums were still constantly full, and non-pauper cases were being sent to Kirkham. Dr Iredale had sent Frederick James from Blackpool to Kirkham. Frederick had been held in the police cells at Blackpool for three days. The doctor felt he had had no choice; the man had evaded his keeper once and molested people in the streets. He was afraid the man might do someone harm.

The master told the guardians. 'There is no proper accommodation in the workhouse for lunatics, but evidently, the medical gentlemen of the district considered there was.'

The man was eventually found a place in an asylum, but it had cost the union three pounds. The chairman thought the only thing they could do in the future was to send the lunatics outside the county.

Religion played an important role when it came to sending children out of the workhouse. Mr Parkinson, a Protestant, asked to take a fifteen years old Catholic boy, George McMullen, out of the workhouse as a servant. Guardian Mr Finch went to the Willows to ask the priest if George could go to Mr Parkinson's. Father Gillows refused to allow the boy to live in a non-catholic's home. The clerk informed the guardians that they were well within their rights to send the boy to Mr Parkinson. They held a vote. They voted seventeen to three to send the boy.

Mr Parkinson, however, withdrew the offer, and George McMullen was sent as a servant to a Mr Dewhurst of Great Eccleston Lodge, who was a Roman Catholic.

Sending a child to live with a person of a different religion was not the worst-case scenario for a child.

In October, two domestic servants Racheal Hope, aged twenty-one, and Agnes Waller, aged twenty-three, who had given birth in the workhouse, left Kirkham for Manchester. When they arrived in Manchester, they left their luggage at the station and went into the city with their children with plans to abandon them.

Rachael Hope left her twins, Charles and Cyril, under a hedge on Manor Street, Ardwick, wrapped in a shawl with a note saying 'Whoever finds these twins, I should like them adopted by some kind lady. They are a fortnight old born on the 1st.'

Albert Waller, aged eleven days, was left at 17 Dover Street Chorlton-cum-Hardy. After being found, all three babies were taken to the infirmary at Withington Workhouse where Charles Hope died from pneumonia and Albert from diarrhoea.

Detective Sergeant Bloomfield, who investigated the crimes, found Rachael working as a servant in Salford and Agnes working in Chorlton. At the inquest, the nurses at the Withington Infirmary said that the babies were well when they entered, and the deaths had nothing to do with exposure.

Withington Workhouse Doctor, Dr Orchard, said that the cause of death for Charles was exhaustion from the convulsions, which were probably set up by the pneumonia, and Albert's death was caused by diarrhoea, which allowed pneumonia to set in.

Summing up the judge said, 'The exposure had nothing to do with the deaths, and because there was no half-way house between a verdict of natural causes and one of manslaughter, they could not go any further.'

The jury returned a verdict of death from natural causes.

At one time, the workhouse could hold two-hundred and sixty paupers, but now that had been reduced to just under two-hundred mainly because married couples over sixty years now slept in private rooms and inmates were forbidden from sharing beds. Although there were only four patients in the infirmary, the body of the workhouse was full. In the workhouse, there were one-hundred and seventy-six paupers with one sleeping in the reception ward. At the end of the year, it was agreed to hold a special meeting the following January about building the new workhouse. The only work carried out at the Wesham site was extending the boundary wall to the north-west corner of the land. The southern boundary was sealed with a wooden fence, and four-hundred yards of tubular fencing sealed off the other boundaries.

At a special meeting, in January 1902, the chairman, Mr Gill, gave an overview of the reasons for the new workhouse.

He said, 'Four or five years ago, owing to the numbers in the house, and the local board inspectors report, that the Fylde Board of Guardians must provide more accommodation or add to the house. They had plans for a new boardroom and endeavoured to buy more land adjoining the present house. The price and restrictions were such, however, that the land did not meet with their requirements. The late chairman, with his usual foresight, bought from various landowners some 23 acres of land at Wesham for a little over £3,000, the same land today would cost £6000. The land is now paid for, and plans had been decided upon and passed by the Local Government Board.'

Adding, 'The building of the house was deferred, however, owing to the high price of material, and the small number of inmates in the house, and the prospects of an old age pension. Lately, the local government board inspector and some guardians had complained about the accommodation. We cannot alter the plans without going again to the local board. In my opinion, the plans seemed to be a very complete arrangement, and the building, if required, could be enlarged at very little expense or trouble. There was accommodation for 304 inmates. The accommodation for the staff was large. The reason for that, was the Local Government Board insisted on a certain size for a certain number of the population, but they need not staff it fully, even if they build so large an accommodation.'

Finally, he said, 'The rate, from what he could gather, would, at the present time, not exceed ½d in the pound over what they were now paying, and after spending all the money he did not think it would exceed a halfpenny in the pound. Blackpool would have to find about £1,500 a year and the other portion of the union £1,300. It was not a big rate for a place like Blackpool, where a penny in the pound produced something like £2,000, and I don't think Blackpool people need complain. At the moment, building material is cheap, and there would be fair competition if the work commenced at once. The site is a fine and suitable one, and the building would have a south aspect and be near the main road.'

Some guardians thought that they should only build the boardroom and the infirmary, which would free up space at the Kirkham site. However, the government inspector at the meeting thought this would increase the costs, as they would have to have twice as many staff.

Mr Westby asked what accommodation would be provided for married couples.

To which W. S. Hodgson replied, 'For the last forty years, there has not been more than one couple in the house who would live together when they came in. Most of them said they had had enough of one another outside.'

After further discussion, the guardians voted twenty to seven to start building the new workhouse. It was to have seven main blocks, several smaller ones, and an infirmary which could hold one-hundred and two patients. The new building was planned to cost forty-three-thousand, nine-hundred and ninety-four pounds, with furnishing raising it to fifty-thousand pounds. Provisions would be made to hold three-hundred inmates but no children.

The materials used were to be the best quality. Dressed with Accrington pressed brick, with facings of terracotta and stone. Glazed bricks would be used in the dining hall and various other parts of the interior.

The guardians, even with the loan for the new workhouse, had the poor rates under control. The county rates, however, continued to increase. The guardians, according to the chairman, had no choice but to smile and pay. For the first half of the financial year, the council asked for seven-thousand six-hundred and ninety-six pounds an increase on last year's rate, which was six-thousand, six-hundred, and ninety-five pounds. The finance committee reported that the rateable value of the union was seven-hundred and forty-thousand pounds, seven hundred and twenty-five pounds. The one and a half penny rate, required for union purposes, brought in four-thousand, six-hundred, and twenty-nine pounds, and the rate for county purposes, which was four pence, released about eight-thousand pounds.

1902 was the year of King Edward VII's Coronation, and the guardians celebrated it by decorating the workhouse. The inmates were given a meal, similar to the Christmas dinner, and the master hired a Punch and Judy show for the children. Afterwards, the inmates were taken for a two-hour drive in the country-side in chartered conveyances. The outdoor paupers were given a double allowance of relief to celebrate.

The number in the asylums in June were as follows: Lancaster had thirty-eight, Whittingham had fifty-one, Rainhill had three, Prestwich had thirteen, and Winwick had eleven. Mr Crossfield proposed that a deputation should visit the five asylums that the Fylde now used. Mr W. S. Hodgson pointed out that an allowance was permitted for a first-class railway ticket and fifty-seven shillings and sixpence for food for three members to visit each asylum. Anything above that would have to come out of the pockets of the guardians.

The guardians were split on asylum visits. The auditor thought the visits were more about pleasure than business. Mr W. Hodgson thought if they were started again, the numbers visiting should be controlled and the costs detailed more fully. Mr Dickinson thought they were a waste of time, while Mrs Ashworth thought that the visits were essential, and that it was not right to be content with the official's reports only. A delegation was not sent.

The guardians later held a discussion about the Poor-Law-Conference which was being held at Preston the following week.

Mr Westby said, 'I notice the three delegates appointed had all been to previous conferences. I had been to one in 1895, and I must say it was one of the best picnics I had ever been to. They easily surpass the visits to the asylums. There is, however, no benefit to receive from them, at any rate, I did not learn anything.'

Mrs Ashworth was one of the guardians appointed to attend the conference.

Mrs Ashworth said, 'I have attended previous conferences and had paid my own expenses when not a delegate. I remember the conference alluded to, but it was not a picnic to me, as I went straight to the meetings and straight home again.'

The guardians decided to board out a boy called Clarkson to a joiner and builder, Mr Ainsworth of Blackpool, who would contribute five shillings a week towards his pay until he was sixteen. The builder then decided not to take the boy unless he was bound apprentice, which Mr Westby disagreed with. Mr Westby was himself a builder and had offered to take the lad earlier in the year without him being bound, but, because the boy wasn't fourteen, he couldn't take him.

Mr Westby said, 'I do not object to the boy learning a trade, far from it, but I object to the £20 premium. People had taken boys from the house to teach them a trade, and all that had been necessary was to pay the boy's 3d. a week pocket money, and to put 9d. weekly in the bank. If we paid the premium, more boys would be put in the house.'

The chairman said, 'This is an exceptional case as the lad was exceptionally smart, and we should give him a chance to become a respectable citizen. He was without father or mother, and it was the duty of the guardians to do the best they could for him. We would be justified in paying a premium and make the lad into a good citizen, rather than he did become a tramp.'

Wesham ratepayer, Mr E. Kent of Garstang Road, wrote to the guardians, saying, 'I, as a property owner, and having a large family to support, think it a shame that I should have to help to give another man's child a trade when I cannot afford to give my own children one.'

Chairman, Mr Gill, disagreed saying, 'It sounds strange to me that a union only paying 8½d. in the pound for in and outdoor relief, the lowest in England, could not afford £20 in order to make a boy a respectable citizen. We have very few children in the workhouse, and we ought to do the very best we could for them. At Rochdale, the children cost from 12s. to 20s. per week, whereas the paying of the premium of £20 would only mean about 4s. 6d. a week. If we send the boy on a training ship, they would have to pay 5s. a week. Do you not think that with the few children they had, was it not the wisest thing to do the best they could for them. The lad was going to a good home, and the guardians would probably someday have him coming back and telling them he thanked them for what they had done for him."

The guardians voted seventeen for, to fifteen against and the boy was apprenticed for twenty pounds.

Arthur Mellor from Wakefield left his three children in the workhouse after his wife died. Later, he refused to pay their maintenance or take them out of the workhouse and a warrant for his arrest was issued. On the 6th of August, he was arrested and sentenced to twenty-one days' hard labour at Lytham Court. When he was released, he went to Blackpool and again left his children in the workhouse. He was re-arrested and again jailed.

In October, Mr E. Lodge Solicitor of London wrote to the guardians saying the children's mother had left an estate of two-hundred and twenty-five pounds. After the maintenance costs were paid from this legacy, the father was released from prison. A month later, the children were still in the workhouse. The father was, according to the mother's solicitor, living a vagrant's life in Blackpool and was not fit to have the children.

The guardians acted.

They resolved that under the provisions of Section 1 of Chapter 56, of the Poor Law Act of 1889, the children would be placed under the control of the guardians until such time the children attain the ages of sixteen years, as their father had deserted them.

The children left the workhouse, early the following year. Edith Mellor, thirteen years, was sent to live with a Mr Clarke at Dickson Road, Blackpool. Reginald, aged seven years old, and Kathleen, aged five years old, both went to live with a Mr Wormald at Westgate Common, Wakefield.

The numbers in the house were beginning to go down. There were one-hundred and thirty-three inmates compared to last September's figure of one-hundred and forty-eight, but the building of the new workhouse still went ahead. The clerk advertised for tenders to start building the workhouse which had to be sent in for the 1st of October. There had been a few alterations, and the cost of the new workhouse was now forty-six-thousand pounds. The guardians had permission to borrow up to fifty-one-thousand pounds by the Local Government Board and the architects, Heywood and Harrison of Accrington and Lytham, were appointed.

Mr Wilson was appointed the main contractor who would do the brickwork, excavating, and joinery. A. Pollard of South Shore would cover masonry; Mellows and Co., Sheffield, would fit the plumbing and glazing; Edward Walsh, Accrington, would do the slating; James Watt, St Annes the plastering; and Oldfield, St Annes, the painting. Some outdoor paupers were put to work draining and levelling the land.

The bricks were still being made on the site, twenty-thousand in total, and the guardians set a rate of two shillings per thousand bricks to pay for the cost of filling the clay pits, levelling out the brickmaking area, and making the land fit for agricultural use.

Almost ninety inmates, mainly children, were taken on a trip to Blackpool in September. The group travelled by tram from Blackpool to Fleetwood and spent an hour sailing on the ship 'Pioneer'. Before returning to Blackpool, they were given refreshments in the tram waiting room. Later in the day, they all had a meal in Messers Clark and Heaps, Coffee Palace.

Afterwards, they visited the Winter Gardens, and the elderly paupers had a ride on a roller coaster. The 'Les Montagues Russes' an early French roller coaster, set up in the Italian Gardens. It took the older people for a ride in a car at speeds of up to twenty miles per hour. The elderly people, who had all survived the ride and the children had an evening meal at the Station Coffee Palace, before returning to Kirkham at eight o'clock.

At the end of the year, the clerk reported that there was a woman in the workhouse who weighed thirty-five stones, and the chairman asked if she had been sent out of the workhouse. The clerk reported that she was ill and could not be removed.

One guardian replied, 'No wonder.'

The year 1903 started with the death of the Master, John Osborne Trickey. Two months earlier, he had been diagnosed as suffering from Bright's disease, but couldn't act on Dr Shaw's advice and take a sea trip. On 18 December, he had a paralytic stroke; under the care of Dr Shaw, he regained his speech and use of his limbs. On 15 January, when it looked like he would make a full recovery, he suddenly died from heart failure.

Born in London in 1856, he was educated at Torquay Grammar School. At fifteen, his father bound him apprentice to the merchant navy for five years. He served on a private yacht and later as fourth officer on a P&O boat working between India and China. After getting married, he retired from a seafaring life and took a position at Lancaster Castle Prison. He had become chief warder by the time he left for the Fylde Union Workhouse, where he worked for fourteen years until his death.

Mrs Trickey hadn't worked long enough for the union to receive a pension, so she stayed on as matron. Porter John Fowler was promoted to master and his wife to assistant matron. The guardians then advertised for a new porter and portress.

Twelve people applied for the role of porter and portress, and four were selected for interviews: James and Margaret Howard of Preston; George and Amie Graves of Blackpool; Henry and Margaret Turner of Fulwood; and Francis and Elizabeth Hudson of Kirkham. Mr and Mrs Howard were appointed, with salaries of twenty-pounds and sixteen pounds respectively, complete with furnished apartments and uniforms.

Mr W.S. Hodgson, Chairman of the New Workhouse Buildings Committee, reported that there should be sufficient water on the site for the requirements of the house. The matron had tested it for washing and found it was satisfactory. If the water were also found to be suitable for cooking purposes, they would draw the supply of water from the land and not use Fylde Water's supply. John Nickson of Kirkham was appointed clerk of the works for the new workhouse, and the first tranche of the loan was taken out of fifteen-thousand pounds from the Public Works Loan Board at a repayment rate of three and a quarter pence.

The foundation stones of polished grey Aberdeen granite were laid in July. The first by Mr Gill, bearing the following inscription, 'This stone was laid on the 2nd July 1903, by John Gill, Chairman of the Board, 1901–1903, Guardian twenty-six years.'

The second stone was laid by the ex-chairman, Mr W.S. Hodgson, and was inscribed as follows: 'This stone was laid on the 2nd July 1903 by Mr William Segar Hodgson J.P. Chairman of the Board of the Guardians, 1875-1901, guardian forty-three years.'

The future Master and Matron Edwin and Emily Perry at the main entrance 1907.

Afterwards, the guardians had refreshments in a marquee. Mementos of silver trowels and mallets were presented to both men.

By this point, the forty bricklayers on the site had built the administrative block, which just needed to be roofed. The female block had reached the first floor, and the foundations for the men's block and the married couples' block had been laid.

The half-yearly Lancashire County Council rate was increased by five-hundred pounds to eight-thousand-five-hundred pounds, and the amount for poor law was five-thousand-five-hundred pounds. After the Balfour Act was passed, the school penny was abolished, and the county council funded education through the rates. Another three-thousand, three-hundred and seventy-five pounds in rates were raised for educational purposes. All the townships contributed apart from Blackpool, who had its own education authority.

Mr Bradly wanted to know if Ribby-with-Wrea should be exempt from the rate because they had a free school. The clerk said that all townships, except Blackpool, should pay the three pence rate, and if any township benefited from a trust or fund, they would be credited with that amount from Lancashire County Council.

Mr Jenner Fust visited the workhouse and suggested more help for the nurse who had thirty-six patients in the infirmary including three in the lying-in wards and one case of cancer, Jane Wolfedice, who had been treated in the Manchester Cancer Hospital. Also, in future, to help prevent the spread of smallpox all tramps entering the workhouse were to be bathed, have their clothes disinfected, and undergo a medical examination.

The guardians decided to appoint Mr Hallsworth as a visiting dentist for a salary of ten guineas. The clerk reported he made his first visit in August, and some children wished he hadn't. The dentist said that the teeth of the children were in a bad condition, and it was necessary to extract eighteen teeth and fill four. The dentist recommended that the children be provided with toothbrushes and shown how to use them.

After the dentist's visit, the children could look forward to the annual trip to the seaside. This year's trip was to St Annes. The auditor allowed two shillings and sixpence per inmate for the trip on waggonettes to the resort.

The number of people receiving indoor relief on 1 July that year was one-hundred and forty-one, the same number as last year. The number receiving outdoor relief, on the same date, was four-hundred and thirty. These numbers had been static for years, but the numbers in the asylums continued to climb.

On 1 July, it was recorded that there were one-hundred and thirty-two patients of the Fylde in the asylums compared with one-hundred and sixteen the previous years. Throughout the country, the number in the asylums had increased by three-thousand. According to the chairman, out of the ten-thousand in the asylums, only two-hundred and ninety-three were lunatics, the rest were in the asylums because of the amount of alcohol they drank.

The Reverend W. T. Mitton, Vicar of Kirkham, wrote to the guardians saying: 'We are going to dispose of our old hearse, and if the guardians would like to have it as a gift, they are welcome.'

One guardian proposed they should accept it, and another suggested that it should go into a museum, and a third asked if it would collapse under the weight of a corpse. The matter was passed to the house committee. They declined the vicar's offer.

The guardians weren't always sympathetic to people's request for help.

Three men asked the guardians to provide work for them so that they could maintain their families. Mr Blundell moved that they should put them to work breaking stones at ten shillings per week.

Mr Bradley disagreed saying, 'The best thing to do with some of the men who applied for such relief, would be to shoot them. The offspring followed in their footsteps. If we give them 10s. per week and not very much work the men would come, but if they were found plenty to do, they would soon be missing.'

The matter was passed to the workhouse committee.

By January 1904, the one-hundred men employed at the new workhouse had built and roofed the four main blocks. The foundations for the boardroom, infirmary, and vagrant's block had not been started, but the foundations for the laundry and bakehouse were finished. The highest part of the new workhouse was above Weeton reservoir. Enough pressure would not be available for the new fire system, so a water tower was built costing an extra one-thousand-five-hundred pounds. The guardians also borrowed an extra one-thousand-five-hundred pounds for the boiler and heating apparatus.

In April, Mr William Hodgson was elected chairman for the first time, his cousin and former chairman, Mr William Segar Hodgson, was again co-opted onto the board and stayed as chairman of the new workhouse buildings committee.

The Fylde was going through an economic distress and, in February, the workhouse was nearly full with one-hundred and ninety-three inmates. In Blackpool, there was a lot of desertion cases, both husbands leaving their wives and wives leaving their husbands. The guardians began looking into the cases in more detail to see if the parties were colluding to defraud the union.

Extra work was found in Blackpool for the able-bodied by labouring on the Blackpool Promenade extension program. In the workhouse, the men had gone from breaking stones to breaking Haslington Flag, which was used to make the setts for road making. These setts were smoother than stones, but the horses struggled to grip on them. Crushing sandstone was another way of keeping the paupers busy. Able-bodied female inmates, by law, couldn't be employed breaking stones, but they could be employed crushing sandstone.

Lancashire County Council, despite the struggling economy, again increased the amount they needed, in September, by five-thousand pounds to eighteen-thousand, one-hundred and forty-seven pounds. This figure didn't include the poor rate. The council spent the money on Elementary and Higher Education, Kirkham Police Division, Preston Sessions, Amounderness Hundred Bridges and Amounderness Main Roads.

The call in the pound was now ten pence. Broken down it was eight pence in the pound for the county rate and two pence for the poor rate. The guardians had two members on the county council and asked for an extra representative on the council, to gain more influence and reign in the council's spending, which they thought was too excessive. The request was declined.

Mr Jenner Fust reported on his inspection of the workhouse.

He said, 'The vagrant wards are in wings, and if the main building was on fire or full of smoke there was no escape from the cells. I suggest you put a door at the end of each of the vagrant wards to facilitate escape. It would only be a small expense and worth doing. As to the fastenings of the cell doors, the board advised that locks and keys should not be used. The main reason was that, apart from any question of legality of locking the doors, in case of fire it took some time for a man to go to each cell, and fit a key to the door and open it. If they simply had a draw-back bolt, it would be much easier. The present method of fastening at the workhouse consisted of a bolt at the top and bottom. The latter was hardly any use, and it would be more convenient if the ones at the top were brought down about halfway. It would be more easily opened, and there would be no expense in making the alterations.'

He continued, 'The last time I was here, I asked that the medical officer should be instructed to inspect, at regular intervals, all the children, with a view to seeing that they were in good health and not requiring any of his care. I am glad to see that the suggestion was adopted. I am also glad to see that the workhouse committee have made improvements in the way dinner is served to the children and the old people'

They now used calico for tablecloths.

Regarding pauperism on the Fylde, he said, 'You have not been quite free from the increase which has been general throughout the country. Your pauperism was always extremely low but still showed an increase. It's eight per thousand of the population against seven per thousand on the 1st of January of last year, against an average of six per thousand for the previous five years.'

Last year's figures could be broken down into districts.

On September the 1st last year, the Kirkham District had a population of twenty-four-thousand, two-hundred, and seventy-nine, of which there were one-hundred and thirteen paupers, including forty-four children, either in the workhouse or receiving outdoor relief. This represented four point six per thousand of the population.

In Blackpool, the population was fifty-thousand, five-hundred, and thirty-three, there were two-hundred paupers, including ninety-six children a rate of four point one per thousand. Fleetwood, with a population of eighteen-thousand, eight-hundred, and eighty-five, had eighty paupers, including forty children, a rate of four point two. The total number of paupers in the three districts was four-hundred and three, including one-hundred and eighty children. In the workhouse there were one-hundred and fifty-four paupers, the number of children under sixteen years being thirty-eight.

The Committee in Lunacy reported on a visit to the workhouse.

There were three men and six women in the workhouse, who were classed as lunatics, but they were all cases that could be treated in the workhouse. The dietary was adequate, and the arrangement for employing the patients were satisfactory. The day room was very cheerless, and the accommodation of the workhouse was inadequate.

It was decided to split the Blackpool Medical District into two wards: north and south. The existing doctor, Dr Butcher, was made medical officer for the north ward and an advert was placed for a doctor for the south ward. Dr Merrell was appointed medical officer for the south ward on a salary of forty pounds, plus vaccination fees.

The pauper children were protected by the union. In the days before social services, the guardians worked closely with the N.S.P.C.C. and the courts. In that year, a case of child neglect came to Kirkham Court, before the former chairman and judge, Mr W. S. Hodgson, who used his experience in both roles to attain the best outcome for the family.

Grace Entwistle was brought before the magistrates at Kirkham Petty Sessions for neglecting her three children: James, aged twelve; Elizabeth, aged eleven; and Grace, aged four. Inspector Kingwell of the N.S.P.C.C found the children living with their mother in the front room of a house on New Row, Kirkham; the father was missing.

In court, the inspector said, 'The room in which they lived gave forth an abominable stench, and the bed on which they slept was absolutely rotten with filth, while the only covering they had was a wet sack. The children were in a pitiable condition. Their heads were literally being eaten by vermin. The girl, Elizabeth, looked as if a poultice of scabs had been placed on her head; this was caused through vermin bites. I requested the mother to go into the workhouse along with the children, but she declined. After threatening to take the children from her and have her locked up, she consented to go into the workhouse. She left the workhouse after a few weeks, and I later found the children in a house devoid of any furniture and sleeping on stone flags. The children were again covered in vermin and were taken back to the workhouse.'

Judge, W. S. Hodgson, told Grace Entwistle, that he would send her to prison, but if she went back to the workhouse with the children, they would adjourn the case to which the mother agreed. The court then issued a warrant for the father's arrest for neglecting his family.

The guardians did their best to represent the poor and the ratepayers. However, the female guardians were best at representing the children and women paupers. That year a nurse and suffragette, Mary Johnson, was elected as a guardian, and, from day one, made her views known.

She complained about the children in the house, some of whom had ringworm and had been going out of the workhouse and mixing with other children. She said that at one time there was only one hairbrush, which would account for cases spreading. They were not fit to go to school; in fact, one girl was not fit for the union. The matter was referred to the house committee.

At the end of the year, the numbers in the workhouse were still high with one-hundred and eighty-three inmates.

On New Year's Day 1905, Mr Fielding and his party gave the inmates a 'capital nights' entertainment, consisting of songs and recitations. The adult inmates were given gifts of tobacco, pipes, cups and saucers, and stockings. The children were given toys.

After twenty-eight years-service, Mr Gill was presented with a self-portrait. Mr William Hodgson, at the ceremony, talked a bit abought the changes on the Fylde since 1878.

He said, 'When Mr Gill was appointed, there were only five members elected from Blackpool, and today there were 16. The population of the union then was 30,000, and now it's over 100,000; the population of Blackpool was 7,092, and now it's over 50,000. The rateable value of the union has risen from £249,920 to £848,145, and the rateable value of Blackpool from £82,274 to £460,310.'

The call for the second half of the year was the biggest the union had ever had: sixpence in the pound for county education expenses; sixpence in the pound for other county council expenditure; and three pence in the pound for poor-law purposes. This gave a rate for the entire year of two shilling sixpence, paid in two instalments of one shilling and three pence.

The clerk stated that the sixpence rate for twelve months poor law was higher because the union needed a surplus in the bank. In 1898, the Guardians had six-thousand pounds in the bank; in 1900/01 over seven-thousand pounds; 1902, six thousand pounds; 1903, eight thousand, two-hundred, and twenty-one; and in 1904, two thousand, seven hundred, and seven pounds. At this present time in March, they had nothing at all.

He added, 'I am providing for a balance of at least £2,000 to stand as credit for the board 12 months hence. Then we have to provide £2,500 loan and interest payments on the new workhouse and £4,600 for lunatics in the asylums.'

Rates were paid by homeowners, businesses, and landowners. The Fylde was still a rural place despite the growth along the coasts. In April, after seven new guardians had been elected onto the assessment committee one of them, Mr H. Crossfield, talked about the imbalance of the land rates aiming his remarks at the Blackpool Guardians.

He said, 'There ought to be some means of fixing a comparative value. As an instance of the irregularity, the village I represent, Freckleton, had a rateable value per statue acre of £1 14s. 7d, Warton's value was £1 13s. 9d, Clifton £1 13s.1d, Lytham was rated at £1 2s. 4d. The value of Newton-with-Scales was £1 2s. 4d. and across a lane was Salwick at £1 10s. 9¼d. The most ridiculous of all was the valuation of Treales, Roseacre, and Wharles at 18s. 9d. Medlar-with-Wesham, with a railway to boot, was £1 0s. 8d. Kirkham's rateable value was £1 13s. 11½d, and Blackpool's £1 10s. 2½d. They had a foreshore too and it's not rated at all; before long, they would be letting fresh air. Fleetwood which used to be a rabbit warren and appeared to be one still, its land had a value of 13s.

11½d. per acre and Marton nearly drowned in water and affording special facilities for ducks to swim all over the moss was £1 13s. 8d. I have come to the conclusion something was out of joint. I want an assessment committee of sensible men, who would stand fair and square and act fearlessly.'

Mr Bradley disputed his figures because he hadn't included buildings. The matter was passed to the assessment committee to deal with.

Mr Jenner Fust inspected the workhouse.

He said, 'The means of escape in case of fire were not all that could be wished. The fastenings on the cells of the vagrant's ward, I am glad to see had been altered. There was now an escape door from the end of the corridor on the main side, but there should be a second key. On the female side, there was only one key to the door, and although this was supposed to be continually in the lock, it occasionally got removed. I suggest there should be another key under glass fastened against the door.'

He continued, 'There is, on the upper floor, a canvas shoot which one hoped would be found useful if a fire should occur, but in order that it might be used to the best advantage there should be occasional trials. I would suggest that, at regular intervals, it should be thrown out of the window and anyone who felt inclined might try the experiment. I have known instances were these shoots had been used in the manner I suggest, and the master and matron had set a very good example by going down the shoot, to show how they should be used. If you only got the children to amuse themselves, in that way, it would do a great deal of good.'

There were lots of problems with the old workhouse building, but the inspector didn't worry too much about them, as the new house was in the process of being built. Some other points were, however, mentioned by him which could be remedied without out too much cost.

He said, 'The bathroom attached to the receiving wards on the female side of the house is very dark. The windows were not large and, having been painted a dark brown colour, allowed very little light in. The medical officer has 33 patients to look after, ten in beds, a lying-in-case, two locked cases (lunatics), and a bad cancer case. You still only have one nurse, and I still hold the opinion that you should strengthen the nursing staff.'

The two points were passed to the house committee.

A boy, who had lived in St Annes with his parents, both of whom had just died, was sent to Penrith to live with his grandmother. It was the mother's last request that this should happen, and the boy was happy living with his grandma. The problem was that the Fylde Guardians had abolished non-residential relief and refused to pay the four shillings outdoor relief for the boy.

The Penrith relieving officer said, 'I'm glad the Penrith Guardians adopted a better policy. They considered every case on its merits and were not bound down by resolutions. If the Guardians of the Fylde Union were humane and intelligent men, they would reconsider their decision.'

The motion banning non-resident relief was passed in 1877, and another case was brought before the guardians in December. Mr Laycock wanted it rescinded after a seventy-six-year-old lady living in Blackpool, but having settlement in Burnley, was refused three shillings weekly relief. He also pointed out that a circular in 1900 was issued by the Government not to encourage persons over sixty years of age to enter the workhouse, but their action, in this case, was contrary to the spirit of that circular.

Kirkham Vicar, Reverend Mitton, said, 'Blackpool was a nice place to live, and if they granted relief in one case, there would be a lot of people wanting to live there on the same terms. I appeal to members to look on this matter from the standpoint of a business principle. It would be a dangerous thing to abolish this rule.'

Mr Laycock's request was lost with only seven guardians voting for it.

The number of children dying in the union, during the early 1900s was higher than usual, but no single reason was attributed.

Year	Children born in the union	Number of children's deaths	Percentage
1902	1,323	120	9.0%
1903	1,299	122	9.4%
1904	1,192	127	10.7%

On 31 October, the Annual North-Western Poor Law Conference was held at Southport. Usually, the guardians weren't interested, but that year eight members wanted to go. Only three were allowed to have their expenses covered by the auditor. Messers Richardson, Laycock, and Westby were elected to go on behalf of the union. Miss Johnson, Mrs Webber, Mrs Scott, Mr Gill, and Mr Kemp paid their own way to the conference.

1905's conference covered three main points: transferring the control of vagrants from the guardians to the police; underfed children attending schools; and the diet in workhouse infirmaries. The Fylde had vagrancy under control, but in other parts of Lancashire, it was not so.

Mr Leach of Rochdale talked about the problem at the conference.

He said, 'In my union alone, there was no fewer than twenty thousand tramps to be dealt with last year. The idea that the majority of such people are old and unable to work was exploded by Dr Rhodes analysis of cases of the Chorlton Union. Dr Rhode found that only three tramps out of a thousand were over sixty years of age, while over six hundred and fifty were between the ages of twenty and fifty. Sixty per cent are from the prosperous counties Lancashire and Cheshire; twenty per cent from Manchester alone [Lancashire and Cheshire were the only counties in the country not in recession]. Wales and Scotland together only contribute six per cent, but Ireland is accountable for sixteen per cent.'

Some delegates wanted forced emigration, whereas some wanted to create labour and farm colonies to hold the vagrants in. The government inspector Jenner Fust was at the conference, and he didn't think passing the problem to the police would create greater uniformity by handing over the management of tramps. The motion was defeated. The motion for providing free meals to children was also defeated. The general view was if you feed them breakfast and then dinner, the parents would be left with more money to spend on drink. Most guardians thought that nearly all pauperism was caused through drink.

Miss Johnson talked about the conference at the board meeting.

She said, 'You would think they were signing the treaty of peace between Japan and Russia. First, one delegate jumps and says if the word 'the', 'and' or 'which' is omitted or knocked out, then I would support it. One thing I admired was the way guardians jumped up immediately as the papers were read. The evils mentioned never existed in their unions. According to Father Roach's paper on 'administration of union infirmaries and nursing in workhouses' better treatment was meted out to the inmate in prison hospitals than in their own infirmaries. I hope that when the new house was occupied, the nursing would be on a par with the building.'

In November, Mr Westby mentioned that there was nearly a waggon load of old iron sitting about the workhouse, and seeing that the market for this was rising, he thought, as a businessman, it would be better to sell it. The harness, 'had never had a brush upon it' since the death of the late master and it was no use lying about. If they had a cob, they might get one too large for the harness.

Mr Crossfield reminded him that before old iron, harnesses, or even cabbage leaves are sold, the matter must be brought before the board, or some members will be selling the workhouse next. They did, however, sell the workhouse pigs.

Near Christmas, Miss Johnson brought forward a motion on behalf of the Lytham Branch of the British Women's Temperance Association, asking the guardians not to supply the inmates of the workhouse with beer at Christmas. The clerk remarked that it had been twenty years since they last supplied the inmates with beer, but Mr Bradley said that they would not refuse any beer if it were sent in.

For Christmas, the inmates had the usual meal of roast beef and plum pudding. The matron had made twenty-five plum puddings which weighed nine pounds each. Nineteen of the plum puddings were consumed – an average of about one pound of pudding, per head, including the sick and the children. A man called Bob Heatley, aged seventy years, died from heart failure two days after the boxing day meal.

Miss Johnson told the story, 'One of the old men had died from over-eating. I have been in a great many workhouses but had never heard of the guardians killing anybody by feeding them too well. The old man in question had been in the hospital a great many weeks but pleaded with the doctor to be allowed to partake of the Christmas dinner. After having a second helping of pudding, he died, but he died happy.'

He had had no sympathy from the guardians, who found Miss Johnson's story hilarious. Bob Heatley was buried in St Michaels Graveyard on 30 December.

The guardians received a letter in 1906 from the Union of St Giles, Camberwell, requesting support in repealing the Vaccination Act, which was becoming unpopular as smallpox outbreaks were becoming rare and the high vaccination costs. Smallpox vaccinations had been compulsory since 1853.

There were four main clauses to the circular:

> 1. That the Local Government Board be requested to take steps, at an early date to promote legislation for the repeal of the compulsory vaccination.

The Fylde Guardians were against this clause. The Fylde was reliant on tourism, and they thought an outbreak of smallpox in the resorts would be a financial disaster for the area.

> 2. That they be asked to take steps to promote legislation to place vaccination officers under the entire control of the guardians, and thereon that such officers do not institute proceedings for non-compliance with the Vaccination Acts, without the consent of the guardians.

The Fylde Guardians agreed with this clause. Due to the costs involved with vaccinations, the guardians felt they should have the oversight and control over it, and not the magistrates.

> 3. That the payment of both public vaccinators officers be by salary and the fee system abolished.

They agreed to this as they could pay an officer a salary of five-hundred pounds, to do nothing but vaccinate people, making it cheaper than the fee system which cost seven-hundred and fifty pounds the previous year.

> 4. That longer time be given to conscientious objectors in which to apply for exemption certificates, and that the means of obtaining such certificates be simplified by providing for conscientious objectors, making a statutory declaration

> before a justice of the peace, and for forwarding the same to the vaccination officer.

The guardians were against this clause.

The clerk explained why, 'This recommendation really meant that all a man need do, was to make a declaration before a magistrate that he was a conscientious objector, and then take it to a vaccination officer who would give a certificate. At present, if a man wanted a certificate, he had to appeal before two justices in a court.'

Only the father could apply for his family as a conscientious objector, except in the cases of widows and single mothers.

Despite all the talk about the smallpox vaccinations, the local board inspector mentioned to the guardians that there were eleven cases of unvaccinated children in the workhouse, some of whom had been there over two years. It transpired that members of the visiting committee had signed in the visitor's book that there were no cases of unvaccinated children.

The chairman said that it was a case of serious neglect on the part of somebody, but he thought the chief responsibility rested on the workhouse master. All the children were vaccinated by Dr Weeton, and safeguards to prevent it from happening again were put into place.

Old people could now keep any money they had when entering the workhouse. However, the able-bodied still had to hand any money over to the master, who placed the entire amount in the common fund.

In January, a woman entered the workhouse with thirty shillings in her possession, and the following month a man entered with ten shillings. This incident started a conversation about whether it was right that they should be entering with that amount of money because, in theory, they were not destitute, and how much should be taken from them.

Miss Johnston ask the chairman if he was aware that criminals, whilst undergoing periods of incarceration, were allowed to earn money.

To which Mr Hodgson replied, 'I am not a prison authority, you'd better ask them.'

Miss Johnson said, 'Suppose a man who is imprisoned for begging and has some money in his possession. What had he to do when he comes out?'

Mr Crossfield answered, 'Stop out of prison and spend it.'

Miss Johnson, 'Yes, but what if he comes out of prison with no money in his pockets.'

A guardian, 'Come here.'

Miss Johnson, 'I think something ought to be done in the matter. At least a little money might be given to a sick man or woman on leaving the workhouse hospital. Of course, they don't want to come here and have a good time.'

Chairman William Hodgson ended the conversation by telling Miss Johnson, 'The best thing you could do is give notice of motion of some resolution, and then the question can be considered properly.'

The finance committee announced that the rateable value of the union was three-hundred-and-twenty-four-thousand, four-hundred, and forty-eight pounds, on which a penny in the pound released three-thousand, four-hundred, and thirty-five pounds. The estimated expenditure for the next six months for poor law was eight-thousand pounds. In addition, eighteen-thousand pounds would be required for county council purposes. The committee recommended a call of two pence in the pound for poor law and ten and three-quarter pence in the pound for county council purposes, seven pence out of the county rate was solely for education. The call was, however, still the lowest in the country.

Mr Jenner Fust inspected the workhouse.

He said, 'I'm glad that the workhouse would be ready shortly for occupation. The old one could scarcely earn any praise from me. I have nothing to complain of, with the exception that I found some of the boy's beds had not been made properly. You have a number of boys attending school, and they seemed to me to be an uncommonly poor set. The general impression they left on my mind was that a number of them required special treatment, inasmuch as they seemed to be mentally deficient. I think it advisable that they should be given special training; otherwise, they might become a charge on the rates for the rest of their lives. I say this not only from feelings of kindness towards the children but also on the point of economy in order that if possible, the children might be made self-supporting in after-life.'

The workhouse committee recommended employing a trained nurse on a salary of twenty-five pounds to assist the current nurse. Miss Johnson thought they should reconsider. She could not understand how they were going to get a trained nurse for such a low salary.

She added, 'Seventeen years ago, when I came out of training school, I received £30 a year at my first appointment, and in view of the different character of nurses nowadays I think £25 was far too little. Further, I do not see how the thing was going to work satisfactory, for the present nurse who was untrained received £30 a year. I do not object to a trained nurse being appointed, for the place now was badly in need of reorganisation.'

Mr Jenner Fust supported the recommendation of the workhouse committee to employ an extra trained nurse.

He said, 'On more than one occasion, I had brought to your notice the very small character of the nursery staff at the workhouse. On the last return, you had 35 patients and only one nurse, whereas the next worst union in this respect had one nurse to every 18 patients. The general proportion throughout the country was one for every 12 patients. I am inclined to agree with the suggestion that the salary they were offering was rather small, but I would much prefer that they should try to get a nurse at this figure than do without one. As to the accommodation for another nurse, he had made inquiries in the matter and found that it was ample. The present nurse, I understand, had had three years' experience in an infirmary, but I do not know whether that qualified her for being a trained nurse.'

Despite Miss Johnson's concerns, an advert was placed for a trained nurse on a salary of twenty-five pounds and six applicants applied for the post. Three were asked to attend the next meeting of the board. Miss Cameron, from Liverpool; Miss Cochrane, from Lichfield; and Miss Blackburn, from Thorp Bridge, near Huddersfield. Miss Cochrane was awarded the position.

Despite some guardians' reluctance to send deputations to visit the asylums that year, some were still sent. A report from the guardians who had visited the various asylums was submitted. Mr Laycock, who visited Lancaster, said that they had forty-odd cases in the institution, which was in a very crowded state. Mr Peel visited Whittingham and reported that they had seventy-eight patients there and, unfortunately, only one out of that number was likely to recover.

All the Lancashire Asylums were full, and a new one was being planned for. Mr William Hodgson, the chairman, discussed some theories to the recent increases of lunacy.

He said, 'Some time ago, it was stated that one reason was the increase in the comfort and better treatment of lunatics in asylums, which had caused people to send their relatives, unfortunately afflicted in this way, to public institutions rather than keep them at home. That could be no reason for the continued increase. It was also attributed to the increased drinking facilities, though there was no doubt that indulgence in this direction was responsible for a large percentage of those persons who found themselves in the asylums, still during the last year or two, the amount of intoxicants consumed in the country had been decreasing, whilst on the other hand, the number of lunatics had been going up, so that, though there was little doubt that it was one reason why they had to deal with such a large amount of lunacy, it did not form a real basis for the continued increase. It was necessary to look elsewhere.'

He asked, 'What is the cause? It might be due to the increased hurry, incidental to modern life. They found that in these days of telegraphs, telephones, express trains, and the like, that businessmen tried to crowd into the short space of a few hours an amount of work which would probably have occupied their ancestors for a week. If such were the case, they would expect to find from the returns that we had a large percentage of businessmen in these institutions, but the returns did not show it. Therefore, we must look elsewhere, and the question came, is education to some extent responsible for the position in which we are placed."

He inquired, 'Is the constant pressure that was exercised upon extremely young children, who were forced to go to school in their early years, must have some extent an unfortunate effect upon the brains capacity of those who were subjected to. Whether it was or was not responsible for this continued increase, I do not know, and I am not prepared to offer an opinion on the matter. At the same time, we could not shut our eyes to the fact that, year by year, the returns showed an increase. It was the fashion to appoint a Royal Commission on almost everything, and I think it would be advisable if the Government were to appoint a commission to examine the question of lunacy and see if steps could be devised to prevent its rapid increase; otherwise I am afraid that before many years, almost half the population would be confined in the asylums. It was a most serious question, and I recommend it to the notice of everyone, suggesting that they should make enquiries in their own localities and see if there was any reason why this increase should be maintained.'

Concluding he said, 'I had an opportunity of conversing with a medical specialist at Prestwich Asylum, and he had gathered that there were not so many patients confined in lunatic asylums as a result of drinking excesses as was generally understood. A large percentage was accounted for by hereditary tendency and a large percentage to the stress of present-day life. It was of the utmost importance that they should concentrate their attention upon the question, and try to ascertain the cause of this increase and not only that but to remove it if it was within the powers of man.'

Mr Laycock said, 'There is no doubt that they were driving their children educationally at top pressure. While however, they were feeding their minds, they were neglecting their bodies, and consequently, they lacked stamina to receive education.'

In October 1904, the N.S.P.C.C. had opened a branch in Blackpool. Previous to this, Blackpool and the Fylde formed part of the Preston District and complaints of cruelty were investigated by the Preston officer. The Fylde Guardians contributed three guineas to the charity.

At a meeting in Blackpool Town Hall, early in 1906, the first full year's report for the new district was read out.

> The Fylde Poor Union has a population of 100,000 and covered an area of 56,356 acres. During the year of 1905, the Fylde Officer, Mr A. Brooker, investigated 97 complaints, of which 93 were found to be true. This involved 275 children and involved 125 offenders (58 males and 67 females). Of these cases, 31 were reported by the general public: 32 by the police; 19 by public officials; 15 by the society's inspector. In 74 cases, a warning notice was sent, seven were prosecuted and convicted, and 12 otherwise dealt with. Of the 275 children affected, 268 were related to the offenders. There

> were 144 boys and 131 girls, of whom 41 were babies under two years of age; 266 supervision visits were made.

The society thought supervision visits did the 'greatest work for children'.

Broken down the cases dealt with were as follows: Blackpool, thirty-eight; Bispham and Thornton, fifteen; Fleetwood, nineteen; Kirkham, fourteen; Lytham and St Annes-on-Sea, three; Poulton and Hardhorn, eight.

Miss Johnson stated that one Sunday in October, she visited the workhouse and promised to give the children some marmalade, which had been given to her by a lady who had made too much. She brought a big pot down that morning and had asked the master if it might be given to the children. He said, 'certainly not', and she would like to know the reason for his actions. The board from time to time accepted gifts and had agreed to accept beer at Christmas, and she failed to see what harm the marmalade would do the boys. They had bread for dinner, and she thought the marmalade would go well with the bread.

The chairman told her that they had had some trouble, through food being brought into the workhouse from outside, and he thought the master had taken the proper course in refusing it. If the dietary was at fault, they must alter it, but they could not permit gifts of this sort. Mr Kemp took exception to Miss Johnson's remark that the boys had bread for dinner, saying that they had beef twice a week and plenty of vegetables.

Mr Webber was about to add something when the chairman said that he'd thought the matter had proceeded far enough, and the next business was proceeded with.

The guardians applied to the Local Government Board to allow the children to be temporarily housed at the new workhouse infirmary until cottage homes could be built. The board considered the blocks of the new infirmary did not lend themselves conveniently to the separation of the sexes, and that, apart from this, it did not appear that one of the new infirmary blocks would afford sufficient accommodation for the sick of both classes. The board suggested that as soon as the sick persons at present in the old infirmary had been removed to their new quarters, the building might be used for the reception of the children until more suitable accommodation could be provided.

At a meeting of the workhouse committee in June, it was decided to discontinue the use of tinned beef in the house for at least two months, after a food scare in Chicago. After the two months, the guardians decided to use up the remaining tinned meat and start purchasing fresh meat.

All this was due to a book released by Upton Sinclair, 'The Jungle' which told a story about an Eastern European immigrant, who worked in a tinned meat packaging plant in Chicago. He wrote the book to highlight the terrible conditions they worked under. However, it was the stories about the rotten meat used in the process, the rats which fell into the grinding machines and the stories of human body parts entering the food process which caused the biggest sensation. When people fell into the vats of boiling fat, they were supposedly left for some time before being removed, and most of their body would dissolve. The machinery had fast-spinning chopping blades, and if a worker lost a hand or fingers, the machines were not switched off, and both practices let human body parts contaminate the tinned meat.

Mr Jenner Fust retired that year and was replaced by Mr A. B. Lowry. Shortly before his retirement, he went through some facts and figures with the Fylde Guardians. His district was a comparatively large one comprising of thirty-three unions, thirty in Lancashire and three in Cumberland. The best union was the Fylde, and at the finance committee's meeting on 29 August 1906, there was not one single application for outdoor relief from the Fleetwood District. This was the first time that a district had nobody applying for relief in the union's history.

He compared some Lancashire unions with the Fylde's. West Derby in Liverpool, was part of Lancashire at this time.

	Largest	Smallest	Fylde
Acreage	Kendal 189,349	Manchester 1,646	56,799
Population	West Derby 529,684	Lunesdale 6,948	93,697
Indoor Paupers	West Derby 5,207	Lunesdale 17	201
Outdoor Paupers	West Derby 5,646	Lunesdale 61	574
Rateable Value	West Derby £2,834,664	West Ward Cumberland £84,641	£859,124
Rates in Pound	Salford 8 1/2d	Garstang 2d. (next lowest to Fylde)	1 1/4d.
Rate/ Population	Manchester 6s. 11d	Fylde 10 3/4d	10 3/4d.

The Fylde had the best levels of pauperism to population at one in one-hundred and twenty-one, the next best was Haslington at one in one-hundred and thirty-two, the worst was Wigan at one in forty-one. The average for Lancashire was one in fifty point seven.

The workhouse was overfull with two-hundred and fourteen inmates: sixteen above its capacity. The new building was badly needed, but due to bad weather over the last winter, the work was delayed. The chairman was asked when they might expect the new workhouse to be finished ... in about twenty years called out one guardian.

Miss Johnson said, 'People outside seem to know more about this than we do.'

The completion of the contracts was on 31 July, and the guardians could impose penalties if it wasn't completed by then. Further delays followed, and the opening was put back to 1 November.

A new committee was formed to furnish the new workhouse the 'furnishings committee' It consisted entirely of men. Mr Laycock moved that two ladies be added to this committee.

He said, 'By mistake, the ladies have been left off the committee. We all recognize that ladies could do a very great amount of good in poor law work, and in view of this, I think it was only right that they should lend their assistance in what was a most important matter. We all know that if we wished to furnish are houses, we consulted the ladies.'

Mrs Webber and Mrs Stott were added to the committee. The committee ordered unclimbable wrought iron fencing, tip-up beds for the vagrant's ward, gas lamp fittings, gale bedsteads, and tables for the dining room. The total cost for furnishing the workhouse was one-thousand pounds.

For the new workhouse Mr James Kinloch of Fulwood was appointed engineer for the boiler room, on a salary of two pounds per week. In December, the new well and water tower were completed and could now supply eight thousand to ten thousand gallons of water a day. The workhouse was being cleaned, and Italian tilers were laying the floor tiles. The opening was, however, further delayed until March 1907.

The last Christmas dinner in the old workhouse was held on 26 December. Mr Fielden of Lytham gave a concert. The outdoor paupers received an extra sixpence for Christmas Week.

At the first meeting of the finance committee in 1907, there were one-hundred and forty requests for outdoor relief. To speed things up, it was decided that Blackpool and Fleetwood's relieving officers should have a phone fixed in their offices. The medical officers could also use these phones.

In the workhouse, during the first two weeks of January, fourteen paupers were admitted, thirteen discharged, and three died. The total in the workhouse was two-hundred and twenty-one against two-hundred last year. One of the fourteen admitted was a woman who the guardians thought had only entered the workhouse to take revenge on her husband by trying to get the guardians to prosecute him for failing to support his family. As a test, they put her to work at the washtub: the worst job for a female inmate. She left the house the next day.

The guardians told the master that when a person entered the house with money, they would now decide who had it taken from them and placed in the common fund and who could keep their money but pay for their maintenance.

On 27 March 1907, the new workhouse was officially opened by William Hodgson in place of William Segar Hodgson who was ill. On the 4, 5, and 6 of April, the building was opened to the public.

At the entrance to the workhouse, a stone archway led into the site where the vagrant's block stood. The porter's living rooms were to the left and the porter's office to the right, both of which overlooked the entrance gate. The male and female receiving rooms, day rooms, bathrooms, clothes store, and steam disinfector were all situated here.

In the centre of the site stood the administration block containing a large central dining hall with glazed brick walls and an open-timbered pitch pine roof. It was built like this so it could double up as a church. A large house for the master, the main kitchen, scullery, and storerooms were all attached. The laundry, bakery, boiler, and engine and pump house occupied the ground floor immediately at the back of the administrative block.

Radiating to the right and left were the various pavilions all connected by an open covered corridor. The females occupied the east side and the males the west side. The accommodation for the able-bodied and aged inmates consisted of two large three-storey pavilions, with day rooms and dormitories. On the far-right hand side stood a two-storey pavilion for mothers and infants and infirm females, behind this building stood the water tower. There were also two-room cottages for married couples.

On the North of the site were the infirmary buildings. These included a nurse's home and two, two-storey pavilions which provided accommodation for fifty patients of each sex, plus all the necessary medical equipment.

On the South-western side of the grounds were the offices and boardroom. It had a large entrance hall leading to four committee rooms. A wide flight of stairs led to the first floor, where the boardroom was situated. In this room, there was seating for fifty members, each guardian was provided with a locker, and the woodwork throughout was of oak. It was light and airy with a six-foot dado rail extending around the room. The boardroom was entered through two folding oak doors surrounded with carved oak. There was also on the same floor the clerk's office, assistant clerk rooms, lavatories, and retiring rooms. Also, in the building, with a separate entrance, were the outdoor relief office, containing waiting-rooms and conveniences, and the registration office with a strong room.

From the well beneath the water tower, water was pumped up to the tanks at the top and distributed over the entire building. This water was used in the laundry, boiler house, all sanitary purposes, and the fire system. For cooking and domestic purposes, the Fylde Water Board's water was used.

The heating, throughout the whole building and the hot water supply, was worked from a central station with the assistance of rotary pumps an equal temperature could be maintained. Telephones were placed in the different departments to summon nurses' and officials in emergencies. There was a morgue and enough pigsties to hold forty-eight pigs.

For the new house, it was decided to employ four new officials: A female cook, Miss Emily Sykes, and a laundress, Mrs M. D. Trueman, both at twenty-five pounds a year plus uniforms. They were both required to assist the matron when needed. An extra two properly trained nurses at twenty-five pounds a year, including uniforms, were appointed. The visiting committee decided to stop using blue serge uniforms for the staff, and they all received two printed dresses. Nurse Cochrane would move to the new house with the adults, and Nurse Redfern was to stay with the fifty children in the old house. Two foster parents were recruited to look after the children. Mr and Mrs Magson were given the position as the children's superintendents. They were paid twenty-two and thirteen pounds respectively.

By mid-June, some guardians wanted to delay the move to the new house, but with the new officials arriving and with no proper accommodation in the old house for them, it could not be put off any longer. The present master and matron, Edwin and Emily Perry, organised the moving of the inmates into their new home on 20 June. The able-bodied walked, and the less able went on carts, leaving the children behind in the old workhouse.

Moving Day

The New Workhouse

The first meeting in the Wesham Boardroom.

On 17 July 1907, the Guardians held their first meeting in the new boardroom at Wesham. A photograph of the event was taken by the press.

A new committee was formed, the 'cottage homes committee', who would report back to the guardians on all matters concerning the 'home' as the old workhouse was now known. The Wesham Workhouse would be known as the 'house'.

When the union was formed, the guardians were all men and conservative. Later women joined the board giving the guardians a different mindset, especially concerning women and children. Then Miss Johnson, a suffragette, became a guardian; as a former nurse, she often went against the grain but for good reasons. She, however, was not popular with the other guardians because she was, in their opinion, often underhand. As an example, if a guardian visited the workhouse, any complaints were meant to be written in the visitor's book, but Miss Johnson would write letters to the board in London. That year, two new guardians were elected Mr Hartley Lee, a socialist of Fleetwood, and Mr Albert Ellis, a Blackpool Labour Councillor; both held the guardians in contempt.

The cost of building the new workhouse was discussed.

The total estimated cost for the building was forty-six-thousand, two-hundred, and twenty-six pounds, fifteen shillings, and nine pence, and the actual cost of the building was forty-seven-thousand, six-hundred, and fifty-four pounds, nineteen shillings, and sixpence: a difference of one-thousand, four-hundred, and twenty-eight pounds, three shillings and nine pence. In addition to these amounts, there were the architect's fees of two-thousand, six-hundred, and fifty-two pounds, and fourteen shillings; special items at six-thousand and fourteen pounds, eighteen shillings, and two pence; and a further three-thousand-five-hundred pounds were spent on the furnishings; making a total of fifty-nine-thousand, eight-hundred, and twenty-three pounds, and eight shillings.

All the guardians, except Albert Ellis, were satisfied with the cost and quality of the new workhouse.

Mr Hartley Lee proposed that a woman with six children, whose husband was in prison, be given eight shillings weekly arguing it would be the lesser evil than bringing the children into the workhouse.

The chairman said, 'The public have no right to keep the children of a felon outside the house.'

Mr Hartley Lee of Fleetwood took exception to the remarks. He said, 'We have no right to throw on the children any stigma attached to the parents. I think the chairman had no right to bring up a matter like that in the manner they had done.'

Mr Hodgson ignored him.

The nurses asked for six additional pairs of clogs, six collars, and six capes. They also requested a competent pauper woman to look after the nurse's rooms and cook their meals, as well as a little more variety in the food. Mrs Mary Tattersall of Knutsford was appointed nurse to make up the three required at the new workhouse. When she arrived the other two nurses resigned.

Mrs Cochrane's resignation was due to ill health. Miss Mary Ann Lilly's reason for resigning was given, when the twenty-eight-year-old nurse applied for a position at the Ormskirk Union. She was asked why she left the Fylde Union.

She replied, 'Because I was unhappy.'

Ormskirk's clerk, 'Why were you unhappy?'

Mary Lilley answered, 'Because the off-duty time was unsatisfactory, and the food was not good.'

Superintendent Arthur Magson asked the master for all the keys belonging to the old workhouse and told him he could not enter without his permission. It was planned to move the children temporarily into the old infirmary, once it had been cleaned and decorated. The rest of the old workhouse would remain empty.

Mr Lee suggested that variety should be introduced in the decoration of the old premises to make the children long for something better.

He said, 'They would be spending money well in making them desire to grow up useful and industrious citizens with a comfortable home of their own. Breed them in slums, and they would produce men who were no credit to them, but let them be brought up in the best surroundings and they would bring up a race of good men. It was a matter of economy. In many cases, they apparently spent money extravagantly, but if it was applied to the children, it was well spent, for the public in the future would reap the benefit.'

Miss Johnson agreed.

She said, 'The children should not go there without a thorough cleaning of the premises. In those rooms, people had had every disease under the sun. It was just as cheap to have pretty colours as dull ones in decorating.'

Now that the workhouse was in the Parish of Wesham, the paupers were to be buried there. After the first person had died, the master reported that it would cost one pound to bury the paupers in St Joseph's graveyard compared to seven shillings and sixpence at Kirkham. The clerk enquired, and the priest told him that they had to pay the grave digger between seven shillings and sixpence and ten shillings for each burial, according to the depth of the grave, so the charge could not be less than twelve shillings and sixpence or fifteen shillings. The priest would conduct the funerals and provide a grave for twelve shillings and sixpence. If the guardians paid for the grave digging, he would charge them five shillings.

Miss Johnson said, 'It was a little thing to do when they were dead to bury them in their own ground, but how was it that Kirkham could bury them at 7s. 6d.'

Guardian and Kirkham Vicar W. T. Mitton said, 'It's because we keep a regular man. In this case, they don't.'

The Vicar of Lund, Reverend Smith, also a guardian, said, 'Our sexton is paid 13s. for each grave he digs.'

Mr Lee asked, 'What objections could there be to the paupers being buried in Kirkham. There would be very little difference in conveyance. Are we compelled to bury in the parish?'

The chairman stated that they were not. Reverend Smith added that they charged double fees when bodies were brought from another place. The offer of twelve shillings and sixpence was excepted.

It was decided that parents in the workhouse could only visit their children once every three months. Mr Lee was against this; he thought it was the duty of the guardians to foster parental feelings as much as possible. They must not punish good parents for the sake of bad ones.

Mr Woods said, 'I always thought it was better that the children in the institutions should be kept as far as possible away from the parents. I think the period named was ample if the visit extended over a couple of hours.'

Miss Johnson said, 'In my experience, bad mothers only developed love for their children when they entered the workhouse.'

Dr Shaw had been the workhouse doctor since 1893, and he hadn't had a pay rise, even though the number of patients had increased by a third. He asked for a pay rise of fifteen pounds taking his pay to fifty-five pounds, plus that the guardians, in future, provide the drugs required. Nearly all the guardians supported the pay rise. Mr Lee did not.

He said, 'I believe in starting from the bottom, and increasing the wages of the poorer paid servants.'

Dr Shaw received a pay rise. He now earned fifty-five pounds as medical officer for the workhouse and forty-five pounds as medical officer for the Kirkham District.

Deputations were now sent out regularly to visit the Lancashire Asylums. Mr Kemp went with seven guardians to Whittingham, he reported that four of the eighty-one patients were in bed, and likely to be on the rates for some time to come. Mr Woods went to Lancaster. He reported they were given every opportunity for asking questions. All the patients looked well except one.

Mr Hartley said, 'At Whittingham, some of the patients thought they were quite rational and healthy enough to come out and wanted to know how long they were going to keep them there. We spoke to the doctor about a few, who agreed that they appeared all right at that moment. One of the ladies pointed at us, and another said, 'You shouldn't point to gentlemen: that's not etiquette.' One very stout lady said, 'I am strong and healthy, and why do you keep me here, there are many more crackpots out of the house than there are inside.'

Mr Crossfield, said, 'They had not yet been to Prestwich, but if they arrived back safely, they would report back.'

Miss Johnson told the guardians, 'The asylum gardens had beautiful flowers, and the doctor told me that it helped lift the inmates up. The same idea should be adopted in our grounds. It would make their officers stay longer if they got them to take a pride in it.'

Mr Lee complained that notice was given of the visits to the asylums and made some sarcastic remarks.

To which the chairman replied, 'The authorities would not admit us if we did not give notice, because the patients are scattered all over the place, and it took an hour or so to get them together.'

Mrs Webber reported on Winwick; she said, 'There were thirteen women and six men from the Fylde in Winwick Asylum. Some were very sullen, and some excited. One woman was very foul in her language. There were three in the hospital, one being very far gone in consumption. Several seemed rational, though all but one seemed fit cases. The exception was a Kirkham man, though it was said he occasionally got depressed. I asked the doctor if he would not get a bit depressed under similar circumstances, and he said perhaps he would. I think there is no, perhaps about it. Patients were only allowed out on parole very rarely, and I would like this altering. The matron admitted that some of the inmates who were suffering from senility, rather than heredity insanity, would be better in the workhouse. Many were detained longer than they need be because they were useful. I know of a man who was in the asylum nineteen years. He brewed the beer, but when he refused to do it any longer, they discharged him.'

One of the old men in the workhouse refused to do the work which he had been allocated. He was seventy-one years old and complained his work was too hard. He was sent to prison for fourteen days. A woman in the house had entered with thirteen pounds when she left she had one pound deducted for her month's stay.

Mr Lee told the guardians he was going to bring a motion forward saying that the guardians should advertise the fact that poor people could receive free vaccinations.

He elaborated, 'I came into contact with someone who had a child attending elementary school, and this child had contracted fever from another child, with the result that it lost time at school, and its parents were put to a great deal of expense and trouble which might have been avoided if the parents of the child from whom the disease was contacted, had known that they could obtain medical assistance free. Considering the subsequent effects of the disease, he thought it would be a real economy to have posters issued dealing with the matter, and they would have a healthier childhood, manhood, and womanhood. I move that posters be issued in all poor neighbourhoods throughout the Fylde District informing that when parents were unable to provide proper medical aid for their children, they were entitled to medical attention free, and that the acceptance of such did not disfranchise them or pauperise the parents.'

Mr Ellis seconded, he said, 'There were a large number of poor families who attempted to nurse their own children themselves because they could not afford to send for a medical man. But what form the intimation should take was a matter for discussion. The new Education Act, which came into force New Year's Day, provided that all elementary school children would be brought under the observation of a medical officer, as well as their surroundings. If we could assist the educational authorities in bringing home to the parents the fact that they could obtain free medical assistance without losing their franchise, I think we should do it.'

Mr Kemp thought the posters were a waste of money; all poor districts knew they could have the doctor's services for free if required.

Mr Crossfield added, 'They have free education and free breakfasts, and if the resolution had included free rent, he [Mr Ellis] would have seconded it. I do not think they should spend ratepayer's money in sending the bellman round to tell the people to go for relief. They were always being called extravagant, or something else, and if they were not careful, they would have a reputation like Westham or Poplar.'

Mr Lee replied; saying, 'When I appeal to people's selfishness, I always feel a bit ashamed of myself, but I had hoped to appeal to their better natures. I know, I have made out a bad case. I had not appealed to them as fathers and humanitarians. They only have their sanatoriums because they were forced to have them for the safety of the well-to-do. They only have their infectious diseases hospitals for the protection of the well-to-do. I had thought that they as guardians, and therefore humanitarians, would have hoped as far as possible to stamp out disease, but by mistake, he had appealed to their selfishness. But, like other people who had made mistakes, I have touched the right spot … I have appealed to their pockets. What did it matter if they had to keep children for the rest of their lives because of some ailment left by disease? We are guardians of the poor, and I think the expense they would have to bear would be increased by their short-sighted policy. It would be economical for them to undertake the medical assistance of the poor. I think we should help citizens, and then there would be less need for places like the Kirkham Workhouse. I am sorry I do not appeal to their better nature, but instead their selfishness, I only wish I could.'

The vote was taken. Two for the motion the remainder against.

There were two-hundred and fifty-nine inmates in the workhouse by the end of its first year, and the male's side of the building had five more inmates than there was accommodation for. The workhouse committee decided to place the men in the male attendants' rooms. The workhouse had a baker who visited three times a week for fifteen shillings; the guardians decided to appoint a permanent baker on a salary of twenty-five pounds with rations and uniform.

The expenditure on paupers in 1908 was twelve-thousand, six-hundred, and fifty-nine pounds, against eleven-thousand, three-hundred, and sixty-five pounds last year. In 1901 it was seven-thousand, four-hundred, and sixty-nine pounds; and in 1895, five-thousand, eight-hundred, and sixty-three pounds. Broken down, that year's figures for indoor relief were one-thousand, eight-hundred, and thirty-four pounds, and outdoor relief at two-thousand, three-hundred, and twenty-five pounds. The maintenance of lunatics cost three-thousand-eight-hundred pounds, and the salaries of officials cost one-thousand, six-hundred, and eighty-seven pounds. Buildings and repairs were at four-hundred and fifty-three pounds, loan charges at two-thousand, three-hundred, and six pounds, and other expenses three-hundred and twenty-one pounds. The call was three pence for poor law and eleven pence for county purposes.

Chairman of the visiting committee, Mr Gill, appealed to the guardians to keep costs down. They were paying three pounds per day in coal; forty-five shillings a day for butcher's meat, pickles, cheese, eggs, bacon, and other sundries; twenty-five shillings a day for flour; one shilling for spirits; two shillings for tobacco; and thirty shillings for milk. The expenditure on gas was eighty pounds for the quarter.

Miss Johnson said, 'The Chairman of the Finance Committee seemed to think the guardians should economise, but in her opinion, it was the officials who should be careful. Almost every time I visit the house, I had to put some lights out, and I think someone ought to be made responsible because it was not for a guardian to come here and have to turn out the lights.'

Mr Yates disagreed, 'I had been at the workhouse at dusk on several occasions, and the corridors were so dark I had to have a guide going in front of me with lighted matches.'

The chairman thought the workhouse committee ought to keep a careful supervision over various outlets, so as to reduce expenditure as much as possible.

Since the building work on the workhouse had been completed, Guardian Ellis had complained about the cost and workmanship on the house. The complaints which Mr William Segar Hodgson had to defend, as the building committee chairman, led to him refusing to come to a meeting ever again.

Mr W. S. Hodgson said, 'For nearly 50 years, I have had the pleasure of coming to this board, but since Mr Ellis became a member that pleasure had been greatly diminished, and it is my intention not to come again.'

By November that year, the entire board had had enough of Mr Ellis. At a meeting, the auditor, the subcontractors in masonry and plastering, the architects, and Mr F. Broughton, chief contractor, went through Mr Ellis' complaints.

1. Mr Ellis claimed the contractor charged for washing the workman's clothes when most of this was done by the master and inmates. The auditor had proof that the contractor had done his work in this regard.

2. Mr Ellis' next objection was that the contract for the twenty-two inspection covers was seven pounds and the price charged was nine pounds. The architect stated that the chambers had to be deeper than the original specification.

3. The next objection was to the eighteen-thousand, four-hundred, and sixty-two square yards of pointing. Mr Ellis stated that level joints had not been made but line joints to save putting up scaffolding. The auditor thought, although not according to specification, full value had been obtained.

4. Another objection was twenty-five pounds for specially made brick angles. The auditor stated they were over and above anything in the original specification.

5. Mr Ellis pointed out the contract price for three-hundred and twenty-two superficial yards of six-inch brickwork in mortar, including pointing and best red facing, was given at two shillings and sixpence per yard, but the bill amount was put down at four shillings and sixpence.

The auditor asked, 'I would like to be correctly informed as to what is meant by red facing.'

The architect told him, 'Red facing means the substitution of Accrington bricks, and these were allowed for as extras at the rate of 2s. per yard. It was not intended that ordinary bricks should be used.'

The auditor again accepted this. He told Mr Ellis that maybe he didn't understand the practice in contractors drawing up a specification.

Mr Ellis continued, 'The contract price for laying 472 feet of terra-cotta coping was 3½d, but I found that a shilling a foot had been charged.'

The auditor replied, 'I have the bills before me, and find that a clerical error had been made in this matter. There had really been a saving on this work of £13 18s.'

Mr Ellis went on and on, cheap wood used, overcharged for decorative stones, concrete, the foundation stone laying, stone steps, bricks, and plastering.

When Mr Ellis had finished, the auditor summed up.

He said, 'I have been through every item in the contract, and I have come to a conclusion. I have found both under and overcharges which, however, were justified on explanation, and I have arrived at figures which I have decided to allow. Personally, I could not say whether the work was well done or not. That was not a matter for me. I have had advice of an independent architect, and on that advice, I was satisfied that the work was well done. The local board architect had also been around the buildings, and he was satisfied that the work was carried out according to the plans.'

Mr William Hodgson closed the meeting saying, 'I do not think Mr Ellis has presented his case in a strong manner, which he has made much out of. In work like this, which amounted to £60,000, it would have been impossible to have had no discrepancies, but those which had been revealed were, in my opinion, very trifling.'

The new well didn't work as expected, and it was sunk further down. A new pump house was built, by John Haslam of Kirkham, to pump the water up into the tower for one-hundred and sixty pounds. The well, it was claimed, could now supply one-thousand gallons an hour. The covered corridors between the male and female accommodation were open to the elements, and it was decided to close them up with bricks and windows. Wesham Parish Council applied to the guardians to use the board room for their meetings, which was allowed.

In the home, Mrs Hull, the assistant foster mother, found bruises on a small boy. She spoke to Superintendent Arthur Magson, who in her opinion did not take the relevant action. She then wrote two letters of complaint one to Dr Shaw and one to the clerk. The cottage homes committee held an inquiry on 24 April but found no grounds for complaint. They did, however, caution Mrs Hull, as to the consequences of her interfering with the discipline of the home or disobeying the superintendent.

Mrs Hull then sent a letter of complaint to the Local Government Board.

A sub-committee was formed, who held another inquiry to find out how the boy, Clements, received the bruises. The foster parents and several children were questioned; Clements himself could not say how the bruises were caused. The clerk thought that the bruises were probably caused by the boy falling off a swing.

At the meeting, Arthur Magson reported that, owing to the lack of hot water, there was a difficulty in bathing all the boys on one day. The delay could have stopped him from noticing the bruises. The committee recommended that the superintendent devoted two evenings weekly for the purpose of bathing the boys and that he be furnished with a suitable cane for the infliction of corporal punishment, plus, a book be provided in which the superintendent must enter all offences by the children and the punishment administered.

It was also moved by Mr Lee, and seconded by W. Kirkham at the next guardians meeting, that, 'This committee having very carefully inquired into the circumstances of the complaint or allegations made by Mrs Hull, find that there is no foundation for such charges and the children in the homes appear to be carefully looked after and happy.'

It was carried unanimously.

Undeterred Mrs Hull wrote two more letters of complaint and the subcommittee recommended that Mrs Hull be called upon to resign. If she didn't resign, the clerk was ordered to give her one month's notice. She resigned, leaving on 6 June, and was replaced by Mrs Edith Usher of Liverpool.

As far back as 1845, there were strict rules concerning the punishment of children. In the book, 'The General Orders and Instructional Letters of the Poor Law Commissioners', the rules are listed concerning the punishment of children.

> Art. 45. No Corporal punishment shall be inflicted on any female child.
>
> Art. 46. No corporal punishment shall be inflicted on any male child except with a rod or other instrument, such as shall be seen and approved of by the Board of Guardians or the Visiting Committee.
>
> Art. 47. No corporal punishment shall be inflicted on any male child until six hours shall have elapsed from the commission of the offence for which such punishment is inflicted. (presumably to let tempers calm.)
>
> Art. 48. Whenever any male child is punished by corporal correction, the master and school master shall (if possible) be both present.
>
> Art. 49. No male child shall be punished by corporal correction, whose age may be reasonably supposed to exceed fourteen years.

The book also gives reasons for the rules.

> The Commissioners are satisfied that good temper, joined to firmness and self-command, will enable a skilful teacher to manage children with little or no corporal punishment. The frequent use of corporal correction is the common resource of teachers who, from their idleness or other defects, are incompetent to acquire a command over children by a knowledge of their characters and by gentle means.
>
> For these and other reasons, the Commissioners have

> prohibited the corporal punishment of female children, which they believe to have been by no means frequently employed in workhouse schools, and they would discourage all corporal punishment of pauper children to the utmost of their power. They confidently look forward to an improvement in the schools for the training of pauper children, and they do not doubt that such an improvement will bring with it the gradual disuse of all objectionable modes of correction. In the pauper school, established at Norwood and organised by Dr Kay, under the sanction of the Commissioners, the use of corporal punishment has almost entirely discontinued.

There were forty-four children in the home; one was George Flood who the captain of the training ship *Indefatigable* had sent back because he was subject to epilepsy.

Four other children in the home were the Taylor children, victims of child neglect. In September, last year, Annie Taylor and her brother Robert Taylor of Tyldesley Road, Blackpool, were both sent to jail for six months with hard labour for child cruelty. The pair had told the relieving officer, Thomas Dixon, they were man and wife and that the children were theirs. The case came to the attention of the N.S.P.C.C. when the eldest child, Jane, was arrested for 'larceny' when begging for food.

Inspector Brooks, who investigated the case, told the court, 'Every room had a terrible stench, and the baby was sucking out of a furred and dirty bottle. Enough to kill any child. The children had to beg for bread, and only the previous week, the eldest child had been charged in court with stealing. The only food in the house consisted of dry crusts of bread and a pint of milk.'

Using the Poor Law Act 1889, the guardians motioned, 'That Jane (11), Robert (6), Martha (2), and Lionel (8 months) shall be under the control of the guardians of this union, until the boys attain the age of 16 years and the two girls reach the age of 18 years, and taken out of the control of Annie Taylor who is, at present, in prison for cruelty against the children and is not a fit person to have the custody of her children.'

For the children born in the workhouse, the address 1 Derby Road would now be placed on the birth certificate. This would remove the stigma of being born there. At the home, a new assistant matron was employed. She was also to be the cook. The adult paupers were not officially allowed to go to the home, but the guardians obtained permission to allow responsible paupers to assist the matron at the children's home when extra hands were needed.

At the workhouse, Miss Johnson asked Mr Ellis to visit the infirmary. He later wrote a letter to the clerk.

> 82 Central Beach, Blackpool, Aug. 13th, 1908
>
> Dear Mr Brown,
>
> After the board meeting yesterday, I visited two of the wards in the hospital and was most distressed to find many of the patients apparently neglected. I had no time to interview you afterwards or would have done so, but take this opportunity of making my complaint. I do not know who is responsible for the state of affairs, but I am of the opinion that an appeal to your humanity will prevail upon you to do your part to remedy it.
>
> Kellet: This man showed me his feet. Cakes of dirt were upon them, and he complained they had not been washed for five or six weeks. Candish: says his leg had not been dressed for three weeks, and he has never seen a night nurse in the ward. Woods: Inmate twelve months, bad leg, reports doctor only looked at it three times this year. Edwards: Inmate two years; reports doctor only examined his leg twice this year.
>
> I discount a great deal of what they told me, but what is seen, must be accepted as correct. In the isolation ward, there was a case of paralysis, and a case of phthisis, an infectious disease. Both patients said their feet were neglected. I am not ashamed to say that I wept, and I hope something may be done between this day and the next board meeting. On inquiry, I found six pairs of slippers in the ward for all the patients, and on seeing patients visit the lavatory in their shirts, was astonished to learn that no cloaks are provided. It appears to me that the nurse is overworked and that a superintendent nurse is required for administrative purposes.
>
> Yours truly
> Albert Ellis,

> P.S. Externally everything appeared very clean and comfortable.

After some discussion some supporting Mr Ellis, the majority not, the chairman spoke on the subject.

He said, 'I am sorry, Mr Ellis is not present, because his case thus lost a great deal of its strength. If you study the letter carefully, it would appear that it had not made a very deep impression on the minds of those who conceived the allegations, or they would have taken immediate action. About twenty-four hours after Mr Ellis made his visit at the instigation of Miss Johnson, I went around. I interviewed every man in the absence of the nurses and found a great many were perfectly satisfied. They had no charges to make and were comfortable and well looked after. One said that the doctor did not take sufficient care and that he had not seen him from Mondays to Friday; another complained about the cheese and said it did not agree with him; another said the beef was not good for him; another said his leg was neglected three months ago, but he had had nothing to complain of since. He was put to work, but it was too hard. That work was carrying food upstairs to the other patients. One said the nurses were a little forgetful.'

He added, 'I saw the nurses. They said that the nurse on night duty made a visit to the wards every hour. They said they did not always go into the male ward because the men said it disturbed them; they stood at the door and looked in, and if they saw any cases needing attention, attended to them. The patients were washed every day and bathed once a fortnight. The doctor said he did not attend every day. He telephoned to the master, and if there were any cases needing immediate attention, he came to the house. There are no grounds for the charges either against the nurses for neglect or the doctor for inattention.'

Mr Ellis' letter was left to 'lie on the table'.

Mr W. S. Hodgson had still not returned to the guardian's meetings. Mr Bradley commented on the valuable services Mr Hodgson had rendered the board and moved that a letter be sent asking him to attend the meetings again.

The Reverend C. F. Smith said, 'I saw Mr Hodgson this morning, and though I offered him a lift in my carriage he declined to attend. I am ashamed that such a rude thing should have been said to Mr Hodgson in that room by brand-new members whose manners are not particularly good.'

The clerk was asked to write to Mr Hodgson, asking him to attend future meetings.

There were hardly any able-bodied females in the house to help the matron, and a new seamstress was employed for seven shillings and five pence per week; there were only five old ladies in the sewing room who didn't stop all day, according to the visiting committee. To help a Foster knitting machine was purchased for seven pounds. The guardians also had to employ a laundress, another job which was traditionally done by the female inmates. Miss Mary Reeve of Essex became the laundress on twenty-five pounds per annum.

At the same time, Miss Allen of Lytham asked for permission to introduce Brabazon work into the house. The charity provided about five pounds' worth of material which when made into an end product was sold for about nine pounds. The work was done, as a rule, by men who worked with mats and carpets. The society took out the money they had provided, and the rest was given to the union. The guardians thought if the paupers were put to work, it should be for the union and the request was declined.

Mr Robert Blacoe resigned as relieving officer. These jobs didn't come vacant very often, and eighty-eight applicants applied for the post. All classes of trade were represented, including a fish salesman, an undertaker, a solicitor's clerk, a warehouseman, a policeman, a publican, a quarryman, school masters, printers, a confectioner, a draper, a grocer, and railway clerks. There was also a lady applicant from London. Mr John Jump received the post.

Mr Robert Blacoe had worked for the union for seventeen years and was entitled to a pension. The pension awarded would be $17/60^{th}$ of his average salary for the last five years of one-hundred and sixty-five. He retired on a superannuation of forty-six pounds.

The Fylde had an excellent new workhouse which had cost sixty-thousand pounds to build and had only cost the ratepayers an extra three-quarter pence on the rates. It had been a fractious year for the guardians and most wanted Mr Ellis, the main source of discontent, to resign, but he didn't. After being proven wrong, the guardians hoped Mr Ellis would be more respectful in the future. The year closed with two-hundred and fifty-nine inmates in the workhouse and forty-four children in the home.

In January 1909, the new pension scheme was introduced for people over seventy years of age. The maximum a person could claim was five shillings if their income was below ten shillings per week. There were five different pensions awards ranging from one shilling to five shillings per week, with five different coloured pension books: one shilling for terra-cotta, two shillings for orange, three shillings for drab, four shillings for cream, and five shillings for blue. The money was drawn at the post-office. According to the Chancellor of the Exchequer, David Lloyd George, he estimated six-hundred-thousand would be in receipt of the pension, and in a stroke these people would be removed from the poor-law system.

Not every person over seventy was entitled to a pension; 'shirkers', people who haven't worked to maintain themselves in the past, people detained in lunatic asylums, habitual criminals and habitual drunkards, and people in receipt of outdoor and indoor relief were all excluded. However, people who had claimed medical and surgical assistance from the union, people in workhouse hospitals or infirmaries, or people who had claimed for payment for their dependents' burials were exempt, and could still claim their pension.

In the home, a boy set fire to his bed, and the guardians decided to buy twenty Kyl-Fyre, three Minimax, and three Underwriters fire-fighting extinguishers. The boy was placed on the punishment list, and because of his ill effect on the other children, he was sent to reformatory school.

The master bought four dozen clogs for the small children in the home.

Miss Johnson said, 'I have seen one of the babies wearing a pair of clogs, that would have been more suitable for a man ploughing a field.'

Miss Johnson also entered into the visitor's book that a boy was suffering from ringworm but was not separated from the other boys. Dr Shaw reacted to this report by saying that the boy was not suffering from ringworm and not a case for isolation. He added that he very much resented this kind of mischievous interference with his medical work.

Miss Johnson asked, 'Why was he not going to school then, I understood from the superintendent that he was suffering with ringworm.'

Chairman, Mr Hodgson replied, 'Evidently from your own saying you know nothing about it. You state you had asked the superintendent, and from his report, you have made this report.'

Miss Emma Lowe was appointed assistant matron on eighteen pounds per annum plus rations, and another boy was sent to the home from the training ship *Indefatigable* because he had nowhere else to go during the August holidays.

Responding to the 1908 Children's Act, which prevented children being placed in adult prison, the clerk of justice asked the Fylde Guardians if they could send children convicted of a crime to the old workhouse and use it as a borstal. The guardians agreed and told the clerk they would charge one shilling and sixpence per day per child.

Every year, in April, a temporary chairman was appointed, and the nominations were taken for a new chairman for the preceding year. Mr Gill was appointed temporary chairman, and Mr Hodgson was again nominated as chairman. Mr Brandwood thought that Mr Hodgson was an excellent chairman, especially after the past two years of ill-feeling, but after the fullest investigation into the building of the new workhouse, he hoped they could move forward in harmony.

Mr Ellis could not let go, 'While agreeing it would be a mistake to attempt to make any change in the position of chairman, I take exception to the remark made by Mr Brandwood, that the fullest investigation and inquiry had been made with regards to the building of the workhouse. That was not true. They had 'burked' the inquiry, and I do not think such a statement should be allowed to go forward without contradiction.'

Nor could his socialist second in command, Mr Lee who added, 'The inquiry into the building of the workhouse had been hindered on every hand by members of the board. If the minutes for last year were read, it would be found that Mr Ellis' remarks were perfectly true. I submit that Mr Hodgson is entirely unfitted for this position.'

This was the first time since the union was formed that somebody had been against the former chairman being elected, and the boardroom went into uproar over these remarks.

After order was restored, Mr Lee continued, 'That morning Mr Hodgson had told me that only one out of every thousand tramps moving about the country was a genuine man. I hope the press would hand that on, and let the public know the kind of man they were electing for their chairman. The man believed that 999 out of every 1000 of the working men of this country who were compelled to tramp were "rotters".'

There was more uproar, and shouts of 'turn him out' 'send him to Fleetwood'. and 'our time is worth more than his speech.'

Mr Lee undeterred continued, 'In committee, he said that a respectable working man would have his tools with him. I am producing this as evidence that Mr Hodgson is not fitted for the position of chairman.'

An indifferent William Hodgson told Mr Lee, 'The business is the appointment of a chairman. If you propose another, it would be all right.'

Mr Lee, 'I don't do that.'

Mr Crossfield said, 'Mr Hodgson would find a good many backers in the board, men with level heads and common sense and not humbugs.'

Mr Ellis asked, 'Are you going to allow a member to call his colleagues 'humbugs' without asking him to withdraw. It is improper.'

On the vote being taken, Mr Hodgson was appointed, with only Mr Lee voting against. Mr Hodgson responded to the appointment by saying the less said about what had taken place, the better; every man was entitled to his own opinion.

Last year's overspending on necessities was mainly down to the poor bookkeeping by the master. There was also an acrimonious atmosphere between the staff, for which some guardians also blamed the master. However, no action was taken as Mr and Mrs Bamber resigned.

Six married couples were interviewed at a meeting on 5 May. Frank Culshaw, a former relieving officer of Blackburn, and Eleanor Culshaw were appointed master and matron. It was an unusual appointment because they were parents with a baby. The child could live in the master's accommodation, and when it had attained the age of two, Mr and Mrs Culshaw would have to repay the child's rations whilst theirs were free.

People with money were still asked to pay for their own maintenance.

A St Annes woman entered the workhouse with one pound and nine shillings, she had four shillings deducted for the four-night stay. Another woman entered the house and gave birth to a daughter on the same day as she had arrived. She had thirteen shillings and ten pence in her possessions, all of which was placed in the common fund.

Mr Brandwood said, 'We can't turn her out penniless. She would probably go out soon.'

The guardians decided to refund the money.

Fred Kirby also came to the notice of the guardians; he was having a bad time.

When Fred was away on business, his wife sold their house and disappeared, leaving the children living on the streets of Blackpool. The children were taken into the cottage homes until Fred returned. He then left the children with his brother and went to make his fortune in Canada. After six months, the brother stopped looking after the children, and they were sent back to the homes. It didn't work out in Canada, so Fred found work as a cattleman to pay for his passage back to England. On his return, he fell ill. When he had recovered, he was then arrested for leaving his children chargeable to the union. He couldn't pay the two pounds and sixteen shillings of arrears and was jailed for twenty-one days.

Some alterations were made at the new workhouse. They erected a greenhouse, some stables, a shippon, and a coach house; using the remaining bricks left on the site. The farm committee purchased six calves and nineteen small pigs for the able-bodied to look after. The well was only providing three-thousand-five-hundred gallons, and it was sunk deeper passed the gravel and into the sandstone. The stone breakers started braking Welsh granite, which was used to make curbstones. John Hardman, aged twenty-nine, a vagrant, refused to break his thirteen c.w.t of stone and caused two shillings and sixpence worth of damage to his cell. He was sentenced to seven days' hard labour.

At Christmas, Miss Johnson read a letter from the Lytham Branch of the British Women's Temperance Association, a society Miss Johnson, as a suffragette, would have been a member of. The letter requested that beer not be given to the inmates of the workhouse at Christmas. The guardians ignored the letter.

1910–1919

In 1910, Fylde Rural District Council started renting the old porter's lodge and stone yard at the old workhouse for seven pounds per annum. They had been storing their steamrolling engine in the old fire station next door after the Kirkham Fire Brigade moved to the Kirkham Gas Works yard. The master received a ten pounds pay rise this year, but he also had to start paying for his child's rations. He was charged two shillings and sixpence weekly until the child reached the age of seven.

The new workhouse was again opened to the public to allay criticisms about the size and cost of the institution. On 9 July, between 2 p.m. and 4.30 p.m., three hundred people looked around the buildings. Most, according to the guardians, were satisfied with what they saw.

The Fylde's consumption cases were sent to the Sandgate Sanitorium, which like the asylums were constantly full. Cases of consumption were delayed in being sent there, and in cases where there was no chance of recovery, they were sent back to the institution. There was nowhere for them to go. To remedy this, the guardians decided to erect two Pagoda Shelters, one for the males and one for the females. The wooden buildings came flat packed and cost forty-five pounds each.

Robert Stewart, a former boy of the workhouse, had finished his training at *T.S. Indefatigable* and had gained a place on the White Star Ship *R.M.S Baltic*. Life in the homes wasn't ideal for children, but there was a worse path a child could take.

During the Victorian Era, there weren't any child adoption services, and people advertised providing a service to adopt unwanted children for a fee. Many provided a good home for the children, but a good percentage didn't. 'Baby farming' as it was called, led to infants being neglected and, in some cases, being murdered. The worst case involved Amelia Elizabeth Dyer, who was executed aged fifty-six years, on 10 June 1896, after seven corpses of babies were found in the River Thames. She had been baby farming for between fifteen to twenty years, and it was thought she could have murdered up to four-hundred babies.

Amelia Elizabeth Dyer

Part of the Children's Act 1908 was set up to prevent baby farming, and from January, the relieving officers were appointed infant protection officers. The guardians also passed a motion which allowed a maximum of two infants in any dwelling. Any cases of the practice investigated by the police would, in future, be brought to the attention of the guardians.

On 17 April, the flags at the children's home and the workhouse were at half mask after the death of William Segar Hodgson. Chairman William Hodgson's sadness at losing his cousin was lessened when two of his biggest critics, Guardians Lee and Ellis were not returned in the April elections. William Hodgson was again elected to the position of chairman.

Some unions wanted to provide labour colonies for habitual vagrants.

Mr Crossfield motioned that, 'Labour colonies be established either by a combination of unions subsidised by the Government, or under state control for the detention of habitual vagrants.'

He thought that they ought to teach and train these people to stand on their own two feet and keep them out of the way of other men, who were really looking for work.

The chairman thought, 'It would be a costly exercise. They would have to decide as to the length of detention because the men would have to be kept for such a period as to affect a real and lasting improvement. Nothing contributed more to the increase in vagrancy than the difference in the treatment meted out by various unions. I think the colonies should be managed by the state, with local committees to which the inmates could make any representations they desired.'

The guardians voted by thirteen votes to eight to support petitioning the Government in the setting up of labour colonies.

The cost of indoor maintenance for the first six months of 1910 was one-thousand, eight-hundred, and thirty-five pounds plus one-hundred and thirteen pounds for the asylums. In 1909 it was one-thousand, six-hundred, and eighty-eighty pounds; in 1905, seven-hundred and seventy-five pound; and in 1901, five-hundred and sixty pounds. Outdoor relief in 1910 was one-thousand, four-hundred and thirty-two pounds; in 1909 it was one-thousand, three-hundred, and thirty-eight pounds; in 1905 one-thousand, one-hundred, and seventy-seven pounds; and 1901, eight-hundred and eighty pounds. The indoor maintenance had more than tripled in ten years, but with the large increase of staff and two sites to maintain this was to be expected. The call of two and a half pennies in the pound for poor law was, however, still one of the lowest in the country.

All punishments were recorded in the punishment book. Most were for men deserting their families and leaving them chargeable to the union. Some of the other misdemeanours could also land a pauper in Kirkham Court.

Kennedy Thomas, a thirty-two years old, was a vagrant who absconded over the gate after refusing to break his thirteen c.w.t of stones. He was sentenced to fourteen days for each offence and sent to prison for twenty-eight days.

Harvey George, fifty-five years old, was also a vagrant. He refused to perform his two tasks of one day's 'spade labour' and breaking thirteen c.w.t of stones. He was sentenced to seven days in prison.

Alfred Mansergh, an inmate, aged fifty-seven years, returned from leave drunk and damaged a door. He was sentenced to twenty-eight days in prison.

Some cases were dealt with by the master, like Susannah Kirby for refractory conduct, using obscene language, threats, and striking the master. She was sentenced to six hours with only bread and water.

In the year of 1911, the police informed the guardians of three cases which fell under the 1908 Children's Act.

1. Florence Burke of St Annes had failed to notify the coroner of the death of a child she had taken into nurse.

2. The death of Edith Thornton, in May, a child being nursed for a fee and not registered; a report by P.C. Byron stated that the child had received every care and medical attention.

3. Mrs Ada Croft of 1 North Albert Street, South Shore. She had had a child to nurse for a fee and reward, since the 29th October 1910, but was not registered.

Dr Couper told the guardians, 'Ada is in poor health and will shortly undergo a severe operation. She pleads ignorant of the 1910 act requiring notification.'

In all three cases, the guardians decided to take no action.

The smallest committee was the boarding out committee, which consisted of three guardians who met every three months. Two of the committee members that year were Mrs Kershaw and Mrs Walton. The other, Miss Lea, also had the role of Local Government Board Inspector, who, along with the district doctor and relieving officers, visited the boarded-out children and reported their finding at the committee's meeting. The minutes were discussed and approved at the guardians meetings.

At June's meeting of the committee, the minutes went as follows:

> Annie Lister is employed part-time in Blackpool Market; the inspector recommends that the board pay a little more relief in this case with a restriction that the child's employment in the market be discontinued. The house where the child resides was, on the inspector's visit, in a rather untidy condition.
>
> Doyle's Children, the inspector reported that the oldest sister of these children was doing her utmost to look after these children, the home was in a very clean state on her visit, but the bedroom accommodation was very limited, there being only two beds for six children. Recommended that a little more relief be paid in this case and that steps be taken to obtain another bed. (Albert Doyle was sent to St Vincent's Training ship in January 1912, aged fourteen.)

Three Grundy Children, the inspector reported that the house these children lived in, was in a rather untidy condition, the walls needed colour washing, and the sleeping accommodation is unsatisfactory, she recommends extra relief in this case.

Dickinson's Children, the inspector reported that the boy and girl who are boarded out with a brother and sister both need Sunday clothes; otherwise, the homes are satisfactory. (William Dickenson started work in September 1914, and his allowance was stopped.)

Wright Child, the relieving officer stated this child was in a good home in Fleetwood.

Boarding out was a way of preventing children from entering the cottage homes. Somebody, usually a family member, would offer to foster the children, and, after their house was inspected, the committee set an allowance for each child for a period of between ten to fourteen weeks. The allowance would be reviewed at the end of the allotted period. When the children reached fourteen, they were expected to find work, and the allowance was stopped. If the committee thought the foster parents needed help with clothing or furniture, it was provided. They also had the power to remove children to the cottage homes, if they thought the children were not looked after properly.

When the Chippendale Children needed boarding out, the guardians went into an agreement with their grandfather, Joseph Ellenden, of 27 Albert Street, Blackpool. Relieving officer, Hugh Parkinson, and Dr Robinson considered the home satisfactory. Joseph Chippendale, six years old, Mary Jane, five years old, and John James, four years old, moved into their grandparents' home. They were given an allowance of three shillings per week per child.

The children's progress was recorded in the committee's minutes over the months and years that the children were under the guardian's protection.

In July 1911, the union dentist examined the children and extracted several teeth. John was provided with a new pair of boots.

In February 1921, Joseph Chippendale left school and started work, and John James Chippendale received glasses

> free of charge from the union. When Mary Jane Chippendale reached the age of 14 years, she was found employment. On November 29th, 1922, her allowance was reduced from 9s. to 3s. per week. She ceased working through illness in February 1923, and her allowance was increased back to 9s. She returned to work, and an allowance of 12s. was paid for the remaining child. By July 1924 all the Chippendale children were in work and, as assistance was not required, all allowances were stopped.

In January, a report showed that seventy-two people came off outdoor relief the previous year and onto the old-age pension: twelve from Fleetwood, eighteen from Kirkham, and forty-two from Blackpool. In the workhouse, forty-three old people were eligible, but only nine took the five shillings pension.

After a full year of the new pension system, two problems arose which the guardians discussed. One was people claiming a pension, then spending all their money, and returning back to the workhouse.

Mr Bradly said, 'Some would claim their pension, spend the weekend getting drunk, and return to the workhouse on Monday. I want to know if there are any provisions against this.'

Mr Hodgson told him there was nothing that could be done apart from passing a resolution and forwarding it to the Local Government Board.

Another was that the poor law system was set up so that a man could claim relief to support his family, but a woman could only claim for herself or her children. This created an anomaly in the system. An old aged couple could both claim outdoor relief of three-shillings each, but if the man reached seventy before his wife and claimed his pension of five-shillings, the wife was disqualified from claiming outdoor relief, so as a couple, they were one-shilling a week worse off. However, if the woman reached seventy before her husband, he could still claim outdoor relief, so as a couple they could claim eight shillings a week.

During the last five years, the guardians had dealt with thirty-seven cases of consumption, at an aggregated cost of eight-hundred and thirty-seven pounds and eleven shillings. The average cost of sending each patient to the Sandgate Sanitarian was twenty-four pounds and three shillings. The average length of stay in the institution was twenty-two weeks. The highest amount paid for one patient was one-hundred and seventeen pounds and six shillings for a stay of eight-hundred and seventy-two days in the sanatorium, which the patient, a boy, completely recovered. The lowest amount paid was one pound and ten shillings for a man who stayed a week.

The guardians were flexible with consumption cases, which weren't strictly pauper cases. A baker from St Annes, with eight children, asked for three of his children, who were suffering from consumption, to be sent to a sanatorium. The man, who earned thirty-four shillings a week, offered to pay three-shillings a week towards the maintenance of the children. The difference would cost the guardians one-hundred and fifty pounds a year and some, including the clerk, were against it.

Chairman William Hodgson explained, 'I would like the board to look at these cases from a very broad standpoint. There was no doubt, technically speaking, they were not entitled to give relief of that kind. The applicant was earning far beyond the average wage, but it was quite true he had a big family. They were not entitled to consider the man, and if they refused to send the children away, the sanitary authority could not take it up under the present circumstances. The other children would run a grave danger of being infected, and the result would be the applicant would be unable to maintain his family and would be chargeable to the board. It was far better to spend a few shillings or a few pounds in preventing what was almost a certainty, than to let things take their ordinary course and the other children become infected.'

He continued, 'As to the question of who should do it, the clerk was quite right. It was the duty of the sanitary authority, but under the present circumstances, the sanitary authority was not in a position to do it. At best, the action the board took was only a temporary one. That the question would have to be faced by some authority before long, was undoubtedly true. Parliament had taken the matter up, and undoubtedly some steps would be taken before long.'

After putting it to the vote, the guardians decided to send the three children to the Sandgate Sanatorium.

Some cases were straight forward, such as Mary Parker of Blackpool, who was sent to Lancaster Asylum, where her husband was a patient. She had one-hundred and three pounds, fifteen shillings and two pence in the Post Office Bank and nine pounds and seventeen shillings cash at home. The family didn't want to be involved, and the clerk was told to sell all the furniture and pay any rent due. All the money collected would be used to cover the cost of her care.

The fight against smallpox continued. The vaccination returns from July to December showed that there were one thousand, one-hundred and forty-seven births. Of these, six-hundred and fifty-nine were successfully vaccinated. There were two-hundred and forty-one conscientious objections, ninety-one children died before vaccination, forty-five were postponed for medical reasons, seventy-seven left the district, and thirty-four were unaccounted for.

Mr Helliwell continued his campaign against 'idle men'.

He moved that, 'This board is of an opinion that able-bodied men who refuse to attempt to maintain themselves or their wives and families should be more stringently dealt with, and that for this purpose, legislation should be introduced at an early date, whereby such men could be detained and colonised by the Government at labour colonies.'

Elaborating he said, 'I think every member of the board was fully aware of the class of people to which I refer ... it was to those men who had got families and did not try to look after them; those who were strong and able to work, but would not try to keep themselves, those 'sharps' as they might call them, who were trying to live on anybody else, so long as they did not keep themselves. I think the time has come, now that we have a Government who were trying to help those people, who were trying to help themselves, that we should get hold of these people who will not help themselves. We want those men taken over by the state, and put in a colony of some description where they would be made to work or else be allowed to starve. I think that if they could provide a colony, after the style of a reformatory in which to place those men until they redeemed themselves, it would be a great saving to the country, and they would see happier homes. I am of the opinion that the Local Government Board should be pressed to bring in a scheme on the lines suggested by him.'

Mr Crossfield pointed out, 'We passed a resolution last November and sent it to the Local Government Board, with regard to the habitual vagrants, and in view of the fact that if a man neglected his wife and children, he would be summoned by the N.S.P.C.C., or else by his wife for neglect. I do not see that such a resolution was necessary. I do not think we should keep pestering the Government Board, with resolution after resolution, and I move a direct negative to the motion.'

Miss Webber pointed out that the resolution did not apply to those men who were out of work but to those who did not try to get work and who, she thought, ought to be compelled to work. Prisons were not stringent enough. The men would rather go to prison than the workhouse, and so long as they had a man like Winston Churchill at the head, they would never have prisons severe enough.

Miss Johnson took a harder line, 'I think the guardians ought to do something to make these men work. It is quite true that the Bible says that those who will not work, shall not eat, so what have we got to do with them. I should shoot them.'

The motion was passed and forwarded to the Local Government Board.

After Ernest Clark's mother was jailed for six months for child cruelty, Miss Johnson passed a motion asking the guardians to adopt the boy: which was passed. In June, the mother was released from prison and asked for her son to be returned. The guardians wrote back saying that the child would stay with them until she could prove that he will be well cared for and have a good home.

Nearing the end of the year, Mr Greenhalgh resigned as the dentist for the children's home and was replaced by Dr Buckley of Poulton. Dr Wigglesworth of Kirkham Number One District was replaced by Dr Alexander Smith.

The master and matron also resigned and were replaced, unusually by an unmarried couple. Seven couples had applied for the post including the porter and portress, Mr and Mrs Sharples, and one of the union's clerks and his wife, Mr and Mrs Rees. Mr Herbert Ashworth, a hospital steward of Manchester, and Miss Harriett Tattersall, a head nurse from Luton, were appointed – they eventually got married.

Matron Harriett Ashworth with one of the nurses. (Photo Courtesy of Janet Davis)

The adult outdoor paupers received an extra one shilling for Christmas, plus sixpence for each child, they had received the same amounts in June to celebrate the Coronation of King George V and Mary.

The Fylde Union rates in 1912 were very low, mainly because Blackpool's rateable value was so high, with a comparably low population. This year's call was set at two and a half pence in March and two pence in September. This was on a valuation of nearly one million pounds, which in March raised twenty-nine-thousand, one-hundred, and seventeen pounds of which nineteen-thousand, one-hundred and seventy-six pounds went to the county council.

Township	Rateable Value	Call	Township	Rateable Value	Call
Bispham	£22,759	£1093	Marton	£10,055	£580
Blackpool	£530,601	£5527	Wesham	£11,663	£656
Bryning with Kellamergh	£1120	£66	Newton with Scales	£1914	£112
Carleton	£7902	£444	Poulton	£15,596	£871
Clifton with Salwick	£6920	£420	Ribby with Wrea	£3353	£200
Eccleston with Larbreck	£1837	£107	Singleton	£3805	£227
Elswick	£1800	£106	St Annes	£93,839	£4849
Fleetwood	82,854£	£4904	Thornton	£31,540	£1817
Freckleton	£5076	£293	Treales Roseacre and Wharles	£7477	£438
Greenhalgh	£3002	£176	Warton	£2412	£137
Hardhorn with Newton	£7576	£447	Weeton with Preese	£5642	£338
Kirkham	£11708	£677	Westby with Plumpton	£9270	£554
Lytham	£74,353	£4083	Totals	£954,091	£29,117

Calls for March 1912

The guardians still visited the five Lancashire Asylums, but now they also sent a delegation to visit the training ship. Mr Richardson was in charge of the visit to the ship.

He reported, 'The deputation visited the training ship in the Mersey, and interviewed all 14 boys belonging to the union; we also made an inspection of the ship. The members were well pleased with all they saw, and are content the action of the board of sending suitable boys is to be commended.'

Last year, Commander Butterworth of the training ship forwarded a letter to the guardians. It was sent from Mr Cunningham, asking for his son to be returned home. The guardians thought the boy should remain and would not assist in his return. He stayed on the training ship for another year. Vincent Cunningham was then discharged from the *T. S. Indefatigable* and joined the Royal Navy. The Captain of the ship *Clio* informed the guardians that Harold Boothby was being transferred from his ship to *S.S. Advocate*.

In June that year, the Government's new national insurance scheme started. Previous to this, workers escaped being drawn into the poor law system by contributing to a friendly society, which would pay-out in cases of illness or unemployment. Now workers earning under one-hundred and sixty pounds a year were provided with health insurance. They had to contribute four pence a week, whilst the employer paid three pence, and the Government two pence. This provided them with ten shillings per week for the first thirteen weeks, and five shillings for the following thirteen weeks, after that they had to apply for poor relief. The scheme was administered through the existing 'friendly societies' but could also be accessed through the post office. The post office was an inferior option, as more benefits were provided through the societies.

Workers in certain industries, which went in circles of employment to unemployment, were compelled to join the National Insurance Scheme Number Two, which they had to contribute two and a half pence per week, the employer two pence a week, and the Government three pence. After being unemployed for a week, they could then claim seven shillings a week, for up to fifteen weeks, after that they had to claim poor relief.

The introduction of the old aged pension for the over seventies and the national insurance scheme for workers between sixteen and seventy was another nail in the coffin of the poor law system. Under the 1911 Act, the treatment of T.B. became free for all workers, which again took some of the responsibility from the guardians.

Entering the workhouse with a national insurance card was now similar to entering with money. So later in the year, the guardians wanted to know how many paupers for the last two weeks, beginning 1 October, had entered the workhouse with insurance cards. The clerk reported that six people had entered the workhouse in possession of the cards. There had been thirty-six vagrants passing through the tramp wards of which twelve had cards. The workhouse officials were ordered to keep a careful record of all the tramps admitted who were in possession of insurance cards.

These changes meant less able-bodied paupers were entering the workhouse. Of the two-hundred and twenty paupers in the house, one-hundred and ninety were over sixty years of age. Fifty years ago, the matron had an army of female workers, who helped her with the running of the workhouse. Now that work was done by employees.

The staff now employed by the union were:

Relieving officers: John Jump, Thomas Dixon, and Hugh Parkinson.

Master and matron: Mr and Mrs Ashworth.

Children's home superintendents: Arthur and Sarah Magson with assistant Emma Lowe.

Porters: John and Mary Sharples.

Engineer boiler room: James Kinloch.

Nurses: Florence Barton, Sarah Arkless, M. Hicks, Gertrude Greenhow, and A. McGreevor.

Cook: Margaret Ainsworth.

Laundress: Sarah Wilson.

Gardener: Mr Dowman.

Dentist: W.R. Buckley

District medical officers: William Wright Shaw, William Smith, James Anderton, A.M. Eason, Dr Merrall, W.R. Robinson, T.W. Butcher, and C.H.S. Winter.

Valuation officer: William A. Goss.

As well as paying the salary of the above staff, the guardians paid the pensions or superannuations of three former employees, William Thompson, Emma Trickey, and George Blacoe.

On the men's side, the workhouse daily routine was not directly affected by low numbers of inmates. The men were still employed on the farm with its pigs, cattle, and arable land. The feeble men helped the gardener in the greenhouse, vegetable gardens, and flower beds. In August, the gardener, Mr Dowman, was told to give them a lecture and demonstration on pruning. The tramps still had to break stones.

The Children's Act had been in place for four years, and the guardians started summoning people taking in children to nurse and not following the proper procedures. Legal proceedings were taken against Mary Walton of 7 St Walburgas Road, Blackpool, after she had taken a child Clifford Wright to nurse and had not given notice.

The children were still living in the old workhouse infirmary, and the guardians were under pressure to do something with the old workhouse and provide proper accommodation for the children. Mr Harrison was appointed the architect to help advise on the best possible course of action.

There were three options under consideration.

1. Selling the land at the old workhouse and adopting the scattered house scheme. This scheme involved having a central administration hub, and renting homes for the children to live in. The guardians could increase or decrease the amount of homes rented depending on the number of children, and some guardians thought it was a more natural way for the children to live. The old workhouse land in the town centre was worth three shillings and sixpence per yard. Land for the administration hub could be bought elsewhere for ten pence. It was cheaper to set up, about eight-hundred pounds, but in the long-term, it would cost more money. The neighbours could, however, become hostile to the children, and a matron was needed for each house.

2. The Group Home System was were semi-detached homes were built to house ten to twelve children, along with an administration block. This kept the children in one area, and the children could live as separate 'classes', boys, girls, or feeble-minded (children who couldn't be sent to the asylums for various reasons). The homes were built, so if in the future the Government arranged different ways of homing the children, the houses could be sold on as normal housing stock. The downside was that the initial cost was higher, at about eight-thousand pounds.

3. Redevelop the old workhouse. This was never going to happen. The old house had been condemned for the adults to live in and the Local Government Board would never sanction its use for children.

Option three was disregarded. The guardians were split on the other two options. It was decided to send a delegation to visit the only two unions who had adopted the scattered home system, Blackburn and Oldham. Miss Johnson decided to go behind the boards back and wrote to the Local Government Board.

She wrote,

> At the Fylde Union Lancashire, the guardians are now considering the best scheme to adopt for housing their poor law children. The board are partly divided on the question, which is the best plan? The 'cottage grouped homes' or the 'scattered homes.' As one of the guardians, in support of the 'cottage grouped homes' that you were in favour of them, I should be very grateful if you will kindly let me know which system you would adopt if you were a guardian of the Fylde Union.
>
> I am yours faithfully, Mary Johnson, Poor Law Guardian for Lytham.

The board forwarded the letter and the reply to Clerk Fred Brown. It was read out at August's meeting.

> I am directed by the Local Government Board, to acknowledge receipt of your letter of the 24th and to state that they regret that the matter to which it relates is not one in regard to which they can undertake to advise. They have found it necessary to make it a rule to abstain from advising individual members of local authorities or private persons on questions such as you have submitted to them.
>
> I am, your obedient servant,
>
> J. S. Davy, Assistant Secretary.

It was decided, after twelve months of debating, to adopt the group home system. The old workhouse would be demolished apart from the old infirmary where the children lived. Three semi-detached homes would be built along Moor Street and an administration block on Station Road.

1913 would turn out to be a quiet year for the Fylde Guardians but not for relieving officer, Hugh Parkinson, who lived at 5 Byron Street, Fleetwood. A tramp applied for relief, and when he was refused, he smashed three large

This grainy picture shows an aerial view of the Cottage Homes in 1930. The two-storey old infirmary is still standing.

plate glass windows at the officer's house. The guardians gave Mr Parkinson three pounds and tens shillings to repair the damage.

The Lytham Ladies Committee gave their annual tea and entertainments night to the sick and old folk in the workhouse in January. They provided tea for the old people over sixty and the sick in the infirmary. A concert was held in the dining room where thirty-six children from Lytham St John's School Choir sang a selection of songs. Piano solos were played by Muriel Cartmell, Mildred Gledhill, and Mary Ormerod. Percy Birley of the Villa, Wrea Green, sang several songs accompanied by Mr Hoyle and Eva Winchester. Mr and Mrs Pearson and Miss Parsons met all the expenses.

When Blackpool retired police officer Sgt Kendall was sent to an asylum, the guardians ordered the clerk to look into ways of paying his maintenance. Sgt Kendall had been receiving a pension of thirteen shillings and one penny per week, and after he was sectioned, the Blackpool Watch Committee decided to give his wife eight shillings per week to live on. The clerk told the union collector to apply for the remaining five shillings and one penny to pay for the policeman's maintenance. The committee would only allow the union to take three shillings and one penny, which they had to accept.

In July, the King and Queen visited Kirkham. The Royals planned to travel through Kirkham on their way to Blackpool from Preston; this route passed the old workhouse. The guardians decided to build a stand in front of the old house, to allow the old people and children to see the royal couple as they were driven along Moor Street.

The plans were finally passed for the cottage homes, and a building committee was formed. The committee appointed Thomas Croft and Sons Ltd. to build the new homes. There were twenty-one children in the home. In the house, in December, there were one-hundred and twenty-two men and ninety women. Out of the two-hundred and twelve paupers, seventy were in the sick wards, and over one-hundred and forty were over the age of sixty. These figures show that the Government's unemployment schemes were working.

There are two good examples of refractory behaviour in the punishment book for this year.

1. Arthur Taylor, who had stolen a pair of clogs from the receiving ward, was jailed for 14 days.

2. Thomas Brown, aged sixty-six, had assaulted the master by throwing a plate of food over him. He also received fourteen days imprisonment.

At Christmas, the dining room and infirmary were both decorated.

Dr William Wright Shaw, Mrs Ashworth, and the nurses in the infirmary 1913. (Lancashire Archives)

On Christmas morning, Henry Langton Birley of Carr Hill House, carried on the long tradition of his family by giving the adults either two ounces of tobacco or four ounces of tea and one pound of sugar, as well as giving sweets for the children. On Boxing Day, amongst the usual rations was; an extra three-hundred and eighty pounds of pork, one-hundred and twenty pounds of beef, three-hundred pounds of Christmas plum pudding, eighteen gallons of beer, ten dozen mineral waters, four-hundred and eighty pounds of potatoes, two-hundred and eighty pounds of swedes, one barrel of apples for apple sauce, one c.w.t onions for stuffing and three-hundred and sixty pounds of Christmas cake were consumed. The dinner was served at twelve noon and tea at five pm. The evening's entertainment started at six-thirty pm. The first part consisted of songs, sang by the staff and friends. The second part was a farce titled 'Ici on Parle Francais' put on by the staff.

The Fylde Union was known as the A1 Union, the best in the country, because of its low rates and its first-class workhouse. The main problem was the large turnover of staff, especially the nurses, this problem, however, was about to be dwarfed ... the clouds of war were gathering.

In 1914, with fewer and fewer able-bodied paupers entering the workhouses, and more and more of the inmates being old or infirm, the Local Government Board made some changes to better reflect how the institutions had changed.

The word 'inmates' would now be used instead of 'pauper' and the word 'workhouse' was dropped for 'institution'. The building would now be known as the 'Wesham Institution'. As well as the word changes, the classes of inmates would be changed according to age, character, and any disease of body or mind. The power would be placed into the hands of the medical officer as to which classes the inmates would be placed in. The guardians could now co-opt people onto the board with no previous knowledge of poor law.

William Hodgson said, 'This principle of co-option had been a great success in educational affairs, and I believe it would be a great advantage to the board.'

Another change, in April, was when the Neutral Deficiency Act of 1913, came into force. The guardians were sent a circular explaining the new act which defined the four grades of mental defectiveness.

1. Idiot: people defective in mind as to be unable to guard against common physical dangers.

2. Imbecile: could protect themselves from common dangers, but unable to take care of themselves. Imbeciles were not idiots but were incapable of managing themselves or their affairs, or, in the case of children, of being taught to do so.

3. Feeble-Minded: required care to protect themselves. Feeble-minded people were neither idiots or imbeciles, but if adults, their condition was so pronounced that they require supervision and control for their own protection or the protection of others. If children of school age, their condition was so pronounced that they, by reason of defectiveness, appear to be personally incapable of receiving proper benefit from instruction in ordinary schools.

4. Moral Defectives: moral defectives were people who, from an early age, displayed some permanent mental defect coupled with strong vicious or criminal propensities on which punishment had little or no effect. Unmarried mothers also became absorbed into this category.

There had been a steady decline in tramps admitted for the last fifteen years, especially noticeable since 1910. In 1913 the average number of tramps in the Wesham tramp ward per night was two. In May, Mr Crossfield, who had been to the North-Western Vagrancy Committee Conference, announced the commencement of the new ticket system.

The 'way ticket system' was where a working man in search of work was given a ticket or passport. This ticket allowed him to pass through a county, from union to union. It entitled the man and each member of his family to half a pound of bread and two ounces of cheese each when they arrived at the ward named on the ticket. The bearer would only be detained for one night and was given no task of work. He would be released immediately after breakfast. Ordinary casuals still had to perform work and were detained for two days.

The final work was carried out on the new homes. Mr Fox of Lytham laid the linoleum floors, and Pearson and Fairclough of Kirkham laid new paths and removed the soil. Two new walls with railings were built along Moor Street and Station Road for six-hundred and thirty pounds. The children could now leave the old infirmary and move into the six new Cottage Homes: numbered one to six.

Now that the cottage homes had been completed, four foster parents were appointed: Mrs Nuttall, Miss Wilson, Mrs Broadly, and Miss Lowe. They received a salary of thirty pounds plus uniform and rations. Miss S. A. Heywood was appointed relief foster mother.

Cottage Homes, Moor Street, Kirkham (Lancashire Archives)

Two more former homeboys had left the training ship. Stuart Steward left to work for the Cunard Line, and John Magee left for *S.S Gloucestershire.*

The first effects of the war were felt when the county treasurer wrote to the guardians saying that, because of the increase of police duty, the amount required for the second half of the year would increase by one penny in the pound.

When a soldier or sailor, including territorials, were called up for duty, his family was entitled to claim outdoor relief. The relief paid out to the families was reclaimed by the guardians through the National Relief Fund. The matron was part of the Army Nursing Reserve and was put on standby. The guardians appealed, and, in December, the War Office wrote to the guardians, stating that, under the circumstances, Mrs H. Ashworth will be relieved from duty as a member of the Territorial Force Nursing Service.

Despite the war starting, life still went on as normal.

Wesham Parish Church, where most paupers were buried, asked for a contribution of twenty-one pounds towards a new burial ground, and the guardians agreed to the request. A new clerk was appointed to help the master. He received a salary of twenty-five pounds plus accommodation, uniform, and rations.

The Blackpool Grocers' Association wrote requesting that the board, in future, should stipulate in advertisements that tenders would only be received from traders who were ratepayers in the union. The grocers' felt that they were only asking what was due to them and the traders in the district.

The clerk said, 'Apart from tea, proprietary articles, and flour, all articles were purchased in the district.'

The registrar of births and deaths for the Lytham Sub-District, Robert Waring resigned. At the age of seventy-six, he was the oldest registrar in the country. He had been the registrar for marriages since 1862, and births and deaths since 1876. He received a pension of thirty-one pounds.

1915 started with the now annual concert put on by the Lytham Ladies Visiting Committee, along with the St John's School Choir.

Although the cottage homes and institution were now separate, the cottage homes sent all the large items of laundry, such as sheets and blankets, to the Wesham Institution. Any bread or cakes needed at the home were baked at the institution and sent down to them.

Children entering the home were until this year admitted at Wesham. They were bathed and cleaned and then sent to the home in new clothing. However, from this year they would be admitted directly into the cottage homes and their clothing sent to Wesham to be cleaned and then stored.

The guardians purchased five pounds worth of books, and a library was opened in the homes.

As the war rumbled on, the Government started interning foreign aliens, and the British born wives of these men could claim maintenance from the union. The Fylde had fourteen cases. The twenty-five pounds and five shillings paid out in relief by the union was refunded by the Government.

On the training ship, John Gregson, who had become ill, was sent to Birkenhead Borough Hospital; he was suffering from phthisis. John's mother was an inmate at the Wesham Institute. The Birkenhead Union wrote to the Fylde asking them to except John's settlement and pay the twelve shillings cost of his weekly care. The guardians excepted the settlement claim.

Two more boys left the training ship, which had increased its cost by one shilling per week. The boys would now be sent mainly to Naval Ships. Edward Boardman and Robert Taylor were both sent to the *S.S Oxfordshire* Hospital Ship.

Colonel Coates of the Royal Army Medical Corps inspected the old infirmary after the guardians had offered the army the use of the empty building. The Colonel later wrote back, thanking the guardians, but said no small hospitals were being accepted at the present time. The War Office proposed to use Winwick Asylum for injured soldiers, but the Lancashire Asylums Board was fighting the proposal. Dr Goodling was against the army taking over Winwick.

He said, 'I have accommodation at South Shore for the reception of the wounded, and had offered to find double accommodation if required. The War Office replied that it was not yet required. Their idea seemed to be to get large institutions so that they could put large numbers of wounded soldiers in them. The idea is prevalent that in small institutions, the men got treated too well.'

Mr Helliwell disagreed, he said, 'The times were absolutely exceptional. The accommodation at the small hospitals was nothing as compared with the accommodation at Winwick. The real fighting only commenced last week (Battle of Neuve Chapelle). It is our duty to have the best places possible to enable soldiers to get better, so that if the war was not over, then they would be able to return to the fighting line. We are engaged in a fight such has never been known in history, and our duty was to help the Government all we can.'

The clerk interrupted, 'Perhaps I could shorten the discussion. This morning, I received a letter from Winwick Asylum Authorities intimating that a patient sent there from the Fylde last week had been removed to Lane Hill. It appears to me that the building has already been taken over by the Government, and the wounded were well on their way.'

Mr Bradly of Wrea Green, who seemed to know what was coming in this war, added, 'No doubt they would take more institutions before long, and the old workhouse at Kirkham would probably be taken. All available institutions would be wanted before this war finished.'

In June, the army opened a tented camp at Weeton for two-thousand territorials and volunteers from Lancashire; this camp swelled to over twelve thousand soldiers. The military authorities changed their mind about the old infirmary. Colonel Harrison asked to use the infirmary as a general hospital for the troops based at Weeton Camp. The guardians agreed but stipulated that no infectious cases could be admitted there.

Some of the staff joined the army. The master's clerk, Stanley Cottrell, joined the Royal Field Artillery. He asked for his post to be kept open until his return, and that the board made up the difference between his army pay: this was agreed to. Mr Walter Moorfield was appointed temporary master's clerk. He earned ten shillings weekly with food when on duty but slept out.

Sister Ada Johnson, as a member of the Queen Alexandra's Military Nursing Reserve, was called up. She was posted to Malta; her position was also kept open for her. The guardians insured the institution against enemy aircraft for ten-thousand pounds.

Dr William Wright Shaw suffered a heart attack and died this year. He was only the third doctor to hold the post of workhouse doctor since the union was formed. The first was Dr Gradwell serving from 1838 to 1840; followed by William's Father, Thomas Shaw, 1840 to 1883; and William who had replaced him. The post being held by one family for seventy-five years was probably a record for the country, according to the chairman. To help the nurses, two ward maids were appointed on a wage of sixteen pounds per annum.

Up to the year ending September, four-hundred and fifty-eight vagrants were admitted into the tramp wards. The year before it was one-thousand and thirty-one vagrants. The average for the last five years was one-thousand-six-hundred vagrants. Stone breaking was becoming rarer, which meant a loss of income for the guardians. They still made a profit on the pigs though. The profit from the pigs for the last five years was an average of ninety-four pounds.

Baby farming still went on.

Sgt Sample of Blackpool Police reported that Mrs Langley, of 7 Eden Street, Blackpool, had received a child named Ivy Armstrong to nurse for a reward and had not notified them.

Dr Dunderdale said, 'Mrs Langley was in ill health.' She was cautioned by the clerk.

The Chief Inspector of Blackpool reported that Martha Thompson of 23 Belmont Avenue, had taken a child to nurse and maintain for a reward. The child Richard Henry Prest, aged five years, who seemed well cared for. The clerk was instructed to caution her.

1916. The Battle of the Somme was on the horizon, and the army would need specialists in the form of field doctors who could not be trained up like the infantry and artillery in a matter of weeks. The military asked the guardians which medical men under the age of forty-five years and employed by them could be spared for military service. Dr Buckley gained a commission into the Royal Army Medical Corps in April. He offered to resign, but the guardians said it was unnecessary and he should visit them when on leave.

Dr Merrall, the medical officer for the Blackpool Southern District, also left for the army. Dr Hodgson was appointed the acting doctor whilst he was away. Dr Hodgson wrote to the guardians stating that due to his work for the war office, he was unable to attend to the public vaccinations. Dr Reid of 250 Lytham Road took over the role of the public vaccinations officer. Dr Cockcroft of the Blackpool Northern District also applied for a commission into the army, but he wasn't successful. He joined the Navy the following year.

In April, Dr Anderson of the Poulton District died. The guardians used this as an opportunity to divide the Poulton Medical District into two separate districts. Thornton had changed from a small village into a town of four-thousand, six-hundred, and sixty-nine inhabitants; nearly half of the eleven-thousand, eight-hundred, and twenty-five of the Poulton Medical District. Dr W. A. Riddell was appointed the medical officer the Poulton District on a salary of twenty-six pounds, and Dr Rhodes for the new Thornton Medical District on a salary of sixteen pounds.

Kirkham Number Two District relieving officer, Mr Jump, thought he would be liable to be called up for military service any time soon and asked the guardians to appeal to the military tribunal service for an exemption or make provisions for his family. The tribunal spared him from military duty.

Another effect of the war was the increase in the costs of food. The guardians asked the master to experiment with bread making by using potatoes. The house committee reported that no noticeable savings could be made using potatoes, and the experiment was discontinued. The cost of funerals for the institution's inmates was increased. Both Christ Church Wesham and St Josephs increased the cost from twelve shillings and sixpence to fifteen shillings owing to the additional expense of drainage.

The numbers being injured in the war was becoming apparent.

The military authorities told the Warrington Union they were taking over their infirmary to create a one-hundred and twenty-beds temporary war hospital. Warrington then wrote asking the Fylde Guardians to take one-hundred patients from their infirmary. This was agreed to but then rescinded, because of the large numbers of soldiers being billeted in Blackpool. The military then took over the Wesham Institution's infirmary and opened the Fylde Military Auxiliary Hospital for one-hundred and twenty soldiers. The army had total control of the building, but the guardians set the following conditions as the union doctor, nurses and staff would work in the building.

A. The military authorities must pay 2s. per patient, or such a sum in excess if the costs are more than that amount.

B. That a certain number of orderlies are supplied to help in the wards and paid for at the above rate.

C. That the necessary clothing be provided by the military authorities for all patients.

D. That a military medical officer attends for disciplinary purposes and help in the treatment of the cases if such becomes necessary.

E. That any patients suffering from infectious or contagious diseases be sent away for treatment.

Colonel Coates agreed to the terms but asked the guardians to provide all the necessary equipment for the soldiers in the infirmary and then charge it to the Ordnance Stores.

Fylde Auxiliary Military Hospital

The Fylde Guardians joined a protest supporting the county asylums in 1917. They were against soldiers returning from the war and being treated as pauper lunatics. The asylums were forced into a position by the Government, where they claimed from the soldier's war pensions to pay for their maintenance.

Miss Johnson passed the motion, which Reverend Cotton supported saying, 'It would be a scandal to the country if we allowed men who had risked their life and limb to be reduced to pauperism on their returning to this country.'

William Bradly's prediction was coming true. Colonel Coates asked the guardians to provide an additional fifty beds for returning injured soldiers. The satellite hospital would come under the command of the 1st Western General Hospital, Fazakerley, Liverpool. Mrs Hale of Mowbreck Hall donated geese and chickens to the forty-four soldiers in the military hospital.

The military patients created a lot of work for the institution's staff.

The laundress, Annie Worthington, who now had to clean the Army's laundry, received a pay raise of five pounds taking her salary to thirty-seven pounds and ten shillings. The military then installed new equipment in the laundry to help her. The guardians agreed to purchase the machinery at the end of the war. They also decided to give the master, matron, cook, and porter a pay raise and then claim the money back from the military authorities.

Despite the fifteen-pounds pay raise, the master and matron resigned, leaving for Brentwood. Six applicants applied for the Ashworth's former post: Mr and Mrs Warren, Howden; Mr and Mrs Willis, Cleobury Mortimer; Mr and Mrs Broad, Ashton-under-Lyne; Mr and Mrs Swaffield; Scollcotes, Hull; Mr and Mrs Seeley, Salop (Shropshire); and Mr and Mrs Pickford, Todmorden. Richard and Rosetta Willis were appointed master and matron.

Some more staff left for the army. The temporary clerk was called up. It was decided to offer the post only to a discharged soldier. Albert Kirby became the temporary-temporary clerk for seven shillings and sixpence per week.

The Kirkham Number Two District doctor, Dr Smith, joined the 27th Brigade Royal Field Artillery. He was injured on the Western Front on Sunday 27 May 1917. Lieutenant William Alexander Smith died from his wounds on 3 June aged thirty-five years of age.

He was buried in Aubigny Communal Cemetery, Pas-de-Calais,

> 'The Beloved Husband of Elsie Smith of Wesham, Kirkham, Lancashire.'

William's brother, Dr G. B. Horrocks, took over his Wesham practice and became the doctor for Kirkham Number Two District.

Dr Parkinson was called up in May and went into the army. In September, Dr Cockcroft was called up for naval duty. Dr Wylie medical and vaccinating officer was also called up. He was struggling to get a locum and asked the guardians to support his appeal against being conscripted.

In the military hospital, entertainment was put on every Thursday, for the troops by the Entertainments Committee of the Fylde Auxillary Military Hospital. This group was allowed a free hand in the hospital, but by December, complaints were raised by the union staff about the entertainments lasting until the early hours making it impossible for them to carry out their duties.

Future permission to hold whist drives and musical entertainment would now only be given as long as they ended before nine p.m. The Kirkham Red Cross also applied to entertain the troops, orderlies and nurses with whist drives and tea. This was again granted as long as it finished by nine p.m.

Since the end of the Boer War, in 1902, the number in the vagrancy wards had been continuously declining. This year the Joint Vagrancy Committee decided to close the wards at Wesham, Blackburn, Chorley, Garstang, and two in the Ormskirk Union for the duration of the war. All vagrants would be, in future, directed to the Preston tramp wards, which were central to the ones closing. The costs of running the Preston wards were to be shared between the unions whose wards were closing

---

At the start of 1918, there were two-hundred and thirty-two inmates in the house and fifty-one children in the home. The complaints about the whist drives mentioned in December's meeting were published in the newspapers, prompting this letter which was sent to the guardians.

> The Square Dec. 22th 1917.
>
> The committee who have weekly whist drives in hand at the Fylde Auxillary Hospital Wesham, have instructed me to write to thank you for permission to hold them on December 20th and 27th. They regret they cannot do so at such a short notice, as

all arrangements were cancelled on receipt of the clerk's letter of the 10th inst. saying whist drives had better not be held for the present. In the report of the board meeting of December 19th, given in the "Lancashire Evening Post" of the same day and the "Preston Guardian" of December 22nd, Mr Helliwell of Blackpool is reported to have said, "that the entertainments committee had taken advantage of the liberties in the house." And Mr R. Woods had said also "that the entertainments had lasted, in many cases until 2 or 3 a.m." The committee beg to state that the guardians have been misinformed, and suggest that these gentlemen be asked to substantiate their statements if correctly reported in the press or withdraw them, as it has given the public a wrong impression.

The only time the committee enter the house is when they signed their names in the visitor's book, and they do not re-enter it. The weekly whist drives given by the committee have always finished at about nine o'clock, and the only time late hours were kept was until 1 a.m at a public dance and whist drive in the assembly hall on November 22nd for which the guardians gave special permission. The committee has in hand a large sum of money subscribed by the public for these entertainments, and they gather from the press that the guardians do not wish them to be discontinued altogether. They have no desire to encroach upon the guardians prerogative in any way but suggest that if the guardians care to fix a new list of dates upon which whist drives may be held in the wards, some arrangements may definitely be come to, and they will undertake as previously, that the entertainment conclude by the time fixed by the guardians.

Signed D. Parkinson Hon. Sec.

Mr Helliwell, in answer, said, 'I do not think it is necessary for me to reply to the letter. We, as guardians, are responsible for good government of the house, and we have taken the necessary steps for that government.'

Miss Johnson said, 'I object to that committee sending such letters. The cook has left because she was kept up until three o'clock in the morning and then had to rise again at five for her ordinary duties.'

The vice-chairman finished with, 'Treat it with the contempt it deserves. Let the matter rest at that.'

These responses were also reported in January's newspapers, which annoyed the Fylde Auxilary Hospital Entertainments Committee further, and they stopped holding whist drives on 16 January. Unrepentant, the guardians contacted the Surgeon General, based in Blackpool and asked him to provide entertainment for the soldiers.

Mr Hale of Mowbreck Hall, whose land ajoined the workhouse, was appointed by the Canadian Red Cross Society as a representative to visit any Canadian soldiers in the hospital, and the whist drives were restarted by his wife. Later, two more groups the Kirkham Red Cross Society and Wrea Green Red Cross Society also started holding whist drives, and both agreed that the drives and refreshments would finish by nine p.m.

The army opened a third auxiliary hospital in April, in the Kirkham and Wesham Council School. Major Reeves asked the guardians if the whist drives could be moved into the dining hall to entertain the soldiers from the school which was agreed to.

The war was still in full flow. The Mayor of Blackpool invited the guardians to Blackpool where a tank was set to visit in the second week of February, promoting the purchase of war bonds. The guardians had already invested five-thousand pounds in 1917 with bonds set at a rate of five per cent.

Much of the care the soldiers received was undertaken by the institution's seven nurses and doctor. The guardians claimed the costs back from the Government. The cost of care for the soldiers, this year was five-thousand, five-hundred, and eighty-eight pounds, two shillings, and twenty-one pence. This money also covered the extra forty pounds paid to the doctor and the wages of thirty-two shillings for the clerk and store keeper at the auxiliary hospital.

Some of the other union officials, who had extra work from the army, could claim a war bonus; the nurses received a bonus of twenty-six pounds and ten shillings. Relieving officers John Jump, Hugh Parkinson, and Thomas Dixon all applied for war bonuses and were allowed an extra thirty-five pounds a year from 1 July.

Since the union was formed, able-bodied women either looked after their children themselves or joined them in the workhouse. The only other option was to pay a baby farmer to look after the child. Although the baby farmers were now watched by the police and N.S.P.C.C, it was not a good option for the child. Three to four cases on the Fylde ended up in court yearly, but this was mainly for not informing the authorities that they took in babies to nurse.

One ward in the institution was for pregnant paupers. Margaret Lucene, aged twenty-seven years and able-bodied, gave birth to an illegitimate child. She left the institution on 25 August, but she could not find a place in a nurse home for the baby. She then asked the guardians if she could place the child in the cottage homes until she found somewhere to live.

Clerk Fred Brown, talked about Margaret's case at September's meeting.

He said, 'A child has been born in the house, but at the time the mother declined to hand over the child to the guardians, stating that she would take it with her to Blackpool and place it to nurse, but if she failed to find a suitable place she would communicate with me. I think the time has come when better protection should be made for children when they leave the house. Twenty years ago, I would not have advocated such a course, but when the flower of our manhood was being drained on the battlefield, it behoved them to look strictly to the welfare of the children. A big percentage of the children from one to twelve months, taken from the house died each year. The board now has the chance of starting a scheme that would help mothers, whose affection for their children prevented them parting with them even to a board of guardians.'

He wanted the option of allowing children to be placed in the cottage homes by able-bodied women and allowing them to stay outside of the institution but making them pay for their child's maintenance.

Mrs Webber was against it, 'The mother has taken upon herself the responsibility of motherhood, and she ought to be made to discharge her responsibility. Why the ratepayers should be called upon to maintain illegitimate children passes my comprehension.'

Chairman Mr Hodgson, agreed with the clerk, 'Referring to the circumstances in this particular case, the question occurred to me more than once, whether the time had come when they would have to make provisions for such cases. I do not believe public action on the lines indicated would increase illegitimacy. There were a certain number of people who would go wrong whatever happened, and who met with misfortunes. It was the duty of the state or a public authority to make such provisions that the children might develop into useful citizens.'

The guardians decided to help her. Margaret Lucene's child was taken into the cottage home, and she had to pay four shillings weekly for the child's maintenance. Another woman, Mrs Dagger, gave birth in the hospital and asked to leave the child until she could find work. The clerk pointed out that her husband and other children were at present in receipt of assistance and, under the circumstances, they decided not to grant permission.

The Ministry of Health was established that year. The ministry's role was to coordinate all matters referring to the health of the public. They took over all local authority health-related duties, national insurance, planning, housing, environmental health, and poor law. The guardians would now answer to the Ministry of Health and not the Local Government board.

Even before this act, the Ministry on Reconstruction had been looking at transferring these powers to county councils and borough councils. It would be another twelve years before the guardians were replaced, and life continued in the institution, where the gardener and labour master resigned. He was replaced by Thomas Taylor.

In the cottage homes, a receiving room was opened to admit the children. A domestic servant was employed at the cottage homes to help with the children.

In 1919, with the fighting over, and hardly any soldiers in the hospital, the guardians asked for the infirmary to be released earlier than the army had planned. The army moved out and sold all the furniture, bedding, and clothing to the guardians for five-hundred pounds. By July, there was just the medical and surgical stores remaining, which were removed by the army. All three auxiliary military hospitals in Kirkham were closed.

Now that the old infirmary was empty, the Kirkham and District Branch of the Comrades of the Great War asked the board to meet a deputation, who wanted to lease the old hospital as a club room. This group would eventually become the Kirkham Royal British Legion. The request was refused, because of the close proximity to the homes and the unsatisfactory approach to the building. There had also been a lot of problems with the soldier's behaviour when the hospital was still open.

The guardians also started keeping an eye on the numbers of ex-soldiers entering the re-opened casual wards. A total of twenty-two discharged soldiers and sailors were admitted into the institution's casual ward during the month of June.

Though the fighting ended in November 1918, peace wasn't declared until the signing of the Treaty of Versailles in 1919. To celebrate the end of the war, a bank holiday was created, 'Peace Day' on 19 July. To help the paupers celebrate, the guardians gave each adult in receipt of outdoor relief, one shilling and sixpence and nine pence for each child.

The call for this year was four and a half pence on an assessable value of one-million, fifty-eight-thousand, eight-hundred and sixty-eight pounds. Forty-thousand pounds was for county council purposes. Blackpool had the highest assessable value at six-hundred-and-thirty-one-thousand, two-hundred, and twenty-two pounds. Second was St Annes at ninety-eight-thousand, eight-hundred, and sixty-one pounds; Third Fleetwood at eighty-nine-thousand, three-hundred, and eighty pounds; Fourth Lytham at seventy-eight-thousand, one-hundred and twelve pounds; Fifth Thornton at thirty-six-thousand, two-hundred, and seventeen pounds. Poulton came sixth at sixteen-thousand, two-hundred, and fifty pounds, and Kirkham seventh at twelve-thousand, eight-hundred, and eighty-six pounds.

Inspector Cooke, of the N.S.P.C.C, asked for Mary and Dora Cardwell, fourteen years and nine years, to be admitted into the cottage homes. They were the illegitimate children of Ellen Cardwell who had been recently jailed for three months for child neglect. In May, the guardians took over parental control of the children. Now that the war was over, the annual trip to Blackpool restarted, and the children were taken to the seaside for the day and given one shilling to spend.

Thomas Dixon resigned after thirty-nine years as the relieving officer for Blackpool. After the post was advertised, two-hundred and thirty-one people applied, of which ten were interviewed. Before the post was awarded, the guardians divided Blackpool into two separate relieving districts: The north district with thirty-eight-thousand, six-hundred, and fifty-seven inhabitants and The south district with thirty-five-thousand, four-hundred, and twenty-nine inhabitants. Hardhorn-with-Newton was moved from the Blackpool District into the Fleetwood District. The Fleetwood officer received an extra ten pounds to compensate for the extra work.

Mr George Rees, aged thirty-eight, the chief assistant clerk at the institution, was given the role of Blackpool North District, relieving officer. John Jump, aged forty, the relieving officer and registrar for the Kirkham Number Two District, was appointed to the Blackpool South District. Both were paid one-hundred and twenty pounds as relieving officers, union collectors, and children's act and infant life protection officers. They earned an extra fee of one-hundred and ninety-pounds as registrars of births, deaths, and marriages, and vaccination officers. All fees and salaries included travelling expenses: there was no war bonus.

Johnson Cardwell, the assistant overseer of Marton, aged thirty-eight, was appointed to John Jump's former post of relieving officer, union collector, vaccinations officer and infant protection officer at a salary of one-hundred and twenty pounds, plus war bonus of ninety-pounds.

Due to the fact that you had to live in the district you served, all three men had to move home before the start date on 1 January; Johnson Cardwell had no problem, but the other two were struggling to find somewhere to live. There was a chronic shortage of housing in Blackpool; the construction of houses had stopped during the war.

The guardians purchased two homes for the officers: 1 Westbourne Avenue for the Blackpool South District for one-thousand-six-hundred pounds, and 9 Raikes Parade in the North District for one-thousand, three-hundred and seventy-five pounds. Both men had to pay an annual rent of thirty-five pounds.

When Mr Thomas Dixon retired on 31 December, the guardians worked out his pension at 36/60th of his salary and fees for the last five years. He retired on a yearly pension of three-hundred and two pounds, eighteen-shillings, and ten pence.

One of the main reasons given by the nurses for leaving the Fylde Union was the fact that they were paid quarterly and by cheque, which in some cases could mean waiting fifteen weeks to be paid. One nurse also thought they lost a day's pay a year, two days in a leap year.

Mr Shea passed a motion in August, 'That salaries of all union officials be paid monthly instead of quarterly, and that payment be made in cash.'

As from August, the salaried officials were paid monthly. Mr Cross who was the union assessor, had his pay increased from three-hundred pounds to four-hundred pounds plus a war bonus.'

The clerk was paid a set amount by the guardians; he then paid for any staff he needed out of this money himself. He received five-hundred and twenty-five pounds a year from the union of which he paid his staff three-hundred and thirty pounds. Mr Brown was also the clerk of the education committee, pensions committee, hospital committee, Fylde Rural Council, and some other governing bodies and actually received one-thousand-two-hundred pounds a year. That year he asked for a pay raise of two-hundred pounds for his role as union clerk. Despite the chairman agreeing to the pay raise, it was voted down by the guardians.

1920–1930

It was 1920, and the British economy was going through a depression with high unemployment, deflation, stagnant growth, and industrial action. Due to the war and the unsettled times, boards of guardians, which would have probably been disbanded by now, received a reprieve. William Hodgson talked on the subject when he was re-elected as the chairman.

He said, 'Some of us a short time ago thought boards of guardians were going to be abolished, but I do not think that would happen for many long years. I am of the opinion that no government would propose to impose upon the country, a scheme costing more, and which would not be anything so effective as the present one. Whilst the work of the guardians during the past two or three years had been easy; I feel right in saying that difficult times were ahead.'

Blackpool's and Fleetwood's economies were struggling to get back to pre-war levels.

Blackpool's main economy was in fact house building, but with the cost of materials still high, hardly any house building was taking place.

In Blackpool there were almost eight-hundred unemployed former soldiers and three-hundred and twenty civilian men, both groups received about twenty-nine shillings a week. There were also seven-hundred and five women and girls out of work, most former munitions workers who received twenty-five shillings per week. In Fleetwood, it was the fishing industry that was struggling. Almost one-hundred steam fishing boats had been commandeered by the Military. Most had still not been returned. Kirkham's cotton mills were running at full strength and the town was not too badly affected by the recession.

Despite the high unemployment, the main costs for the Fylde Union were the maintenance of lunatics at twelve-thousand pounds, followed by indoor relief at seven-thousand pounds, outdoor relief at three-thousand-five-hundred pounds, Union salaries were five-thousand-five-hundred pounds per year, and rations for the staff cost one-thousand-three-hundred pounds.

In March, the finance committee, recommended a call for this year poor law of eight-pence in the pound: double last year's. The expenditure for 1919–20 was twenty-thousand, seven-hundred, and seventy-six pounds against the estimated expenditure for 1920–21 of thirty-five-thousand, eight-hundred, and eighteen pounds. The assessable value of the Fylde was one-million, one-hundred-and-twenty-thousand pounds. For the half-year from March, the rates were set at four pence for poor law and two shillings and three and three-quarter pence for county council purposes.

Mr Bradley thought the Government spent too much money.

He passed a resolution. 'That it is the opinion of the board, the time has come for all public bodies throughout the country to demand the cessation of the Government's reckless expenditure and its continued interference with the finance and right of such public bodies, through bureaucratic and unnecessary ministries, whose orders are forcing up local rates, causing widespread distress with resultant growing resentment on the part of the already overburdened ratepayers and taxpayers.'

He explained his thinking, 'The board are convinced that such methods could no longer be tolerated by the public bodies, and must be met by a firm determination, to resist to the utmost of their capacity, if these things went on any longer the country would be in bankruptcy.'

Reverend Dr Cotton said, 'I notice from this morning's papers that one out of every 65 persons in the country were receiving relief. It was an astonishing fact, and unless something was done about that quickly, they would find themselves in a very difficult position.'

Mr Wallace had another point, 'I am not opposed to the motion, but I do not like to hear some members gloating as stated over the dropping of measures such as the Education Bill etc. and yet they never express any opinion against the employment of troops in Mesopotamia and Ireland at such a cost. The only thing workers got from the occupation of Mesopotamia and Ireland was that they were called upon to pay and send their sons out to be killed for no useful purpose whatsoever. What the board should do was to send letters of protest to Lloyd George and Churchill about the extravagance in maintaining the army's in these areas.'

Some of the initiatives of the 1918 Education Act, were dropped that year due to Government cuts.

In answer to Mr Wallace, Mr Bradley said, 'I deny gloating over the Education Bill, or any other useful bill, but I still maintained that it was quite long enough for a boy to go to school until he was 14. If he is an intelligent boy, he could continue in the higher realms of education by winning his way to university, without any cost to the ratepayers.'

In the asylums, there were two classes of lunatics, 'private and pauper'. Former soldiers and sailors classed as lunatics were somewhere in between. To avoid any stigma attached to being in the asylums and having your maintenance paid by the state, a new class of inmate was created for former servicemen and women: 'service class'.

One former Blackpool soldier who fell into this group was John Fisher. When he was sectioned, the guardians didn't claim maintenance from his family but from the Blackpool War Pensions Sub-committee.

To move patients to and from the asylums, the guardians had previously used a horse ambulance, but now with this mode of transport being outdated for the long journeys, they asked Kirkham Urban District Council if they could use their motor ambulance. No, was the answer.

When the master's clerk applied for a pay increase, the finance committee decided that now the military hospital was closed, his services should be dispensed with. They thought that he had only been employed whilst the army occupied the infirmary.

The master told the guardians that they were wrong; there had been a master's clerk before the army occupied the infirmary.

He said, 'The previous master had had a clerk appointed in 1914, with a salary of £25, rations, and uniform. In April 1915, that clerk was called up for military service, and his place was taken by an inmate of the institution, who left with the former master when he went to Brentwood. The present clerk was appointed in July 1917, and his position was made permanent by the house committee in February 1919. Without clerical assistance, it would be a physical impossibility for me or anybody else to keep all the accounts and books, give out the stores, attend the telephone, and, exercise supervision over the inmates and staff.'

After some discussion, it was decided to stay with the original decision and dispense with the clerk. In future, the work would be done by a boy on leaving school.

How former soldiers were treated was high on the agenda at this time, and the guardians kept pressure on the Government to do what they thought was right for former service personnel.

Mr Wallace moved the following resolution, 'That were men on enlistment into the naval, military, or air forces, were passed fit for service, had been discharged, and were still suffering from disability, or in need of assistance, they should continue to receive a pension and not have to apply for poor law assistance and become chargeable to the local rates.'

He said, 'When the men were asked to join the fight for their country, they were promised an abundance of things. One thing was that on their return there would be a land fit for heroes to live in. One wondered what the men thought when they returned home and found it anything but a land fit for heroes. The men had suffered in their country's cause and for them to become chargeable to any charitable institution was, to my mind, simply scandalous and a disgrace to a civilised nation. I think the Government ought to take all the responsibility and see that if the men were unable to maintain themselves and families, that they were kept for free from poverty and charity. It is the duty of the Government to see that the men do not want for anything. Yesterday, I saw the certificate of a man who had been on all fronts and who had been wounded in France and Mesopotamia, which enabled him to draw the handsome pension of 5s. 6d per week, which, with the present value of money, was equivalent to about 1s. 6d.'

The resolution was carried, and Mr Shea added that at Blackpool the men had to be helped out with a local fund, which was pure charity, to enable them to carry on with a very small pension.

An ex-soldier received a pension, depending on their circumstances, of between five shillings and sixpence to twenty-seven shillings and sixpence weekly, plus allowances for any children: first-child, five-shillings; second, four shillings and two pence; third, three shillings and four pence; and each child after the third gave an extra two-shillings and sixpence, all weekly.

The soldier mentioned by Mr Wallace, was probably unmarried, lived with his parents and uninjured. A former soldier who was disabled and could never work again, or was undergoing treatment received the higher amount. Disabled soldiers who needed a carer could claim an extra twenty-shillings weekly on top of their pension, or if his wife acted as his carer, an extra ten shillings weekly.

The Preston Board of Guardians had a meeting with the Fylde Guardians to discuss the case of a widow and her six children chargeable to the Fylde. She was living in Preston because she couldn't find anywhere to live on the Fylde. The Fylde Guardians still refused to pay outdoor relief to people living outside their area; it was costing the Preston Union forty shillings per week.

After the meeting, the Chairman of the Preston Union, Mr Woodhouse, said, 'The Fylde Guardians had received us courteously but adhered to their previous decision. The only alternatives left were to remove the family to their place of settlement, or to maintain them so long as they were in need. It is impossible for the widow to get a house in the Fylde District, and if we remove her, she would have to go into the Fylde Workhouse. That would mean that her little home would be broken up, and her children would be separated from her and sent to the children's homes. The rule against granting out relief to non-resident poor was a relic of a by-gone age, and I am sorry the Fylde Guardians were not more progressive.'

The woman had cost the Preston Union one-hundred and ten pounds so far, and they appealed to the Ministry of Health.

Alfred Loynes was charged at Blackpool for leaving his children and wife chargeable to the union. Mr Jump, in court, said the man left his wife and two children absolutely destitute. The woman was removed to the institution and the children to the homes at Kirkham.

Loynes in court said, 'I left my wife on affectionate terms on going to work at Birmingham.'

He earned five guineas per week and offered to pay the guardians forty-five shillings per week for their maintenance. The case was adjourned for two months. If he paid what he had promised, no further action would be taken.

The inmates of the institute and the children's homes had their annual trip to Blackpool in June. They travelled not by train, but by motor charabancs. At Blackpool, they visited the Pleasure Beach and went to the pictures. They had a circular tour on the trams and later had dinner at the casino and tea at the Station restaurant, before returning home.

In October, William Hodgson, paid a surprise visit to the cottage homes and found everything in a perfect condition. He thought the children looked healthy and well cared for. He congratulated the superintendent, Mr Magson, on the appearance of the house and the way the children were looked after. Land came up for sale next door to the cottage homes on Moor Street, and it was purchased by the guardians for any future expansion projects. They bought nought point seven acres of land with a four-hundred and twenty-pounds loan from the Ministry of Health. The guardians then leased the land to a Mr Maxwell until it was needed by them.

Back at the institution, a new committee was formed the 'health committee'. When a nurse had her watch broken by one of the inmates, who was making her bed, she complained to the new committee who agreed to pay to get it repaired. Mr Hodgson thought this was illegal.

The chairman of the health committee, Mr Mellor disagreed, 'I am told it is quite in order, my information being that it is done by other unions. If the Government auditor refuses to pass the amount, I shall have no difficulty in finding the money for a refund.'

The clerk said, 'It is quite wrong. The next thing, some of the officers will be claiming for something valuable, £100 or £200 worth of stuff. The union make no contract with their officers to replace these things. If it had been clothing spoilt by the laundry, then we should have been liable. This girl may have been careless in leaving her watch about. Suppose it was a diamond ring she had left, and it had been taken away, would you be liable? You are opening the door to a very serious matter.'

Mr J. H. Counsel said, 'In my experience as a former member of the Salford Board of Guardians, was that officers were responsible for their own articles, and notices were posted up to that effect.'

On 8 November the previous year, the new Unemployment Insurance Act came into force. Prior to this, only four-hundred-thousand workers had insurance against unemployment. However, in 1921, under the new act, it was compulsory for all workers between sixteen and seventy years old, who had health insurance to be insured against unemployment, this was nearly twelve-million people. This meant that after three days, unemployed men received fifteen shillings weekly, and women received twelve shillings. Boys and girls would receive seven shillings and sixpence. The weekly contribution for men was four pence, then their employer would also contribute four pence; women, three and a half pence and their employer three pence; boys, aged 16 to 18, two pence and their employer two pence; girls, two pence and their employer one and a quarter pence.

The only exceptions were agricultural workers, private domestic servants, and people in employment whose terms made it unnecessary to have insurance such as teachers and civil servants.

The health and unemployment insurances were the beginnings of the welfare state, but it didn't have a massive impact on the poor law system. Most working people had previously paid into a friendly society for the cover they now received from the Government. However, with long term high unemployment, it was going to be a difficult time for the guardians, especially for indoor relief. In January, there was two-hundred and thirty people in the institution, last year it was two-hundred and six.

The shortage of houses was a problem. A Wesham resident wrote to the guardians, on behalf of twenty married couples, asking if they could be found accommodation in the institution even though they were working and paying rates. The writer stated that there were fifty to seventy married couples living in apartments in the district in anything but comfortable conditions, and they had come to the conclusion that apartments in the Fylde Institution would be more suitable.

Mr Kemp said, 'We now have an opportunity to use the old infirmary. I think it will be most suitable for such a purpose and at the same time we could make a little revenue from it.'

The request was declined.

Since the formation of the Fylde Union, they had always had spare money in the accounts, but in March last year, they were overdrawn by five-thousand pounds, and in March of 1921, they were overdrawn by fifteen-thousand pounds. The finance committee, with this in mind, set a poor rate of sixpence in the pound raising twenty-seven-thousand-five-hundred pounds against an estimated expenditure of twenty-three-thousand-five-hundred pound: fourteen-thousand pounds for lunatics, twelve-thousand pounds for the institution and cottage homes, five-thousand pounds for outdoor relief, and five-thousand pounds for general maintenance and equipment. The extra four-thousand pounds would be used to start clearing the overdraft; the county rates were set at two shillings and nine pence in the pound.

Mr Bradley suggested that the county rate should be collected by the county people themselves, but Michael Shea pointed out that this would mean duplicating officials.

Despite the high rate and overdraft, Mr Yates reported, 'We are the lowest-rated union in the country, and in view of that fact we have something to be proud of. Some of the union rates in other parts of the country had been increased 100 per cent, so our union was not badly managed.'

In April, Mr Hodgson was again elected chairman.

Mr Bradley said, 'I have served under three chairmen, during the last fifty years, and I knew of none who had done the work better than Mr Hodgson, who had always allowed full latitude to the members'.

Mr W. Yates touched on Mr Hodgson's fairness and impartiality, and Michael Shea, a new guardian, said, 'I describe myself as one of the labour men of the board and identify myself with the remarks of the previous speakers.'

Mr Hodgson replied, 'There were some lively incidents in the years gone by, but today everything was passed practically without comment. I refer to the work of the assessment committee, which is extremely important between the ratepayers and the overseers, and if the day ever dawned when the assessment committees were abolished, it would be hard against the ratepayers who would be unprotected.'

The immediate problem after Mr Hodgson's election was the miner's strike which the railwaymen had just come out in sympathy. The institution was given priority but was still struggling to find coal. They had dispatched a lorry to Wigan, but the wagon returned empty; the driver was just happy to get back alive.

Children had to leave the cottage homes on reaching fourteen years of age. If they consented, some were sent to the colonies. The clerk reported, at September's meeting, that two boys from the children's home were on their way to Canada.

Mr Shea inquired as to what became of these boys. He asked, 'Did the guardians take any reports of them after they landed in Canada? I have heard some rather strange stories for men who had toiled out in the states, to the effect that some of the boys were treated like slaves.'

The clerk said, 'They received reports as to the progress of the boys from time to time, but in view of the question raised I will get the addresses of the boys and communicate directly with them.'

Fleetwood continued to suffer from high unemployment. Reverend Doctor Cotton told the guardians that the relieving officer, Mr Parkinson, was only able to compile forty cases for today's meeting. There was a large number still to be dealt with, and he thought Mr Parkinson should have some help. They decided that the Fleetwood area guardians and the clerk should meet with Fleetwood Council.

Dr Cotton held a meeting with two representatives of the unemployed, the guardians, and Fleetwood Council. One of the representatives of the unemployed stated that in the coming winter months, six-hundred to eight-hundred men would be unemployed owing to the fact that less trawlers were going to sea, and that there had been a reduction in the staff numbers on the trawlers.

The urban council had found work for forty to sixty men, and they offered to find work for more men on Fleetwood's council house building scheme if the guardians paid the one shilling hourly rate. This house building was part of the Government's plan to make a land fit for heroes.

The unemployed reps of Fleetwood protested to the guardians, saying it was unfair to call upon men to go and work alongside others who were receiving one shilling and sixpence per hour, and asked for the sixpence to be paid.

Later, at the guardian's meeting, Mr Whittaker asked if it was fair to the men to work on the housing scheme.

Mr Hodgson said, 'We have to provide a text. We have no authority to relieve able-bodied men without a text.'

'Supposing men put on the 'test' do not carry out a certain amount of work. What will be the result?' asked Mr Shea, who didn't want the unemployed being paid the same as a working man who could be sacked for not doing his job.

Guardian and Wrea Green farmer, William Bradly said, 'The men would be getting as much as a farmhand, and it would be more than farmers would be able to afford in six months time. There would be a lot of trouble in the next 12 months on the wages question. Foodstuffs would come tumbling down in price, and we have to remember that there is competition of foreign nations to meet, and nobody wanted to see this country go down. There was a lot of unemployment during the summer as the result of strikes, and there was a great deal of public works held up owing to the large expense it would entail to carry it out. I keep a large staff of servants, and their keep was officially estimated to cost 18s. weekly.'

Mr Kemp added, 'In the old days, the relief granted was 2d. and a loaf and they had to work the whole day.'

The guardians decided to pay the extra sixpence.

In September, the clerk reported that ex-servicemen were still passing through the casual wards. When this happened, the clerk, with the men's permission, made representations on their behalf to the pensions officer and had their cases investigated. Whilst they were in the house, they were not called upon to carry out any work.

In towns like Blackpool, relief committees were set up to provide additional help to the unemployed. This help was sometimes in the form of money, which was distributed by the police. Blackpool as an unemployment hotspot could also claim money from the Ministry of Health. Preston's unemployment was far worse than Blackpool's with fifteen-thousand people unemployed, including six-thousand females. However, Blackpool's woes were sometimes hidden with hundreds of lodging house owners suffering in silence ashamed to claim any relief.

In the winter, the town was awarded a one-off payment of one-thousand pounds which was meant to be distributed by the poor law officials. This, however, caused a problem, because most of the unemployed were former soldiers, who refused to be drawn into the poor law system. They wanted the police to distribute the money.

Mr Shea said, 'If the money had to be handed over to the Blackpool Corporation, I do not agree that it should be paid through the hands of the police. The workers of the country would resent any such actions.'

Mr Hodgson told the meeting, 'When the Ministry of Health had decided whether a lump sum should be handed over for relief of unemployment, it rested with the guardians, to decide how the money should be administered.'

Although Mr Whittaker agreed to some extent with Mr Shea, he said, 'The question of distribution through the police force was, as far as he could gauge, to avoid overlapping. That authority was already granting certain relief money, and it was felt that the relief should be given through one source entirely.'

Mr Counsel thought they were giving away their rights as guardians. He thought that relief applicants should make their cases known to their relieving officers who would bring it before the relief committee that would grant money on the merits of each case.

The clerk asked permission from the Ministry of Health to pass the money directly to the Blackpool Corporation, whose reply was that it was the duty of the guardians to relieve distress in their union, and it was not open to them to delegate the duty to any other body.

During December, in the Blackpool North Poor Law District, twenty able-bodied people received outdoor relief of ten shillings. In the Blackpool South District, there had only been one case in the last two weeks. However, the Blackpool War Pensions Committee and Blackpool Corporation Unemployment Committee were dealing with two-hundred cases. Some of the unemployed had been given work on the many improvement schemes taking place in Blackpool.

Some settlement cases could turn-up some surprising stories.

In November, last year John Owen, aged forty-four, from Sheffield, walked into the sea at midnight near the Hotel Metropole and drowned himself. His wife went into the water to save him and had to be rescued by two men. The police later dragged John's body from the sea. Why he took his own life was never found out. His wife had a nervous breakdown and couldn't give an account of the evening. She was sectioned and after being in Blackpool Victoria Hospital for six months, was sent to Whittingham Asylum.

The drowned man's settlement was in the Islington Union, and the clerk wrote asking them to take over the maintenance. It then turned out the woman was bigamously married to the man, and therefore the Islington Union said that if her real husband was still alive, it was a matter for him. Mr Brown traced the man, who had gained settlement in Felixstowe in 1915. The Woodbridge Union, Suffolk, took over the maintenance and repaid the one-hundred pounds that the Fylde Union had already paid out.

In 1922, Mrs Holland Secretary of the Women's Branch of the Blackpool Labour Party, asked for permission for a number of ladies to visit the institution and cottage homes; the permission was granted. The chairman pointed out that the board always allowed ratepayers to inspect the premises. The clerk was told to arrange a visit.

In Lancashire, the number of people claiming relief was three point six per cent of the population, the Fylde's was nought point five per cent, the lowest in the county. The assessment value of the Fylde was one-million, three-hundred-and-fifty-two-thousand, five-hundred and seventy-two.

In the institution's house there were eighty-four males and sixty-four females. In the institution's infirmary, there were forty-two males and fifty females. There were also three male children in the institution's infirmary and four female children. In the institution's nursery, there were eleven baby boys and six baby girls. One child in the infirmary was Nellie Bennet, aged fifteen months. Her mother paid ten shillings per week for her treatment. At the cottage homes, there were forty-four boys and twenty-three girls.

In total in both buildings, there were one-hundred and eighty-four males and one-hundred and forty-seven females, three-hundred and thirty-one in total.

There was one less male in the infirmary when Philip Henry Sparrow died. He had left a properly executed will asking for his body to be sent to the School of Anatomy, Manchester. His relatives offered no objections and the master arranged for the body to be removed to Manchester.

The War Department was billed by the guardians for the time when they had occupied the infirmary. One bill was for three-hundred and three pounds, nine shillings, and eleven pence paid to Messers Beaumont and Parkinson for painting the military block. The war office auditor wrote to the clerk saying that since the block had not been painted since 1910, and the occupation was from 1915, the guardians should pay half the costs. The guardians agreed, and the balance of one-hundred and twenty-three pounds and four shillings was struck off the army's bill. The war had finished over four years ago, and with the officials having less contact with the military, all war bonuses were reduced by five pounds and twenty-six shillings from 1 March.

After a person entered the institution, the clerk set about claiming maintenance for them. Each person was named at the meeting, and any ongoing action was reported by the clerk.

These are May's ongoing actions:

> Violet Walsh, a Lunatic. Further inquiries are being made as to any relatives she may have. She was admitted into Lancaster Asylum, and we are unable to get any information from her.
>
> Eileen Wilson & child. They are in the infirmary, and the lady members were asked to interview her regarding chargeability. (She had settlement in the Manchester Union and was removed there on the 12th July).
>
> Jas Brown, a Lunatic. His settlement is still under consideration. (It was later accepted by the Bath Union).
>
> Alfred Longworth, a Lunatic. Blackburn Union will give a decision after their next meeting. (Settlement was accepted by the Blackburn Union; the Fylde Union transferred chargeability and recovered all cost paid out by them).
>
> Daniel Wardle, a Lunatic. Enquiries were being made as to whether the case can or cannot be transferred to the service class.

> Amy Teasdale was ill in the infirmary. (After recovering, she left the infirmary on the 14th June).
>
> Albert Dickinson, a Lunatic. (This case was accepted by the Ministry of Pensions and chargeability was transferred to them).
>
> Elizabeth Fitzgerald, 36 years, a Lunatic. She was a patient in Barnstead Asylum chargeable to Wandsworth Union. She lived with an Austrian, but as they were never married, the man couldn't be held responsible for her maintenance. She had lived in Blackpool for 14 years until 1919, settlement accepted.
>
> Marion Rachel Aske, aged 14. She was being maintained by the Parish of Paddington. The clerk reported she had settlement in Blackpool by residence. (The case was accepted, and she was removed to the Fylde).
>
> Betty Roberts, a Lunatic. Her husband was written to and asked to pay full costs of maintenance. He went to the Blackpool Relief Committee and offered to contribute 10s. (This was accepted).
>
> Sarah Holbrook. Left the Institution before she became chargeable.

When a person moved to a different Union and stayed continuously for five years, they gained the status of irremovability. The Wellington Union wrote to the guardians asking them to accept the settlement of Isabella Picker, age nine years, whose mother lived in St Annes and had gained the status of irremovability. After the clerk had inquired, it was agreed to take the child out of the Wellington Union.

Over the years people with epilepsy were often sent to the workhouse. They would stay for most of their lives. In 1903, The David Lewis Trust opened a purpose-built colony for epileptics; patients from the Fylde were treated there. In this year, 1922, the David Lewis Manchester Epileptic Colony of Alderley Edge wrote saying that owing to the condition of Dorothy Whitehall, it will be impossible for her to remain at that institution and asked for her removal. She was removed and admitted into Wesham.

Baby farming was still going on. Mr Rees, the infant life protection visitor, reported that Margaret Bishops of 21 Boothby Road, Blackpool, had taken to nurse a child named Mary Leila Cooper, without giving notice as required under the provisions of the Children Act. She was summoned to Blackpool Court on 12 June, where her case was dismissed.

Warrants were still issued for men abandoning their families. Since 1 January, twelve warrants had been issued: seven executed, one cancelled, four still in the hands of the police. The sentence for abandoning your family still carried a jail sentence.

The guardians arranged a project with the Fleetwood Relief Committee and Fleetwood Council were able-bodied unemployed men, who reported to the relieving officer, would be directed to a place specified by the council where they would be found work mainly on road-building schemes.

The council would provide the materials and supervise the men. A single man would be paid fifteen shillings per week, less relief from other sources. A married man with one child was paid twenty-four shillings per week plus five shillings for each additional child. The maximum relief paid was forty-four shillings per week and was paid half in money and half in kind. Men employed on task work were paid one shilling per hour.

When the scheme was set up, there were sixty cases. This dropped to an average of thirty-five cases almost immediately. After a year, there were only six applicants, five of whom were over sixty years, and the project was terminated. The total amount paid out in relief by the union was three-hundred and seventy-six pounds

At Christmas time, the adults receiving outdoor relief received an extra two shillings, and their children received one shilling. Another tradition was the donating of money to the cottage home by former 'homeboys'. Richard Whittle and Harold Boothby both donated a pound to the children in the homes. The board wrote a reply of thanks, saying to both that their actions reflected credit on the training both boys received at the homes.

In 1923, the master and matron resigned and asked to be released as soon as possible after gaining a position at Tynemouth. The guardians then passed a motion saying the new ones must be married and that the matron must hold nursing certificates so she could act as the superintendent nurse. This was because the institution had, in reality, become a geriatric hospital. The roles were advertised at one-hundred and ten pounds per annum for the master and ninety pounds for the matron.

Thirty-nine applicants applied for the role, and seven were interviewed.

> Mr and Mrs Perkins, Master and Matron Mitford of Launditch Union.
>
> Mr and Mrs Leyland, Master and Matron of Whitley Union.
>
> Mr and Mrs Carter, Master and Matron of Whitchurch Union.
>
> Mr and Mrs Holbrook, Master and Matron of Cheadle Union.
>
> Mr and Mrs Wilson, Master and Matron of Rugby Union.
>
> Mr and Mrs Lund, Assistant Master and Charge Nurse.
>
> Mr and Mrs Ellis, Assistant Master and Charge Nurse of Haslington.

Mr and Mrs Wilson were offered the position and said that they could start on 10 March. The old master was given permission to leave on 24 February, and the porter and portress were asked to perform the role of master and matron until the new officials arrive.

Of the four assistant nurses, three left in July. Laundress and assistant nurse, Miss Eccleston, resigned. Miss A. Hall left for a three-year nurses training course, and Miss J. Summers left to work for the Cunard Line as a stewardess. The remaining assistant nurse, Miss Fairclough, asked for a pay raise. Her salary was increased to fifty pounds.

This year's poor law rates were a third lower than recent years at three and a half pence for the first six months, and six shillings and six and a half pence for county purposes. The assessable value of the Fylde was one-million, three-hundred-thirty-nine-thousand, three-hundred, fifty-seven pounds, which raised sixty-one-thousand, one-hundred, and sixty-three pounds.

Charges in the asylums were also coming down. Reduced from twenty-seven shillings and five pence weekly to nineteen shillings and ten pence; it was reduced in five stages over the last twenty-four months. The cost for private patients was more at twenty-four shillings and sixpence, but you had the privilege of wearing your own clothes. From March, the asylums under the control of the Lancashire Asylums Board would now be known as County Mental Hospitals, and the patients were now 'mental cases' not lunatic cases.

The cost in March for treating the Fylde's mental patients was as follows: Whittingham Mental Hospital, six-hundred pounds; Lancaster Mental Hospital, two-hundred and twenty-one pounds and ten shillings; Prestwich Mental Hospital, thirty-seven pounds, six shillings, and eight pence; Rainhill Mental Hospital, fourteen pounds.

Some cases were international. Flora Barlow, a 'mental', was brought back from Canada and delivered to the Blackpool Relieving Officer by a stewardess of the White Star Line. Flora had left for Canada with her husband thirteen years ago, and in March 1912, was committed to the public hospital for the insane there.

She remained in the hospital until June the previous year when she was discharged for deportation; her husband was still in Canada. The clerk was instructed to bring the case before the Ministry of Health and Colonial Office. They both wrote back saying the Canadian Government have powers to remove mental patients and deport them. She was admitted to a mental hospital, and the Fylde had to accept her maintenance.

Some cases came from the prison service.

The board had to take over the cost of maintenance of Annie Robinson, who had been removed from H.M. Prison Preston where she was undergoing one-month's imprisonment having been convicted at Blackpool on 13 July. She was sent to Whittingham Mental Hospital. Enquiries were made into her settlement, but she was not able to give any information.

The board also paid out monthly to people in schools, institutions and some hospitals. They paid to Buckley Hall Orphanage twenty-four pounds, one-shilling, and three-pence; Waif and Strays Society, seven pounds, eleven shillings and two pence; Blackpool Victoria Hospital, two pounds, seven shillings, and sixpence; Reverend Strange, Headmaster Kirkham Grammar School, seventeen pounds, ten shillings and ten pence.

One boy at the cottage homes gained a place at Kirkham Grammar School.

In August's meeting, a letter was read by the clerk from the Managers of Kirkham Grammar School, stating that Thomas Ruxton, a boy in the cottage homes, had been awarded a scholarship at the school, after passing a recent examination. The board resolved that the clerk be empowered to sign or get the parent to sign the agreement accepting the same and that further consideration to the matter be given by the cottage home committee.

In September's meeting, Mr Walton, the cottage homes committee chairman, motioned, and Mr Shea seconded, that the board send him as a boarder to the Kirkham Grammar School. The motion was passed.

Girls still left the cottage homes at the age of fourteen to go into service. Rose Knowles was sent into the service of Miss Glendenning of South Shore, Blackpool.

Miss Wilson asked if fifty members of the Blackpool's Co-operative Guild could visit the institution and cottage homes. They were granted permission and afterwards, wrote a thank you letter saying all were delighted with the arrangements made for the comfort of the patients.

The Fylde Coast was a popular place for people to stay when they were ill: this caused a problem. Miss Rossall, a Lytham guardian who had just been elected as first lady councillor for the new borough of Lytham St Annes, passed the following resolution.

That the clerk write to the Ministry of Health drawing attention to the unfair practice of outside areas sending their persons to convalescent and other charitable homes at the seaside and other health resorts, and after gaining settlement, passing them on to the poor law institutions, where they became a lifelong charge.

The clerk was given orders by the guardians, which were recorded in the minute books.

The following orders for January were given to the clerk.

> That Joseph Blackstock be called upon to contribute 10s. weekly towards the maintenance of his wife in the institution.
>
> That enquiries be made into the settlements of Lilian Evans and Clifford Browett, recently admitted into the institution.
>
> That the thanks of the board be tendered to donors of gifts during Christmas week.
>
> That the surgical appliances recommended by the District Medical Officer at Blackpool be obtained for the child Harriet Bee, aged 11 years.

That the necessary repairs required at 1 Westbourne Avenue be carried out.

That Mary Mulholland of Fleetwood be admitted into the infirmary.

February's orders were:

That the offer of Mr James Hall to contribute the sum of 10s. weekly towards the maintenance of his sister at Lancaster be accepted.

That the arrears of maintenance amounting to £14 18s. 0d owing by Samuel Wilder of St Annes be struck off, owing to his poor circumstances.

That the three children of William Wright of Fleetwood be admitted into the children's homes.

That the recommendations of the Blackpool North Relief Committee, for the tender of £85 from Mr Miller for necessary structural repairs required at 9 Raikes Parade Blackpool, be accepted.

That Mrs Eastwood be called upon to contribute 15s. weekly towards the maintenance of the husband Frederick Eastwood whilst chargeable at Whittingham.

That enquiries be made into the settlement of James Fielding and John Williams.

That year Blackpool planned to hold an eight-day carnival to try and revive the tourist industry. The Superintendent of Police wrote to the guardians asking to use the old infirmary to billet one hundred police officers required for duty on the roads for the Blackpool King's Carnival, which was held from the 8th to the 16th of June. The request was granted, and no charge was made for the use of the building.

The carnival, which composed of giant figures and decorated cars, was a great success, with two million visitors including the King and Queen. Another carnival was held in 1924, but this was the last. The police spent more time dealing with drunkenness and violence than road duty, and the parades were stopped.

1924, the first quarter's expenses for the institution were two-thousand, five-hundred, and fifty-seven pounds and for the cottage homes three-hundred and eighty-four, a decrease on the previous quarter. The cost per head at Wesham was ten shillings and two pence per week and seven shillings and sixpence in the cottage homes which included provisions, clothing, heating, and lighting. If salaries and loans plus interest and repairs were added, it worked out at one pound, four shillings and one penny per head and fifteen shillings in the cottage homes.

A small part of the costs was the subscription to the North-Western Vagrancy Committee, which the Fylde was part of. Some guardians were against paying this.

The clerk talked about the committee's role, 'The committee was brought into being in order to bring about uniformity in vagrancy administration, and its work is of great importance. In the area covered by the committee, there are 50 unions representing an assessable value of 40 million. The Fylde Board are contributing £358 towards the cost of the committee, and this sum was higher than that contributed in some of the unions in consequence of the call being made on the assessable value of the union, which is at present nearly £2,000,000. Vagrancy can only be dealt with by combination among the unions, and those institutions that were situated on the main roads always got more vagrants than those away from big industrial centres. The present system is to supply vagrants away from big industrial institutions, and the casuals then had no excuse for begging.'

If the police dealt with a case, which they thought belonged to the poor law, they would bill the guardians.

On Sunday, 13 April, the police were called to a ship at Fleetwood where a man, John Burke, had gone insane, or mental as was now correct term. He was taken to the police station. The police contacted the relieving officer, who told them he would bring a doctor in the morning but would have nothing to do with the case tonight. The Superintendent of the Police then contacted the master at the institution, who refused to deal with the case unless he had an order from the relieving officer.

Inspector Swaits eventually took the man to the Wesham Institution, where he was admitted on humanitarian grounds. The man was eventually taken before a judge by the Kirkham relieving officer and sent to Whittingham.

The police sent three claims for the expenses incurred whilst dealing with the man, but Mr Parkinson refused to pay. The police took the guardians to court for the one-pound, fifteen-shillings and six pence.

In court, Mr Parkinson said that in his opinion, he had no power to give an order for admission into the institution, as the man had not been certified and there was no accommodation for lunatics. The master of the institution, Rowland Wilson, was also in court, he told the Judge that there was a padded room at the institution, but they had no attendants to deal with lunatics. The Judge sided with the police and awarded costs.

At the next meeting, Mr Shea asked the clerk about the court case. The clerk said, 'After deliberating for twenty minutes in private, the magistrates made an order against the guardians, but I still think I was right.'

Mr Shea questioned, 'Do we take it now that the police have a perfect right to send anybody here without an order?'

To which the chairman replied, 'We do not think so.'

Mr Shea asked, 'Suppose similar cases arise. Cannot instructions be given that the person shall be taken back from this institution to the place from which they came?'

The clerk answered, 'I have always given instructions that the person should be admitted, and a legal form can be gone into afterwards. It is strictly on humanitarian grounds that these instructions are given.'

Mr Shea replied, 'I object to the police taking away the rights of the guardians because we are supposed to be here to protect the rights of the public.'

The conversation ended there.

In the institution, there was an Australian, William John Ward, who asked the guardians for help in returning home. During the war, William had failed to join the Australian Forces, so worked his passage to England and joined the army here. After being discharged from the army, he went to

Fleetwood to find work but ended up in the Wesham Institution. The clerk wrote to the Agent-General of South Australia who replied he was unable to help the man. Representations were sent to Mr Ward's family, and thirty-seven pounds was cabled to pay his passage from London to Adelaide.

The man should have sailed on 2 December, but the ship was full, and the only way to get on the next vessel was to pay a further two pounds. The guardians decided to pay an extra five pounds, which would include the man's fare to London plus a few extras. Before this happened, they had to gain permission from the Ministry of Health.

Mr Schofield said, 'I have taken a deep interest in this case, and am glad to hear our efforts have been successful. I desire to know, however, what would happen if the Ministry of Health refused to sanction the grant.'

The chairman said, 'We will raise the money one way or another, for the man must be sent back to his own country.'

The guardians were given permission to help Mr Ward. The following year, on his way back to Australia, he wrote thanking the guardians for the help and assistance given in enabling him to return home.

If the guardians felt a child was being neglected or abused, they could pass a motion and take parental control of the child.

After the mother of Lillian Eaves was jailed for three months for child neglect, at Fleetwood Court, Lillian became chargeable to the union. Mrs Walton motioned that all rights and powers of the parents over Lillian Eaves, aged fifteen years, be vested in the guardians under subsection 1 of the Poor Law Act 1899: which was carried.

Mrs Walton became involved with another case. She wanted Eleanor Edwards, daughter of Alice Edwards, to be taken into the cottage homes at a payment of five shillings per week. She admitted that she knew very little about the case but was interested in the child's welfare.

The guardians had allowed a few cases of children entering the homes whilst the mother stayed outside and paid for the child's maintenance, but it was not generally allowed.

Mr Shea, who supported Mrs Walton, said, 'It was rather peculiar, but I brought a similar case forward a few years ago and was rather severely talked to for my audacity. The only danger in accepting such cases was that we would have to enlarge our cottage homes. I know already of three or four cases who are awaiting the result of our action this day. I do not think the fee of 5s. should be fixed until further investigation has been made.'

Mr Mellor, who had more detailed information, said, 'I have interviewed the woman, who is earning 15s. a week, and she is paying 10s. per week for a child to be nursed out. She found she could not clothe herself, and unless the child is taken into the homes, she would have to come in herself and bring the child into the workhouse.'

Mr Shea asked, 'Has the board accepted similar cases?'

The chairman replied, 'Yes, more than once.'

Mr Bradly said, 'There is no doubt about it, if we accepted that case, they were going to leave themselves open to a grave danger. It was not fair to the ratepayers to accept such cases, and they as guardians would not be doing their duty if they did so.'

The guardians voted against allowing the child to enter the homes. The girl's mother, Alice, ended up in Croydon Mental Hospital, where she died on 19 November.

Mr Wallace would have allowed Eleanor into the cottage homes. When Mr Mellor reported on the North-Western Poor Law Conference held at Lancaster earlier in the year, he reported that much of the discussion veered around the question of dealing with the unmarried mother, and of course, the question of expense had to be considered.

An indignant Mr J. Wallace said, 'It was always alike when money was wanted, the guardians always stated it could not be found. When the war was on, people never troubled to ask where the millions a day came from to slaughter people. It was only when money was wanted to keep people alive, healthy, and happy that the question arose, where was the money to come from? It was as easy to find it as tumbling off a chair, if only they went the right way about it.'

The guardians were an umbrella organisation, working with groups distributing relief, like the Blackpool and Fleetwood Relief Committees and War Pensions. Another group was the Blackpool and Fylde Society for the Blind. On the Fylde, only nine per cent of blind people claimed relief.

The Blackpool and Fylde Society for the Blind was supported in three ways, by voluntary contribution, voluntary donations and by Lancashire County Council and Borough of Blackpool. Like former First World War soldiers, the Fylde's blind didn't like to ask the poor law for assistance. Grants were being paid by the blind society to many cases which would have otherwise required assistance from the guardians, and the funds in the society were not sufficient to bear the whole of this expense.

A meeting was arranged, where they asked the guardians if they could distribute relief on their behalf, and make some working arrangements in cases where blind people are in receipt of poor law assistance.

At the meeting, William Hodgson told them, 'There is no doubt you needed assistance, and that must be given to you to enable you to carry out your work. It should, however, be clearly understood that the question of maintaining the destitute was one for the guardians alone. No, board of guardians had the right or power to hand over their duties to any other society. The question was, how were they going to assist the society, which was doing such work.'

He continued, "In the Fylde Union area, they had 137 blind persons, 12 of whom were receiving relief. There was a number of cases where they disliked applying to the board for relief because of a certain amount of independence. For the life of me, I cannot see the difference between the board of guardians or any other body granting relief. The only difference was that it was a different authority. The fact remains it is given. I do not think they could attach great importance to a feeling of that kind, however estimable it might seem to some people. The blind people were no different to anybody else in that respect."

The only help the union could offer was a yearly donation of fifty pounds, and to save any overlapping in the giving of relief, the guardians asked the blind society for a list of persons they helped, in turn, the clerk sent the society a list of persons receiving outdoor relief.

When a former serviceman applied for poor relief, his war pension was taken into account, and this reduced the amount he received.

Mr Whittaker thought it was unfair and passed this motion.

That a letter be sent to the Ministry of Health stating that in considering applications for assistance from ex-servicemen, the relief committee's concerned view is, with regret, that they are required to take into account, for the purposes of calculating the total income of the household, any 'disablement pensions' received, and consider that as any such pensions is for 'services rendered' they should not take same into account, for the purpose of calculating the total income, as so far as it exceeds 8s. per week.

When a child whose parent received relief was in need, the school could now apply to the guardians on the child's behalf. The Blackpool Director of Education asked the board for glasses for Nelly Davies and Dora Mayfleet. The relieving officer was told to obtain the glasses. The Blackpool School's Medical Officer informed the guardians that Edith Smith, who was suffering from enlarged tonsils, needed operative treatment. Instructions were given to Dr Cockcroft from the clerk.

Harriot Nichol, a girl in the homes, was, according to the homes committee, 'a most unsuitable girl to mix with other children.' When she reached fourteen years in 1922, she had to leave the homes. The guardians thought she was unsuitable for service, and she was sent to the Waifs and Strays Home. Now, sixteen years old, she was asked if she would consent to be emigrated to Canada. Harriot agreed to this, sailing on 13 June 1924, costing the union twenty pounds.

Harriot would now be far beyond the reach of the guardians and was vulnerable. Mr Shea wasn't happy and passed this motion, 'That the Ministry of Health take such steps, as may be devisable, to get the Canadian Government to make it compulsory that all houses in the dominion be examined and approved before any children are drafted to there from England and Wales, and that frequent visits are made by government officials to the houses where children are taken.'

In 1925, the guardians received a letter from the Overseas Settlement Office, reporting on Harriet Nichol. The office wrote that she appears to have a good home and is doing well.

Clerk Fred Brown received six-hundred pounds per year from the board for himself and his assistant clerks. Compared to other unions, he was poorly paid, and at a special meeting of the finance committee, it was decided to employ the three assistant clerks directly. The committee had compared the Fylde Union with other unions. After taking into account the rateable value and population, they recommended appointing Henry Blacoe as chief assistant at two-hundred and twenty pounds a year, Fred Taylor second assistant at a similar salary, and Joseph Langley third assistant at fifty pounds. They also decided that the clerks could retain any offices they now held but could not to accept any others without permission of the board. The assistant clerks remained under the full supervision of Mr Brown. This was a large pay rise for Fred Brown.

Discussing the recommendations, Mr Whittaker pointed out that, in effect, the resolution meant increasing the clerk's salary by five-hundred and eighty pounds and contended that it would be a waste of public money.

'It would be a mistake to accept the recommendation,' agreed Mr J. Wallace of Blackpool, 'I think it would be better to refer the matter back to the finance committee. I am entirely opposed to the question of salary. Any business firm granting an increase of salary would expect some further benefits from it, but in this case, I can see none. I move that the whole matter be referred back.'

Mr Schofield contended that no good would come from referring the matter back. It was a question of justice to the three clerks in question, and the salary they were paying the clerk was less than the surveyor of a small place like Thornton was receiving.

Reverend King thought, 'It was not right to expect Mr Brown to find clerks out of a meagre salary of £600, which reflected no credit on the union. I think the finance committee's recommendation is a proper one."

After a vote, the committee's recommendations were adopted, and as the clerks were now employed directly by the union, they were now entitled to a union pension when they retired.

The clerks were central to the entire operation of the union. Below are four cases which the officials discussed at some of that year's meetings.

1. The Rochdale Union asked the Fylde Union to take over the case of a William Whiteside, aged forty-three, who was in their institution and was said to have resided in Blackpool and Fleetwood. The clerk said that the man had been in and out of the Fylde Institution fourteen times since 1912; the last time he left was in June last year, and he supposed they would have no option but to accept him.

2. Chairman of the Blackpool South Relief Committee, Mr Brandwood, told the board that at a meeting of his committee this morning, it was decided to recommend that the board take out a warrant for the arrest of a woman who had deserted her child and left it chargeable to the ratepayers.

The guardians' opinions were split. Mr Wallace thought that taking out a warrant and dragging this poor-unfortunate woman to court would not benefit the board or the woman, or do any good to the ratepayers. Michael Shea agreed. He thought the day had gone when magistrates would issue warrants against women for such an offence.

Mr Counsell disagreed. He thought that the woman had no right to desert her child. It was a cruel action and they ought to proceed with the prosecution. Mrs Walton thought that perhaps as a result of the woman being brought to court and punished, the guardians might do the child a good turn by adopting it. A warrant for arrest was issued.

3. The police sent the clerk a bill after a man was found in Marton, certified insane, and then removed to an asylum. The bill was for sixteen hours work at three shillings per hour with meals supplied, amounting to two pounds, twelve shillings, seven pence. Mr Shea wanted to know when the man actually became chargeable to them. Would it be immediately after his arrest or immediately after he was certified to be insane?

Mr Hodgson answered, 'We have no liability until the man actually became chargeable to us. I do not think we would have any chance if we contested the case. Perhaps the account was high, but if we were to fight the matter, we would probably have to take it to the High Court. The union and the police had always worked harmoniously, and I don't think any good would come of getting into an antagonism with the police.'

Mr Shea replied, 'The charge seems to be extortionate. I myself do not get 3 shillings an hour,'

The chairman replied, 'Probably, some of us have missed our vocation, Mr Shea. If we get cross with the police, they would say it was no business of theirs and throw the whole responsibility of looking after insane people onto the union officials, and in that case, it would cost the guardians more. I would advise that the amount be paid, and nothing more said about it.'

Mr Wallace asked, 'Would it not be possible to draw the attention of the police to the excessive charge?'

The chairman replied, 'I don't think it is advisable. The police are generally very kind and do a lot of work for us.'

The matter was then dropped.

4. During the summer, the Blackpool South Relieving Committee recommended that a sum of twelve pounds owed by a woman for her husband's maintenance in a mental Institution should be struck off. Mr Counsell objected. He thought further investigation should be made into such cases, saying that he was not satisfied with the way in which such matters were conducted, and thought that the relieving officers were not sufficiently keen in their efforts to regain the money and were a little bit too lenient towards the persons concerned.

Adding, 'I have every confidence in our officers, but I think they could make a more thorough investigation. I may give notice of motion to appoint a collector to gather in the amounts owing, and I think we might save money.'

Mr Brandwood, replied, 'We also have every confidence in our relieving officers, but this case was a particularly sad one, and the woman could not afford to pay. She has a shop in Blackpool which is very heavily mortgaged, and the original order was made because it was felt that if her husband had been at home, she would have to keep him. The amount in question constituted arrears under the order, but the woman's business was not near so good as it was 20 years ago. We are satisfied that proper investigation had been made. To be continually pressing the woman to pay the amount was like holding her in a vice, and I think the best way was to relieve her of a responsibility which she could not meet.'

The clerk produced a statement which showed that there were thirty-five maintenance cases in arrears in the Blackpool South District, amounting to four-hundred and fourteen pounds, of which one-hundred and forty pounds had so far been collected. The unpaid weekly amounts varied from fifteen shillings to three shillings.

The poor law was a hands-on authority, and in most cases, knew the people they were dealing with and treated them accordingly, but it was going to change.

The Poor Rate Law was passed in 1601, and it was simply for the relief of the poor. Now only a fraction of the money collected was used for poor law purposes; the rest went to the county council. Until 1875, the poor-rate was the only rate, until the general district was established by an act of parliament. In England and Wales, there was fourteen-thousand different parishes, each with their own overseers preparing valuation lists. Over six-hundred unions had assessment committees. The valuation lists were revised periodically, in that year out of the fourteen-thousand parishes, more than one half had not had a revision since 1918, and three-thousand had not had a revision since 1900.

Going through parliament was the Ratings and Valuation Act. This act wanted to abolish overseers and transfer their duties to the local authorities, remove the fourteen-thousand parishes with overseers, merge the county and poor rates into one rate, create new valuation lists every five years, disperse with union rating committees, and create larger rating areas.

It was an existential threat to boards of guardians, and the guardians received a letter from the President of the Association of Poor Law Unions. The letter referred to Neville Chamberlain's remark that the Rating and Valuation Bill was only 'a step towards further legislation,' and that the true intention of the Government was eventually to abolish boards of guardians. He asked all boards to elect emergency committees to watch the course of events, and inform Members of Parliament of the guardian's role so that they would be well informed when the measure came before them.

Referring to the letter William Hodgson said, 'We do not yet know what form the bill was going to take when it's presented. It was no use appointing a committee to fight something not yet in existence. The time was not ripe to deal with the matter. I think the matter could safely be left in the hands of the finance committee.'

This course was adopted.

In September, the institution was nearly full, with one-hundred and sixty male adults, and one-hundred and thirty female adults; when children were included along with the cottage homes the numbers of indoor-recipients was three-hundred and eighty-nine.

	Males	Females	Total
Institution House	107	69	176
Institution Infirmary	53	61	114
Institution Nursery	13	7	20
Infirmary Children	2	3	5
Cottage Homes	39	35	74
Totals	214	175	389

September's Figures Broken Down

The numbers would only increase over the coming winter, and the house committee held a meeting to discuss how to deal with the lack of accommodation and reported back to the board.

The committee reported that the institution at Wesham had been erected nearly twenty years ago, and taking into account that the population of the union in 1901 was ninety-three-thousand and now it was at least one-hundred-and-ninety-thousand, it was only natural that additional accommodation would be necessary.

There were four possibilities:

1. The erection of a new permanent ward or wards.
2. The erection of army huts adjacent to the existing wards.
3. The transfer of a number of men from the male wards at the institution to the old institution near the cottage homes, and using the vacant beds for Infirmary cases.
4. Sending men to neighbouring unions.

Mr Mellor reported, 'The committee had made an inspection of the various day rooms and dormitories. Statistics relating to the accommodation and present numbers in the institution were also investigated, and it was unanimously recommended that additional accommodation be provided at the earliest possible moment. The committee discussed a proposal that the old institution near the cottage homes be utilised, and after examining the probable cost to make it suitable, and also taking into account the stocking and administration of the place, if converted, we were of the opinion that the old institution as a means of additional accommodation was impractical.'

Mr Millar continued, 'Having regard to the fact of a hard winter in prospect and the season at Blackpool coming to an end, it was to be expected that, as usual, there would be a number of men and women coming back to the house. Increased accommodation would, therefore, be badly needed. However, with the much talked of legislation looming in the near future to abolish guardians, together with the high cost of building, it might be advisable to avoid incurring heavy capital expenditure by building temporary army huts, which would be much cheaper if the board's medical officer and Ministry of Health considered the cost of building suitable.'

The board decided to erect a temporary wooden building to provide forty beds and applied to the Ministry of Health to sanction the expenditure of about five-thousand pounds in connection with the erection of the building. The Ministry of Health refused to sanction it and told the guardians to use the spare capacity at neighbouring unions. The clerk was ordered to write to neighbouring unions asking whether they could receive into their institutions cases from Fylde Union and the terms.

The Chorley Union wrote back saying they would accept fifty day-room cases, twenty-five of each sex at a charge of one-pound and one shilling per week, per head. The Preston Union also agreed to take inmates of the Fylde Institution at a cost of one pound per week for each person. At the end of the year, the clerk reported that twenty persons had been sent to Preston, and there were two-hundred and ninety persons in the institution. In December, the pressure was relieved as only twenty-seven persons had entered the house, but fifty-three had been discharged.

The Pontypridd Union sent out a circular letter asking whether the Fylde was prepared to contribute towards the cost of appeal proceedings in a test case with regard to the recovery of relief given on loan during industrial disputes.

During the 1921 National Coal Strikes, the Pontypridd Guardians granted relief to the families of miners, but it was given as a loan and the guardians wanted it repaying. Mr Brown told the guardians that four-fifths of the unions in the country were supporting the Pontypridd Guardians, and the cost of the case to the Fylde Board would not be more than five pounds.

Mr Wallace opposed supporting the Pontypridd Board, he said, 'The miners and the engineers were the worst paid workers, and the probability was that wages might be reduced. I do not see how any workman, out of their meagre earnings, could refund money which had, in my opinion been lent on loan. These people were destitute and would not consider that the money was given from the loan point of view.'

Reverend Cotton of Fleetwood thought, 'If the people were destitute no body of guardians would insist on their repaying the loan, but the question whether the money was given in the shape of a loan, and whether the people were in a position to make restitution, was a vital case.'

The guardians decided to support the Pontypridd Union.

In March 1926, the master and matron resigned after gaining a place at the Rochdale Union.

Chairman of the House Committee, Mr Mellor said, 'I do not think it had passed more pleasant than whilst Mr and Mrs Wilson were in charge, everything has gone on very nicely indeed, and everything in the house would always be found satisfactory. I am sorry personally that they were going.'

Resignations were also received by the cook, seamstress, and the assistant nurse. Mr Miller pointed out that this had nothing to do with the resignation of the master and matron.

Twenty-nine applicants applied for the post of master and matron. Six were interviewed: Mr and Mrs Geoffrey Lunn of Hartismere; Mr and Mrs Parsonson of Malmesbury; Mr and Mrs Procter of Ashbourne; Mr and

Mrs Woods of Tetbury; Mr and Mrs Adams of Patington; and Mr and Mrs J Hayes of Bromyard. Mr and Mrs Lunn were appointed.

The guardians fell out with the board of St. Annes Hospital.

On 12 November the previous year, the Wesham Institution received a telephone call at ten-thirty p.m. The master answered it. He told the matron that a doctor wanted a case removed at once from the hospital at St. Anne's. The matron suggested that they should hold the case over until the morning, but the doctor said they were short of beds and that a lying-in-woman had to be accommodated on the operating table. The doctor was then asked to phone the relieving officer for an order. Despite this, the woman was brought into the institution at eleven-fifty-five the same night; she had given birth to a child at ten o'clock.

The guardians were unhappy with the woman's treatment and told the clerk to write to the hospital 'as strongly as you can' asking for an explanation. The first letter didn't receive a reply, and the clerk wrote again. The guardians received an explanation letter in January.

> St. Annes Hospital, Inglefield, 8, St Annes-road East. December 28th.
>
> Dear Mr Brown, your letters of December 9th and 23rd have been placed before the governors, and I am asked to write to you. I am sorry that your letter of December 9th was not formally acknowledged in due course, but I must ask you to believe there was no discourtesy intended. The facts are as follow. The letter did not reach the secretary until December 12th. It came to me on the 13th and was placed before the visiting committee on the 15th when the secretary was instructed to put it before the house committee, which he did on the 21st at which meeting I was asked to obtain a report from the doctor, which I received on the 23rd and which is now in my possession.
>
> It is to be regretted that at your meeting on the 23rd certain comments on the case, were made which reflected upon St Annes Hospital, and its staff, and were reported in the public press, and I am asked to say there was not the slightest justification for any such reflection.

> The St. Annes Hospital is not a maternity home, and there is not (so far) any accommodation for maternity cases. The doctor was called to this woman about 7.30 p.m. She was then in labour. Her life was in danger, confinement was impossible where she was, and it was equally impossible and dangerous than to send her to Kirkham. The only place available at once was the hospital, and every bed was occupied. But even if this had not been the case, the danger to herself and other patients would have been too great a risk. She was delivered in the operating theatre. The doctor, matron, and hospital staff never left her until the doctor pronounced it safe to send her to Kirkham, in the borough ambulance accompanied by one of the nurses, all danger then being over. The doctor and the hospital staff did everything they possibly could for this poor woman.
>
> Although, it was obviously not a hospital case at all, was never entered in the books, and never came before the governors, after seeing the reports in the newspaper's, calculated to damage the reputation of the hospital and its medical staff, a special meeting of the governors was called, and I was requested to send this explanation to you and at the same time, a copy of it to the newspapers, which contained an account of the proceedings of the guardians at their meeting on the 23rd of December. May I add, with respect, such cases like this have a legitimate claim on the guardians, and so far from comparing your displeasure my colleagues think that the doctor and our staff deserve the thanks of the patient, the guardians, and the public generally.
>
> Believe me yours faithfully S. Louis Stott Chairman of the Governors.

The letter was read out at the guardian's meeting. Chairman William Hodgson, said that the letter was one of the most ingenious letters he had ever heard. It gave information as to the internal management of the hospital, which I think no member of the public could ever anticipate, which would certainly not have been disclosed if it had not been contained in that letter. It was signed by the Chairman of the Governors.

The case was reported as an emergency and a legitimate case for the union, but Mr Hodgson disagreed.

He said, 'The women had maintained herself and her two children and had made all necessary arrangements for her confinement. She secured the services of a midwife and the services of another woman to look after her, and when the time arrived, she sent for the midwife, who in turn sent for the doctor, the latter in his judgement ordering her removal to the St. Anne's Memorial Hospital, to which place she was conveyed in a taxi. She was confined on the operating table. The woman was removed an hour after delivery of her child on a night when it was 15 degrees below freezing point. Was there any man in the boardroom who would allow his wife to be treated in such a manner? ('No'). There was no individual, he felt sure, having a woman in those circumstances in the house, who would not find every accommodation rather than have her taken under the conditions to another place at that hour of the night.'

After he had had his say, knowing it would be reported in the papers, the matter was dropped.

Lancashire County Council wrote to the Fylde Guardians asking for their opinion into how the new assessment areas should be created. Mr Hodgson thought that Blackpool would not be part of the Fylde Union, but without Blackpool, it would be too small to be an evaluation area. It would have to be expanded by the addition of the Preston and Garstang Unions, excluding the County Borough of Preston.

He added that the position of the individual ratepayer under the new act would be greatly worsened, as regards to the efficiency and economy which the act was supposed to affect. It would be impossible to have efficiency in every union, and as far as the economy was concerned the act, in spite of what politicians said, would undoubtedly mean an increase in the cost of administration, as many officials would have to be compensated and others appointed.

He moved the following resolution: 'That in the opinion of this board, the Unions of Fylde, Preston, and Garstang should be one assessment committee with the exceptions of the County Boroughs of Preston and Blackpool.'

The resolution was passed unanimously, and a copy was sent to Lancashire County Council.

The council decided to divide Lancashire into twenty districts. The Fylde, excluding Blackpool, joined with the Garstang District. The new assessment committee would consist of eighteen members and have its centre in Kirkham. Two guardians from the Fylde's largest districts were elected onto the new committee, E. Mellor of Fleetwood and J. Pearson of Lytham St. Annes. The rest of the committee was made up of councillors: Lytham St. Annes Borough, three; Fleetwood U.D., three; Kirkham U.D., one; Poulton-le-Fylde U.D., two; Thornton U.D., one; Fylde R.D., two; Preesall U.D., one; Garstang Guardians, one; and Lancashire County Council, two.

Blackpool's Assessment Committee consisted of twenty members. Five of which were guardians elected by the board for a term of three years. John Kemp, John Duckworth, Frederick Brandwood, Arthur Drinkwater, and John Counsel.

A woman wrote to the guardians from Blackburn asking if they could possibly put her in correspondence with a widower or bachelor forty or fifty years of age. The clerk, Mr Brown, a bachelor, read out the letter.

It went, 'I am 34 years of age and am tall and fair. I am a cook in my present situation. I am finding life rather quiet, as I do not know anyone in this town and I very seldom go out. I do not care to meet men in the street. If you could put me in touch with anyone, I should be very pleased. I am fond of children, and I would not object to a widower with children. I shall be pleased to hear something soon.'

Mr Shea joked, 'I move the letter be left with Mr Brown.'

A recent outbreak of smallpox in Fleetwood had cost the guardians two-hundred pounds. Even before this outbreak the Ministry of Health had been concerned with the large reduction in the take-up of vaccinations on the Fylde.

Returns for the year ending 31 December 1924 showed that the Blackpool North District had six-hundred and five births with two-hundred and seventy-four unaccounted for in terms of vaccinations, Blackpool South District also had six-hundred and five births, of which one-hundred and ninety-one vaccinations were unaccounted for. Fleetwood District had six-hundred and fifty-nine births, and one-hundred and forty-two unaccounted for vaccinations. Kirkham District had twenty-three births against eleven vaccinations in 1923. The Ministry of Health wanted an explanation. The vaccination officers were brought before the Board.

Mr Jump of Blackpool South, said, 'Quite a number of those unaccounted for were the children of people only temporarily resident in Blackpool, and it was very difficult to get to know where they had gone.'

Mr Cardwell of the Kirkham District reported, 'Fifteen children born in the institution had been removed to places unknown.'

Mr G. Rees of Blackpool North said, 'That of the children unaccounted for, 122 had removed to places unknown, 87 had removed to other districts, non-vaccinated 75. Of the latter number, they were mainly cases where parents refused to vaccinate their children for various reasons. Every effort was used to persuade parents to have their children vaccinated, but the result was very disheartening.'

Mr Hugh Parkinson of Fleetwood summed up by saying that due to the large numbers of anti-vaccinators in the district, and the entire absence of prosecution, parents took no notice of visits or of the forms.

In 1917 the vagrancy wards had been closed at Wesham for the duration of the war. They re-opened in 1918, and the numbers passing through went as follows.

Year	31 March	30 June	30 September	31 December
1918	–	40	18	15
1919	57	81	52	92
1920	52	141	249	260
1921	318	669	976	637
1922	424	1140	787	519
1923	683	1129	722	258
1924	144	258	174	113
1925	118	361	–	–

In September, the institution was full with three-hundred and three persons, and the guardians wanted to re-close the tramp wards. The Ministry of Health, however, refused to grant them permission to close the wards because they had resigned their membership of the North-Western

Joint Vagrancy Committee last year. Membership of a committee was an essential part of closing a ward, because it stopped unions closing wards and passing the problem of vagrants onto neighbouring Unions.

Numbers eased in October, with two-hundred and sixty-eight inmates and forty-four casuals passing through the tramp ward in the last two weeks of the month. However, by the end of November, the institution was again full with three-hundred and five inmates.

Mr Brown told the guardians, 'I have written to the Ministry of Health with respect to the male infirmary, pointing out that for several weeks the accommodation has been most severely taxed and on certain dates all beds have been occupied, leaving no provision for admission and treatment of urgent cases. Applications have been made to the adjoining Unions of Preston, Chorley, and Garstang, but they are unable to accept male bed cases, and I have asked if the ministry would make any further suggestions. There are 20 male aged and infirm inmates boarded out in the Preston Union Institution.'

Mr G. R. Snowdon, Government Inspector, replied in writing saying,

> It would obviously be useless now to try and provide additional accommodation, as was suggested last year, by a temporary building. I could quite understand that there might be difficulties in getting neighbouring unions to take hospital cases, as there seems to be little spare hospital accommodation anywhere, but I ask if it would not be possible to clear out some of the old, infirm inmates, or others who were available, and use their present quarters, or part of them, as an extension of the infirmary. I thought that Preston, Garstang, and perhaps Chorley might be able to assist in regards to this class of case, and you might go further afield and try Lancaster, Wigan, and Ormskirk.

The Blackpool Blind Society held a meeting with the guardians. They wanted to employ a superintendent to distribute relief on behalf of the guardians, as many blind people still refused to receive relief through poor law.

Mr Shea, as member of the blind society, said, 'They had had cases where blind persons refused to receive relief. In one instance, a blind person threatened to punch our relieving officer out of the house.'

Chairman, Mr Hodgson, said, 'The position of the guardians was quite clear. It's our duty to relieve destitution and destitution alone, and it was our business to a ascertain what was the nature of that destitution before we grant relief. In 99% of cases, adequate relief was given after investigation by the relieving officers. If they wished it was quite within the power of the guardians to increase the annual subscription, but they could not entertain the idea of allowing cases to be investigated by the official of another body; also, the guardians could not hand over their funds to some other authority to disburse.'

In December, Mr Snowdon had a meeting with the guardians to discuss further the problem of overcrowding, the Kirkham and Wesham Band provided a Christmas concert, and the outdoor relief recipients received two shillings per adult and one shilling per child for Christmas week.

On 31 March 1927, after sixty-five years of service, the Fylde Unions Assessment Committee was disbanded. The Fylde and Garstang Assessment Committee, who took over, had already done its work prior to this and had assessed the different areas. The total value of the Fylde, was six-thousand, six-hundred, and sixty-two pounds, and the finance committee set a call of sixpence. Times the two together and the amount raised was thirty-nine-thousand, nine-hundred, and seventy-two pounds.

Blackpool Corporation	£4220
Lytham St Anne's Borough	£1132
Fleetwood Urban District Council	£510
Kirkham Urban District Council	£61
Thornton Urban District Council	£261
Poulton Urban District Council	£87
Fylde Rural District Council	£391

The rates were now paid on 23 July and 17 December. The last time the Fylde Assessment Committee and Overseers were involved in the rates, last September, sixty-two-thousand and forty-five pounds were raised; forty-four-thousand pounds were for the county rate and eighteen-thousand pounds for the poor rate. For the Fylde's ratepayers, it was a saving of just over twenty-two-thousand pounds.

In October, there were two hundred and ninety inmates in the institution. The board decided to try and reduce the number of inmates by allowing those entitled to an old-age pension to leave and stay with relatives, during periods of overcrowding. Lists of those who qualified to join the scheme were produced by the master. The guardians passed the following resolutions.

a. That inmates named are given reasonable leave of absence, to ascertain and report to the master the result of their enquiries concerning the persons with whom they could reside, accommodation, and similar information.

b. That they be allowed train fares to make their visits.

c. That the reports be submitted to the respective relief committees for consideration with a view to granting outdoor assistance in suitable cases.

The number of inmates stayed below three-hundred until 21 December when it reached three-hundred and nine, climbing to three-hundred and sixteen in March, before dropping back down below three-hundred in April.

At the Wesham Institution, the borehole in the well was blocked and sealed with concrete; only Fylde Water's supply would now be used. Life continued as normal. The aged and infirm were looked after by the nurses, pregnant women came and went, the infirmary treated the poor. The able-bodied women helped the nurses, baker, matron, and laundress, cleaned the wards and toilets, helped in the kitchen, sewing, and generally kept busy and useful.

The men helped the gardener, tended the flower beds, vegetable plots, and orchards. The master set them to work helping with general maintenance or anything he needed labour for. The institution's one-hundred and one pigs, and two heifers were all looked after by the male inmates. Men would be sent to the homes to work in the gardens and allotments and help the superintendent with general maintenance.

At the cottage homes, the children went to the Kirkham schools, until they were fourteen years old and then they had to leave the homes. However, since 1924, all girls leaving school stayed in the house for a period of domestic training. Once trained, they were found a place of employment and sent out of the home. Boys also left aged fourteen, and nearly all were sent to the training ship at Liverpool or to Liskeard Naval College and then a life at sea.

There were a few other options open to the children. Some children, like Thomas Ruxton after finishing at Kirkham Grammar School, could go on to college to lead an academic life. The other options were to join the Army or Air Force or emigration to the colonies. Emigration was voluntary, which some children took to escape from an unhappy childhood.

One was Dora Cardwell, who had entered the homes, aged nine with her elder sister Mary, aged fourteen, in 1919 after her mother was jailed for child neglect. In 1923, aged thirteen Dora was sent to the Children's Rest, Liverpool suffering with tuberculous ankle. Her sister, Mary, had returned to Blackpool to live with her mother Ellen, who now asked for Dora to be returned to her.

The Children's Cottage Homes Committee thought it most undesirable that she be allowed to return to the mother, and the guardians gained parental control until she was eighteen years. When Dora recovered from tuberculous ankle, she was sent to the Girls Training House, 1 Blackburne Terrace, Hope Street, Liverpool. After eight months training, Mrs Walton travelled to Liverpool to see if she would like to emigrate. Dora agreed to be emigrated.

After having a medical, the Liverpool Sheltering Homes Emigration Society approved her application for emigration. In February 1926, the society told the cottage homes committee, that the next party travelling to Canada was mostly boys, and it would be next year before she could emigrate.

The committee then applied to the Salvation Army, who agreed to send her to Canada, but first, she had to have some experience in service in order to gain some references. Dora was sent into service in London; the cottage homes paid for an outfit and travel expenses for the journey from Liverpool to London. On the 19th of August 1927, aged seventeen, she left for Toronto. The care of Dora passed from the homes committee to the Fylde Guardians, who would write to the authorities in Canada, checking on her progress until she was eighteen years old, when she was free to do as she pleased.

Three boys in the cottage homes also agreed to be emigrated: George Goodman aged fifteen, George Hall, aged fourteen, and Oliver Thompson aged sixteen. An application was made to the Salvation Army Emigration and Settlement Office. Medical certificates were sent to the emigration office in March. George Goodman and George Hall were successful and selected for emigration. The boys set sail for Canada on the 29th of July.

Thomas Ruxton, who had left the home and was now a border at Kirkham Grammar School, had the problem of finding somewhere to stay during the school holidays. In Easter that year, he stayed at Nurse Wilson's Home, in August he went to a summer camp in Cleveleys, and at Christmas, his mother, an inmate at Wesham Institution, arranged for him to stay with relatives in Manchester.

John Howison, aged fourteen years, had been abandoned by his parents and ended up in the home. The boy was taken from the homes by his grandparents, who lived in Blackpool. Three months later, in July, the grandparents sent the boy back to the home. John, who was now too old to stay in the homes, was sent to Buckley Hall Orphanage, Rochdale.

Mrs Atkin of Manchester wanted to take her sister, Dorothy Hill, out of the cottage homes. A lady guardian of the Manchester Union visited the house on behalf of the Fylde Guardians. She reported it was not advisable to allow the girl to come to the house because her sister goes out to work.

By 1928, only one in four cases of neglect ended up in court. The guardians believed the police did not think it a priority. The case of John Barrett from Fleetwood was different. The police spent six pounds, eleven shillings and five pence bringing him back from Aberdeen where he was working as a deckhand on a fishing steamer. John's wife and five children had been in the institutions since June 1925 and had cost the union nearly seven-hundred pounds.

Barrett claimed he had not really had the chance to provide for his family.

He said in court, 'Since I came out of the goal sixteen weeks ago, I have had only seven weeks' work.'

He was sentenced to three months' hard labour.

Albert Edward Kearsley was an inmate who was costing the union fifteen shillings a week. He refused to do his allotted work and, as a refractory inmate, was sentenced to twenty-one days with hard labour.

Workhouse Master Jeffery Lund, in court, said, 'Kearsley had been a disturbing influence on all the other inmates at the institution. The present charge was not an isolated instance, but for calculated disobedience, during the whole fifteen months, Kearsley had been at the institution. He refused to do any work, was always idling about the airing court, and would not even gather evergreen for Christmas decorations, or chop a little firewood, or do some decorative gardening.'

Another person in trouble was the Fleetwood District Doctor for his treatment or lack of treatment of a pauper patient. Fleetwood Relieving Officer, Mr Cardwell, had given Mrs Baines an order to take to Doctor Reid for her husband John Baines, suffering from an internal growth.

Mr Cardwell told the guardians, 'I satisfied myself that the case was urgent and issued to her an order on Dr Reid to attend on March 1. On March 4, I saw Mrs Baines in the street in a very distracted manner crying. She said Dr Reid had visited her husband and had said that her husband would require a specialist to see him; the fee would be five guineas. To this, Mrs Baines told the doctor that this was out of the question. Doctor Reid replied, 'If you could get two guineas by this afternoon, I will get the specialist.'

The relieving officer continued, 'The poor woman, driven to despair, raffled sheets among her neighbours, and the man's old mother went around begging to raise the fee. She took the money to Dr Reid, who obtained a specialist.'

The specialist, Dr O'Kane, then visited Mr Baines, who was told, 'If the growth burst the consequences would be fatal. You should go to hospital as soon as possible. You could go to St Joseph's Hospital, Preston where the fee would be two guineas for the first week and a guinea a week afterwards, the operation would cost between five to ten guineas.'

The woman went back to Dr Reid to tell him what the specialist had said, and he replied, 'You are on the parish, to Kirkham Poor Law you must go, or find the money for St Joseph's.'

To which she answered, 'The next time I receive a food voucher, I will see if Fleetwood Council would pay for my husband's treatment at the hospital.'

In the end, she consulted another doctor, Doctor Preston. He did what Dr Reid should have done and sent the man straight to Fleetwood Hospital, where the operation was performed.

On this evidence, Mr Bagot moved, 'That Dr L. M. Reid be suspended from the discharge of his duties as District Medical Officer for Fleetwood District, pending the decision of the Ministry of Health, to the application by the guardians for the termination of the officer's appointment.'

The Doctor was suspended, pending an inquiry by the Ministry of Health.

Five more cases of neglect were discovered by the Fleetwood Relieving Officer. In July, Mr G. F. Maslin, General Inspector, and Dr W. Davidson, Divisional Medical Officer, held an inquiry. Mr Reid was found guilty of neglect and asked to resign; which he refused to do.

The numbers in the two Institutions in February, usually the busiest time, were still high.

	Males	Females	Total
Institution House	100	81	181
Institution Infirmary	56	58	114
Institution Nursery	7	10	17
Institution Children in Infirmary	1	4	5
Total Institution	164	153	317
Cottage Homes	52	35	87
Total Both Institutions	216	188	404

In the Lancashire mental hospitals, there were two-hundred and fifty-three patients from the Fylde. These numbers were now broken down into two groups. Blackpool had one-hundred and sixty-four patients, and eighty-nine came from the remaining Fylde districts.

The unions were told not to send mental patients to the Lancashire asylums with infections, or send any patients from a place where infections existed. In these cases, they had to stay in isolation at the Wesham Institution for fourteen days, until they were given the all-clear. The guardians had to employ two female mental nurses to care for the temporary detained mental patients at the institution. In the casual wards, the workhouse doctor now had to examine every casual that entered. He was paid one shilling per casual.

The guardians made some improvements at the institution. A new oven, costing one-hundred and sixty-seven pounds was purchased for the bake house. Another seventy-five pounds was spent on a new vertical steam engine for the calorifier house, the water tower was repointed with mastic, and R. Wright and Sons enlarged the house committee rooms for ninety pounds and ten shillings.

The biggest improvement was the plan to connect to the electric supply. The plans included a sub-station built near the entrance. Electric lights and fittings would be installed throughout the institution, union offices, and cottage homes. The Preston Electric Corporation gave a quote of a fixed annual sum of two-hundred and fifty pounds and a one penny rate per unit. The work would be overseen by the electric committee.

The days were numbered for the guardians. Going through Parliament was a bill to abolish boards of guardians and pass their powers over to the county councils. The guardians decided to invite some local Members of Parliament, to sit in at one of their meetings to show them the work of the guardians. They would then show them around the institution.

They invited Captain Edward Stanley, M.C. Fylde's Member of Parliament, and Sir Walter De Frece for Blackpool, both Conservatives. They also invited the Liberal Member of Parliament for Lancaster, Mr Robert Parkinson Tomlinson.

On 7 November 1928, William Hodgson gave an extended welcome to Mr R. Parkinson Tomlinson, the only one who had accepted the boards invitation to attend the meeting and visit the institutions.

After the visit, Mr Tomlinson expressed his pleasure at the efficient manner in which the board conducted its business and complimented the guardians and officials. He stated that with the first-hand knowledge he had gained of the work of the guardians, he would be better qualified to take an active part when the Government's proposals for their abolishment came before the House of Commons.

Mr A. Gill, Assistant General Inspector of the Ministry of Health of Out Relief, inspected and complained about the amount of relief given and, in some cases, the reasons for relief were not clear. The guardians found no reason for complaint or to change the way they administered relief.

The inspector also complained about how the relief committee's meetings were conducted. There were four relief committees now, who went through the relief cases for their respective districts: Kirkham, Fleetwood, Blackpool North, and Blackpool South.

The relieving officers were meant to submit relief applications, make a report, and produce the relief order lists and case papers to the relief committee, all before the guardians meetings. At the meetings, the committees went through the relief lists, where the relieving officers had to be present to give any additional information. The applicants were also meant to be present, but the Fylde Guardians didn't apply this rule which was picked up by the inspector.

Chairman William Hodgson considered it impractical in his union, where recipients of relief were generally known by the guardians. He thought that to have all applicants appear before the committee for interviews was impractical due to time restraints. However, in view of the increasing numbers of applicants, he recommended that the relief committees commence their meetings at nine a.m. on board days. This, he thought, would give reasonable time for cases to receive the necessary consideration and finish before the board sits.

At this time there were very few able-bodied entering the institution, but one person who did enter was Miss Jessie Ruxton.

When Jessie was twenty-four years old, she became pregnant and left her family home and moved in with the father. Sometime after 1911, Jessie and the child's father left Liverpool and moved to Blackpool, where they had another three children. When the fourth child, Elsie, was four months old, the father, James Arnott, abandoned his family.

Jessie, who was now thirty years old and living at 10 Heys Street, Blackpool, had no choice but to report to the relieving officer. He gave her and the four children an order to enter the Wesham Institution. Jessie and the two youngest children; Elsie and Norah, were admitted on 5 August 1915, and the two eldest Thomas and Ida; who were both over three years old, were sent straight down to the cottage homes.

At the guardians meeting on 18 August, the clerk was ordered to make inquiries into Jessie Ruxton. Jessie's original settlement was in the West Derby Union, but she had gained the status of 'irremovable' so could not be returned to that union. The clerk wrote to the 'putative' father of the children and asked him to contribute towards their maintenance.

On 18 September, the clerk received a letter from the father saying he refused to pay. He was told legal proceedings would be taken against him unless he contributed. In court, the mother received a magistrate's order, against the father of the children, for a weekly sum of ten shillings.

As Jessie had nowhere to go, she stayed in the institution. At that time, with thousands of troops in and around Blackpool, and no house building taking place, there was a chronic shortage of housing on the Fylde which resulted in increases of rents. The clerk was instructed to take steps for a 'variation in the order' so that the money could be paid straight to the guardians. This was on 1 October 1915. In November, the father left Liverpool for an unknown address. Nothing more was heard from him.

Jessie and her children would stay in the institution for a prolonged period of time.

Thomas Ruxton, who was born on 26 June 1910, lived in the cottage homes until he turned thirteen in 1923. He was then offered a place at Kirkham Grammar School and was admitted as a boarder. In 1927, he gained a Cambridge Local School Certificate but did not gain his matriculation requirements. This was put down to his behaviour. Thomas, now seventeen, couldn't return to the homes and applied to join the Royal Air Force. He wasn't accepted and with his options running out, he had a meeting with his mother and some of the female guardians.

What was said at the meeting is unknown, but Thomas' behaviour showed a 'marked improvement' and he returned to Kirkham Grammar School. Thomas failed again to matriculate in September but was given another chance at Christmas. Despite this, provisional steps were taken for his admission into a training college for the following year. In February 1929, he was told he had passed his exams and arrangements were made for him to attend a college in the summer. On 16 September 1929, Thomas reported to the York Diocesan Training College for a two-year course.

The second child, Ida, was born on 16 June 1912. She was just three when she was separated from her mother and sent to the cottage homes. She would now only see her mother every three months. In June 1926, Ida had her fourteenth birthday, and it was time to leave for a life of service. When the school year finished, Ida stayed at the home until she had finished a short period of domestic training. She was then sent into service with Mrs Swan of Wesham. Ida didn't settle with Mrs Swan, and after being 'placed out' in some other positions and still not settling, her future was discussed. This was at the same meeting with her mother and the female guardians who were discussing her brother's future. Ida's options were limited. She was sent into service again, this time with a Mrs Carlisle of Wesham.

The third child, Norah Ruxton, was born on 6 November 1913. Norah stayed with her mother until the day after her third birthday, so her entrance into the cottage homes was not as abrupt as Ida and Thomas. There were two siblings to guide her when she arrived on 7 November 1916. After her fourteenth birthday, in 1927, she also had a month's domestic training. She was sent into service in January 1928, at the home of Mrs H. Yates, Lytham.

The youngest child Elsie, who was born 19 March 1915, was also sent to the cottage homes, after her third birthday. She turned fourteen in March 1929 and, like her sister, after a period of training was sent into service, with Mrs S. Allen of Ansdell. By that time, Elsie had been in the two institutions for nearly fourteen years and had hated every minute. One thing she could never come to terms with was that, throughout those fourteen years, children came and went, but she just stayed.

Why Jessie stayed so long in the Wesham Institute is unknown. It was unsettled times, with a world war and later mass unemployment. Maybe, Jessie decided it was better to sacrifice her freedom for the benefit of her children. She could solve the problem of only seeing her children once every three months by working in the nursery. When the infants were taken on walks in their prams, there was nothing to stop Jessie from passing the schools at break time.

When Elsie left the Institution, Jessie Ruxton was now free to leave and find a place of employment. A vacancy arose at the Wesham Institution when the seamstress, Helen Bonney, resigned. Jessie applied for the role and became the new seamstress on 24 April 1929 . Now she had a uniform, a salary and accommodation provided. She could start building a new life. She later changed roles at the institution and became the nursery attendant, earning fifty-two pounds and fifteen shillings per annum.

On 25 September 1929, the clerk gave a report regarding the Ruxton Family.

The three girls are in service, and Thomas reported at the York Diocesan Training College for a two year's course on the 16th instant. I have made an application to the Lancashire Education

Committee for a loan to cover his college fees. Resolved that the report be received and approved.

Jessie resigned as nursery nurse in September 1930, and later married David Pitt, a road worker, moving to 38 Birkdale Avenue, St Annes. All the children ended up living a normal family life. Thomas married a teacher and later became the Headmaster at Kirkham and Wesham County Primary School. Ida married and had two children. Norah also got married and moved to Leicester. Elsie married Frank Kay and stayed in Kirkham.

Elsie with her husband Frank Kay centre, Jessie seated, and Nora standing behind her. (Photo Courtesy of Tony and Barbara Kay)

At the start of 1929, Messrs Brassers and Oakley Solicitors wrote saying that Dr Reid did not propose to resign from his office and requested that his salary and vaccinations fees for the quarter, ending March 1928, be paid to his client. The clerk informed the Ministry of Health of Dr Reid's refusal to resign and forwarded the solicitor's letter.

The minister's clerk wrote back.

> I am directed by the Ministry of Health to acknowledge the receipt of your letter, 2nd instant, informing me of the resignation of Dr L. Reid as District Medical Officer for Fleetwood in the Fylde Union, has not been received and a forwarding copy of a letter from Dr Reid's solicitor. The minister, in pursuance of his powers in that behalf, hereby removes Dr Reid from the office of District Medical Officer.
>
> As a result of this consideration, the Ministry of Health does not propose to remove the suspension of Dr Reid from office and will unless Dr Reid himself, within the next seven days, informs the guardians of his intention to resign office, proceed to issue the necessary order for his removal.

Accepting defeat, Dr Reid finally resigned as the Fleetwood District Doctor. The guardians paid him for the ten days of work he was owed, before being suspended, from the 1st to the 11th of April 1928. He was still technically the Fleetwood Public Vaccinator, so, Mr Duckworth motioned, and Mr Drinkwater seconded, that the agreement entered into with Dr Reid as Public Vaccinator of Fleetwood, be put to an end and that the clerk serve upon Dr Reid the necessary twenty-eight days' notice. He was replaced in all roles by Dr J. Wylie.

In July that year, the clerk reported that he had submitted a letter from Miss Lea, the Ministry of Health Inspector, with reference to certain children she recommends should be brought under the boarding out order, and undertakings had been entered into with the following foster parents for boarding out.

Mrs Elizabeth Cardwell, of 109 Alexander Road West, St Annes on the Sea, of her three grandchildren. Jennie Ashcroft, aged 12 years, Stanley Ashcroft, aged 10 years, and Gladys Ashcroft, aged 8 years. Weekly allowance 10s. for each child for a period of ten weeks.

Mrs Elizabeth A. Walker, of 23 The Crescent, St Annes on the Sea, of her two grandchildren, Margery Magdalene (or otherwise known as Walker), aged 10 years, and Kitty Elizabeth, aged 8 years. Weekly allowance 5s. for each child, for a period of 10 weeks.

Mrs Rose Ann Peel of 4 Prospect Road, Blackpool, for Ida Ball, aged 8 Years. Weekly allowance 5s. for 10 weeks.

The committee followed the children's progress over the years and months, they were under their protection.

In September, the homes of the three prospective foster parents were inspected by Mrs Walker and Mrs Cardwell (both of the boarding out committee) and were found to be highly satisfactory. At the end of the ten weeks, the allowances were continued for another thirteen weeks: the three Ashcroft children were given thirty shillings weekly, the two Walker children ten shillings weekly and Ida Ball five shillings weekly.

In December 1929, Mrs Elizabeth Cardwell told the inspector that she was unable to give her grandchildren the necessary care and attention owing to her eyesight; she was nearly blind. Jennie, Stanley, and Gladys were all admitted into the cottage homes.

Ida Ball's allowance was last reviewed in March 1930 for a fourteen-week period. After that, no more is heard of her; presumably, she had gone back to her parents.

In 1930, Margery and Kitty were provided with winter clothing. At Christmas, all boarded out children were given a shilling for Christmas. Margery left school in June 1933 and went into the world of work. The Grandmother was paid eight shillings per week for Kitty's allowance until she commenced work in July 1935, and her allowance was stopped.

This would be the last full year for the guardians after the Government's Act of 1929. This act would transfer all the powers of boards of guardians, and the establishments under their control, to the county and borough councils. After the creation of Health and Unemployment Insurances, the only people applying to poor law for relief were the entirely destitute. Of the thousands of people on the Fylde who served during the First World War, there was none from the Fleetwood or Kirkham districts claiming relief, and only four from Blackpool. In Blackpool, there were nearly five-thousand unemployed, but the Fylde Union only helped about six-hundred and fifty people in the entire union.

People who had a right to help, or would qualify to use the institutions infirmaries, refused because of the stigma attached to poor law and this placed great pressure on other institutions, so as from 31 March the following year, Poor Law Boards of Guardians would cease to be.

Plans to replace the guardians started in the latter months of 1929.

After the bill was passed, Lancashire County Council held a conference with a delegation of the Fylde Guardians, where it was recommended that the present areas of the Fylde and Garstang, excluding Blackpool, form the new guardians committee area.

The new committee was called the Fylde and Garstang Guardians Committee. It would consist of thirty-six members, mainly councillors. Lancashire County Council had three members, Lytham St Annes five, Fleetwood five, Poulton two, Kirkham one, Preesall one, Thornton one, Fylde Rural five, and Garstang five.

The guardians could co-opt eight members to the new committee. In the Fylde and Garstang Union eighty-eight point five per cent of the seven-hundred and two paupers receiving help came from the Fylde. William Hodgson thought the Fylde should have six guardians on the new committee, two of which must be women. The remaining two positions were filled by the Garstang Guardians.

The guardians elected from the Fylde, were Mrs M. E. Walton and Miss J. Rossall, both of St Annes; William Hodgson, Poulton le Fylde; Reverend A. J. King, Thornton; and Mr J. Hill, Fylde Rural District.

Blackpool had a separate committee, called the Blackpool Public Assistance Committee. This committee had twelve members of Blackpool Council and six co-opted members from the guardians.

The Fylde Guardians passed a motion, inviting the Fylde and Garstang Guardians Committee, and the Blackpool Public Assistance Committee, to their meetings from 1 January until 31 March.

The reason why was explained by William Hodgson, 'The object was to enable those members on the new guardians committees, who were as yet unfamiliar with poor law administration, to have an opportunity to come to the board meetings, in order to familiarise themselves with the way in which the business was conducted. Unless they had actually been brought into connection with poor law administration, people were usually completely ignorant of the work done by such boards. We are not putting forth the offer in any egotistical spirit as a board but solely to enable people appointed on the new authorities, to get an insight into the methods adopted by the unions'

He added, 'I don't want to use the words their fall, though that must be in the minds of some. We are face to face with two great and, I might say, insoluble problems: poverty and parasitism. We all know from sad experience how easy it was with a too sympathetic attitude to undermine the independence of man and to teach him not to rely on his own determination to succeed. He came to depend on others in times of hardship. I think it is a gigantic mistake that the knowledge and experience shared by every one of us, and appreciated by the public generally will be lost to a large extent. The Lancashire County Council did not want the new act. On three separate occasions, they protested against it most strongly and passed resolutions saying that their work was sufficient. The Government seemed to entirely ignore the position of Lancashire and took no account of the great difficulties the act would make for the country. Yet Lancashire County Council would do all in its power to make the new act a success.'

On 20 September 1929, the final North-Western Poor Law Conference was held at the Blackpool Central Library; this was the 50th conference. William Hodgson was on the platform and spoke about the end of the Guardians.

At the time of the conference, there was an increase of one-hundred and twenty-two persons on out-relief, but a decrease of twenty in the institution. There were seventy paupers per one-thousand of the population of the Fylde, in receipt of relief, compared with Manchester at three-hundred and thirty-one per one, the nearest to the Fylde was Preston at eighty. The Fylde was the lowest-rated in the country. Next year with only one fund for the entire county, the Fylde's ratepayers would subsidise the poorer areas like Manchester.

The assessment value of Blackpool, for the final year, was five-thousand, and eighty-one pounds, per penny rate; Poulton le Fylde's was ninety-two pounds; Lytham St Annes was one-thousand, one-hundred, and eighty-three pounds; Thornton Cleveleys' was three-hundred and seventeen pounds; Fleetwood's was five-hundred and sixty-nine pounds; Fylde Rural was three-hundred and ninety-three pounds; and Kirkham's was seventy-four pounds. In total, making seven-thousand, seven-hundred, and ten pounds times the six-penny rate.

Blackpool had to pay thirty-one-thousand, one-hundred, and seventy-four pounds, six shillings, and nine pence; Lytham St Annes, six-thousand, three-hundred, and eighty-four pounds, fourteen shillings, and four pence; Fleetwood, three-thousand, five-hundred, and two pounds, and fourteen shillings; Thornton Cleveley, one-thousand, nine-hundred, and eighty-five pounds, ten shillings and three pence; Poulton five-hundred and sixty-three pounds, fifteen shillings, and eightpence; Fylde Rural, two-thousand, two-hundred and one pound, nine shillings, and three pence; and Kirkham four-hundred and forty-seven pounds, nine shillings and nine pence. The rates had to be paid on 3 June and 4 November.

Inside the institution, Mr Frampton of 25 Birley Street, Blackpool, installed the new electrical fittings for two-thousand, two-hundred, and thirty-nine pounds. He was supervised by the clerk of works, Mr L. J. Allen of Blackpool, who was paid six pounds to make sure the work was completed within six months of signing the contract.

Outside the institution, seven electric lamps were fitted on the carriage drives and footways; three were fitted on the outer circuit and four on the inner circuit all for ninety-eight pounds. The lamps were controlled by a switch in the porter's office. Electric lights were later fitted in the cottage homes, by R. Derbyshire and Sons, Blackpool, for two-hundred and forty-four pounds.

The guardians also purchased a new piano for fifty pounds and spent sixty-seven pounds and ten shillings on a new carpet for the enlarged committee rooms. Two settees were purchased and three adjustable chairs for the nurse's house and the other furniture reupholstered.

Some of the able-bodied, who were found work in Blackpool, were paid one shilling per hour and worked between twenty to twenty-five hours a week. During Christmas week, they were given an extra two shillings plus one shilling per child. The guardians could offset this with the profit of two-hundred and seventy-six pounds, made on the institutions farm this year, but as the clerk pointed out, 'We don't pay rates, taxes, wages or for the pig swill.'

At the start of 1930, the guardians were spending more of the Fylde's ratepayers money on modernising the institution, knowing that in March, any money left in the accounts would be placed in one account for all of

Lancashire. Most unions in the country were doing this. Electric lights were fitted by Mr Frampton in the vagrant's ward for one pound, one shilling, and sixpence. In February, engineers started installing a new wireless system in the infirmary with earphones for each bed. Now that they had an electricity supply, new equipment could be purchased to help the staff. The guardians bought a four-roller, belt-driven, ironing, drying, and finishing machine for five-hundred and sixty-five pounds. They also built a new drying house for the laundry.

The guardians gave fourteen members of staff a pay rise which would cost an extra one-hundred and forty-four pounds a year. It was recorded in the finance committee's minute book.

> The finance committee recommended the increases to institution and cottage home officials be made as shown below, with the effect in each case from the 1st of January 1930.
>
> R. W. M. Holmes, Chaplain, £75 to £90 per annum
>
> G. W. Lunn, Master, £125 to £155
>
> F. Lunn, Matron, £105 to £125
>
> R. Parker, Cook, £64 to £65.
>
> B. Armstrong, Seamstress, £52 to £60.
>
> A. Magson, Home Supt., £100 to £120.
>
> S. Magson, Homes Matron, £75 to £85.
>
> M. Hammond, Foster Mother, £50 to £55.
>
> M. Bagley, Foster Mother, £50 to £55.
>
> E. Clegg, Foster Mother, £50 to £55.
>
> M. Winstanley, Foster Mother, £50 to £55.
>
> J. Holmes Foster Mother, £50 to £55.
>
> J. Smith, Foster Mother, £50 to £55.
>
> S. E. Kean, Servant, £35 to £45.
>
> It was further recommended that the application of Miss Kean, servant at the cottage homes, to be classified foster

> mother, and the application of the gardener for an increase in salary, be not acceded to.

Smallpox infections were becoming less common and with the fear of the disease diminishing the take up of vaccinations decreased again in 1929. Three years prior, forty per cent of the children were vaccinated, now it was twenty-five per cent. In 1927, four-hundred and seventy-five children under one year were vaccinated; in 1928, it was three-hundred and forty-seven; and in 1929 there were three-hundred and forty-three children vaccinated. For children over one year, two-hundred and ten were vaccinated in 1927, ninety-six in 1928, and in 1929 only sixty-two.

The total numbers vaccinated in 1927 was six-hundred and eighty-five; in 1928 it was four-hundred and forty-three, and in 1929 the number was four-hundred and five. The revaccination figures showed a fall in numbers from two-hundred and forty in 1927 down to one-hundred and one in 1929.

In March, when the contracts for supplies were awarded, the Lancashire Public Assistance Office, asked to be involved. The new board would not be responsible for vaccinations, and all seven doctors were given notice of termination. Their vaccination contracts ended on 31 March 1930.

On 12 February, the Fylde and Garstang Guardians Committee met for the first time. There would be some continuity as William Hodgson was elected chairman. During the last month of poor law, there were three-hundred and six inmates in the Institution, plus nine at Preston. In the cottage homes, there were eighty-one children. During the first two weeks of March, seventy-five casuals passed through the tramp wards.

At the meeting on 13 March, Mr Drinkwater thought the eleven guineas paid to a woman for dental treatment was excessive. The thirty-five-year-old widow had a pension and received an extra ten shillings from the union. He thought a woman so young and receiving the amount mentioned was unreasonable, when other people are crying out for bread and butter. The clerk was asked to look into the case. It didn't matter for most of the guardians, as two weeks later the board would cease to exist.

At the last meeting, Alderman, William Hodgson, was presented with a canteen of cutlery and table silver. When the meeting was over, and the guardians had finished their business for the last time, the chairman made a parting speech.

Amongst the portraits of former chairmen, William said, 'There was invariably a tinge of sadness at our parting. We would never meet again, and the position was one with which, I am sure, everyone was profoundly touched. Boards of guardians had been in existence a long time, and they had done an immense amount of good work. How much, history alone would show. We had over 600 boards in the Kingdom, and everyone, with a few exceptions, had done their duty to the country. I cannot help thinking that it was a profound mistake for the Government of the day to have swept away a body of such excellent citizens, many of whom, under the new regime, will not have an opportunity again of doing the work or assisting those who would do it in the future.'

He continued, 'I could not help thinking, that the touch we possess of kindness, and consideration, and the help for those unfortunate people who had come to us for assistance, combined with our desire to take care of the interests of those who we represent, would no longer be possible to the same extent. The new representatives would no longer have that direct and personal contact, which will go, and which would never be renewed. I think also that the change was to the disadvantage of both of the public authorities and those who had to find the money.'

Being conciliatory, William said, 'At the same time my remarks must not be taken, as in any way, derogatory to those who succeed us. So far as Lancashire was concerned, the members of the public assistance committee had been very carefully chosen, and they had already shown a keen desire to carry on the work with the same conscientiousness as had been done in the past. I feel sure that there would be nothing lacking on the part of the new committee in their efforts to carry on the work to the advantage of all.'

He added, 'For almost as long as I could remember we have been the A1 Union, and for this, there were three reasons, one being the unique geographical position, the growth of a residential population, and the last and most important, the administration, for throughout the time I have been here, we have been served by excellent officials.'

He asked, 'Are the Social Services of the Country too far advanced for the wealth of the nation as a whole? Could the country bear the cost without serious deterioration? It had been stated that the cost to this country for social services was £335,000,000 a year, or £8 a head. That was a terrific sum, and I believe it was more than any country in the world. When we considered that we live on our trade and that we depend on our prosperity on the selling of our goods abroad, their position gave us very serious thought as to whether we were not spending too much in carrying out what we knew to be to the advantage of the people as a whole. The question arises whether by this system and works, were we reproducing the bad conditions which operated before 1834. We leave this work with the knowledge that we have done our duty, and that we have contributed something to the health and well-being of those who have come within these walls.'

After paying tribute to the clerk, Fred Brown, and congratulating the Preston Union, who had overtaken the Fylde as the A1 Union; Preston had eighty out of one-thousand in receipt of indoor and outdoor relief against the Fylde's figure of eighty-six. Mr Hodgson switched on the new wireless machine and broadcasted a message, and the Fylde Union was no more.

The minutes of the last meetings went as follows:

Board Room Wesham

26th March 1930

At the last meeting of the Guardians, held this day present;

William Hodgson, Esq. Chairman, J. Kemp, Vice Chairman,

Mrs Walton, Mrs Brookes, Mrs Harrison, Mrs Groves, Miss Rossall, Rev J. Cotton, Rev A. J. King, Messrs, F. W. Waring, W. Marshall, J. Cardwell, A. Mills, M. Shea, G. Ramsden, W. Broughton, A. S. Careless, F. J. Ball, F. J. Brandwood, A. Drinkwater, J. M. Whittaker, C. Bagot, J. Clegg, W. Jolly, B. Ashton, J. Pearson, J. Harwood, H. Burrows, J. Fielding, M. Tomlinson, J. Hill, W. Rawstone, H. Whalley, W. Lawson, J. Fairclough, R. G .Kent, C. E. Harwood, J. Porter, G. Gardener, R. G. Thompson, and J. Pemberton, also present

Miss Ashworth, Messrs J. Brookes, W. E. Simpson, and R. H. Cunliffe.

Before commencing the business to be transacted, the chairman referred in appropriate terms to the death of Mr John Duckworth who had represented Bank Hey Ward of the Parish of Blackpool since 1922. A tribute to his memory was paid, the members of the board standing.

Resolved that the clerk convey to Mrs Duckworth and family the board's sympathy in their bereavement.

The following cases were taken as read and signed: None

The following cases were reported upon from the last meeting.

Sarah E. Beattie, Preston Union, written to for decision.

Catherine Kendall, settlement reported to Blackburn Union for acceptance.

Esther Sharp & John Moseley, investigations not complete.

Dorothy Delves, Elizabeth Entwistle, James Cameron, William Shane, Alexander Wilson, all ill in infirmary.

The reports of the proceeding of the Relief Committee at the meeting held this morning were laid before the board and adopted.

The minutes of the proceedings of the House Committee at the meeting held on the 12th instant were taken as read and adopted.

The minutes of the proceedings of the Farm Committee at the meeting held on the 12th instant were taken as read and adopted.

The minutes of the proceedings of the Electric Committee at the meeting held on the 12th 14th & 19th instant were taken as read and adopted.

The minutes of the proceedings of the Finance Committee at the meeting held on the 12th instant were taken as read and adopted.

The minutes of the proceedings of the Cottage Homes Committee at the meeting held this morning were taken as read and adopted.

The minutes of the proceedings of the Boarding Out Committee at the meeting held this morning were taken as read and adopted.

In accordance with notice duly given, Mr Kemp moved:

That upon the recommendations of the Finance Committee, the salary of Mr M. J. Milly, masters clerk, be increased from £45 to £52 per annum with the effect from the 1st instant.

The motion was duly seconded and carried.

Letters read from Bromley Union, asking the board to accept the settlement of Walter Ashworth, his wife Mary Elizabeth, alleged to have been gained, by residence at Thornton for about 10 years. Enquiries prove this to be correct. Case accepted.

Letter read from Miss E. Muishill resigning her appointment as assistant nurse. Resolved that the resignation be accepted, and the filling of the vacancy referred to the house committee. Also resolved that Miss Muishill application for a testimonial be acceded to.

The clerk laid before the board a statement prepared by the Ministry of Health showing the numbers of persons in receipt of Poor Law Relief in England and Wales in the quarter ending in December 1929. Resolved that each member of the board be supplied with a print.

Upon the report of the finance committee, it was resolved that the following cheques be drawn, and the amounts debited to the following accounts and to the credit of the treasurer.

J. P. Langley	Relief Cheque	£90-0-0
G. N. Rees	Relief Cheque	£130-0-0
J. A. Jump	Relief Cheque	£70-0-0
J. Cardwell	Relief Cheque	£50-0-0
Invoice Institution	J. Hope & Sons	£109-10-10
Persons in Hospital	Dr Barnardo's Homes	£7-11-2
	Blackpool Corporation	£8-8-0
	C. E. Garrett	£15-10-0
Rates	J. Rawcliffe	£2-13-0
Books	Shaw & Sons	£2-19-6
	J. Rigley	£67-17-11
Repair, renewals	D. & J. Tullis	£565-0-0
Salaries	Quarterly and monthly salaries	£759-4-1
Vaccination	Quarterly vaccination fees	£12-1-8
Superannuation	E. Trickey	£8-5-8
	F. H. Brown	£8-13-9
	C. F. Dowford	£1-4-0
Books	J. Cardwell	£1-4-0
Repairs, renewals	L. J. Allen	£48-0-0
Microphone House Co. Ltd.		£390-10-0

The following orders were made;

That inquiry be made into the settlement of Louis Holroyd, recently admitted into the institution.

That the offer of William Whiteside to contribute 15s. weekly towards the cost of his wife's (Ida Whiteside) maintenance at Lancaster Mental Hospital be accepted (on recommendation of Blackpool South Relief Committee)

That upon the recommendations of relief committees, the following amounts of arrears for maintenance be written off.

Kirkham District:	Ruxton Children:	£15-2-6
	Mary A. Pickup	£2-17-9
Fleetwood District:	McGuckin (child)	£6-10-0

That the common seal of the board be affixed to the agreement now submitted, entered into with the Microphone

House Co. Ltd. for the installation of a wireless apparatus at the institution for the sum of £390-10-0.

That the common seal of the board be affixed to contracts for supplies to the institution and cottage homes for the six months commencing 1st April next.

It was resolved that the question of gas supplies, including certain renewals at the institution and cottage homes, be treated as one of urgency and further resolved that the electricity committee be given full power to order and execute any works they think necessary, also to purchase fixtures and fittings.

The clerk reported that the relieving officer's books had been examined and found to be correct. Reported expenditures ordered to be entered viz:

Outdoor Relief	11th Week March Quarter 1930	£56-19-6	J.P. Langley
	12th Week March Quarter 1930	£98-5-1	
	11th Week March Quarter 1930	£59-5-0	G. N. Rees
	12th Week March Quarter 1930	£84-9-7	
	11th Week March Quarter 1930	£74-7-0	J. A .Jump
	12th Week March Quarter 1930	£137-16-0	
	11th Week March Quarter 1930	£134-5-6	J. Cardwell
	12th Week March Quarter 1930	£68-14-6	

The clerk reported that the master's and house superintendent's day books had been examined and found correct. The other books required to be kept by these officers had also been inspected. The following are the amounts of invoices of goods received. Ordered to be entered viz:

11th and 12th Weeks March Quarter 1930	Institution	Cottage Homes
Provisions	£156-5-6	£36-14-3
Necessaries	£35-3-2	£43-19-2
Furniture Property	£18-3-11	£7-11-6
Repairs	£44-14-3	£22-4-6
Pigs	£12-0	
Garden	£12-16-3	
Clothing		
	£272-17-1	£125-7-11

The lists of requirements of the master and home superintendent having been read, it was resolved that orders be issued for the items named therein.

The following numbers are reported to be in receipt of indoor assistance,

	Males	Females	Totals
Institution House	90	67	157
Institution Infirmary	65	61	126
Institution Nursery	16	6	22
Children, Institution Infirmary	2	3	5
Totals	173	137	310
Cottage Homes	49	29	78
Totals	222	166	388

At the conclusion of the meeting, a vote of thanks to the chairman, moved by Mr Kemp and seconded by Mr Careless, was unanimously carried with acclamation and it was resolved that the board records its very high appreciation of Mr Hodgson's services as Guardian of the Poor Law for half a century and as Chairman of the Board since 1904, the courteous manner in which he had conducted the proceedings, his impartiality and fair rulings which have, at all times, commanded the esteem and confidence of every member.

In responding, the chairman gave a review of the work of the Fylde Guardians from its inception, pointing to the favourable position held by this board for very many years, and that up to the date of ceasing to function as an ad hoc authority, the guardians have unfailingly and conscientiously carried out their duties.

Votes of thanks were also unanimously passed to the chairmen of the committees; as follows.

Mr J. Kemp Finance Committee

Mr J. Mellor House Committee

Mr W. Broughton Cottage Homes Committee

Mr A. J. Careless Electricity Committee

Mr R. G. Thompson Farm Committee

Mrs Walton Boarding Out Committee

Mr J. E. Ball Blackpool South Relief Committee

Rev J. Cotton Fleetwood Relief Committee

Mrs Walton Kirkham Relief Committee

Resolved that this Board of Guardians desires to place on record its high appreciation of the manner in which clerk, Mr Fred Brown, has carried out his duties during the long period of 32 years, the excellent advice he has always given, his wide knowledge of the poor laws and administrative ability, which have been at all times at the service of every member of the board.

1930–1939

Fylde and Garstang Public Assistance Committee, Lancashire No. 3 Area

When Lancashire County Council took over from the Fylde Guardians, the institution changed its name to the Wesham Public Assistance Institution. There were three districts, Kirkham Number One, Fleetwood Number Two and Garstang Number Three, each with their own relieving officer. There were eight committees, relief, finance, institution, cottage homes, boarding out, and farm. The other two were the Garstang Institution Committee and the Fylde Institution Committee. These two committees oversaw the work the former workhouse visiting committees undertook. All committees came under the umbrella of the Fylde and Garstang Guardians Committee, who answered to the Lancashire Public Assistance Committee.

Blackpool, which was now totally separate from the Fylde, used the Wesham Institution for their indoor relief and were charged by the county council for their maintenance. The atmosphere was more relaxed in the institution, but it was run on the same lines. It was full, with two-hundred and ninety-eight in the institution, with five from the Fylde in the Preston Institution and six at Garstang: a total of three-hundred and nine. Of the inmates, one-hundred and eighty-eight were from Blackpool and one-hundred and twenty-one were from the remaining part of the Fylde. Under the new system, because all institutions were owned by the council, they could be sent to any of the former poor law institutions in Lancashire.

The vagrants were rarely put to work; due to the recession and mass unemployment, most were desperate men and women looking for work and, in most cases, too exhausted after travelling all day. They were still given a bath, after which they now received canvass slippers to keep their feet warm, something to eat, and somewhere to sleep. In the morning, they were free to go in search of work.

Apart from the resignation of superintendent and matron, because of Mr Magson's health, life in the cottage homes continued as normal. John Burton, aged thirty-two, and Laura Burton, aged thirty-three, former assistant superintendent and matron of the Sheffield Cottage Homes, replaced them. Arthur Magson died in March 1934.

A former homeboy, Richard Whittle, who now lived in New York and worked as a bus conductor, sent two pounds every Christmas to the children in the homes. In his letter, sent in December 1934, he referred to the death of Mr Magson saying he was a 'man of sterling character, patience, and understanding.' The man also mentioned 'Blackpool Day'.

He wrote, 'How I remember Blackpool Day. The days I spent in the homes are buried in my memory, and I take pride in saying that I am still a 'Home Boy'.

The children now went on a two-weeks annual summer camps. This year's camp was at Knott End.

People still claimed outdoor relief. The main recipients of this relief were widows and old-people, who struggled to survive on their pensions and needed help to pay their rents. Some workers who were paid in piece work, mainly cotton weavers, could also claim outdoor relief. The Kirkham cotton industry struggled during this decade, and the mills were often on 'short time working'. The workers who didn't earn enough turned to the assistance committee.

Between the people who still qualified for outdoor relief and the ones with unemployment insurance were a group who claimed, 'transitional benefits.' There were three types of people who claimed this benefit. Old people who had been in employment for many years but who, in recent years, had paid few contributions. People who had recently come into employment and who had only paid a small number of contributions. The third group were people who knew how to work the system, ones who did just enough work to claim transitional benefits.

Sir Frances Floud, Permanent Secretary of the Ministry of Labour, described the third group as, 'The ones at the bottom of the scale, who are no more within the employment field and do little work at any time but are able to satisfy the relaxed transitional conditions.'

The problem the government had was that when the unemployment scheme was set up in 1920, it had a surplus of twenty-two-million pounds from workers contributions. By December 1930, the fund was in debt by fifty-seven-million, two-hundred-and-ninety-thousand pounds and was growing at a massive rate. The group claiming transitional benefits consisted of nearly four-hundred thousand people.

The Government thought the system was open to corruption. People were claiming the benefit, although they weren't entitled to it. The two main groups were married women, who should have been supported by their husbands, and weekend, casual, and seasonal workers, It was decided that, from June 1931, all transitional cases would be means-tested and applicants would have to go before a committee.

The work of reviewing cases of transitional benefits would be the responsibility of the guardians. Clerk Fred Brown thought that there would have to be two relief committee meetings, each week at Kirkham, Fleetwood, St. Annes, Lytham, and possibly Thornton.

He said, 'It is going to be a big tie on the guardians, we have to review cases sent from the labour exchange every week. Your decisions will be final, subject to the confirmation of the Lancashire Public Assistance Committee; it will be necessary for thorough investigations to be made.'

When a guardian asked why they should carry out the work, William Hodgson, replied, 'It is going to be an extremely unpleasant duty, but your loyalty demands that you should do your duty to the applicants and to the country in the national crisis through which we are passing. I think everyone should do their best to assist.'

The relief committees would deal with each case from their area and report their decisions to the guardians, who would pass on the information to the Lancashire P.A.C.

By March 1933, the numbers in the Wesham Institution had reduced to two-hundred and sixty-five, with twenty-six boarded out, from a high point of three-hundred and forty-eight at the same time the previous year. The transitional cases in the Kirkham District numbered five-hundred and fifty, while Fleetwood had nine-hundred and sixty-eight. The numbers receiving outdoor relief in the Kirkham District was one-hundred and ninety. The biggest problem for the Fylde was the number of casuals passing through the casual wards; it was averaging at seventy-five per week.

Kirkham Relieving Officer, Mr J. P. Langley, had a breakdown in February and went off sick; he was granted more time off in May. In September, he resigned, and Mr E. V. Jackson, the temporary transitional clerk, replaced him as the relieving officer for the Kirkham District on a salary of two-hundred pounds plus ten pounds travelling allowance. The pay was on a scale, but as he had his relieving officer's certificate of the former Poor Law Board, he went onto the maximum pay.

Leaving your family chargeable was still an offence. Fred Keirle, thirty-five, of Blackpool Old Road, Marton, was found guilty of leaving his wife chargeable to the Fylde and Garstang Guardians Committee: he pleaded guilty.

He told the Court, 'I have been away looking for work. I was at Fleetwood trying to get a job on a trawler, and the day before, I was in London. I made my way back by getting lifts on the road.'

When Keirle handed himself into the Kirkham Police, he only had a half-penny on him. After he offered to pay the two pounds and nine shillings owed to the guardians, he was remanded on bail until 25 June.

In November 1933, the four cleaners at the institutions had their wages reduced. Mrs Jane Rossall defended the pay cut by saying the cleaners were engaged during the war years when wages were high. They had a fortnight holiday each year and only worked six days a week. The committee was more liberal with the people receiving relief and the staff over the Christmas period. Inmates received two shillings per head, with one shilling for casuals, and three shillings for the staff as well as an allowance of one shilling and sixpence per child for toys. The people in receipt of out relief received two shillings for adults and one shilling and sixpence for children.

At the start of December, after fifty-two years of service, Fred Brown gave notice of resignation due to ill health. He didn't get to see his retirement. Fred died on 22 December 1934. The Lancashire Evening Post ran an obituary

> The death of Mr Fredrick Henry Brown, of Bodminville, East Beach, Lytham, which occurred about midnight on Saturday, had removed a figure who occupied an important position in the life of the Fylde for half a century. Mr Brown, who was 67 years of age, has been in failing health for some weeks, and within the past two months had tendered his resignation

from several of the offices he held. In accordance with those notices, Mr Brown would have terminated his appointments on January 31st, 1935. The three principle posts held by Mr Brown were: Clerk to the Guardians Committee to the Fylde and Garstang Area, Clerk to the Fylde Rural District Council, Superintendent Registrar for the Fylde Area. He was also the clerk to the Local Education Committee and to the Fylde Joint Hospital Committee.

A native of Lytham, Mr Brown was a bachelor. Fifty-two years ago, as a boy, he began work at the Old Kirkham Workhouse, where the poor law offices were then situated, as an Assistant Clerk to the late William Thompson. In 1898, Mr Brown himself became the Clerk to the Board of Guardians for the Fylde and held that position until the Board of Guardians was swept away, and the management of the poor law centralised in the Public Assistance Committee of the Lancashire County Council about four years ago. He then became clerk to the Fylde and Garstang Guardians Committee under the County Public Assistance Committee. It was from this position he tendered his resignation three weeks ago, and on that occasion, Alderman W. Hodgson, Chairman of the Committee, paid a tribute to Mr Brown's fine record and stated that he knew Settlement Poor Law from A to Z and from Z to A. Mr Brown's association with the Fylde Rural Council began 36 years ago. He was appointed Clerk in 1898, having previously been an assistant in the same office. In 1898, Mr Brown also received an appointment as Superintendent Registrar for the Fylde Area, an office that has grown enormously in importance during his tenure.

When Mr Brown was appointed to those positions, they were regarded as part-time offices, but with the amazing development of the district, his work increased manifold, and made tremendous calls upon his energies, in spite of repeated additions to his staff. In private life, Mr Brown was a keen lover of sport, and in his younger days was well known locally as an athlete and cricketer. His interest in coursing was not generally known, but for many years he was a member of the Altcar Coursing Club, along with his brother, the late

> Charles Brown. His dogs ran under the name of K. Brown, and two years ago his border, Bedouin, won the North Meols Trophy. He was an old member of the Royals and St. Annes Golf Club, being Hon. Treasurer up to the time of his death. Mr Brown was identified with St. John's Church, Lytham, having held positions as Church Warden and Sideman.
>
> He was replaced by Fred Taylor, the assistant clerk.

After a Government Act, all transitional benefit cases would now be dealt with by the new unemployment insurance committees, from 1 February 1935, and the transitional committees were disbanded.

Mr Hodgson said, 'The work of the transitional committees come to an end this month, and we have done our work in a most admirable way, particularly at the beginning when it was a duty of great responsibility and great difficulty. We had imposed upon us some very difficult and intricate cases, and we had taken great pains, with the assistance of the staff in their investigations. The members have done right down good work, sometimes entailing long hours and a considerable amount of odium, as all public men had to bear, but in this instance, in a most accentuated form. We carried on, and now our work was being transferred to another authority. That authority will not be in any way responsible to the ratepayers, as you know. But I am certain of this; they will not do the work any better than the transitional committees have done in the past. I doubt very much whether those who will have to apply to them will receive any better treatment than they did from the transitional committee.'

In March, there were twenty-one deaths in the institution, and a guardian asked why it was so high. Clerk Fred Taylor, said that most of the deaths were of people who had recently been admitted. In April, there were twenty deaths. The clerk reported that the majority of deaths were persons over sixty-five years of age, with three being between seventy-six and eighty, another three between eighty-one and ninety, and one being over ninety-five.

The running costs at the institutions were higher in 1935 than in 1934, but still the second-lowest in the county. In December, the average weekly cost per head over the last twelve months was sixteen shillings and sixpence per head at the institution and eighteen shillings and two pence in the cottage homes.

There was a large turnover of staff that year, and when two more staff resigned a guardian asked the master for an explanation.

He said, 'A night sister left after two and a half years' service to take a course at a training college. The other sister has been with us a considerable time, but the heavy mental work had caused her a considerable strain.'

The year closed with two-hundred and ninety-four inmates: one-hundred and ninety from the Blackpool area and one-hundred and four from the rest of the Fylde. On Christmas Day, the Mayors and Mayoresses of Lytham St. Annes, Fleetwood, and Blackpool, visited the institution, along with some guardians. The wards were decorated, and every inmate received a gift. Entertainment was provided for the inmates on Boxing Day.

The board meetings weren't much different than the old guardians meeting's. This is from October 1936.

Lancashire Public Assistance Committee

Area No. 3 Fylde and Garstang.

Union Office, Wesham, Kirkham.

7th October 1936.

At a meeting of the Guardians Committee held this day, present:-

Sir William Hodgson, Chairman.

Miss Rossall, Miss Ashworth, Miss Harrison, Messrs W.Jowett. W. Holt, C.H. Riley, J. Hill, J. Tomlinson, T. Ledger, C. Rowley, B. Ashton, A. Swarbrick, W. Rawsthorne, T. Pemberton, F. Wood, J. Postlewhite, R.G. Thompson, J. Harwood, J.W.Chapman, W.E. Simpson, F. Wilkinson, T. Clegg, W. Jolly, W.J.Porter, J.W. Fitzherbert-Brockholes.

The minutes of the last meeting were taken and read and signed.

The following cases were reported upon from the last meeting:-

Patrick McKenna and John Warrender, settlement reports forwarded to the Superintendent Relieving Officer.

Ada Calvert, reported to the Public Assistance Officer as a departure from the public assistance committees rules.

The reports of the proceedings of the relief subcommittees at meetings held as below were taken and read and adopted:-

Fylde Institution: Meetings held 2nd and 16th September 1936.

Resolved the following recommendation be reported to the Public Assistance Committee:-

That the public assistance committee make representations to the Milk Marketing Board for a revision of their terms and conditions of supply of milk to Public Assistance Institutions, to enable contracts to be entered into, for supplies, not less favourable than those operating prior to the constitution of that board.

Garstang Institution: Meeting held 1st October 1936.

The minutes of the proceedings of the Cottage Homes Subcommittee, at meetings held on the 2nd and 16th September 1936, were read and adopted and it was resolved that the following recommendations be reported to the Public Assistance Committee.

That the permanent staff be increased by one relief foster mother and that the services of Miss N. Blezard be continued in the meantime as temporary relief foster mother.

That the following quotations be accepted:-

Potatoes: Thomas Jackson and Sons, Kirkham, Lancashire, Grown at 3/6d. per c.w.t.

Irish Roll Bacon: J. Coupe, Wesham, at 1d. per lb.

Girls Pilot Cloth Coats: J. W. Stringer Ltd, Lytham, at 16s. 6d. and 19s. 6d.

Boys Serge Knickers, J.W. Stringer Ltd, Lytham at 3s.3d. per pair.

The minutes of the proceedings of the Farm Subcommittee, at a meeting held on 2nd September 1936, were read and adopted and it was resolved that the following recommendations be reported to the Public Assistance Committee:-

That the following quotations be accepted:-

3 tons thirds at £6.15. 0. per ton.)

3 tons Indian meal at £6.5.0. per ton.)

3 tons barley meal at £8.5.0. per ton.)

1-ton bran at £6.15.0.)

1 c.w.t. fish meal at 14s.)

Preston and District Trading Society

Mr T. Clegg moved in accordance with the notice given: That upon the recommendations of the Fylde Institution Subcommittee, after reports by the medical officer, Fredrick Davies, aged 46 years, a patient in the Fylde Institution under the provisions of section 24 of the Lunacy Act, 1890, be discharged into the care of his wife, Mary Ann Davies at 5 Melling's Lane, St Annes. The motion was duly seconded and carried.

Six selected candidates for the appointment of non-resident engineer at the Fylde Institution were interviewed, and it was resolved that Mr Harry Brook of St Annes be appointed in accordance with the terms of the advertisement and subject to the public assistance committee terms and conditions of appointment and to the officer residing, whilst holding the appointment in either Kirkham or Wesham.

Notices from the following Mental Hospitals were read:-

County Mental Hospital, Whittingham

Discharge, recovered, of Fred Wardle on the 28th of September.

Discharge, recovered, of Elizabeth Brown on the 29th of September.

County Mental Hospital, Lancaster

Discharge, recovered, of Lily Hogarth on the 3rd of October.

Discharge, relieved, of Arthur Jacob Cross on the 3rd of October.

County Mental Hospital, Winwick

Discharge, relieved, of Elsie Muriel Jackson on the 12th September.

The Colony, Langho

Discharge of Marion Emma Cowling at request of husband on 6th October.

The following settlement reports received from the Superintendent Relieving Officer were submitted:

William Sutcliffe, chargeable in Fylde Institution, accepted by the County Borough of Grimsby.

Mary Elizabeth Finnigan, in receipt of out relief at Thornton, accepted by the County Borough of Manchester.

Alfred Eli Alonzo Waring, in receipt of out relief at Thornton, accepted by the County Borough of Blackpool.

George Cook, in receipt of out relief at Thornton, accepted by the County Borough of Manchester.

William Isaac Young, chargeable in the County Mental Hospital, Lancaster, accepted by the County Borough of Salford.

Edward Tillyard, chargeable in Garstang Institution, accepted by the County Borough of Cambridge.

Jack Rhodes, chargeable in the Cottage Homes, Kirkham, accepted by the County of York, West Riding.

Read letter from Miss Alice Mason, resigning her appointment as night sister at the Fylde Institution, to terminate on 4th November 1936. Resolved that the resignation be accepted, and the filling of the vacancy be left in the hands of the institutions subcommittee.

The following numbers were reported to be in receipt of indoor relief:-

Chargeable to Lancashire P.A.C.	Men	Women	Children	Total
Fylde Institution	26	18	2	46
Garstang Institution	6	2	–	8
Cottage Homes Kirkham	–	–	48	48
Total	32	20	50	102
Chargeable to Blackpool Borough	Men	Women	Children	Total
Fylde Institution	37	57	1	95
Garstang Institution	4	–	–	4
Cottage Homes Kirkham	–	–	19	19
Total	41	57	20	118
Grand Total	73	77	70	220

In January 1937, ten people died within forty-eight hours of entering the institution. Guardian Walter Rawsthorne of Freckleton thought people who were dying should stay where they were and not be moved in the final hours of their life. One sixty-three-year-old man had died in the ambulance on the way to the institution. Four of the patients lived with relatives, two with friends, one in a lodging house, and one was a farm servant. The average time between admission and death was twenty-two hours. The clerk provided the guardians with a report.

Deaths recorded for the year ending the 31st of March 1936 were one-hundred and ninety-eight in the Institution. Of these, forty-two were under sixty years, sixty-nine between sixty to seventy years, sixty between seventy to eighty years and twenty-three over eighty years.

Eight people died within seven days, ten people within six days, Six people within five days, nine people within four days, eleven people within three days, thirteen people within two days, and twelve people one day.

The details of the ten who died in January, plus the one in the ambulance, went as follows:

Name	Age	Address from whence admitted	Sickness as shown on admission order or Doctor's Certificate	Lapse of time between admission and death	Further Information
Yates Taylor	32	2 Charnley Rd, Blackpool	Pulmonary Congestion	30	
Arthur Edward Heard	72	44 Berwick Rd, Blackpool	Cerebral Haemorrhage	22 1/2	
George William Taylor	70	13 Avenue Rd, Normoss	Cerebral	30	
James Anderton	60	Staining Wood Farm	Cardiac Disease	24 1/2	Buried by County
Robert Baker Dawson	63	74 London St, Fleetwood	Paralysis Agitans	22	
Frederick Owen Forrest	64	11 Sandgate, Blackpool	Myocarditis	14	
Thomas Callaghan	63	12 Seed St, Blackpool	Cardiac Failure, Moribund	Died before admittance. No inquest, Myocaritis	Buried by County
Thomas Doig	83	3 Pickup St, Blackpool	Heart and Kidney Disease	5 1/2	
Richard McGinn	69	25a Marsden St, Kirkham	Cerebral Thrombosis	20	
Mary Ellison	75	1, Oxford Rd, Fleetwood	Senility	47	Inquest, Death fell at home
Charles Hodgson	62	67 Harris St, Fleetwood	High Blood Pressure	19	14 days order, No Inquest

Mr Hodgson told him, 'The matter of people dying soon after admission to the institution is general. Other institutions suffer in the same way. There does not seem to be any remedy. The relieving officer is bound to move when he gets a medical certificate.'

Clerk, Mr Taylor, said, 'No other course of action appeared open to the relieving officers other than the removal of the patient to the infirmary when this course was recommended by a medical practitioner and desired by relatives or the householder.'

In April, Sir William Hodgson was again elected Chairman of the Fylde and Garstang Guardians. On 9 April, he would have completed fifty-six years of service as a guardian. He thought the change from the poor law had not been for the better.

He said, 'I regret the change, and whilst I might be prejudiced in the matter, I think the old boards took a greater interest in the work than the present authorities. The old boards had responsibility, but that responsibility had been taken away and is now vested in the county councils who to a great extent are an overriding body. We do not feel the same weight of freedom, and today we are confining our activities.'

The new regime was better for the inmates or patients as they were meant to be called, as they had greater freedoms to come and go and could wear their own clothes. Another improvement was when people in the institution, were given an allowance of two shillings from their pensions to spend. This, however, was not extended to imbeciles, because the guardians thought some of the other inmates would take advantage and steal the money.

The unemployment was high at this time, but the guardians struggled to fill female attendant posts. Any temporary posts were advertised through the Royal British Legion to help get First World War veterans into work. For male attendants, the guardians had no problems in finding applicants. That year, one-hundred and seventy-three men applied for a vacancy for a male attendant. They included: a lay reader, pork butchers, brewery salesmen, unemployed variety artists, and an unemployed tackler. Seven were interviewed: William Barnes, Kirkham; William Bray, Whittingham; William Danson, Wesham; Frank Hargreaves, Lancaster; Harold Yeoman, Clitheroe; and Joseph Searles, Lancaster, who was awarded the post.

In August, there were two-hundred and seventy-three inmates, one-hundred and sixty-six were chargeable to Blackpool, and one-hundred and seven to Lancashire County Council. Fifty inmates had been admitted during the month, along with one-hundred and ninety-one casuals. In October, two-hundred and fifty-five casuals past through the tramp wards.

The two district relieving offices were in Fleetwood and Kirkham. Kirkham's was in a bungalow opposite Flaxfield Mill. Fleetwood's office had a set of stairs at the entrance, and with mainly old people claiming relief, the guardians decided to build a new office with a more accessible entrance. In December, they planned to buy a plot of land on Warrenhurst Road for one-thousand-eight-hundred pounds to build the new office. They didn't buy the land, and instead purchased a building for the new relieving office, 110 London Street, Fleetwood.

If you claimed help for your rent, it was called 'domiciliary assistance'. Some guardians complained that lodging house owners claimed this relief which, in effect, was subsidising a business. There was nothing which could be done about it though. A person received a fixed sum for one to two months, when it would be reassessed by the relief committees.

In March, there were eleven deaths in the institution. Five were between seventy and seventy-five, three between seventy-five and eighty, and two over eighty-five years.

Again, referring to the cases of inmates who died shortly after admission Mr Rawsthorne said, 'It seems to me a very hard-hearted method to send people to the institution when they are dying.'

Mr Lunn, the master, told Mr Rawsthorne that in July sixteen people died in the institution. Mr Rawsthorne wanted to know how long they had been in the institution.

Mr Lunn said, 'One died within two days of admission and four within seven days. One case was from a lodging-house.'

Walter Rawsthorne replied, 'It seems to me there has been no improvement since the discussion of the matter some time ago about sending people who are already dying to the institution. If a man is dying, he should not be carried about but allowed to stay where he is.'

The number in the institution stayed at the three-hundred mark and plans were in place to build extra wards for twenty-thousand pounds. There were twenty proposed extension programmes in Lancashire, and Fylde's was sixth on the list.

In January 1939, the master, reported an increase in the number of casuals during 1938. It had been two-thousand-five-hundred compared to two-thousand, four-hundred and forty-two in 1937. It wasn't a large increase, but with unemployment coming down, it was a surprise.

Mr Hill asked if the casuals got better treatment off the beaten track. The Chairman of the Institution's Subcommittee, Mr Clegg, had interviewed some casuals, who expressed satisfaction at the treatment they received at Wesham.

He added, 'It is better than some places, and I am satisfied the casuals are as well looked after at Wesham as anywhere in the country. Some of them tell me during the summer that they come this way because they are making more for Blackpool in search of work.'

A special subcommittee held a meeting to discuss the terms and conditions of the staff which had been recommended by the Lancashire Public Assistance Committee. They recommended:

1. That the salary for non-residential assistant nurses in public assistance hospitals and infirmaries be fixed at £2 2s. per week together with meals when on duty and uniform valued at £5 per annum.

2. That the Lancashire Public Assistance Committee approve the adoption of a working fortnight, not exceeding 108 hours for the nursing staff in hospitals and infirmaries under their control and that the necessary arrangements to implement this decision be made as soon as possible.

3. That the scale of salaries of master's and matron's be amended, and the existing salaries reviewed, as from the 1st April 1938, in accordance with the table set out in the report of the special subcommittee. (The new rate gave the Master a £30 pay rise taking his salary to £200.)

4. That all laundry staff (other than officers in charge) scrubbers and cleaners, employed in the committee's institutions, be employed and paid by the hours worked at the rate of 9d. per hour and meals be not provided.

In February, the clerk gave a comparison of the costs between the old board and the new public assistance board. There had been a continual increase in costs since 1930. During the last eight years, there had been a decrease in inmates, amounting to about fifteen per cent. However, there had been an increase of thirty per cent in staff and nearly a one-hundred per cent increase in salaries. Outdoor relief had cost one-hundred and thirty pounds a week in 1930; now it was four-hundred and seventy.

Institution's Staff

	1930	1939
Medical Officer part-time	1	1
Master	1	1
Matron	1	1
Sisters	3	3
Assistant Nurses	13	13
Cook	1	1
Assistant	Non	1
Chaplains part-time	2	2
Religious Instructors part-time	2	2
Organists part-time	1	1
Baker part-time	1	1
Porter	1	1
Porteress	1	1
Seamstress	1	1
Laundress	1	1

	1930	1939
Laundry Workers	Non	3
Cleaners	4	7
Engineer	1	1
Gardener	1	1
Gardener Labourer	Non	1
Joiner	1	1
Bricklayer	1	1
Stoker	1	1
Assistant Stoker	Non	1
Master Clerk	Non	1
Male General Assistant	1	2
Nursery Attentants	3	3
Barbour, Bathman	1	1
Female General Assistants	1	1
Assistant Master	Non	1
Storekeeper	Non	1
Mental Attendants	Non	8
Painter	Non	1
Totals	45	67
Staff Salaries	£3,500	£6,140
No. of inates chargeable daily average	295	255
Casuals for year	2546	2,600
Cost per head per week	15s. 8 1/2d.	21s. 3.8d

Cottage Home's Staff

	1930	1939
Superintendent	1	1
Matron	1	1
Foster Mothers	6	6
Relief Foster Mothers	1	2
Assistant Foster Mothers	1	1
Dentist part-time	1	1
Medical Officer part-time	1	1
Seamstress part-time	1	1
Totals	13	14

	1930	1939
No. of Children daily average	74	78
Staff Salaries for year	£660	790
Cost of maintenance per child per week	15s. 8d.	18s. 10d.

Out relief

	1930	1939
Kirkham District		
Relieving Officer	1 (part-time)	1
Relieving Officer's Clerk	Non	1
Fleetwood District		
Relieving Officer	1 (part-time)	1
Assistant Relieving Officer	Non	1
Relieving Officer's Clerk	Non	1
Junior Clerk	Non	1
Garstang District		
Relieving Officer	1 (part-time)	1
Totals	3	7
Salaries for year	£660	£1360
Average weekly cost out relief	£130	£470

Administrative

	1930	1939
Clerk (part-time)	1	1
Assistant Clerks	2 part time	2
Junior Clerk	1	1
Totals	4	4
Salaries for year	£1228	£850

The guardians had different views regarding the increases.

Mr Rawsthorne said, 'We have not to look far to find out how the annual increases in the county rate came about. If the increased cost of the Fylde applies to all institutions in the country, then to my mind a serious blunder was committed when the poor law work was taken out of the hands of the boards of guardians and placed in the hands of the county council. I remember the remark by Sir William Hodgson at the time of the changeover when he commented that the step was the wrong one to take. The returns now before us proved him right. The old boards of guardians worked the poor law system far more economically than the county councils. There had been nothing but increases in expenditure since the changeover, and they would never stop. No one would quibble about a little extra for the poor people, but the cost of administration had got to a terrible state.'

Mr Ledger of Wesham disagreed with him, saying, 'The additional costs, were due to a different type of patient being taken in, especially people mentally affected. It was the duty of the county council to look after that type of person.'

Mr Chapman of Great Eccleston a Garstang guardian, said, 'The administration of poor law was more efficient under the old boards of guardians, but they could not lay the blame on the public assistance committees. The guardians committees sometimes passed recommendations on to the public assistance committee without giving serious thought to the financial obligations involved. Some of the blame rests on our own shoulders.'

Mr Wilkinson thought the old boards were cheaper because of the long hours and low wages that the staff endured.

Guardian Clegg, of Fleetwood backed him up, 'We now have three staff shifts instead of two, and the care of mental cases costs about £1,000 a year for mental attendants. The object of the changeover in poor law was, I think, was to enable each district in the county to help one another, and I think that has materialised. We now have a type of older and more infirm patient who require more looking after. I cannot see anything extravagant in the report.'

In April, William Hodgson was again elected to the position of chairman.

On his election, Mrs Rossall said, 'Sir William's Judgement was always sound. Whether he agrees with us or not, we are sure of a fair hearing.'

William Hodgson replied, 'It is very difficult to administer relief so that it will not do any harm, but will do good. Do not let sentiment run away with discretion. It is very easy to be sentimental and to give money in relief that is sometimes going to do more harm than good.'

Mr Evan Eaves of Fleetwood was appointed the assistant relieving officer for the Fleetwood District. He had been the relieving officer's clerk for the last four years. However, his appointment was disallowed by the Lancashire Public Assistant Committee because he didn't have his relieving officer's certificate. Mr A. J. Rosser of Chesterfield was appointed in his place.

Mr and Mrs Sharples retired. Edwin and Mary Buckley were appointed the new porter and portress in September. Another old employee who retired was the Reverend R. W. M. Holme, Vicar of Weeton, after thirty-seven years as the institutions chaplain. Reverend Sleigh, Vicar of Wesham, replaced him.

The institution was a good place to help down and outs.

William Mitchell, a labourer who had lived in a hut on allotments in Fleetwood, was arrested for being drunk.

Police Superintendent Hinds told the Judge, 'The man had no income, no known relatives and the hut he lived in was verminous and filthy. He has nothing to sleep on but old rags and paper, and I think he ought to enter an institution. He drinks methylated spirits.'

William was bound over for twelve months as long as he entered the Wesham Institution.

The Wesham Institution had two observation wards for mentally ill patients. One patient, eighty-three-year-old James Ball of Blackpool, borrowed a knife from eighty-one-year-old Alfred Booth which he used to take his own life.

At the Coroners Court, Alfred Booth said, 'I have known James for over a year and saw him sat on a bench outside the observation ward and went over to speak to him. James told me he wanted a smoke but didn't have a knife to cut the tobacco. I gave him an old penknife to cut up his tobacco and, just at that moment, he was called inside by a nurse. He forgot to hand the penknife back to me. I knew he was not allowed to take a knife into the ward, and I would have got it back from him if he had not had to leave me so quickly. I was doing him a good turn in my way by lending him the knife.'

Thomas Whiteside of Wesham, an attendant, was checking the patients in the observation ward on Friday night, and on reaching Ball's bed found bloodstains on his clothes. Ball was moving his hands about beneath the sheets, and Whiteside discovered the man had wounded his throat with a penknife.

Mr Lunn, the master told the coroner, 'Certain patients are allowed out of the ward to get fresh air. A male attendant is detailed to watch about 12 of them and is instructed not to let any man wander from his side. It is the duty of the attendant, as far as possible, to keep the men occupied with something. The transfer of the knife from Booth to Ball should not have been permitted. I take a serious view of the matter and will go through the regulations again with my staff.'

The War Years

The first mention of the war was in January 1939, when it was suggested by Mr Ledger and adopted to train the staff in anti-gas measures. The training was undertaken by the Local Authorities Joint Committee Instructors. By the summer, the County Air Raid Precautions Committee had earmarked the Fylde Institution for the storage of medical and other emergency equipment for use during air raids. In September, the Lancashire Public Assistance Committee were warned that the supplies of fish could not be guaranteed, as the Admiralty had recalled the whole of the fishing fleet to home ports. The A.R.P opened a regional operations post in the union office block.

In September 1939, twenty-four evacuees arrived at the institution. The hours of duty were abandoned, and staff were expected to remain on the premises after normal working hours and undertake additional duties. Fylde Rural District Council asked to use the fumigation facilities to clean bedding which had been issued to refugees before being returned to A.R.P. stores.

The assistant master, Edward Townson, who wanted to join the army, had to apply for 'a release from duty' as his occupation was on a list of occupations reserved by the Ministry of Labour. The guardians voted twelve to six to release him for the duration of the war. All workers employed to replace staff joining the forces were made known that it was temporary and, on the employees return, they would be dismissed.

Mr H. Binns also left for the army and was replaced by the first-ever female clerk, Mary Lamount. Doctor W.A. Kerr, the medical officer for Fleetwood, also left for the forces.

The planned extension work was cancelled, along with the plans to build a recreation hall for the children at the cottage homes. Extra accommodation was built at Wesham but not for the inmates. The Ministry of Health decided to build an emergency hospital on the site, for evacuee patients from hospitals in cities under threat from German air raids. The five wooden hut buildings could hold one-hundred and eighty patients. The electricity bill increased with the building of the huts and premises used by the A.R.P., and the master was ordered to install separate water and electric metres for the hutments, and charge the A.R.P for the electricity they used.

Kirkham and Wesham Fire Brigades were part-time, and Blackpool Fire Brigade strengthened the areas fire protection for the war by opening a satellite fire station in Wesham, with a fire engine and full-time crew. In December, the institution's staff were trained in anti-gas and decontamination measures.

Wesham Park Hospital

In 1940, the administration of outdoor relief paid to old-age pensioners was transferred from the Fylde and Garstang Guardians to the National Assistance Board. The pensioners received a supplementary pension as from 3 August. This removed a considerable amount of work from the relieving officers, and the districts were reorganised. The Garstang Relief Area was amalgamated with Fleetwood's and the rural part of the Fleetwood District was transferred into the Kirkham District.

Sir William Hodgson explained the decision, 'The County Public Assistance Committee had set up a small subcommittee, which had spent time considering the matter. The position was a rather delicate one in view of the promises made to Garstang when it was amalgamated into the Fylde Union. Relief cases in the area on the July 10th numbered 53, but with the removal of the old-age pensions the number was now only 37. The subcommittee concluded that the best way to deal with the matter was on the lines recommended. Obviously, we cannot have one man in charge of 37 cases only.'

Garstang Relieving Officer, Mr Chapman, who had held the post for twenty-six years, was offered a position in another part of Lancashire and compensated for his loss of office.

Unofficial foreign war refugees started landing in Fleetwood and were housed in two schools in the town. The clerk, on behalf of the guardians, began working with Mr Hewitson, Chief Billeting Officer; The Ladies Committee of the British Legion Club, Fleetwood; Women's Voluntary Services; the Clerk to Poulton U.D.C; Donors of Gifts; and Owners of Canteen Shelters. They all helped with the reception, accommodation, and general welfare of those landed in the town. Temporary relief was paid out to the refugees.

The biggest increase in costs at the start of the war was the transportation of coal, which went up by three pence per ton for journeys up to three miles and one penny per ton for journeys over three miles. This raised the coal contract price by eleven pence per ton.

The Blackpool Fire Brigade inspected the institution, and they recommended the purchase of more extinguishers. The master purchased three soda acid extinguishers, one foam extinguisher, and two carbon tetrachloride extinguishers.

Mr Townson wrote to the guardians in March saying he was not successful for enlistment and requested that they consent to him joining the Finish Army. He was told the decision on 1 November was only for the British Army, and his request was declined. He resigned, but then later withdrew it and returned back to work.

All the clerks applied for military service, and the master asked that at least one be retained. The guardians could block an employee's application to join the army, but if someone wanted to join the forces, they would support them. The master was told to replace the clerks leaving with ones above military age. On 12 June, Mr Hodgson and Fred Davies were engaged as temporary clerks. The master's clerk and the assistant clerk left for the army the following day. When G. E. Buck, the clerk and storekeeper, was called up, the master wanted it to be blocked. Mr Buck was asked if he wanted to go to the army by the guardians, which he did, and he was released.

Of the male residents in the 'house', only the porter and master were left, and there was no night supervision. To reduce the demand on staff, the casual wards were closed. It was also decided that one member of the permanent male staff slept in the male house block in rotation. The nurses, who lived in, had to have permission to leave the site, but now with the casual wards closed and nobody at the gate they could sneak out into town. Three nurses who left the institution without permission were caught and reprimanded by the vice-chairman.

In the summer, the hutments were almost ready, and Mr H. J. Norfolk was appointed clerk and storekeeper for the emergency hospital for three pounds per week. Gas, water, and electric were connected to the hutments, and the maternity ward in the house was converted into an operating theatre. This meant removing the coal heater stove, leaving no heating in the ward. Electric heaters were fitted; the cost was borne by the Ministry of Health.

During the First World War, the army asked the guardians when they needed their help, now with their power greatly diminished, the Ministry of Health told them what they wanted them to do.

The Ministry of Health wrote to the guardians to tell them their plans for the Emergency Hospital. They asked that:

1. The male and female infirmary blocks to be made available entirely as an emergency hospital, and with the new hutments, administered as such.

2. The use of the seclusion block as an X-ray department and dispensary store.

3. The use of the nursery block as residential quarters for medical staff.

4. House inmates to be transferred to other institutions, and the male and female house blocks to become the institution's sick wards.

The guardians were against this. They thought it would be easier to leave the ill patients in the infirmary and move the inmates out of the main house block who were generally fitter. The house block would then be part of the emergency hospital. The Fylde Guardians Subcommittee's provisional report requested that:

> 1. The construction of additional huts to meet the needs of emergency requirements, including quarters to accommodate resident staff.
>
> 2. The adaption and use of the whole institution as an emergency hospital.
>
> 3. The use of the male and female house blocks as an emergency hospital, the sick wards remaining undisturbed.

On 20 September, the subcommittee met with Dr Hall, to discuss the arrangements of the emergency hospital.

Dr Hall told them, the county medical officer was told to make emergency arrangements at existing hospitals and institutions with as little disturbance as possible to peacetime users of the premises, and, that in the present stage of the emergency, there is no possibility of the arrangements suggested in one and two of the provisional report being adopted.

Dr Hall explained, 'The house wards at the institution, whilst not of hospital standards, are far more adaptable for temporary and emergency hospital use than other institutions in the county and that the use of these blocks should be made available for patients from the infirmary where serious casualties might be expected. The administrative difficulties of dual users of the institution will obviously be great, and in discussions on this matter, I assure members I will assist all I can. The immediate requirements are the facilities for commencing the work, of adopting the nursery block as residential quarters for medical personnel.'

The subcommittee had no power to refuse the ministry's requests and motioned:

> That every facility be affected in the carrying out of the proposals as outlined in the Ministry of Health's letter of 20th August.
>
> That one of the cottages at the children's homes Kirkham be made available immediately for the reception of children

> from the institution's nursery to enable builders to commence conversion of the nursery into residential quarters.
>
> That arrangements for children displaced from the cottage homes to proceed to either Lancaster or Padgate Homes (Warrington).
>
> That the transfers be arranged of suitable house inmates capable of attending to themselves to the Garstang Institution and tentative arrangements for the remaining house inmates to other county institutions.
>
> That efforts be made for the transfer of a number of uncertified mental patients now in the sick wards and whose treatment in the house wards will prove especially difficult.

More organisations started using the institution for their individual war efforts.

The Home Guard was given permission to use the field at the institution for training purposes and to use the water tower as an observation post. Two-hundred and twenty cases of condensed milk and fourteen c.w.t of syrup were stored at the institution by the Woman's Volunteers Service. An emergency first aid post was opened in the casual ward. Weeton R.A.F Station had been using the disinfection facilities to clean infected kit and bedding and asked to keep using the facility, but with the emergency hospital opening, the request was declined.

Nurses were in short supply, so, starting 3 September, a two-week intensive training course was held at the institution for nursing auxiliaries. One nurse, Miss Whalley, was in trouble with the matron, due to her failure to observe the blackout regulations by 'shewing' an unscreened light after an air-raid warning and by her refusal to obscure it when told.

Coal prices increased again. Emergency coal was moved from Northumberland and Durham to Lancashire, and the Chairman of the Lancashire Associated Collieries increased the cost of coal due to the extra transportation costs by eleven pence per ton. Coal deliveries were made to the institution, whether it was needed or not, as railway coal wagons had to be emptied immediately on arrival at Kirkham Railway Yard.

Under the Fire Watch Orders of September 1940, a fire watcher had to be present at all times at the institution. The only male officer on night duty was on the male mental wards, but the order had to be implemented immediately. Luke Kirby was employed as night fire watcher at two pounds and ten shillings. He was allowed one day a week off.

In October, four trained nurses, two assistant nurses, and ten nursing auxiliaries arrived for duty at the emergency hospital. As the hospital was still empty, it was made available for the reception of mothers and children evacuees. One-hundred and nine arrived on the 11th and most left on the 13th moving to their reception areas. Nearing the end of October, another three-hundred and ninety-eight evacuees arrived at the hospital. One-hundred and ninety-nine left on 26 October, one-hundred and ninety-nine remained for further treatment. The drains for sewerage failed in the huts, and all patients had to be transferred to the Bury Institution on 15 November.

The fight against conscientious objectors began.

In December, a letter was read from the Lancashire Public Assistance Officer to the effect that any officer or servant whose salary or wages is paid out of the county fund, and where they were on the permanent or temporary staff, and registered for his Majesty's Forces as conscientious objectors, shall forthwith inform the Clerk of the County Council, and such officer or servant shall then be offered the alternative of either:

> A. Continuing in his present post at the prevailing standard rate of army pay and allowances of a private soldier 3s. per day for subsistence or his present remuneration, whichever shall be less.
>
> Or
>
> B. Taking leave of absence without pay for the duration of the war, in either case, the superannuation rights be preserved.
>
> In the event of any officer or servant being granted by the tribunal exemption subject to remaining at his present post, he shall be subject to terms of (b) above. Any such member who accepts non-combative service in the forces shall from the date of taking up such service, be treated as coming within the terms of the resolution of the County Council passed on the second day November 1939.

At the end of the year, there were one-hundred and fourteen adults and sixty children chargeable to Lancashire County Council, and one-hundred and twenty-seven adults and twenty-three children chargeable to Blackpool.

In 1941, the Blackpool Fire Brigade asked to be allowed to feed and accommodate their officers at the institution. The guardians refused, saying they would help during an emergency, but not on a day to day basis. The mortuary was extended to hold twelve bodies, and a bier room and viewing room were added. In the union offices, a food control office was opened, when rationing was introduced. They also stored extra foods outside of rations, which were given free, milk, cod liver oil, and fruit juices for children. The group were charged forty pounds a year rent.

The A.R.P opened a Local A.R.P. report centre, and Kirkham Urban and Fylde District Council asked permission to use facilities for 'stoving' of clothing and bedding of contagious diseases in their districts. The guardians allowed this, and set a tariff of five shillings per stoving, in all cases, where the fumigation house is used. Mr Carlisle, the baker, was made full time to cope with the increased workload.

The Government set up 'first line rest centres' where persons whose homes had been damaged in air raids could go to for temporary accommodation. The guardians worked with the Women's Volunteers Service to set up and run the forty-two rest centres in the Fylde and Garstang Districts. A full-time organiser was employed to look after the rest centres.

In February, after the drains were fixed, refugees started to arrive again. In May, all one-hundred and forty-two evacuees in the emergency hospital were moved out and transferred to other institutions to allow for the reception of one-hundred and twenty patients; sixty came from London and sixty from Wrightington Hospital. Ten cases of scabies were admitted at the same time: four were evacuee children, and the rest were from Kirkham. A few weeks later, forty-two patients arrived at the hutments from Birkenhead, all bedridden.

In September, the fire watcher left. Under wartime law, all male employees could be compelled to do forty-eight hours each month of fire watch duty.

The Fylde Institution Subcommittee held a meeting and decided:

> That all male staff aged 18 to 60, excepting three who are exempt by reason of being in the Home Guard and Special Constables, be included in a rota for fire watch duties, 15 males being available and fire watching 10 hours on one night each week. There are, in addition to the fire watchers, the night duty female staffs who are always available in emergencies.
>
> That they are provided with adequate equipment and helmets. The subcommittee also recommends the purchases of ladders, to be placed at suitable selected parts of the institution.
>
> That proper and adequate sleeping and restroom, bedding, sanitary, and washing facilities be provided in the female casual block, and a phone is fitted in the fire watch restroom.
>
> That arrangements for payment of a subsistence allowance as scale, and if required, refreshments for which charges will be made accordingly.

Some more work was carried out at the institution.

Loudspeakers were fitted in the hutments, and the first aid post in the casual ward was extended by adding a gas cleaning station. However, the most urgent problem was the provision of air raid shelters. The institution had no cellars and, at first, they planned to build four surface shelters to hold fifty people. Experiences at institutions in areas of intensive enemy air raids found these shelters impractical, and the plans were abandoned. It was decided to strengthen one room in each of the following areas: male house, female house, male and female infirmary wards, admin block, and resident medical officers block. Blast walls were built a short distance in front of the downstairs windows. Ladders with access to roofs were placed around the building to fight incendiary devices.

In September, the guardians looked into building air-raid shelters at the cottage homes for the children. They had cellars in the old infirmary, but the distance from the cottages made it impractical, so they decided to build surface shelters, this was on 17 September. The following week on the 24th a lone German plane dropped four bombs on Kirkham. One landed in the cottage home's yard, smashing all the windows and blowing down a wall. The children had a lucky escape. None of the children or staff was hurt, and the children were moved into the other cottages until the damage was fixed.

At the end of the year, plans for an extension to the emergency hospital were put in place for infectious cases, comprising of six wooden huts fifty-four feet by sixteen feet and a further three huts thirty-six feet by sixteen feet for patients and staff. Only two were built.

Even before the new hutments had started to be erected at the start of 1942, there were five-hundred beds at the institution. More patients arrived forty from Bolton and ten from Birkenhead; fourteen patients arrived from Rawtenstall and twenty-eight from the Fishpool Institution. The number of inmates fluctuated between four-hundred and five-hundred, and with all the additional work the master and matron asked to be moved up the pay scale. They moved to grade three on the scale, which was for institutions with between three-hundred and fifty-one to five-hundred inmates. The master's pay went from two-hundred pounds to two-hundred and seventy pounds, and the matron's pay from one-hundred and fifty pounds to one-hundred and seventy pounds. Their daughter, Miss Lunn, passed her final examination in nursing and won a silver medal at the Queen Victoria Royal Infirmary, Preston.

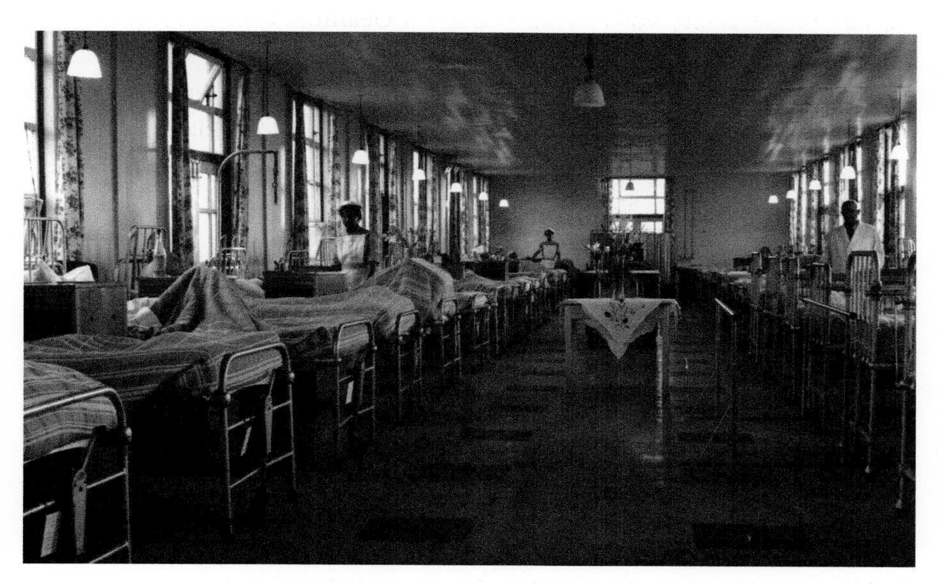

Ward Five of the Hutments in 1951, (Photo Courtesy of Yvonne Blundell)

The metal railings fronting the Wesham Public Assistance Offices was handed over to the Ministry of Supply to cut down as scrap for the war effort. The railings at the cottage homes were also taken. The guardians wanted to plough the unused land at the institution and grow arable crops, but with clay just below the surface, it wasn't possible. They decided to let the land to Mr Shorrock of Chapel Farm, Mowbreck Lane, who paid twenty-five shillings rent per annum, for grazing his cattle on the fields north of the institution. He had to keep the fences in repair as part of the deal.

Ever since the union was formed, they awarded contracts for essential supplies. However, in February, due to the consequences of rationing, the usual advertisements for tenders was dispensed with and wholesale suppliers used. Only coal, coke, and meat were contracted.

This year saw the de-reservation of the male staff. The guardians struggled to fill vacancies and started asking the Ministry of Labour officials to suggest suitable persons to apply for vacancies when presenting themselves to the Ministry of Labour offices.

The Army would write to a person and tell them they were liable to be called up, and the guardians could ask for it to be deferred, which often happened. The deferrals were for between one to six months. John Barnes, Thomas Bullen, Frank Scott, and Norman Gregson were told they were liable to be called up in April. Thomas left one month later on 21 May, Frank Scott had his call up deferred until June at which point, he failed his medical, Norman Gregson's call up was deferred until September, and John Barnes who was aged forty-two years wasn't called.

The relieving officers of Lancashire were supervised by the superintendent relieving officer, who made complaints against the Fleetwood officer for not undertaking his duties. The Fleetwood relief subcommittee held a special meeting on 29 July, and went through the complaints.

> Compilation of Papers.
>
> It is admitted that very few case papers are compiled by the relieving officer. This work is done by the assistants from notes made by the relieving officer, after a personal interview of the applicants. The relieving officer states that all first applications for assistance he has personally interviewed approximately 95% of them, making appropriate notes of his interrogations for later embodiment on case papers.

Computation Sheets

Computation of scale allowances have been carried out by the assistants.

Visitation of Homes

Visits to homes of relief applicants and relief revision cases are done mostly by assistants.

Registration and Hours

During official registration hours at Thornton, Poulton, and Cleveleys the relieving officer is always available and does actually interview applicants for assistance, quite half his time is taken up in dealing with relief cases.

Increase in Registration Duties-Maternity Homes

The maternity homes are wartime emergency hospitals, and, in any case, they are visited only outside normal office hours.

Relief Pay.

Relieving officer states he is rarely absent during pay at Fleetwood Office. At sub-stations, where the numbers receiving pay are small, the work has been done by the assistants in company with the clerk. The arrangements for relief payments in the Preesall and Garstang Area are with the approval of the committee.

Cash.

It is correct that the relieving officers assistant has a key to the safe, and the committee sees no objections to this, being fully satisfied as to the integrity of the present assistant.

Duties Allocated to Assistants are:

Assistant relieving officer: Relief pay, visits through-out the districts, and investigations.

Relieving officer's clerk: Occasional visits to local relief recipients, writing up of case papers from instructions, computation of scales of relief, and general clerical duties.

Mental Patients.

Relieving officer states, he has only allowed his assistants to deal with these occasionally. He states he is aware of his statutory responsibilities and that he will carry them out.

Office Hours.

The suggestion that, except for attendance at meetings of the relief subcommittee, the relieving officer only visits the office for a few hours each week and on these occasions acts in an advisory capacity only is without foundation; the relieving officer affirming he is at the office at all times during normal office hours when not taking official registration hours, or dealing with mental cases or outside on official relief duties.

Specific Relief Cases Referred for Consideration of the Committee.

Eleven cases referred for special consideration were examined. They fall generally into two categories:-

1. Wrong computations of relief.

2. Entries on sheet (e) by assistants which would, on the face of them, indicate a lack of sympathy and understanding on the part of the investigator, resulting in harsh treatment and relief not according to scale or similar neglect.

As regards (1) the cases cited are in respect of cases, which have not been differentiated as between the contributions to household income by relatives living at home, the computations having been made under the regulation with respect to dependent children, instead of non-dependent relatives residing with applicants. Similar mistakes should not in future occur.

As regards (2) the relieving officer and the committee are satisfied that some of the observations written on sheet (e) by the assistant are of a nature which would not be written by a relieving officer himself, carrying out duties as the committee would desire. The entries are in terms which would not be used if the relieving officer himself had written them. Throughout his long period of service, the relieving

> officer has given satisfaction to the committee and to relief recipients in his sympathetic understanding, and treatment of all applicants. All the cases still chargeable have been reviewed, and fresh orders where appropriate made.
>
> Administration Generally.
>
> The relieving officer, expressed his serious concern at the position he finds himself, owing to his dual appointments, and the increasing duties not only of registration, but the greater times required in dealing with cases in a district, which has been enlarged with the addition of Garstang Rural and Preesall Urban District. The number of cases in those districts do not reflect additional work entailed. He states that within his capacity, he had devoted as much time to his relief duties as he possibly could.

To help the relieving officer, he was provided with a motorbike, and a deputy registrar was appointed. On 12 August, the subcommittee reported back to the inspector.

> The Registrar General has approved the appointment of a fresh deputy registrar of births, deaths, and marriages, and that he will now be in a position to so arrange registration duties which will enable him to devote considerably more time to his relief administration. He is expectant that his arrangements will permit him to devote the majority of his time to his duties as relieving officer, but having regard to all circumstances, he regrets he must decline to give a written assurance that, in future, he will devote the bulk of his time to the personal discharge of his duty as relieving officer, as requested by the Public Assistance Officer.

The year ended with two-hundred and sixty-seven inmates in the house, one-hundred and fifty-nine evacuees, and seventy-eight children in the cottage homes.

The Fylde Institution's nursing staff in 1943, consisted of two-ward sisters, one-night sister and fourteen assistant nurses; it was difficult owing to sickness and changes of staff to maintain a twenty-four-hour duty roster. The master struggled to fill most vacancies. In July, the staff vacancies were one female attendant, two cooks, two clerks, and five assistant nurses. The guardians told the master to try and fill the kitchen, laundry, and cleaning vacancies with part-time labour or with volunteers through the Woman's Volunteer Service. The bricklayer, Mr R. Gillet, should have retired on 1 January 1941. He was sixty on 14 January but was kept on for another twelve months. The lack of staff made it impossible for people to go on leave, and the male attendants were paid a week's wage in lieu of a week's holiday.

The nurses who worked in the emergency hospital were recruited from the Civil Nursing Reserve, and Dr Hall asked the master if he would open one of the unused huts to provide accommodation for the nurses. The master refused because of the extra work it would entail in opening it.

The master reported the highest percentage of bedridden cases to be admitted into the house. Of the one-hundred and ninety cases admitted from Blackpool, one-hundred and seventy went straight to the sick wards; this was ninety-one per cent. There were one-hundred and twenty-five admissions from the county area, of these one-hundred and seven, eighty-five per cent, went to the sick wards. The guardians arranged a conference with Dr Hall, as it was becoming impossible for the master and matron to provide the care the patients needed in the house and oversee the running of the emergency hospital.

The conference held on 21 July compiled the following joint statement.

> The position with regard to the institution house staff had been eased by the appointment of a cook and attendant, the deficiencies now being clerical. There are, however, still five vacancies as assistant nurse, for which no applications are being received and the civil nursing reserve, who have been posted for the emergency medical service work, are being used in the general hospital wards.
>
> Discussion also took place upon the many problems the master and matron have had to contend with since the opening of the emergency hospital, especially in regard to the civil nursing reserve and it was generally agreed that consideration might be given to the drawing up of a scheme for separate administration of the hospital, including the emergency hospital,

> and your subcommittee supports the suggestion that the Lancashire county medical officer prepare a detailed report for consideration by the guardians committee of separation of the hospital from the institution.

Dr Hall made a report which he sent along with the joint statement to the Lancashire Public Assistant Committee.

> Following up on the conference with the Fylde Institution Management Committee, I have carefully considered the question of ensuring the proper staffing of the E.M.S Hutments attached to the Fylde Institution. The facts which were elicited at the conference were:
>
> 1. That members of the C.V.R were unwilling to be posted to this institution.
>
> 2. That the resignations were unduly frequent.
>
> 3. That the billeting arrangements were unsatisfactory and were not supervised by the matron of the institution.
>
> 4. That the willing assistance of local members of the W.V.S had not been gained.
>
> In view of these facts and taking into account the general services provided by the institution for the hutments, it appears to me that any new arrangements should be solely directed towards ensuring a full staff for nursing of the emergency medical service's patients, leaving the question of a more comprehensive hospital scheme until the termination of the war. I suggest therefore that a matron be appointed at the E.M.S scale, for the number of beds in the hutments. The duties of the matron would be concerned with:
>
> 1. The control of nursing and domestic staff, engaged for the patients in the hutments, including the supervision of the billets for living-out members of staff.
>
> 2. The care of the patients in the hutments, including their diets.

3. Complete responsibility of a matron for the administration of the hutments as distinct from the institution and infirmary.

He recommended that the deputy matron at the E.M.S was promoted to matron of the E.M.S. The Lancashire Public Assistance Committee responded to the report. It was not supportive.

F. Taylor, Area Public Assistant Officer, 29th August.

1. It is difficult to see how young women about to become nurses can demur at being posted to Fylde, except on hearsay. Such cases would be rare. The fact is there are 48 C.N.R nurses here now to 122 E.M.S. patients.

Of these 48, bearing in mind, the hutments have not yet been open 3 years:

17 have been here over 2 years.

11 have been here over 1 year.

20 have been here under 1 year.

2. During the 8 months January 1st last to date, 17 C.N.R. nurses have left or been transferred. Reasons were as follows:

health grounds 4, for training 3, transferred to be near home 3, confinements 2, to be married 1, return to fever nurse 1, recalled by St. John's Military Hospital 1, transferred at matron's request as unsatisfactory 1, absconded with married parents 1, Total 17.

3. Matron has not been asked to supervise outside billets. The difficulty with regards to billets is mainly due to so many wives of members of the forces from the local camps living in the district. Matron has several times gone about the district, as far as Dowbridge to ask people she knows to take in nurses, for whom there was difficulty in finding billets.

4. The local W.V.S were quite willing to assist and endeavoured to do so but were unable through shortage of local labour. I reported this to the committee more than once.

> There are 122 E.M.S. patients, of these only 10 need dressing, and no less than 50 are up, many going out each day and are not really patients. 16 Birkenhead and 11 of our own, are public assistance inmates.
>
> I concluded a matron would not have sufficient work to do in the hutments. Your matron has done this work for nearly three years, most of the time without pay and latterly for only £20 p.a. including all the initial work of allocating ward furniture, equipment, instruments, and utensils, marking all articles, preparation of staff rotas, and the reception over this time of 1,100 evacuees. The committee knows the work the matron has done to the sacrifice of her own leisure and holidays. The patients have always been well looked after, and there has been no complaint that can be substantiated from staff and patients.
>
> To appoint another matron at this stage would be an affront to your matron in which, if conscientious service has any virtue, I hope you will not acquiesce. If the application of the Rushcliffe Scale of salaries has any bearing on the matter, matron is prepared to forego this in respect of the hutments rather than be belittled in the eyes of her staff with whom she is held in respect.

The guardians ignored the report. A new matron was appointed for the hutments, the assistant matron, Mrs Price, staying as the assistant matron. As there were fifteen small children held in the institution, one of the unused hutments was opened as a nursery, and a nursing and child's attendant was employed.

By the end of the year, there were two-hundred and seventy-five inmates and one-hundred and thirty-four refugees at the institution.

By 1944, the threat from air-raids had greatly diminished, and the guardians asked the Ministry of Health if they could remove the blast walls protecting the windows to let more light in, but the request was declined.

It was, however, to be an allied plane that caused the biggest loss of life on the Fylde.

In 1944, an American Consolidated B-52 Bomber from Warton Aerodrome crashed during a storm. The plane came down in the centre of Freckleton destroying the infant class of the town's school, the Sad Sack Café, and three houses. The accident cost the lives of sixty-one people. At the school, thirty-eight children and six adults were killed. Only three children survived from the infant department. Fourteen people were killed in the café; seven Americans, four R.A.F personal, and three civilians. All three-air crew lost their lives.

Freckleton Air Disaster (Lancashire Archives)

The event was recorded in the guardians' minutes.

> At the meeting on the 6th of September, before commencing the usual business, the chairman referred in appropriate terms to the distress and suffering in the village of Freckleton, through the crashing of an aeroplane in the village on the 23rd ultimo. Members stood in silence, and the area officer

> was directed to convey the sympathy of the committee to relatives throughout Freckleton Parish Council.

The area officer opened the rest centre on the day of the crash. It was also minuted.

> The area officer reported upon the opening of the rest centre at Freckleton on Wednesday 23rd and succeeding day owing to the distressing calamity caused by a plane crashing during a storm, and a report was made available to the members present.

Despite the accident, in November, the Ministry of Health closed all rest centres in towns with populations of less than forty-thousand. The ones in the Fylde and Garstang District were closed and the equipment recovered and stored ready for collection by the ministry.

The running of the Fylde Institution was overseen by the Fylde Institution Sub-committee, where most of this information comes from. This meeting in March was the last recording of the committee's minutes. They went as follows.

Lancashire Public Assistance Committee

Fylde and Garstang Area, Public Assistance Offices, Wesham, Kirkham

15th March 1944

At a meeting of the Fylde Institution Subcommittee held on this day, present:

Mr T. Clegg, in the chair

Miss J. Rossall, Miss D.P. Healey, Miss M. Baron, Messrs J. Turner, C.H. Riley, J. Postlewhite, A.J. Smethhurst, W. Rawsthorne, T. Ledger, J. Hill, W. Jolly, J.W. Chapman, E.W. Worsley, W.J. Porter, and T. Warbrick.

The minutes of the last meeting were taken and read and signed. For roll call, there was one man. Mr H. King, stoker, resumed duty on the 5th instant after almost 6 weeks absence, through sickness and debility. Miss Ida Shorrocks and Miss Hilda Dean have been engaged as assistant nurses, via the appointment officer and the county medical officer. Commenced on 7th March 1944. These are two of the extra five nurses sanctioned by the P.A.C. The laundress, Mrs Mary Small, has informed matron she wishes to be relieved of her appointment for domestic reasons as soon as a successor can be found. The positions of portress and female general assistants are still vacant.

Resolved that the master's report be received and that Mrs Small application to be allowed to terminate her appointment without the service of the usual notice be acceded to. Further resolved that the post of laundress be reported to the Ministry of Labour and also advertised and that the chairman and vice-chairman be authorised to consider applications and make the appointments.

Letter read from the County Medical Officer of Health that he has been notified that the Ministry of Health, are unable to approve the recommendations of the guardians committee with reference to the removal of protective blast walling at the Fylde Institution at the present stage of the war.

A report of dry rot in the maternity block now used in connection with the emergency hospital scheme, together with a request from the county architect to carry out works remedying this was received and considered. Resolved that the committee give authority for repairs stated in the report to be carried out as very urgent.

Correspondence with regard to deliveries of coal to the Fylde Institution under the fuel contract orders was read. Resolved that consideration of this matter be deferred till the next meeting of the committee. The master to submit a further report as to stock and deliveries.

The area officer submitted correspondence which has passed between Councillor Norcross of Middleton and the Public Assistance Officer, Preston with reference to the classification of Miss Doris Pashley, County Borough case in the Fylde Institution, also with respect to transport facilities for persons visiting the institution. Resolved that a copy of the master's report with regards to classification and the general observations of the committee thereon as now discussed be sent to the public assistance officer.

Resolved that the provision of a steam press for the laundry and tar spraying of footpaths in the institution's grounds be carried out during the financial year 1944–45, the estimates of expenditure for the ensuing year having allowed for these works.

At the end of the year, the numbers claiming outdoor relief went as follows

Subcommittee	Dates	Applications for out-relief
Kirkham	15th November	12
Kirkham	6th December	20
Fleetwood	15th November	12
Fleetwood	29th November	46
Fleetwood	6th December	5
Garstang	30th November	7

In the Kirkham District for the last five weeks, ending 2 December, three-hundred and twenty-seven pounds, nineteen shillings, and sixpence was paid for outdoor relief, and in the Fleetwood District (including Garstang) one-thousand, two-hundred, and eighty-one pounds, four shillings, and sixpence were paid out. In the institution, from the Fylde, there were forty-three men, fifty-three women, and thirteen children at a total of one-hundred and nine. In the cottage homes, there were thirty-three children from the Fylde. From Blackpool, there were sixty-eight men, eighty-eight women, and fifteen children. In E.M.S hospital, there were fifty-two men, eighty-nine women and two children evacuees.

William Hodgson (Lancashire County Council)

Nearly, two months before V.E. Day, the last of the old guardians, Sir William Hodgson, died aged eighty-eight years. At the meeting on 7 March 1945, the guardians referred to his passing.

> The chairman and other members in appropriate terms, referred to the great loss sub-stained through the death of the chairman of the committee, and it was unanimously resolved that a record be made of the outstanding services rendered by the late Sir William Hodgson as Guardian of the Poor for Poulton-le-Fylde for the long period of 64 years, and as Chairman of the Fylde Board of Guardians and this committee continuously from 1904 to the date of his passing, during which time the committee have always had the highest admiration for his wide knowledge, sound judgement and advice and outstanding abilities as chairman. He, at all times, was genial and courteous and together with his other qualities received the esteem of everyone who were favoured with his acquaintance, and the members have not only lost a fellow guardian but a true friend. Tribute was paid to his memory all standing, and the clerk was directed to convey to relatives the condolences of the committee in their loss.

The Final Years

At the Fylde Institution, the problem with the staff shortages continued long after the War. The guardians tried to deal with the problem by moving the refugees back home, but it was problematic with thousands of people on the move. By June 1946, some had been returned to London, but it still left one-hundred and eighteen refugees. Fifty of these were eventually sent to Ormskirk, and the guardians asked the Ministry of Health that if the rest were not moved nearer to their homes, would it be possible to transfer nurses to the Fylde. In August 1946, there were four-hundred and nineteen inmates, two-hundred and nineteen were chargeable to Blackpool, ninety-two to the county, and one-hundred and eight were refugees. There were seventy-five children in the homes: thirty-five from Blackpool and forty from the county area.

The Fylde Institution Subcommittee carried on running the institution, and the Fylde and Garstang Guardians Committee oversaw the outdoor relief. Their powers were greatly diminished, and they were just waiting for the end of the guardians.

In March 1947, the Lancashire Public Assistance Committee started preparing for the end. The first institution to go was the cottage homes on 1 April 1947. The governance passed to the Children's Welfare Committee. The National Assistance Act 1948 finally saw the end of guardians of the poor. The National Assistance Board would take over all the roles previously undertaken by the guardians. The new board had to provide assistance to people in need, and all local authorities had to provide accommodation for the aged, infirm, or in circumstances were people were in need of care and attention, which was not otherwise available to them. People in accommodation, and who were able, were still expected to pay for their maintenance. Discipline was imposed with the threat of a ten pounds fine or one month's imprisonment. Persons who failed to maintain themselves when able could be imprisoned for a term not exceeding three months.

The vagrants' wards would now be known as reception centres; their purpose was to encourage vagrants to live a more settled life. If a person constantly resorted to using a reception centre, when they were capable of maintaining themselves, they could only stay for forty-eight hours and were given tasks of work. These were the only people who were set work.

On 31 December 1948, the management of the Fylde Institution passed to the Committee of the Blackpool and Fylde Hospital Management. The building was renamed Wesham Park Hospital. It had eighteen wards and was divided into two. The house part for non-sick patients, basically an old people's home. It had sixty-five beds for males, seventy-four beds for females, three beds and eighteen cots in the nursery, four male and four female beds in the receiving ward, and four beds in the married quarters.

The other part was a geriatric hospital. In the infirmary for males, there were forty-six sick and twenty-two mental patients' beds, and fifty sick and twenty-two mental patients' beds for females. The hutments consisted of five wards, all containing thirty-six beds and two wards of sixteen beds for infectious diseases. In total, a three-hundred fifty-eight-bed hospital. Mr Lunn, the master, was now known as the administrative officer; his wife was still the matron. Both retired in April after twenty-three years at the institution, the longest-serving master and matron. The porter and portress also retired. The new porter was now the deputy administrative officer, and the role of portress was abandoned; her replacement was now to supervise and direct the cleaning staff.

The hospital remained short of staff until 1960. These shortages made the work of the nursing staff difficult. New nurses were sent straight onto the wards without training. The wards were full of old people with broken limbs, bedridden for months without the opportunity to start walking again, which led to the hospital being constantly overfull and with a growing waiting list.

At the first meeting of the hospital management board the medical officer, Dr Hilliard said, 'In the first place I should like to compliment the staff in their work, which is often uninteresting, thankless, hopeless, and dirty.'

The hospital was modernised. A hairdresser was employed, a tuck shop selling sweets, tobacco and cigarettes was opened. New furniture was purchased for the patients, and the toilets and washing blocks improved. Day rooms were added to the wards, and lifts built. All the open corridors in the hutments were closed off and the whole hospital re-roofed. A great deal of effort went into modernising the staff living quarters to help recruit and keep them. To make more space, the former female casual ward was converted into accommodation for the resident domestic and cooking staff. A tennis court with a pavilion and a putting green were built; the hospital paid five-pounds a year for the psychiatric patients to use the Wesham Institute's Bowling Green.

In the old Kirkham Workhouse, there was, for many years, no nurse and later only one nurse. If there was any proof that it wasn't a workhouse anymore, it was the number of nursing staff needed.

In 1959, the medical staff consisted of: administrative staff, six; tutorial staff, one; sisters and charge nurses, twelve; staff nurses, nine; pupil assistant nurses, thirty-two; enrolled assistant nurses, twenty-one; nursing assistants (psychiatric), ten; nursing auxiliaries, nineteen; other ward orderlies, eight. In total, there were one-hundred and seventeen medical staff.

The work previously done by the inmates was now undertaken by thirty-six domestic staff, ten kitchen/catering staff, seventeen laundry staff, thirty-five miscellaneous staff, and twelve others working in the stores and administration. In total, there were one-hundred and ten non-medical staff. Two-hundred and twenty-seven staff were doing the work which was done by three people one-hundred years ago.

Problems with overcrowding continued. In early 1960, the old aged people in the 'Highlands', the new name for the house part of the hospital, belonging to Blackpool Borough were moved to old people's homes in the Blackpool area. Then, the ones belonging to Lancashire County Council were moved. By November 1964, all the non-sick elderly people had left the Highlands, and the wards were modernised to cater for the sick aged. In 1969, the seclusion block was demolished and replaced by a Psychiatric Out-Patient and Day Clinic. New concrete section wards were built in 1969. In 1970, a new shop was opened by the Friends of Wesham Park Hospital.

The three-hundred and ninety beds geriatric hospital lasted until 2001, when it was closed. The infirmary and hutments were demolished, and housing built on the site. The house part was converted into offices for the N.H.S. and the story of the Fylde Guardians and the Union Workhouse ends.

The information in this book comes from three main sources.

Books.

1. The Act for the Amendment of the Poor Laws, with a practical introduction, notes and forms, John Frederick Archibald (1835).

2. The History of the Poor Laws: with observations, Richard Burns (1767).

3. A History of the English Poor Law, Sir George Nicholls (1854).

4. The General Orders and Instructional Letters of the Poor Law Commissioners, with an extensive index (1845).

Archives.

In the Lancashire Archives, Bow Lane, Preston are the Guardians Minute Books and Committee Minutes. All can be viewed in the file, Poor Union Fylde (P.U.F.). The minutes of the Public Assistance Institution can be viewed in the files Wesham Park Hospital (H.R.W.P.); this file also holds the Punishment Book and the Creed Register.

Newspaper Archives.

From 1862 onwards, most of the guardians meetings were recorded in the Preston Chronicle and Preston Herald, and in later years in the Lancashire Evening Post.

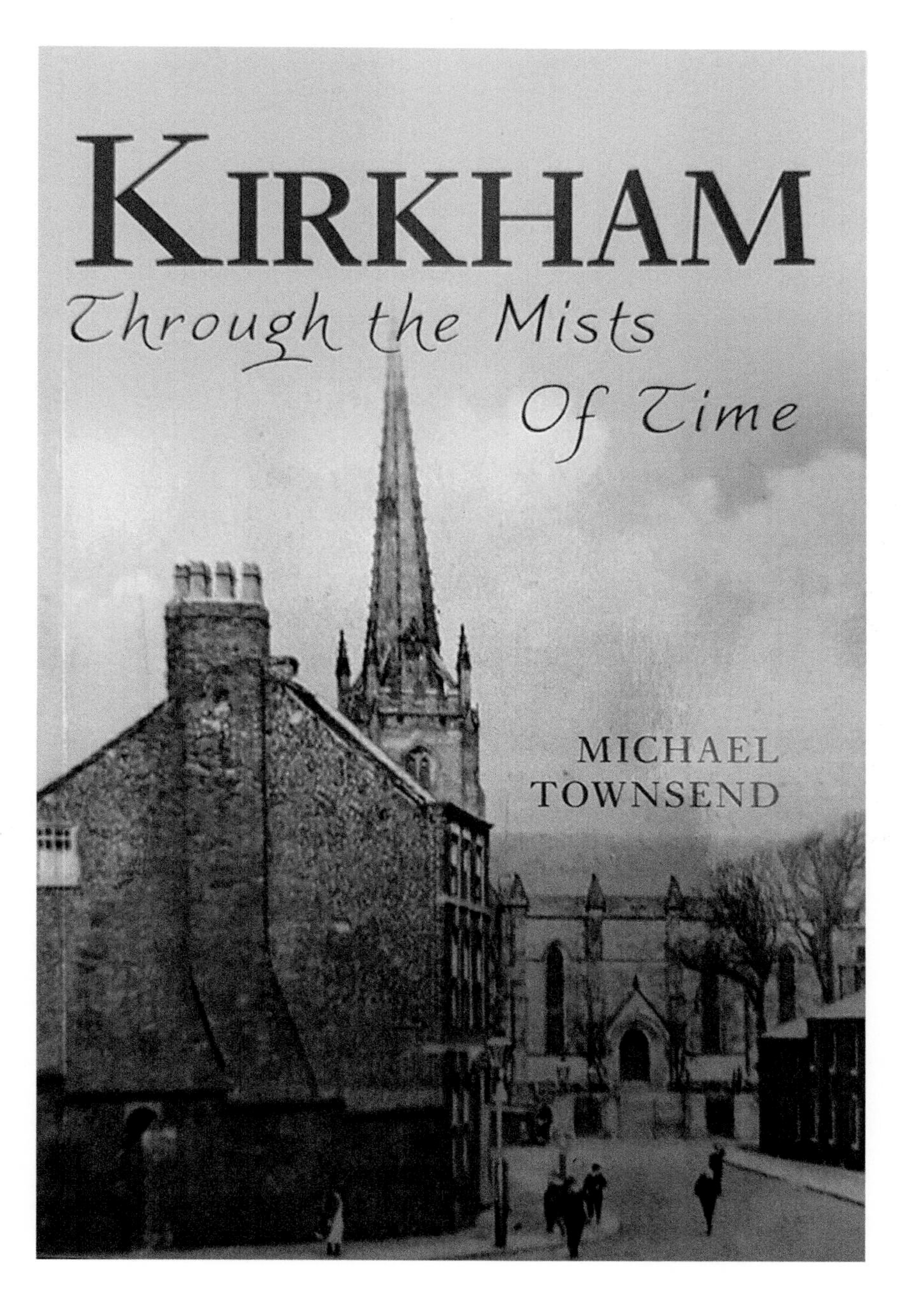

More information on Kirkham is contained in my first book, *Kirkham, Through the Mists of Time*. If you would like a copy, they can be purchased, through Amazon or come and visit Kirkham, and purchase it from the Book, Bean and Ice-Cream, Poulton Street, Kirkham.